HOUSE

European Union Committee

9th Report of Session 2007–08

FRONTEX: the EU external borders agency

Report with Evidence

Ordered to be printed 26 February 2008 and published 5 March 2008

Published by the Authority of the House of Lords

London : The Stationery Office Limited
£23.00

HL Paper 60

CONTENTS

Oral Evidence

Note: References in the text of the Report are as follows:
(Q) refers to a question in oral evidence
(p) refers to a page of written evidence

FOREWORD—What this report is about

The twenty-seven Member States are an area of increasing prosperity, and with external land borders of 8,000 km and sea borders of 80,000 km, migration to these countries is a considerable attraction for those seeking the chance of a better life, or simply trying to escape from their own countries for whatever reason. The abolition of nearly all the internal borders makes it all the more important that the external borders should be efficiently policed, and that there should be close cooperation between the border guards of the different States. The management of that cooperation is the task of Frontex.

Frontex is a relatively new agency, set up less than three years ago, and operational for barely two. As the importance of its work is increasingly recognised, its budget has doubled every year, and much is expected of it by the institutions and the Member States—perhaps too much. We have looked at its constitution and working methods, and at what it has achieved in the course of its brief existence; and we have made suggestions as to the direction its future work should take, and how its accountability might be improved.

Immigration affects the Member States differently. Some have no external borders other than their airports; others, and Malta in particular, are by their position particularly vulnerable to illegal immigration on a scale they can barely cope with. We have made suggestions as to how such immigration is best managed, what part other Member States can play in sharing the burden, how Frontex is best placed to assist, and how the humanitarian problems might be handled.

The United Kingdom would like to participate fully in Frontex, but the Court of Justice has ruled that it cannot. We have considered how this country might nevertheless play a part in the operations organised by Frontex, and make use of its great experience in the efficient policing of borders to assist the other Member States.

FRONTEX: the EU external borders agency

CHAPTER 1: INTRODUCTION

The subject of our inquiry

1. Twenty-two Member States of the European Union are now full Schengen members.[1] They operate as a passport union without internal borders. The external land, sea and air borders of any one of them form the external borders of all of them; each of them relies on the security of the border controls of all the others.

2. In the circumstances the need for cooperation at the external borders of these States hardly needs emphasising. The first requirement is the need for a common source of information, and this was the subject of our report last year on SIS II.[2] But just as important is to have a mechanism for direct cooperation between border posts and those manning them on land, sea and air. The first Schengen Information System has been in force since 1995, and one might have expected a mechanism for direct cooperation to have been in place many years ago. In fact it is less than three years since the Regulation was adopted setting up a European Agency for the Management of Operational Cooperation at the External Borders of the Member States of the European Union—Frontex, for short. It is this Agency which is the subject of our inquiry.[3]

3. Many of our witnesses have stressed that Frontex is a new arrival on the European scene. General Ilkka Laitinen, the Executive Director, told us: "We have only been in existence for two years ... which is a relatively short time for a European Agency" (Q 219). Javier Moreno Sanchez MEP described Frontex as "a baby which was born just two years ago and which needs the support of its parents".[4] But the baby is growing fast, and so is its budget. The importance of robust border control is, if anything, increasing. So is the potential for Frontex to assist in this. We accordingly thought this a suitable time to examine the current work of Frontex and to suggest how it might develop in the future.

4. Between 1999 and 2003 we examined different aspects of Schengen and the EU borders in four separate inquiries[5] and, as we have mentioned, we

---

[1] The Schengen Implementing Convention took effect in 1995 for ten of the Member States. Germany, France and the Benelux countries were the five original Schengen States, joined by Spain, Portugal, Italy, Austria and Greece. In 2001 the Convention took effect for Denmark, Sweden and Finland (and also for Norway and Iceland, the other two members of the Nordic passport union). Since 21 December 2007 it has additionally been in force for all the ten Member States which acceded in 2004 except Cyprus, a total of 24 States. The airport controls for the nine new States will be lifted only on 30 March 2008.

[2] *Schengen Information II (SIS II)*, 9th report, Session 2006–07, HL Paper 49.

[3] We explain in Chapter 2 the difference between the external borders of the Schengen States and the external borders of the Member States, and the effect of the accession of Romania and Bulgaria.

[4] Q 87. See also Jonathan Faull Q 47.

[5] *Schengen and the United Kingdom's Border Controls*, 7th Report, Session 1998–99, HL Paper 37. *Enlargement and EU External Frontier Controls*, 17th Report, Session 1999–2000, HL Paper 110. *A Common Policy on*

reported on SIS II last year. These reports form a useful background to our current inquiry, and show how matters have developed over the past decade. Where appropriate we have referred back to them.

Conduct of the inquiry

5.   The inquiry was conducted by Sub-Committee F, whose members are listed in Appendix 1. We issued a call for written evidence in July 2007; this is reproduced in Appendix 2. In reply we received evidence from the 16 persons and bodies listed in Appendix 3. Between October and December 2007 we heard oral evidence from 30 witnesses. The Home Office arranged visits for us to the border controls at Heathrow and the juxtaposed border controls at Coquelles and Calais. We took evidence in Brussels from witnesses from the Commission and from Members of the European Parliament. At the end of October 2007 we spent three days in Poland. We took evidence from the Executive Director and officials of Frontex, which has its headquarters in Warsaw, and from a Minister at the Ministry of the Interior and Administration. We also took evidence from the Commander in Chief of the Polish Border Guard, and spent a day at Dorohusk on the Polish border with Ukraine. To all those who helped in the arrangement of these visits, and to all our witnesses, we are most grateful.

6.   We were fortunate to be assisted during the course of our inquiry by Dr Valsamis Mitsilegas, Reader in Law, School of Law, Queen Mary College, University of London, and by Major-General Adrian Freer, formerly Coordinator of the Kosovo Protection Corps, who advised us on operational matters. We are most grateful to them for their help and advice.

Structure of this report

7.   In the next chapter we examine the purpose of the borders of the EU and how they operate in practice. The following chapter looks at the setting up of Frontex, including the special position of the United Kingdom. Chapters 4 and 5 analyse the work of Frontex and joint operations, while Chapter 6 looks at the recent Regulation on Rapid Border Intervention Teams. Chapter 7 deals with a number of miscellaneous issues. We then make suggestions as to how Frontex should develop in the future. Finally we summarise our conclusions and recommendations.

8.   **We recommend this report to the House for debate.**

Illegal Immigration, 37th Report, Session 2001–02, HL Paper 187. *Proposals for a European Border Guard*, 29th Report, Session 2002–03, HL Paper 133.

CHAPTER 2: BORDERS

The significance of national borders

9. "National borders are hugely symbolic. They define the territory over which a state exercises sovereignty; they are an integral part of its identity; and they traditionally represent the point at which a person seeking to enter the country must demonstrate their admissibility." These are the opening words of our report on the Proposals for a European Border Guard.[6] To this we would add that national borders also define differences of jurisdiction, of legal systems and, usually, of language. These are important for the purposes of our inquiry, but the most important of all is that the borders between Member States and third countries also usually represent a sharp contrast in economic prosperity.

10. Mr Liam Byrne MP, the Minister of State at the Home Office with responsibility for immigration, explained this graphically: "The World Bank in *Global Economic Prospects*, which was published last year, forecast that something like a billion people will join the labour market in the developing world between now and 2025. The International Labour Organisation estimates that there is a five-fold difference in household income between low income and high income countries. My warning is that over the next 20 years the pressure on Europe's borders will not diminish. It will grow and it will grow sharply. We are already seeing that pressure across the Mediterranean" (Q 475).

11. We accept this view. **The migratory pressure on Europe's borders will grow because there are a growing number of failed states where a combination of economic incompetence, uncertainty of property rights, corruption, internal conflicts, political anarchy and repressive regimes has created intolerable conditions for the local population. Conditions may also be intolerable in states where poverty is endemic, or in those which, though once prosperous, are now ravaged by war. It is therefore inevitable and predictable that people will attempt to escape to countries which they see as offering a chance of a better life.**

12. The needs of Member States for economic migrants from outside the EU will vary, but most have benefited from migration both from within and from outside the Union.[7] United Kingdom Prospects, a quarterly report from the Centre for Economics and Business Research, published on 27 December 2007, estimates that the growth of the United Kingdom GDP will be maintained at 1.8% in 2008 only because of an increase in the number of predominantly unskilled economic migrants entering the country, mainly from the Eastern European Member States.

13. Many of those seeking to escape from countries at or near the bottom of the United Nations Human Development Index are likely to be the more talented. Yet these are the people those countries particularly need to retain

---

6   29th Report, Session 2002–03, HL Paper 133.

7   For the specific benefits to the United Kingdom, see our report *Economic Migration to the EU*, 14th Report, Session 2005–06, HL Paper 58. The House of Lords Select Committee on Economic Affairs is currently inquiring into the Economic Impact of Immigration. Evidence given to that inquiry can be found at www.publications.parliament.uk/pa/ld/ldeconaf.htm.

if they are not to stay anchored near the bottom of the Index, unable to rise because they increasingly lack the talent they need.

14.   It is only natural for those in developing countries who wish to improve the economic prospects for themselves and their families, and who can see that crossing the border into the EU is likely to help them to do just that, to attempt to do so. Any detailed analysis of the root causes of migration, the merits of EU migration policies, the capacity to absorb the numbers involved, and what should be done to regulate migration flows, are all outside the scope of this inquiry. We have proceeded on the premise that the current EU and national rules to regulate immigration are there to be obeyed, and that borders and border guards are there for this purpose. We are however mindful that the developing cooperation of national border guards at the external EU borders takes place in the context of the rules of public international law designed to ensure the safety and dignity of human beings.

15.   The larger the Schengen area, and the greater the freedom of movement within it, the greater the burden which falls on those borders which become the external borders of the EU, and the greater the responsibility of those who guard them. The duty to guard what were previously only national borders becomes a duty owed to all the Schengen States. The changes which took place at the end of 2007 are particularly significant for the States with the Eastern land borders. Twenty years ago it was the Western borders of those States which were designed to keep citizens of the former Soviet bloc from escaping to the economic nirvana of the EU;[8] today it is the Eastern borders of the same States which have the duty of regulating the flow of immigration into the EU from other States which formerly were part of the Soviet bloc. This is the reason why the Polish border guard has had to be built from scratch.[9]

16.   The external borders of the Member States are defined by Article 1(4) of the Regulation setting up Frontex as "the land and sea borders of the Member States and their airports and seaports, to which the provisions of Community law on the crossing of external borders by persons apply". We consider these in turn.

The land borders

17.   The land borders to which an important part of the work of Frontex relates— those of the Member States—are not the same as those of the Schengen States. They do not include the border between Russia and Norway, which is a Schengen Associated State but not a Member State; but they do include the external borders of Romania and Bulgaria, which are Member States but not yet Schengen States.[10]

18.   Until May 2004 Finland, Germany, Austria and Italy guarded the main Eastern land border of the EU, which was 4,095 km long (2,545 miles).

---

[8]   At that time, the European Economic Community.

[9]   Mr Wieslaw Tarka, Under-Secretary of State, Polish Ministry for the Interior and Administration, Q 355.

[10] We do not consider the border between Sweden and Norway, since it is a Schengen Associated State, nor the land borders with Switzerland, which from 1 November 2008 will become a Schengen Associated State.

TABLE 1

The Eastern external land border of the EU before 1 May 2004

Border between		Length in km
Finland	Russia	1,340
Germany	Poland	454
Germany	Czech Republic	810
Austria	Czech Republic	466
Austria	Slovakia	107
Austria	Hungary	356
Austria	Slovenia	330
Italy	Slovenia	232
Total		**4,095**

19. After the accession of ten new Member States on 1 May 2004 the place of Germany, Austria and Italy in guarding the Eastern external land border was taken by Estonia, Latvia, Lithuania, Poland, Slovakia, Hungary and Slovenia. When Frontex started its work, before the accession of Romania and Bulgaria on 1 January 2007, the external land border was 6,220 km long (3,866 miles).

TABLE 2

The Eastern external land border of the EU from 1 May 2004

Border between		Length in km
Finland	Russia	1,340
Estonia	Russia	455
Latvia	Russia	276
Latvia	Belarus	161
Lithuania	Belarus	651
Lithuania	Russia (Kaliningrad)	272
Poland	Russia (Kaliningrad)	232
Poland	Belarus	418
Poland	Ukraine	535
Slovakia	Ukraine	98
Hungary	Ukraine	136
Hungary	Romania	448
Hungary	Serbia	174
Hungary	Croatia	344
Slovenia	Croatia	680
Total		**6,220**

20. Neither of these two tables includes Greece. Although of course a Member State, it was not then geographically part of the main body of EU States, although its borders with Albania, the Former Yugoslav Republic of Macedonia (FYROM), Bulgaria and Turkey were external land borders of a Member State and hence part of the responsibility of Frontex. However the accession of Romania and Bulgaria has changed matters radically. Greece has now joined the main continental bloc, so that the Eastern external land border now runs from the Arctic to the Black Sea and the Aegean, and is 6,378 km long (3,964 miles). As a result the West Balkan States have become an enclave whose collective land frontiers form a lengthy and sensitive part of the external borders of the EU, adding a further 1,580 km (982 miles) to a land border now totalling 7,958 km (4,946 miles).

TABLE 3

The external land border of the EU from 1 January 2007

Border between		Length in km
Finland	Russia	1,340
Estonia	Russia	455
Latvia	Russia	276
Latvia	Belarus	161
Lithuania	Belarus	651
Lithuania	Russia (Kaliningrad)	272
Poland	Russia (Kaliningrad)	232
Poland	Belarus	418
Poland	Ukraine	535
Slovakia	Ukraine	98
Hungary	Ukraine	136
Romania	Ukraine (East and West of Moldova)	649
Romania	Moldova	681
Bulgaria	Turkey	259
Greece	Turkey	215
Greece	Albania	282
Greece	Former Yugoslav Republic of Macedonia	246
Bulgaria	Former Yugoslav Republic of Macedonia	165
Bulgaria	Serbia	341
Romania	Serbia	546
Total		**7,958**

21. Frontex cannot lose sight of other land borders; the problems they raise are often wholly disproportionate to their length. A month after it began operations Frontex found itself in the front line when, in November 2005, hundreds of mainly sub-Saharan nationals breached the borders of the Spanish enclaves of Ceuta and Melilla in Morocco.

22. The Schengen Evaluation Working Party consists of experts from the Member States whose remit is to evaluate against key performance indicators, on behalf of all the states, the manner in which checks and surveillance are carried out at external borders, their practice when issuing visas, police and judicial co-operation at internal borders, and the use of the Schengen Information System. This evaluation mechanism serves to check that Member States implement the Schengen *acquis* properly. But its other—and recently its more important—purpose has been to evaluate whether the Member States which acceded in 2004 fulfilled the conditions laid down for applying the Schengen *acquis*.[11] Before the Schengen area was extended to the nine states which joined it on 21 December 2007,[12] an elaborate evaluation took place of the quality of the border protection. Teams of experts examined the border posts and the areas between them and reported back to the Council with recommendations for improvements. Most of these recommendations have been acted on, and the borders are more secure than they were.[13]

23. Anyone remembering the problem of policing the short common border between Northern Ireland and the Irish Republic during the Troubles, or the Sino-Hong Kong border, will readily understand the difficulty of guarding a border some 8,000 km long against large numbers of determined and sometimes desperate immigrants. However good the border posts may be which guard the main crossing points, in between them are long stretches of border, often sparsely populated, sometimes through country which is difficult to police. Even if they are fenced, this is of little use unless they are also guarded, which in the nature of things they cannot always be. A border is only as secure as its least well guarded area, and it is this area which will attract illegal immigrants.[14]

24. With frontiers of this length, and very large numbers of border guards, there may also be a problem of corruption. Border guards are not usually well paid compared to other workers, and those on the East of the frontier considerably less well than those on the West. We think it likely that even the best guarded border posts may not prove too much of an obstacle to immigrants who are well funded.

25. The enlargement of the Schengen area was an opportunity for the British press to comment on the security of the new borders. Much of the comment

---

[11] Plan for the management of the external borders of the Member States of the European Union agreed by the JHA Council on 13 June 2002 (Document 10019/02).

[12] Cyprus was the only one of the ten which did not join.

[13] The reports of the Schengen Evaluation Working Party are classified, but on 7 September 2007, less than 4 months before the enlargement, the Working Party reported concerns about the continuing entry of Croatian residents into the territory of Hungary and Slovenia with an identity card only, something which had been identified during a land-border mission as far back as May 2006. The working party continues its evaluation of border security of the Schengen States.

[14] We have referred in our reports on *Schengen and the United Kingdom's Border Controls* (7th Report, Session 1998–99, HL Paper 37) and *Illegal Migrants: proposals for a common EU returns policy* (32nd Report, Session 2005–06, HL Paper 166) to the pejorative use of the term "illegal immigrant" in this context, with its imputation of criminality. While this is the term used by most of our witnesses, a number prefer the term "irregular migrants". However "illegal immigrant" is the most commonly used English expression, and "illegal" is the word used in Article 63(3)(b) of the EC Treaty and in Regulation 863/2007. We have therefore used this term, but emphasise that it will include persons whose intention is to settle legally in the EU.

we saw was adverse. By way of example, an article in the Sunday Telegraph of 16 December 2007, subtitled *"Eastern defences are undermanned and overwhelmed"*, tells of a visit to Beregsurany on the border between Hungary and Ukraine, where officials said they caught fewer than a third of those attempting to cross the border illegally.

The Polish-Ukrainian border

26. In the course of our visit to Poland, on 24 October 2007 we visited Dorohusk to see in operation a border post on the eastern external border of the EU. The border with Ukraine is at that point formed by the River Bug, and Dorohusk is one of the main road entry points from Ukraine. The border post was rebuilt in 2004 and is one of the most modern and best equipped on the Polish border. It is well equipped to monitor traffic on the arterial road, but like all land border posts it covers a large surrounding area which it is not so well placed to supervise.

27. Earnings in Poland are low by EU standards, but are still some four times higher than in Ukraine, and higher still compared to some of the other countries of the former Soviet Union to the East of Ukraine. The pressure from migrants seeking to enter the EU from and through Ukraine is therefore very great. Much of the migration is organised, and we were told of groups from Moldova, Georgia, Chechnya, Pakistan, Vietnam and as far afield as China (QQ 332, 340, 347). Other main concerns of the border guards are entry of criminal gangs from the East, and the smuggling of cigarettes, alcohol, drugs, and works of art.

28. Much of the traffic in the opposite direction consists of articulated trucks exporting goods from, principally, Germany to Ukraine and beyond. On the day of our visit there was a queue of lorries well over a mile long waiting to pass into Ukraine. In that direction the chief concern is the smuggling of stolen luxury cars.

29. In addition to the oral evidence which we took (QQ 314–350), we inspected the border crossing itself, we saw the equipment for detecting illegal immigrants in use, and we saw the practical liaison between the Polish and Ukrainian border guards.

Juxtaposed border controls at Coquelles and Calais

30. The nearest the United Kingdom comes to a land border with a Schengen state is the terminus of Eurotunnel in France, at Coquelles. The Home Office arranged for us to visit on 8 January 2008 the juxtaposed controls there and at the ferry port of Calais. The controls at Coquelles have existed since 1994, and the agreement now allows staff from the Border and Immigration Agency (BIA) and HM Revenue and Customs (HMRC) to apply United Kingdom immigration law within this very limited area of France, and so to control passengers and vehicles travelling to the UK before they leave France. The agreement covering Calais does not allow participation by HMRC. Replies to a number of detailed questions from the Committee are printed with the written evidence on page 161.

31. In 2006 BIA, as a result of its juxtaposed controls in France, stopped 16,898 people from crossing the Channel illegally in trucks and refused 6,801 people entry.[15] Examination of both passengers and freight vehicles is by targeted

---

[15] These figures are taken from Security in a Global Hub, paragraph 3.2, but have been updated by the Home Office. The great majority relate to Coquelles and Calais, but they also include some from other juxtaposed controls: Dunkerque, Boulogne, Paris, Fréthun and Lille. There are also juxtaposed controls in Brussels.

selection. At Calais over 80% of passengers identified as requiring detailed examination are subsequently refused entry. Forged documentation features in a third of those cases. Calais identifies more forgeries than any other BIA control.

32.   We saw in action the targeted searching which screens freight vehicles to prevent clandestine entry to the United Kingdom. The use of gamma ray scanners is not permitted in France where the presence of humans is suspected, but we saw in use the following new detection technology:

- passive millimetre wave imager, which uses natural background radiation to generate an image of the interior of soft-sided freight vehicles;

- CO_2 probes, which operate by detecting in a vehicle the elevated levels of CO_2 exhaled by humans;

- body detection dogs; and

- heartbeat detectors, sensors which when placed on the main chassis of a vehicle can within seconds detect the presence of a hidden person.

33.   We were very impressed by this equipment: its sensitivity, and the way it was handled. One thing which surprised us was that, after lorries have successfully cleared the detectors at Calais, and can therefore be presumed not to be carrying clandestines, they have to wait near the ferry berths in an area which is accessible to determined immigrants. We were told that every year some 1,500 clandestines are found to have boarded lorries at this point, and that the area which is fenced is larger than it need be, and the fencing inadequate. This seems to us to be the one weak point in an otherwise excellent system which is greatly to the benefit of the United Kingdom. We are glad to hear that British officials are addressing this question with the French authorities, and **we recommend that more effective fencing should be put in place as a matter of urgency**.

Maritime borders

34.   The maritime borders of the EU are nearly 80,000 km (50,000 miles) long, and getting on for half of this (34,109 km or 21,199 miles) is the vulnerable Southern maritime border.

TABLE 4

The Southern maritime border

Country	Length in km
Portugal (including the Azores and Madeira)	2,555
Spain (including the Canaries)	4,964
France	4,720
Slovenia	48
Italy	7,600
Greece (including over 3,000 islands)	13,676
Malta (including Gozo)	253
Cyprus[16]	293
Total	**34,109**

---

[16]   This relates to the southern part of the island under the control of the Republic, and excludes the British sovereign base areas.

35.   Greece with its 3,000 islands has the longest maritime border of any Member State, longer even than the United Kingdom. Most of the islands are very close to Turkey, a fact exploited by many criminal gangs which seek to infiltrate them. The Black Sea borders of Romania and Bulgaria, 572 km (358 miles) long, are now equally at risk from criminal gangs operating from Turkey.

36.   Only a minority of illegal immigrants enter the EU through the sea borders. Nevertheless, when the media consider the work of Frontex, they tend to focus on the Southern maritime borders. It is operations on those borders which consume the majority of that part of the Frontex budget which is spent on operations. The journeys from West Africa to the Canaries (and hence onwards to mainland Spain), and from North Africa across the Mediterranean, can be very perilous when undertaken in small and inadequately equipped craft.

37.   In 2006 media interest concentrated mainly on immigrants from West Africa aiming for the Canaries and Spain. In 2007, as immigration from West Africa decreased and a greater proportion of immigrants were leaving North Africa and aiming for Italy and Malta, it was there that media interest was directed.

38.   Malta is in an especially sensitive geographical position. The LIBE Committee of the European Parliament,[17] on a visit to Malta on 23–25 March 2006, were told by Mr Tonio Borg, the Deputy Prime Minister and Minister for the Interior, how difficult it was for a country such as Malta, with a surface area of 316 km^2 and a population of 400,000, to cope with the influx of migrants and asylum seekers arriving on the island: 1,388 in 2004 and 1,822 in 2005.[18] The average annual number of arrivals was equivalent to 45% of Malta's annual birth-rate. One person arriving illegally in Malta is equivalent, in terms of population, to 140 in Italy, 150 in France or 205 in Germany. On the basis of the country's size, the numbers are even larger: one immigrant would be equivalent to 953 in Italy and 1,129 in Germany.

39.   These are the migrants who reach Malta. An unquantifiable number perish in the attempt; a great many more would perish were it not for search and rescue operations mounted by the Member States on the Southern maritime border, and especially by Malta, whose search and rescue area goes all the way to Crete in the East.[19] We believe that the media descriptions of these events are often partial and incomplete, condemning expressly or by implication the countries bordering on the Mediterranean which are mounting search and rescue operations. In the view of General Laitinen they tend to ignore the main *modus operandi* of the human smugglers and facilitators in the central Mediterranean, which he described as making the journey become a search and rescue operation which guarantees reception and a way to the closest haven (Q 246).

40.   An event which received very wide international media coverage in May 2007 was the apparent disappearance of a boat with 53 Eritrean nationals on board. Major Andrew Mallia of the Maltese Armed Forces came to London and gave us evidence which we found impressive and compelling. Since he

---

[17] The Committee on Civil Liberties, Justice and Home Affairs.
[18] The figure for 2006 was 1,780; for 2007, up to mid-December, it is 1,698.
[19] Faull Q 54.

was personally involved in this, we think it useful to summarise his account in some detail (Q 385).

BOX 1

The disappearance of 53 Eritrean nationals

When the call was initially received the boat was 200 km from Malta, closer both to Libya and to Lampedusa. The call as usual provided a satellite telephone number which was on board the boat. All the boats are equipped with a satellite telephone, given to them by the traffickers, which allows them to call for help, and because it has an embedded GPS, it also provides the navigation details. That is standard procedure. On receiving the call about six o'clock in the morning, because the position was still within the Libyan Search and Rescue Region, our first step was to inform the Libyan authorities. We did not receive a response from them so we continued to monitor the progress of this boat by regular contacts with these people. At one point, they stated that they were in a position within the Maltese Search and Rescue Region, their craft was adrift and they required assistance. We immediately deployed a vessel and also an aircraft because sometimes the positions are not exact. Two hours after the initial alert we had an aircraft on scene—which also took those pictures which were shown in the media. The craft did seem to be adrift.

It took seven hours for our boat to transit from Malta to the position—which gives you a feel of how far away it was. During that time the aircraft was withdrawn for refuelling and sent again to the position. On arriving it did not find a boat either in the position where it had been initially sighted nor within a substantial radius around it. We had also alerted merchant shipping but we received no reports of the sighting of this craft. Our vessel began a search during which it found a second craft with 25 people on board which had just capsized. It rescued those persons and proceeded directly to Malta because a number of them required medical assistance. The next day we flew a further sortie with an aircraft and also liaised with the Italian Rescue Co-ordination Centre to fly at least one sortie in the area and ask any other aircraft in the area to keep a sharp look out, and they found nothing. Given that a number of the people on board were wearing life-jackets it is highly unlikely that a boat like that would sink without leaving at least minimal trace. Some three days later we noted on a couple of Eritrean websites that this craft had been reported to have arrived again in Libya; they had lost their way and had landed again in Libya. That is the only further information that we have.

We reacted fully in accordance with our search and rescue plan. The only unknown was that when we got there we found another craft, so instead of searching for longer we had to return to base. We did search the area extremely well, both ourselves and the Italians. We can find a drifting object quite easily but a boat being driven in a particular direction is very difficult to find. We could not really have done much more and I have my doubts whether this craft disappeared as completely as was said by the press.

Air borders

41. The air borders of states are the most secure because it is very difficult for would-be immigrants to land otherwise than at an international airport where their status will always be checked. The airports of the new Schengen states will join the system only on 30 March 2008.

42. On Tuesday 4 December 2007 we visited the border control at Heathrow. We viewed the border controls for outbound and inbound flights, and had explained to us the reasons incoming passengers were selected for fuller checks, and the nature of those checks. We saw the Iris Recognition Immigration System (IRIS) enrolment station in the departure lounge, and had a demonstration of document forgery detection techniques. Finally we had a question and answer session, the results of which are printed with the written evidence on page 154.

The position on Schengen

43. Maritime borders are by and large more secure and easier to guard than land borders. It is often clearer exactly where a sea border lies, and crossing the border is frequently more difficult, so that it is usually easier to identify and to intercept persons attempting to cross it: "21 miles of sea is the most effective border control you can have".[20] When the Schengen *acquis* was incorporated into the law of the EU by the Treaty of Amsterdam, one reason why the United Kingdom negotiated an opt-out was because this country's frontier controls "match both the geography and traditions of the country and have ensured a high degree of personal freedom within the UK"; whereas in mainland Europe, "because of the difficulty of policing long land frontiers, there is much greater dependence on internal controls, such as identity checks."[21] The United Kingdom and Ireland participate only in those parts of the Schengen *acquis* concerning criminal law and policing.[22]

44. In February 1999, in the course of our inquiry into Schengen and the United Kingdom's border controls, Ms Kate Hoey MP, then a Parliamentary Under-Secretary of State at the Home Office, was asked whether the Government was maintaining its position on frontier controls with the rest of the EU only until it was satisfied that external border controls of other EU members were adequate, or whether this was seen as a permanent position. She replied that there was no chance that the Government would in the foreseeable future feel that there was no longer any need for these frontier controls.[23] In the current inquiry we put to Mr Liam Byrne the question whether it was not now time for this country to become a full Schengen member. He replied: "Possibly, but not yet. Speaking candidly, until we have greater confidence than we have today in the strength of the external border, I do not think that would be something that I could recommend yet" (Q 475).

45. **Given the views of successive Governments on the comparative strengths of the United Kingdom and Schengen borders, it seems to us that "Possibly, but not yet" will for many years to come be the reply to the question of the United Kingdom becoming a full Schengen State.**

---

[20] Dodd Q 467.

[21] White Paper Fairer, Faster and Firmer—A Modern Approach to Immigration and Asylum, Cm 4018, July 1998.

[22] Ireland opted out only because of its wish to maintain the Common Travel Area with the United Kingdom.

[23] *Schengen and the United Kingdom's Border Controls*, 7th Report, Session 1998–99, HL Paper 37, Q 319.

Guarding the United Kingdom's borders

46. In the course of taking oral evidence we heard from Home Office Ministers and officials about current developments in the guarding of the United Kingdom's borders: the creation of the Border and Immigration Agency (BIA), the Prime Minister's announcement in July 2007 that it was to integrate its work with Customs and UK visas to establish a Unified Border Force, and the review of this by Sir Gus O'Donnell which culminated in the publication in November 2007 of the report *"Security in a Global Hub"*.[24] These are matters of great importance, and this evidence, together with our visits to Calais, Coquelles and Heathrow, allowed us to form our own views about the management of this country's borders. This in turn made a useful background to our assessment of the work of Frontex.

47. The case for Britain remaining outside Schengen is that we can protect our borders better than the Schengen states control their own external borders. We therefore find it astonishing that although there is an elaborate system for allowing certain persons from outside the EU temporary or limited entry to the United Kingdom, there is no way in which the BIA can know whether these time limits and conditions are being complied with, because there is no routine recording of entries into or departures from the United Kingdom. As Mr Byrne accepted, "one of the most basic requirements of a border control is the ability to count people in and to count people out of the country"— and, he added, "you had better make sure that the person you are counting in is the same person as you are counting out" (Q 457).

48. We are glad to know that the Minister accepts the importance of remedying this defect. He told us that passenger screening systems would be put first on the high risk routes, and "the point at which we hit 100% high risk groups will be substantially in advance of 2010" (Q 457). However it will be 2014 before the gap is closed by the full implementation of e-Borders.[25] This undermines the Government's arguments against Schengen. The fact that the Irish e-Borders system will not be ready until even later is no justification for delaying ours. **We believe the work on e-Borders should be brought forward as a matter of urgency to protect Britain's territorial integrity.**

---

[24] Dodd Q 134.

[25] *Security in a Global Hub*, paragraph 3.12.

CHAPTER 3: THE ESTABLISHMENT OF FRONTEX

Background to the Frontex Regulation

49.   The proposal for a European Border Guard which we considered in 2003 can be seen with hindsight to have been too ambitious, and never likely to succeed in that form at that time. But many of the documents proposing such a border guard, and many of the Councils at which they were considered, were also putting forward the less radical alternative of increased cooperation between national border guards.

50.   On 7 May 2002 the Commission presented to the Council and the European Parliament a Communication entitled *"Towards integrated management of the external borders of the Member States of the European Union"*.[26] While the ultimate aim was the establishment of a "European Corps of Border Guards", the Communication proposed as the preliminary steps the consolidation and codification of common rules and standards for external border controls, the creation of an "External Borders Practitioners Common Unit", and other mechanisms for cooperation and the sharing of financial burdens.

51.   There was something in this Communication for all the Member States, since those which were sceptical about the long-term aim of setting up a European Border Guard could still support the suggested preliminary steps. The European Council, meeting in Seville the following month, "applauded" the plan. The conclusions referred to "the intention expressed by the Commission of continuing to examine the advisability of such a [European] police force." Thus it remained unclear whether the long-term aim was to establish an operational force or whether "integrated border management" would stop short of that. On the basis of a report by the LIBE Committee, in December 2002 the European Parliament also approved the plan. The European Council returned to the issue at Thessalonica in June 2003, inviting the Commission "to examine in due course ... the necessity of creating new institutional mechanisms, including the possible creation of a Community operational structure, in order to enhance operational cooperation for the management of external borders."

52.   On 20 November 2003 the Commission put forward the proposal for a Council Regulation establishing a European Agency for the Management of Operational Cooperation at the External Borders,[27] and the Council adopted the Regulation establishing Frontex on 26 October 2004.[28] On 26 April 2005 the Council decided that the seat of Frontex should be at Warsaw.[29] In accordance with Article 34 of the Regulation, Frontex took up its responsibilities on 1 May 2005. On 25 May General (then Colonel) Ilkka

---

[26] COM(2002) 233 final.

[27] COM (2003) 687 final.

[28] Council Regulation (EC) N0 2007/2004 establishing a European Agency for the Management of Operational Co-operation at the External Borders of the Member States of the European Union, OJ L349 of 25 November 2004, p.1. We refer to it as "the Frontex Regulation".

[29] 2005/358/EC: Council Decision 2005/358/EC of 26 April 2005 designating the seat of the European Agency for the Management of Operational Cooperation at the External Borders of the Member States of the European Union.

Laitinen was appointed as Executive Director, and on 3 October 2005 Frontex became operational.

53. In the course of the last two and a half years Frontex has begun to chart a distinct course, but it is far from set in its ways. There are a number of different directions in which it could turn. The Minister thought the timing of our inquiry was "very auspicious";[30] we hope this report comes at a time when we can influence the agency's development.

The legal position of the United Kingdom

54. The Frontex Regulation itself states that "This Regulation constitutes a development of the provisions of the Schengen *Acquis* in which the United Kingdom does not take part ... The United Kingdom is therefore not taking part in its adoption and is not bound by it or subject to its application."[31]

55. The United Kingdom is indisputably not a full Schengen State, nor likely to become one in the foreseeable future. The Schengen States maintained that the Frontex Regulation was a Schengen-building measure, so that the United Kingdom could not be a Frontex State. This was not at all to the liking of the Government. Just as, in the case of Schengen, the Government would like to have the benefits of being a Schengen State without weakening the United Kingdom's external borders, so they would like to participate fully in the organisation and running of Frontex.

56. United Kingdom Ministers have always shown support for Frontex. In the Conclusions of the meeting of the G6 interior ministers at Stratford-upon-Avon in October 2006, chaired by Dr John Reid MP when he was Home Secretary, "Ministers ... underlined their commitment to controlling migration and tackling illegal immigration ... and called on Frontex to be given the necessary support to coordinate meaningful EU level action in this area". Dr Reid subsequently wrote to the same effect to the Minister of the Interior of the Finnish Presidency.[32]

57. Within three months of the Commission submitting to the Council its proposal for the Frontex Regulation, the Government, on the basis of Article 5(1) of the Schengen Protocol to the Treaty of Amsterdam, notified the Council of their wish for the United Kingdom to participate in the adoption of the Regulation. Having been rebuffed, the Government applied to the Court of Justice for a ruling that the Council acted unlawfully in so doing.

58. On 10 July 2007 Advocate General Trstenjak proposed that the Court should dismiss the application, and in a judgment delivered on 18 December 2007 the Court—ruling in Grand Chamber—unequivocally ruled against the United Kingdom. On the principal argument, the Court ruled that the United Kingdom and Ireland cannot be allowed to take part in the adoption of a measure under Article 5(1) of the Schengen Protocol without first having been authorised by the Council to accept the area of the *acquis* on which that measure is based. It stressed that the United Kingdom interpretation would deprive Article 4 of the Protocol of all effectiveness.

---

[30] Byrne Q 450.

[31] Recital (25).

[32] See our report *After Heiligendamm: doors ajar at Stratford-upon-Avon*, 5th Report, Session 2006–07, HL Paper 32, Appendices 3 and 5.

59. The United Kingdom's secondary argument was that there is a distinction between measures which are integral to Schengen and measures which are merely related to Schengen. The Court said that this distinction "has no basis either in the EU and EC Treaties or in secondary Community law'. The Court nevertheless examined the legal basis of the Frontex Regulation to establish whether it properly fell within the Schengen Protocol or whether it was a more general Title IV measure (with the Title IV Protocol applying, which gives the United Kingdom a unilateral option to opt in). The Court found that the Regulation is indeed a Schengen building measure.

60. In evidence to us in connection with our inquiry into the impact of the Treaty of Lisbon Kevan Norris, a Home Office lawyer, referred to the legal basis of the Court's ruling and said that there was nothing in the Protocols to the Treaty of Lisbon which would change this position.[33] It seems to us therefore that **for the present the United Kingdom has to accept that, not being a full Schengen State, it cannot play a full role in Frontex. Subject to that legal limitation, the Government should ensure that the United Kingdom participates effectively in the development and operation of Frontex.**

Gibraltar

61. The Frontex Regulation does not apply to the borders of Gibraltar because, as recital (28) delicately states, "A controversy exists between the Kingdom of Spain and the United Kingdom on the demarcation of the borders of Gibraltar". While Article 12(1) provides for the cooperation of the United Kingdom in Frontex operations, Article 12(3) reads: "The application of this Regulation to the borders of Gibraltar shall be suspended until the date on which agreement is reached on the scope of the measures concerning the crossing by persons of the external borders of the Member States"—a date which shows no sign of approaching.

62. We received from the Government of Gibraltar evidence of its "extreme disappointment" at being excluded even from the ambit of the United Kingdom's limited participation under Article 12(1) (p 153). The evidence refers to lengthy exchanges of correspondence between the Government of Gibraltar and the Foreign and Commonwealth Office stretching from December 2003 to July 2007. We include with the evidence a press release issued by the Government of Gibraltar on 30 July 2004, once it became clear that Gibraltar would not be able to participate even to the extent that the United Kingdom was able to. Gibraltar's chief fear was that, if the United Kingdom were allowed to participate fully in Frontex, its own total exclusion from a measure on external frontiers would further harm its arguments over where that frontier is to be drawn. Perhaps the only favourable outcome of the judgment of the Court of Justice is that this situation has not arisen.

---

[33] Q E518.

CHAPTER 4: THE WORK OF FRONTEX

The statutory tasks

63. The legal basis of the Frontex Regulation is Article 62 of the TEC, within Title IV which governs visas, asylum, immigration and other policies related to free movement of persons. Article 2(1) of the Regulation sets out the six tasks of Frontex:

    (a) coordinate operational cooperation between Member States in the field of management of external borders;

    (b) assist Member States on training of national border guards, including the establishment of common training standards;

    (c) carry out risk analyses;

    (d) follow up on the development of research relevant for the control and surveillance of external borders;

    (e) assist Member States in circumstances requiring increased technical and operational assistance at external borders;

    (f) provide Member States with the necessary support in organising joint return operations.

Joint return operations

64. The last of these tasks is one that we considered in the course of our inquiry into the proposals for a common EU returns policy.[34] For that purpose we took evidence from General Laitinen on 2 March 2006, when Frontex had been operational for less than six months. He told us then that assisting with joint return operations was "not at the top of the priorities",[35] and that is still the case (Q 225). It may be that this will change with the renewed interest in the development of a common EU returns policy. However Mr Byrne is "a bit of a sceptic about Frontex getting involved in joint returns" because of the difficulty of arranging them (Q 484).

65. In our earlier report we emphasised how voluntary return was greatly preferable to enforced compulsory return. Not only was it more humane, it was a good deal more cost-effective, and it was greatly eased by assistance for reintegration, training, education and self-employment.[36] These are matters outside the scope of our current inquiry, but they are reasons why **for the present we would not encourage Frontex to put any more assets into organising compulsory return operations.**

Risk Analysis

66. General Laitinen told us on that occasion that risk analysis "is the inner core of the methodology of Frontex".[37] In the course of this inquiry he said that "the starting point is with the risk analysis" (Q 261). Jonathan Faull, the Director General for Justice, Freedom and Security at the European

---

[34] *Illegal Migrants: proposals for a common EU returns policy*, 32nd Report, Session 2005–06, HL Paper 166.

[35] *Ibid*, Q 583.

[36] *Ibid*, paragraphs 46–48.

[37] *Ibid*, Q 581.

Commission, was of the same view: "risk analysis must be the basis for priority setting by Frontex" (Q 49). We can understand why the work of the Risk Analysis Unit is central to all the other work. The Unit's mission is "to produce appropriate accurate and timely intelligence products which provide the foundation for Frontex operational activities, as well as to keep all principal customers informed of the current illegal immigration situation at the external borders". The Unit regards its "principal customers" as the Council and Commission; we feel the European Parliament should be added to that list.

67. The Unit's tasks are:

- to identify key threats and risks to border security;

- to identify the need for joint operations;

- to identify areas where capacities could be built by technical border control equipment;

- to identify the most effective focus for border guard training programmes; and

- to provide the Member States' border guard services with systematic and immediate early warnings.

The Unit, having identified the need for a joint operation, assists in the preparations, appoints an intelligence officer for the duration of the operation, collects and analyses data during the operation, and passes information—and where appropriate alerts—to the Member States.

68. After the operation the Unit produces a report evaluating the operation. This normally includes:

- analysis of replies to the analytical questionnaire;

- number of migrants, including asylum-seekers;

- routes adopted;

- in the case of airports, entries refused;

- migration trends;

- other irregularities, such as implications for trafficking human beings and drugs;

- international criminal networks;

- comparisons with statistics for previous operations; and

- evaluations by the deployed experts.

69. The evaluation report may ascertain whether the operation induced traffickers to change their *modus operandi* by putting pressure on other illegal points of entry, or maybe by making major changes to the migratory routes. If so, the report may make recommendations for securing other weak or illegal access points, and suggest courses of action to target specific nationalities. It may recommend passing information to Europol or Interpol, which are better placed to investigate the involvement of smuggling organisations and other cross-border crime; we consider the involvement of Europol in Chapter 8.

70. Mr Tom Dowdall, Director of EU Operations at the Home Office and the United Kingdom observer on the Frontex Management Board, explained that the Risk Analysis Unit brings together information provided by the Member States, analyses it, weighs it and on that basis identifies what the course of action should be. In this work it is assisted by a Risk Analysis Network which brings together representatives of the Member States meeting on a quarterly basis. It was in his view a process which was evolving and which needed to improve (QQ 141–142). Major Mallia wanted to see the risk analysis role of Frontex strengthened (Q 399), and we note that development of the risk analysis function plays a major part in the Work Programme for 2008.

Training

71. General Laitinen stressed the importance which he attaches to the training function of Frontex. They have revised and published a Common Core Curriculum for border guard training, which is compiled with the cooperation of the Member States. They are not under any obligation to apply that Curriculum, but only a handful do not yet do so. He told us that Frontex are seeking to have a Common Core Curriculum for mid-level training and have launched periodical four-week courses for mid-level officers. The other part of the training function is arranging courses for the border control authorities, including "land border related training, aeronautical training, helicopter pilot training, travel document detection training, ... and linguistic skills." For 2007 the commitment for training purposes was almost €2 million (Q 223). Mr Byrne told us that the United Kingdom made a significant contribution to training, offering expertise in document forgery detection and the use of detection technology.[38] Given the increasing complexity of some of the equipment used to monitor migration, we think training guards in the best use of the equipment they have is an important element of this task.

72. We believe that training courses for border guards should emphasise the humanitarian background to illegal migration and its causes. We are glad to note the Commission's suggestion that training courses should be organised on asylum law, the law of the sea and fundamental rights.[39] Frontex will also need to ensure that appropriate investment is made in the personal development and capacity of its own staff to enable them to understand this aspect of their work, and the impact that the courses they devise will have on the individuals affected by their work.

What Frontex does not do

73. The list of tasks set out in the Regulation is not illustrative but exhaustive. Frontex could not carry out other tasks without amendment of the Regulation. So far the only amendment has been for the system of Rapid Border Intervention Teams (RABITs) which we consider in Chapter 6. We stress this point because in the course of our inquiry we have heard and read suggestions as to what Frontex might do which are plainly outside its remit, including undertaking (as opposed to coordinating) emergency border

---

[38] Supplementary evidence, p 148.

[39] Commission Communication of 13 February 2008: Report on the evaluation and future development of the FRONTEX Agency, doc. 6664/08, COM(2008)67 final, paragraph 15.

operations and search and rescue missions. This is something which has also troubled General Laitinen. In June 2007 he issued a news release entitled "Frontex—Facts and Myths". He pointed out that the activities of Frontex were supplementary to those of the Member States; with its (then) 82 staff it was not intended to be a substitute for the thousands of border guards of the States. It had no operational personnel or equipment of its own, and its sole role was integration and coordination. As the Regulation says, "Responsibility for the control and surveillance of external borders lies with the Member States".[40] Mr Javier Moreno Sanchez MEP told us: "Frontex is a tool, not a panacea" (Q 107).

Resources

74.   Frontex started operations in October 2005 with 44 staff. By the end of 2006 this had increased to 72, and by October 2007 to 125. The intention is that in 2008 this should increase to 189. Even so, General Laitinen told us that "During the two years of the agency's existence we have been at the edge all the time when it comes to human resources" (Q 238).

75.   By far the larger part of the funds of Frontex comes from the European Community budget via the Commission, though a small part comes directly from the Member States. The rapid growth of Frontex in its first year of operation led to a large increase in the budget, but this came at a late stage— so late that nearly €3m of the €19m voted for 2006 remained unused. Since then Frontex has further increased in size and in the scope of its operations. The budget was double in 2007,[41] and for 2008 has again doubled: a further increase of €35m has been voted, to over €70m. For operations, this represents an increase of 140%.

76.   There is however no point in giving Frontex more money than it can spend, and it cannot sensibly cope with such an increase unless it has a corresponding increase, or at least an adequate increase, in the staff responsible for spending this money. This is a point which concerns General Laitinen: "… focussing only on the operational expenditure is not enough for a coordinator … if the human resources and the administrative side are not in balance with the soaring resources and financial resources for the operational element the results can be counter-productive" (Q 235).

77.   One of the few controls the European Parliament has over Frontex is in the budget. For 2008 the Parliament voted to give Frontex €30m more than either it or the Commission had requested: €53.5m for the operational budget and €15m for the administrative budget. But the Parliament voted to put in reserve—to freeze—30% of the administrative budget, and only to release it if satisfied that Frontex has improved its accountability and its effectiveness on the ground.[42]

78.   It is not uncommon for the Parliament to make the voting of funds to EU agencies subject to conditions. However in our view it makes no sense to release all the money for the operational budget but only part of the money for the administrative staff without whom the agency could not run. No

---

[40] Recital (4).

[41] The total was €35.3m, of which €20.7m was for operations, €9.4m for staff, and €5.2m for administration (Home Office, p 31). However a subsequent amendment added a further €7m.

[42] Simon Busuttil MEP, QQ 95–101.

organisation can plan how to spend €53.5m on operations without knowing whether it is going to have €10m or 15m to spend on staff to plan and administer those operations. As General Laitinen said, "it is not a good message for the staff, that a European agency is not able to guarantee the salary payments for the entire fiscal year" (Q 238).

79.   **We believe that before the European Parliament considers withholding part of the budget of Frontex, it should bear in mind the importance of Frontex being seen as a secure and responsible employer. Nothing should be done to undermine its operational effectiveness or put at risk the accumulated expertise of its permanent staff.**

80.   It is in any case debatable whether a large increase in the number and scope of operations is the best way for Frontex to proceed at this stage of its development. Mr Dowdall told us: "The United Kingdom view is that [the increased resources] should not fund simply a major increase in operations but should be focused on increasing the quality of the operations which are undertaken, also the quality of the intelligence-gathering machinery and the intelligence itself that is produced and shared with Member States. Those are key areas next year in relation to how that money is spent" (Q 147). He repeated this view when he gave evidence with the Minister; and Mr Byrne himself saw a need for more effective planning and evaluation. Mr Brodie Clark, the Strategic Director for Border Control, thought Frontex should concentrate on operations being relevant and effective, and "delivering something"; it was a matter of concern to him that Frontex should manage its ambitions, "so that it is not trying to do everything all the time" (Q 477).

81.   We share these views. **We believe the increased resources may usefully lead to a modest increase in the number of operations in 2008, but should be concentrated on further increasing the quality of those operations, and of the intelligence-gathering and sharing leading up to them.**

Accountability

82.   Strategic decisions on the work of Frontex are taken by the Management Board set up under Article 20 of the Regulation. The Board consists of one representative from each of the Schengen States. For the reasons we explained in paragraphs 54–60 the United Kingdom only has observer status. The Board adopts the work programme, decides on the organisational structure of the agency, and prepares the preliminary budget. It advises on issues directly related to the technical development of border control. General Laitinen explained that whenever the Board meets—on average five times a year—he gives it a full written and oral report of the state of play of Frontex activities and plans. He thought the sharing of responsibilities with the Management Board was very clear (Q 228).

83.   The Management Board is required by Article 20(2)(b) of the Regulation to adopt an annual report by the end of March each year, to send it to the Council, the Commission and the European Parliament, and to publish it. It follows that the annual report for 2007 will be adopted at much the same time as this report is published, but so far the only annual report has been that for 2006.

84. Frontex has an internal auditor within the agency reporting to the Executive Director and his Deputy. The Internal Audit Service of the Commission has visited Frontex, and the European Court of Auditors has the formal responsibility of auditing its accounts.[43] In the course of our scrutiny of EU documents we have recently looked at the Report of the Court of Auditors on the 2006 accounts.[44] The accounts were approved, and the only comments were such as might be expected when an organisation is just beginning its initial recruitment and expenditure.

85. Apart from formal control of the budget, the Parliament also has less formal ways of supervising the work of the agency, in particular by summoning the Executive Director to report and answer questions. On 11 June 2007 the Deputy Director attended a meeting of the LIBE Committee where he gave a presentation of the Work Programme for 2007 and discussed the events which had then recently taken place in the Mediterranean (to which we referred in paragraph 40). The following month the LIBE Committee organised a public hearing on "Tragedies of Migrants at Sea", and the Chairman of the Committee requested—indeed insisted on—the participation of a representative of Frontex. The inability of any of the three senior officials of Frontex to attend that hearing caused a degree of friction.

86. Mr Simon Busuttil's view was that there was not sufficient accountability (Q 115). Dr Bernard Ryan, giving evidence on behalf of the Immigration Law Practitioners' Association (ILPA), thought that the Management Board was "very close to Frontex in terms of personnel, and although there are reports, beyond that there are not specific structures in place through which Frontex is accountable to and can take guidance from democratic bodies ... it is accountability to the public at large or to the political system at large ... that is lacking" (QQ 428, 432). This is a view shared by the Standing Committee of experts on international immigration, refugee and criminal law (the Meijers Committee): "An institutional mechanism of prompt democratic oversight over operational activities of Frontex is non-existent" (p 168). Ms Muggeridge, on behalf of the Refugee Council, suggested the appointment of an ombudsman or observer to produce independent reports on operations (Q 430).

87. We heard criticism that some information about the activities of Frontex which was or should be in the public domain was not easily accessible, in particular on the Frontex website.[45] While information about risk analysis, operational planning and similar matters must remain confidential, we believe Frontex should take steps to ensure that all information which should be in the public domain is easily accessible.

88. Jonathan Faull thought that, broadly speaking, the current legal framework of the agency ensured adequate transparency and accountability. He added that issues of accountability and monitoring would form part of the review of the existing legal framework in the evaluation report which Article 33 of the Regulation required the Management Board to commission. (Q 75).

89. **We believe that the current arrangements for financial accountability are adequate.**

---

[43] Laitinen Q 229; EC Treaty Article 248.

[44] Document 15146/07.

[45] Ryan QQ 412, 428.

90. **Frontex should raise its public profile by ensuring that information which is or should be in the public domain is easily accessible to the public, in particular on its website.**

91. **Frontex should be more formally accountable to the European Parliament. The Chairman of the Management Board and the Executive Director should, if so requested, appear before the Parliament or its Committees to discuss the activities of Frontex.**

CHAPTER 5: JOINT OPERATIONS ORGANISED BY FRONTEX

Operational cooperation

92. Operational cooperation is the first of Frontex's listed tasks, and the one which appears in the title of the Regulation and the formal title of the agency. More than half of its budget is spent on operations, and 80% of that is on sea operations. When we took evidence from General Laitinen in October 2007 he told us that Frontex had arranged almost 40 operations so far (Q 219); the number is now greater. The United Kingdom took part in six operations in 2006 and sixteen in 2007.[46] We give in Appendix 4 a full list of the operations which have taken place in 2006 and 2007, and details of the United Kingdom's participation. Fuller details of all these operations, and of pilot projects, can be found in the Statistical Annex to the Commission report on the evaluation and future development of Frontex. The Commission states that during the operations in 2006 and 2007 more than 53,000 persons have been apprehended or denied entry at the borders, more than 2,900 false travel documents detected, and 58 facilitators of illegal migration arrested.[47]

93. Each individual Frontex operation is managed by an International Coordination Centre (ICC). Within the ICC there will be a Frontex representative, and representatives from each of the countries which has human or operational resources involved in the operation. The operation is prepared by the host country which, together with Frontex, will draw up an operational plan detailing the areas where the operation will be conducted, the activities it is seeking to combat, and what the operation is seeking to achieve. When the plan is issued, other Member States are asked to pledge assets towards the operation. We assume that plans for an operation are not finalised until it is reasonably clear what assets are likely to be available.

94. The Home Office told us that there was a continuing need to refine the planning of operations to increase their effectiveness. Under "effects-based' planning, the Member States conducting a Frontex operation will agree the aim and purpose of the operation, and ensure that all operational, legal and logistical constraints are understood, and that the operation is achievable with the resources provided. A United Kingdom officer reported that Frontex managers are familiar with the concept; it is a best practice to which they aspire.[48]

95. Once the operation starts, any action to be undertaken by a particular vessel has to be agreed by the national representative; thus if an Italian vessel is operating from Malta and the Maltese overall coordinator wishes to deploy it in a particular place for a particular role, that would have to be agreed by the Italian representative. This may seem cumbersome, but Major Mallia thought it worked remarkably well in practice, and would continue to do so as long as the national representatives on the spot retained the power of decision (QQ 391–393).

---

[46] Byrne supplementary evidence, p 149.

[47] Commission Communication of 13 February 2008: Report on the evaluation and future development of the FRONTEX Agency, doc. 6664/08, COM(2008)67 final, paragraph 9 and ADD 3.

[48] Home Office written evidence, p 34, and further information supplied subsequently.

96. The end of a joint operation does not of course mean the end of the activities that were being carried out; the state responsible for the work will continue it, but without the assistance of other states. Meanwhile the operation needs to be evaluated. The Home Office believe that, though both planning and evaluation are improving year on year, evaluation too needs refinement, mainly because of the unfamiliarity of Frontex with the capabilities of the Member States whose resources they coordinate.[49] We have explained in paragraph 67 how an intelligence officer from the Risk Analysis Unit will collect and analyse the data during the operation, and subsequently evaluate it. Full performance analysis of the operation is vital. **We believe that the host country, and other countries taking part if they wish, should also be involved in drawing up a report after each operation from which lessons can be learned. Frontex should be responsible for coordinating such reports.**

97. A report analysing an operation and evaluating the lessons to be learned from it will be of only limited use if there is no mechanism for ensuring that the lessons learned are put to good use in subsequent operations. We are not aware that this is the specific responsibility of any person or body. Given that the Risk Analysis Unit is closely concerned with the evaluation of operations and the preparation of subsequent operations, we believe that it will be well placed to ensure that the lessons learned are indeed put to good use.

Land operations

98. The operations are designed with specific limited objectives. An example of a land operation in April 2007 was Operation GORDIUS. In recent years Moldavian nationals have been one of the main nationalities of illegal immigrants at the Eastern borders of the EU. In 2006 they produced the largest increase of detected third country nationals targeting the border of the Slovak Republic via Ukraine. Frontex therefore launched a joint operation at the borders of Romania, Poland, Hungary and the Slovak Republic. The operation focused on the border checks of travel documents presented by Moldavian citizens at the border controls. Experts from other Member States were deployed at selected border crossing points and studied the routes used and false or falsified documents.

99. The budget for this one-month operation was €200,000. Romania, Hungary and Slovakia hosted the operation, and experts from twelve other Member States took part, including the United Kingdom. 109 illegal border crossings by Moldavian nationals were detected, and there were 855 refusals of entry.

Maritime operations

100. Maritime operations are on an altogether different scale. During 2006 the main operations, HERA I and II, focussed on the flow of illegal immigrants towards the Canary Islands, identified by a Frontex risk analysis as one of the main routes of entry to the EU.

---

[49] *Ibid.*

BOX 2

HERA I and II

> On 17 July 2006 9 experts from France, Portugal, Italy and Germany arrived in the Canary Islands to support the Spanish in identifying immigrants and establishing their countries of origin. In August and September they were joined by two further groups of experts, including some from the United Kingdom. Together with the Spanish authorities they identified all the illegal migrants, and 6,076 of them were returned to their countries of origin, mainly Morocco, Senegal, Mali, Gambia and Guinea. They detained several facilitators, mainly in Senegal, and prevented the departure of more than one thousand people.
>
> The second module, HERA II, was a joint sea surveillance operation. It began on 11 August and brought together technical border surveillance equipment from several Member States to enhance the control of the area between West Africa and the Canaries, diverting vessels and so helping to reduce the number of lives lost at sea. For the first time such an operation was carried out in the territorial waters of Senegal and Mauritania and in close cooperation with them. In addition to Spanish vessels and helicopters, the operation included one Portuguese and one Italian vessel, and one Italian and one Finnish aircraft. Seven States participated in what was the longest operation coordinated by Frontex with a total budget of €3.5m. During the operational phase of HERA II 3,887 illegal immigrants on 57 cayucos (small fishing boats) were intercepted close to the African coast and diverted.
>
> During the two operations close on 5,000 illegal immigrants were stopped from setting off on their voyages. Frontex, by coordinating the activities of the Member States, helped them to bring the situation under control.

101. Even at the close of HERA II Frontex had been operational for barely a year. General Laitinen told us that between 2006 and 2007 there was a decrease of almost 70% in illegal immigration to the Canaries (Q 219). Mr Javier Moreno Sanchez MEP referred to "the excellent results of Frontex's operations", adding that the Vice-President of Spain had said that Frontex's four joint operations in the Canary Islands during the first eight months of 2007 had resulted in the number of illegal immigrants who had arrived in Spain being reduced by 75 % (Q 90). The Home Office figure was that illegal immigrants arriving in Spain in boats had decreased by 55% in the first six months of 2007 compared with the same period in 2006 (p 34). Over the whole year, illegal migration to the Canaries in 2007 was half what it was in 2006.[50]

102. Some of this decrease will have been due simply to displacement: the use by migrants of different routes. But even making allowance for this, and for the discrepancies between the various estimates, there has clearly been a major absolute reduction in the number of illegal immigrants, and Frontex has plainly made a substantial contribution to it. Mr Byrne stressed that the participation of Mauritania and Senegal was essential to the success of the operation.[51]

103. An even more ambitious maritime operation was mounted in 2007. NAUTILUS 2007 had a budget of over €5m, and concentrated on illegal

---

[50] Home Office supplementary evidence, p 148.

[51] *Ibid.*

migration to Malta. Risk analysis suggested that the Central Mediterranean route from Libya and Tunisia towards the Italian islands of Lampedusa, Pantelleria and Sicily, and also towards Malta, was an area under great pressure, as the islands were themselves a preferred destination for migrants but also to some extent transit points to other countries. The illegal transport of undocumented immigrants is organised by facilitators. For most part, organised criminal groups use old fishing vessels and fibreglass boats. Illegal transport takes place mainly during the night and at weekends; the migrants travel from their countries of origin to the big cities of Libya and its northern coastal region, where criminal syndicates arrange to have them embarked on boats bound for the coast of Italy and Malta.

104. The operation was in two phases, between July and October 2007. At its height nine Member States, including the United Kingdom, were involved, using four offshore patrol vessels, six coastal patrol vessels, three helicopters and four aircraft. A total of 3,173 illegal immigrants were detected, one third in the operational area and two thirds outside it.[52]

105. It is of course the Member States which are responsible for committing their resources to such operations—patrol boats, helicopters, aircraft, and those manning them. A major problem has been the failure of some Member States actually to make available the resources they have promised. In July 2007 the Central Register of Available Technical Equipment (CRATE) was impressive—on paper—and included 21 fixed wing aircraft, 27 helicopters and 117 vessels. Of these, 32 were patrol vessels pledged by Italy, yet Simon Bussutil MEP told us that not one Italian vessel took part in Operation NAUTILUS (Q 88).

106. Major Mallia explained to us that "a pledge does not mean: 'I am giving you this asset and it will be there at a drop of a hat.' It is saying, 'I am making these resources available. Sometimes I will be able to participate; sometimes I will not.'." (Q 395) Nevertheless it seems to us that it is very difficult for all concerned, not least Frontex, to attempt to plan operations without having a reasonably clear idea of the resources they will actually have available. As General Laitinen pointed out, a coordinator must have something to coordinate (Q 231). If Italy, instead of making a generous pledge of 32 vessels, had pledged, say, 10 vessels but made them all available, not only would life have been much easier for all concerned, but the number of vessels available would have been double the number that actually took part in the operation. We consider in Chapter 8 what could be done in the longer term to deal with this problem. For the present, **we recommend that Member States should be asked to pledge to make available for Frontex operations only as many vessels and other equipment as they are actually able to make available when requested.**

Disembarkation

107. We heard about the difficulties facing Member States in the policing of their maritime external borders, especially in relation to the practical management of rescue operations and the disembarkation of intercepted persons. Under the current UN Guidelines, the Government responsible for the Search and Rescue (SAR) region in which survivors are recovered is responsible for providing a place of safety or ensuring that a place of safety is provided. This

---

[52] Frontex Press Kit, volume 2/11, issue 1.

is a place where the survivor's life or safety is no longer threatened, where basic human needs (food, shelter and medical) can be met, and where arrangements can be made for transport to the next or final destination.[53] These Guidelines are useful, but the issue is highly complex. "All Member States are subject to the same international legal framework but it is certainly true that differences in practical application and interpretation of that framework can be different from one country to another and those differences may have an impact on the effectiveness of operations, particularly when vessels from different Member States are acting within the framework of the same operation."[54]

108. Assessments as to whether a migrant will be safe in a particular country (like Libya) may vary. The Guidelines leave unanswered the question of what is to be done when attempts are made to disembark in one state persons rescued outside the SAR region of that state. In the case of the Royal Navy, "if there was a scenario where a rescue was required the way that we would interpret the law of the sea would be to discharge the individuals who were rescued at the nearest port. That would typically be a port in the Mediterranean."[55]

109. Immigrants who reach the Canaries or Lampedusa, or their SAR regions, become the responsibility of, respectively, Spain and Italy. Given the numbers involved this causes those countries considerable problems, but these are insignificant compared to the problems faced by Malta: we have already explained in paragraph 38 how, on the basis of the size of the country, one immigrant in Malta equates to nearly a thousand immigrants in Italy. For this reason Malta will generally not accept the disembarkation in Malta of persons recovered outside the Maltese SAR region unless there are overriding humanitarian considerations. It is this which has led to very unfavourable media coverage in a number of cases.[56]

110. The first rule must plainly be that nothing should be done to endanger life at sea. But subject to this, the present situation cannot be allowed to continue. It seems to us that there are four questions to which the Member States must find an answer:

- guidelines on disembarkation for Frontex operations;

- financial support to share the disproportionate burden falling on Malta;

- a sharing of the burden posed by the immigrants themselves; and

- consideration of possible changes to the rules on asylum.

111. Until now, as Major Mallia told us, the question of guidance regarding disembarkation has been handled on an ad hoc basis. For a particular joint Frontex operation the participating countries discuss the operational plan which, among other things, will address this issue of disembarkation, and a practical solution will be agreed. But it will be a working arrangement for that particular operation, and not based on principle (Q 397). Nor, as M .Gérard Deprez MEP said, should it be the responsibility of the Master of

---

[53] Extracted from the UN Guidelines on the Treatment of Persons Rescued at Sea, adopted by the Maritime Safety Committee by Resolution MSC.167(78) in May 2004.

[54] Faull Q 50.

[55] Byrne Q 480.

[56] Mallia Q 389.

the vessel which rescues persons to decide where they should be disembarked (Q 92).

112. **It should not be the responsibility of those planning individual Frontex operations to decide the rules on disembarkation for those operations. Rules must be formulated which will apply to all Frontex maritime operations. This question must be addressed by the working group developing general guidelines about the law of the sea as it relates to EU States and illegal migration.**

113. Malta is already receiving financial assistance from EU funds. Mr Byrne told us that financial burden sharing was important (Q 484). We agree, but **we believe that a fairer method must be found of calculating and granting financial assistance to those states which bear a disproportionate share of the burden of illegal immigration.**

114. More important than the financial burden is the burden of the immigrants themselves: their temporary presence if they are to be refused entry and returned to their country of origin, or their permanent presence if they are granted asylum.

115. Mr Byrne's view was: "The way we interpret burden sharing is that we do not think we should be moving people around. We think that would create an enormous pull factor that would compound the problem rather than solve it" (Q 484). Major Mallia, while welcoming offers for the resettlement of refugees by other countries, such as the Netherlands and the United States, also warned that there was a danger that this might start "to generate a pull factor" (Q 384).

116. Article 63(2)(b) of the TEC already requires the Council to adopt measures "promoting a balance of effort between Member States in receiving and bearing the consequences of receiving refugees and displaced persons". This provision would be amended by the Treaty of Lisbon so that Article 80[57] of the Treaty on the Functioning of the European Union would read:

> "The policies of the Union set out in this Chapter [i.e. the Chapter on Policies on Border Checks, Asylum and Immigration] and their implementation shall be governed by the principle of solidarity and fair sharing of responsibility, including its financial implications, between Member States. Whenever necessary, the acts of the Union adopted pursuant to this Chapter shall contain appropriate measures to give effect to this principle."

We do not think the Member States need wait until 1 January 2009, when it is planned that this provision will come into force, before giving effect to its principles.

117. The movement of immigrants cannot be divorced from the processing of asylum claims. The Regulation known as Dublin II[58] governs which state should be responsible for the processing of an asylum application lodged in one of the Member States by a third country national. Generally speaking, the state in which a person first arrives is the state with jurisdiction to decide

---

[57] This is Article 63b in the Treaty of Lisbon, but will be Article 80 in the numbering in the consolidated text.

[58] Council Regulation (EC) 343/2003 of 18 February 2003. Council Regulation (EC) 343/2003 of 18 February 2003 establishing the criteria and mechanisms for determining the Member State responsible for examining an asylum application lodged in one of the Member States by a third-country national (OJ 2003 L 50/1)

the asylum application. But this rule does throw the main burden on the border States, and again the burden on Malta is disproportionate; Major Mallia's view was that it should not necessarily be the State of disembarkation which would have exclusive jurisdiction to determine any subsequent asylum claim, particularly where interception of migrants occurred outside that State's SAR region (Q 384).

118. Ms Patricia Coelho, speaking on behalf of the European Council on Refugees and Exiles (ECRE), told us: "... the EU has a role to play in brokering some agreements between EU states in terms of responsibility sharing ... we would go along the lines of reforming the Dublin II regulation ..." (Q 420). Both the ECRE and the UNHCR are on record as wishing to see Dublin II reformed for other reasons as well.

119. It is possible that some flexibility in Dublin II would be beneficial. However any examination of this is a wide topic with profound political implications. It is a matter only peripheral to Frontex, and hence to our inquiry. But **we believe that the fairness and effectiveness of the Dublin II system is something which must be addressed in the second stage of the work on a Common European Asylum System.**

Operational cooperation by the United Kingdom

120. Article 12 of the Regulation, entitled "Cooperation with Ireland and the United Kingdom", provides:

> "The Agency shall facilitate operational cooperation of the Member States with Ireland and the United Kingdom in matters covered by its activities and to the extent required for the fulfilment of its tasks set out in Article 2(1)."

121. It is on the basis of this provision that the United Kingdom has participated very fully in a number of operations, as is clear from Appendix 4. The United Kingdom has no right to participate; in the case of each operation, participation has to be decided by the Management Board. This is done by written procedure, but is nevertheless cumbersome. General Laitinen's summary was that the United Kingdom was "very active in participating in joint operations" (Q 232).

122. These operations include two which (with others) the United Kingdom hosted. Operation Torino involved a number of experts stationed at airports around Europe advising on documents in connection with the Winter Olympics in Turin in February 2006; one of these was an Italian border guard stationed at Heathrow who advised on Italian documents and visas, specifically those in relation to the Olympics. Operation Agelaus, in February 2007, was prompted by a United Kingdom officer stationed full-time in Frontex. It dealt with unaccompanied minors illegally entering the Member States, and involved the collection of information at a number of airports including Heathrow, Gatwick and Manchester.[59] Nevertheless the legal position remains that Frontex operations cannot take place on United Kingdom territory; those operations that do take place here can be planned, organised and executed in parallel with the respective Frontex operations, but they have to be construed as separate United Kingdom operations.[60]

---

[59] Dowdall Q 172.

[60] Supplementary written evidence from Frontex, p 68.

123. The United Kingdom has also participated in three Border Management Conferences aimed at promoting third country cooperation, and also in pilot projects, and has been "very, very active" on the return operations side, compiling best practices and training border guards handling returns (Q 232).

124. The United Kingdom has a seat on the Management Board, but only with observer status. However Mr Dowdall, the United Kingdom representative, explained that the only decisions which, up to October 2007, had been decided by vote were the appointment of the Executive Director and the Chairman of the Board itself. United Kingdom operations were well respected; the United Kingdom view was sought and listened to, and influenced the decisions taken by the Board (Q 144). The United Kingdom participates fully in the preparations for operations, and General Laitinen thought that "in terms of risk analysis and also the joint operations, we do not see any difference between our UK colleagues and the others" (Q 222). However the United Kingdom is involved in funding Frontex only in respect of its share of the cost of those operations in which it participates; in 2006 this amounted to €0.2m, equivalent to just 1.2 % of the budget of Frontex.

125. **The United Kingdom has great experience of controlling sea and air borders, and recent experience of controlling the land border with the Irish Republic. This country has much to offer Frontex and the Schengen States. We hope that the Government will share their experience with them, and that they will make full use of it.**

126. **Improved coordination of border management of the Schengen States will be of direct benefit to the United Kingdom. The Government should make clear to the other Member States that they wish to play as full a part as possible in operations, and should commit resources to them for this purpose. The Management Board should not just allow, but should encourage, United Kingdom participation.**

CHAPTER 6: RABITS

Rapid Border Intervention Teams

127. In May 2005, just as the final preparations were being made for making Frontex operational, the ministers of the interior of the G5[61] met in Evian and discussed the possibility of creating a "European Police" in charge of external borders and able to provide rapid responses for crisis management. This border intervention force could then be the "precursor of a European Border Guard". It is not clear whether this expression was intended to refer to a self-contained European border police force of the type referred to in the Commission Communication of 7 May 2002.[62] If so, we have made clear that this proposal is for the present dormant, if not defunct. If however the G5 were envisaging the use of border guards of one Member State to help another Member State facing unexpected major pressure from illegal immigrants, this is the subject of a Regulation which was adopted on 11 July 2007.

128. Regulation 863/2007 establishes "a mechanism for the creation of Rapid Border Intervention Teams", known by the acronym RABITs. RABITs are composed of national border guards of Member States and are deployed by Frontex at short notice to a requesting Member State which experiences an urgent and exceptional migratory pressure.

129. We asked our witnesses for examples of what might be "a situation of urgent and exceptional pressure"? General Laitinen found it difficult to present a scenario, but suggested as examples the situation in 2006 in Lebanon, or the 2005 assaults in Ceuta and Melilla. It would in any case be "an exceptional situation that we did not have any pre-warning of" (QQ 271–274). Major Mallia thought that RABITs would probably have their major applications on the land and air borders. "They are not equipped to operate in the maritime environment. They will be useful as a rapid reaction force in cases of real emergencies [such as] a sudden influx of South American citizens towards Spain, trying to pass through the airports" (Q 401).

130. Unlike other Frontex joint operations, RABITs would not be planned on the basis of risk analysis as they are intended to deal only with unexpected migratory pressure. There is another important difference. RABITs operations are based on a novel concept sometimes called "compulsory solidarity", which means that Member States are obliged to participate in a RABITs operation. The Regulation provides for the creation of a pool of officers which Member States must deploy "unless they are faced with an exceptional situation substantially affecting the discharge of national tasks."[63] M. Gérard Deprez MEP, who was the Rapporteur of the LIBE Committee for the draft RABITs Regulation and responsible for this key provision,

---

[61] The G5 are the five largest Member States: Germany, France, the United Kingdom, Italy and Spain. When they met in Heiligendamm, in Germany, in March 2006 they were joined by Poland to become the G6. We reported on that meeting, and also on their meeting in Stratford-upon-Avon in October 2006: *Behind Closed Doors: the meeting of the G6 Interior Ministers at Heiligendamm* (40th Report, Session 2005–06, HL Paper 221), and *After Heiligendamm: doors ajar at Stratford-upon-Avon* (5th Report, Session 2006–07. HL Paper 32). The G6 Ministers met again in Venice in May 2007 and in Sopot, Poland, in October 2007.

[62] See paragraphs 50 and 51 above.

[63] RABITs Regulation Article 4(3).

thought that new legislation was needed to extend this concept to all Frontex operations, so that in appropriate cases it would be compulsory to give assistance to other Member States (Q 93). We consider this further in Chapter 8.

Amendments to the Frontex Regulation: the right to carry arms

131. The RABITs Regulation contains a second chapter which amends the Frontex Regulation. Provisions in Chapter II clarify the powers which officers participating in all Frontex operations (not just RABITs) can exercise, and the tasks they can be asked to undertake. These include active border guard activities as set out in the Schengen Borders Code, such as investigating nationality, stamping passports and preventing illegal border crossing. As Mr Vuorensola, the Frontex Legal Adviser, explained to us:

     "Until the RABITs Regulation came into force all the powers that our guest officers in joint operations had were based on the national law of the host Member State, and the possibility of that national law to delegate executive powers to foreigners doing the job, which is usually reserved only to their own national border guards: checking persons, asking for identification and doing other border controlling tasks". In his view these powers could now be exercised as a matter of Community law, and they included the right to carry a service weapon and to use it in self-defence, and in certain other limited cases (Q 275).

132. The right of guest officers to carry and use weapons in a Frontex joint operation was one of the contentious issues when the RABITs Regulation was negotiated. We heard from Major Mallia that "weapons do have a role in border control, unfortunately." He identified two roles in particular: weapons act as a deterrent, and are used for self-protection or protection of third parties. However, not all Member States' border guards are part of the police or army and carry guns or other weapons regularly.[64] For this reason, Article 6(5) of the Regulation places a number of restrictions on the carrying and use of weapons: Member States hosting RABITs operations are allowed to restrict weapons from being carried and used if this is prohibited by the host state's domestic legislation, and to determine which weapons are permissible, and the conditions under which they can be used. An amendment to the Frontex Regulation places similar restrictions on the carrying of weapons in the generality of Frontex operations. Both Regulations include provisions on the criminal liability of guest officers.

133. While the Regulation contains clear restrictions on the use of weapons, Major Mallia thought that more clarity was needed on the status of the individuals deployed, and the legal chain and jurisdiction to which these deployed forces are subject, "because, if something happens, as it inevitably one day will, we will have to see the liability of that deployed border guard. Is he liable to the host state? Is he liable in his Member State? He definitely cannot be liable in both" (Q 401).

134. Frontex have told us in their supplementary written evidence that the amendments to the Frontex Regulation have important consequences for United Kingdom participation in Frontex activities. Both RABITs team members and guest officers in Frontex activities have now been endowed with certain tasks and executive powers which would not be available to

---

[64] "The United Kingdom does not arm its border guards, and is not planning to do so." Byrne, Q 476.

participating United Kingdom border guards. The possible liability of United Kingdom border guards participating in Frontex operations (both joint operations and RABIT teams) is unclear.[65]

135. **The liabilities of guest border guards, particularly those which arise from the use of weapons, need to be clarified in amending legislation. The particular position of participating United Kingdom border guards should also be addressed.**

RABITs training exercises

136. The first trial RABITs exercise took place between 5 and 9 November 2007 at Sa Carneiro airport, Porto, Portugal comprising a total of 16 border guards from 16 Member States, divided into three teams. Eight of them concentrated on front line interviews with arriving passengers, five on examination of suspect documents, and the remainder on secondary interviews of those whose eligibility for admission to the EU was in doubt. The main objectives were:

- to test the new mechanism in real circumstances;

- to test the administrative procedures necessary for deployment within the time limits set out in the RABITs Regulation;

- to deal with operational challenges (national expert pools, list of permissible weapons, databases, etc.) and open questions in advance of real missions; and

- to develop further the management of RABITs within Frontex.[66]

137. The exercise was made as realistic as possible, and the guest officers were therefore asked to bring their service weapons with them. This raised the issue as to whether guest officers were required, as a matter of Portuguese law, to obtain a Portuguese firearms permit before the weapons could be carried in public (Portuguese border guards are required to hold such a permit). Frontex argued that the RABITs Regulation took precedence over national legislation and that guest officers could not be required to obtain these permits. After some debate this was accepted by the Portuguese authorities, but only after they had issued the national permits.

138. This is an important issue. Under Article 10(5) of the Frontex Regulation[67] guest officers are only allowed to carry service weapons in accordance with the law of the host Member State. However, the host Member State may prohibit the carrying of service weapons provided that its own legislation applies the same prohibition to its own border guards. If Portuguese law does not allow Portuguese guards to carry arms without a permit, it is legitimate to apply the same law to guest border guards, and to require them to have a permit; but it may also be very inconvenient to have to wait for a permit to be issued in what is by definition an urgent situation. This issue must be addressed.

139. Following from this exercise, Frontex was able to prepare a series of recommendations for the next exercise due in Slovenia in April 2008. The

---

[65] Frontex supplementary evidence, p 68.

[66] *Ibid.*

[67] As substituted by Article 12(6) of the RABITs Regulation 863/2007.

evaluation of each exercise with a view to improving the process the next time is a constant process. The training programme for officers who will be deployed in RABITs began in January 2008, and 22 courses are planned under the RABITs programme before the end of 2008. United Kingdom officers will be involved in the delivery of RABITs training, but will not have a leading role.

CHAPTER 7: OTHER ISSUES

The applicable law

140. Operations at sea generally tend to be governed by international legal instruments rather than purely national ones.[68] The principal instruments are the United Nations Convention on the Law of the Sea (UNCLOS) and the International Convention on Maritime Search and Rescue (SAR). Both are agreements between States, and Frontex could not therefore be a party to them even if search and rescue was a part of its functions, which it is not, as a number of witnesses made clear.[69] But General Laitinen also emphasised that search and rescue was an international obligation incumbent on Frontex as much as on anyone else—even in the case of those whose distress is deliberately of their own making. It is beyond the remit of Frontex to label an operation as a maritime search and rescue operation; but, as an agency established by States which are subject to international law, it too is bound by that law (Q 246).

141. The Standing Committee of experts on international immigration, refugee and criminal law (the Meijers Committee) sent us, with the evidence which they prepared specifically for our inquiry, comments which they had prepared for the European Parliament in October 2006 on the (then draft) RABITs Regulation. We have printed those comments with the evidence, since they consider in critical detail the operations to which we have referred, and in particular the law applicable to them. The Committee point out that "Member States taking part in pre-border control operations apparently operate under the premise that migrants still within the territorial waters of third countries fall under the exclusive responsibility of third countries". This in the Meijers Committee's view is mistaken; they believe that "Member States participating in such operations may be equally accountable under international law for possible human rights violations ensuing from these operations" (p 167).

142. ILPA too had concerns about activities that are coordinated by Frontex but take place outside the territory of the EU. Dr Bernard Ryan explained that it was very difficult to see that Frontex had, as a matter of European Union law, a mandate to operate beyond the external borders of the EU. He thought that Frontex had stretched its mandate beyond what is set out in the Regulation. He felt that if Frontex was to act extra-territorially its role should be expressly set out, and that this should include explicit guarantees that it was governed by international law (QQ 402, 416, 417).

143. The Schengen Borders Code is insufficient for this purpose. It applies within the territorial waters of Member States but not extra-territorially, and hence not on the high seas—still less in the territorial waters of third states. Dr Ryan pointed out, by way of example, that "the code gives a right of appeal against a refusal of entry; it is a bit hard to see how that is operating in the territorial waters of Senegal, to the extent that Frontex is coordinating refusals of entry to the European Union in some sense there. The code is not designed to address extraterritorial activity" (Q 423). Jonathan Faull confirmed that, while border surveillance can be carried out on the high seas,

---

[68] Mallia Q 371.

[69] E.g. Faull Q 47; Deprez Q 92; Laitinen Q 246.

measures of interception and disembarkation are not covered by the surveillance rules of the Schengen Borders Code but are governed by the law of the sea, and so based on the jurisdiction and national legislation of the flag state of each vessel (Q 78).

144. In May 2007 the Commission, in response to a request from the European Council, published a study on international law in relation to illegal immigration by sea.[70] The study examines Member States' control powers in the different sea areas (internal waters, territorial waters and high seas) and identifies the gaps in the international legal framework applicable to operations at sea which need to be addressed. On the basis of that study an expert group was set up which included experts from the Member States, Frontex, the International Maritime Organisation (IMO), UNHCR and the International Organization for Migration (IOM).[71] When that group met in June 2007 it agreed to set up a drafting sub-group: the Law of the Sea/Frontex Guidelines Drafting Group. The United Kingdom is part of both groups. The drafting sub-group met three times in 2007 and again in February 2008; Mr Byrne told us it was hoped that these guidelines would be formulated early in 2008.[72]

145. If Frontex were itself operating extra-territorially, and carrying out search and rescue and other operations on the high seas, we can see that its power to do so, and the principles guiding it when doing so, should be set out in the legislation establishing it. But so long as such operations, though coordinated by Frontex, continue actually to be carried out by the Member States, we see no need to amend the Frontex Regulation in this respect. However, **given the complexity of the law governing operations on the high seas involving illegal immigration, we think it essential that the Member States taking part in operations coordinated by Frontex should follow clear guidelines clarifying their powers and obligations in the different sea areas.**

Agreements with third countries

146. Operating in the territory of a third state, including its territorial waters, is quite another matter. Here activities coordinated by Frontex cannot be carried out without the agreement of that state; and even with that agreement, there is some doubt as to whether the mandate of Frontex stretches so far.[73]

147. Until now such cooperation has been based on agreements between a Member State and third countries; the legal basis for operations coordinated by Frontex in the territorial waters of Senegal and Mauritania is the bilateral agreements between Spain and those countries.[74] However Article 14 of the Regulation requires Frontex to "facilitate the operational cooperation between Member States and third countries", and allows it to conclude working arrangements with the authorities of those countries.

---

[70] SEC(2007)691.

[71] This is the Expert Meeting on the Study of International Law Instruments in Relation to Illegal Immigration by Sea.

[72] Faull Q 54; Byrne Q 465; Home Office supplementary written evidence, p 152.

[73] See the evidence of Dr Ryan quoted in paragraph 142.

[74] Laitinen, Q 267.

148. Arrangements have already been concluded with the border guard authorities of Russia, Ukraine and Switzerland, and negotiations with Croatia are well advanced. The Management Board has given Frontex mandates to negotiate arrangements with ten other countries.[75] Of these, Libya is the country with which cooperation is most urgently needed, as was demonstrated by an incident in May 2007 when 27 Africans were alleged to have been left clinging to tuna nets for three days and nights while Malta and Libya argued over whose responsibility it was to save them.[76] At precisely that time a Frontex technical mission was in Libya discussing questions of illegal immigration. Given its finding that Libya is "fundamentally a transit country from North Africa to Italy and Malta and thereon to the rest of the EU",[77] the mission concentrated as much on the highly porous Libyan southern border, but it recommended that a structured Mediterranean Sea Border Control Cooperation Framework should be developed to extend maritime cooperation in the Mediterranean to third countries, and that Libya should be invited to play a leading role.

149. However this has not yet led to a working arrangement with the Libyan authorities. Major Mallia told us that he would like Frontex to move ahead at greater speed in negotiating with third states in addressing the problems on the Northern African rim, most specifically with Libya. He thought Frontex could and should take a much more substantial role because it brought with it the weight of the whole Union rather than a single Member State (Q 399). Such an arrangement, once negotiated, could be expected to require Libya to play a greater part in preventing would-be immigrants to the EU from leaving its shores, and taking back those who do leave while they are still in its territorial waters, in its search and rescue area, or on the high seas.

150. Any arrangement would not be with Libya or its Government but with its border control authority; as General Laitinen pointed out, "we do not establish a partnership with a country or a government but [between] the border control authority of that third country and Frontex" (Q 268). However Ms Coelho thought that although Frontex working arrangements with third countries might be regarded as technical low-level operational agreements, an arrangement with Libya was part of a political relationship between the EU and Libya, and "could be seen as the EU agreeing that the way Libya treats people as it does on its borders and within its detention centres is acceptable" (Q 413).

151. Dr Ryan pointed out that "Libya is not a party to the Refugee Convention; we just do not have guarantees about what is going to happen if they are returned" (Q 409). In particular, there are no guarantees that Libya will observe the obligation of *non-refoulement*. Other witnesses also made allegations of abuses and human rights violations to which persons were subjected when returned to Libya and other countries in North Africa.[78] It is precisely because a working arrangement with Libya would be seen as

---

[75] FYROM, Turkey, Egypt, Libya, Morocco, Mauritania, Senegal, Cape Verde, Moldova and Georgia.

[76] Immigration Advisory Service p 164. The time "three days and nights" is also given by the International Herald Tribune (3 June 2007), but The Times says that the men were transferred to an Italian vessel after 24 hours.

[77] Report of the mission, paragraph 9.5. The report identifies five main migration flows: from Sub-Saharan western Africa, from the Horn of Africa, from Morocco and Egypt, from the Middle East, and from the Indian sub-continent.

[78] Muggeridge Q 413; Immigration Advisory Service p 163.

carrying the approval of the whole Union that the Member States should be concerned to influence the terms of any agreement or arrangement that is negotiated.

152. **We believe that working arrangements between Frontex and the authorities of third countries in the Mediterranean could play a valuable part in controlling illegal immigration to the EU. We hope that Frontex will carry forward the negotiation of such arrangements.**

153. **Member States, including the United Kingdom, should however be concerned to ensure that any such arrangements with a third country include meaningful guarantees for the treatment of would-be immigrants repatriated to that country.**

Links with UNHCR and other bodies

154. We welcome the close links which Frontex is developing with UNHCR. In July 2007 Mr Soufiane Adjali was posted as Senior Liaison Officer to Frontex, and we took evidence from him on 23 October 2007 during our visit to Warsaw. He told us that a draft of an agreement between UNHCR and Frontex was then in the course of negotiation, and that Frontex had invited UNHCR to participate in the groups formulating a Core Curriculum for border guards (QQ 280, 299). The view of Ms Coelho was that "development of working arrangements with the UNHCR and IOM may lead to some mechanisms and relationships that can improve the ability of Frontex to respond to humanitarian needs and to see how people, once they arrive at the place where they are diverted or taken to, can be dealt with on reception. We think that the presence of a UNHCR position in the Frontex headquarters in Warsaw is a positive step ..." (Q 441).

155. **We welcome the cooperation between Frontex and UNHCR, and would like to see this extended to other bodies with responsibilities for immigration, asylum and refugees.**

CHAPTER 8: LOOKING TO THE FUTURE

Assessment of Frontex to date

156. Jonathan Faull told us that Frontex was "a small, modestly resourced agency which is really no more than a clearing organisation for assets, ideas and risk assessment made at each Member State's level and then trying to organise a coordinated response to that." On that basis it was meeting the expectations the Commission had for it when it was created, and it was continuing to meet expectations even though these had grown considerably and were continuing to grow (QQ 68, 47). But most of our other witnesses thought it had considerable and growing influence. Dr Ryan's assessment was that Frontex was "more than some passive coordinator of Member States' activity ... [it] has led to a step change in the situation because it is initiating the coordination that it engages in" (Q 436). Major Mallia, giving us Malta's perspective, told us that Frontex was doing things to which previously Malta could not have dedicated all the resources it would have liked, in particular risk assessment and multinational joint operations (Q 400). Tom Dodd, the Director, Border and Visa Policy, gave us the Home Office view that Frontex had done valuable work in improving the capacity of European border guards, but could do more to improve its performance in areas like the planning of operations and work with third countries (Q 140).

157. Any assessment of the results of Frontex operations must be based on a better knowledge of the facts. We have explained in paragraph 102 how it is at present impossible even to guess at the extent to which the reduction in the number of immigrants using a particular route is absolute, and what proportion is simply due to displacement. Mr Byrne wanted to see the United Kingdom participating with Frontex over the next three to five years in more effective evaluation of operations, so that we could better understand the effect of displacement (Q 476). This is a view we share.

158. We also agree with Ms Muggeridge that data should ideally include more than just headcount figures. Referring to the current Frontex statistics on the numbers of people it has stopped from coming or has turned back, she said: "... there is no reference really to the differences within that large group, the different needs of people and what kind of ages or gender or whether any of them were vulnerable people, or whether any of them indeed wanted to seek protection or did seek protection" (Q 433). We agree that such information would be useful; it should be possible to collect it without compromising operations and without disproportionate expense.

159. **Frontex should formulate rules for data collection which will allow a better evaluation of the results and impact of operations. This evaluation should show in particular the kinds of people intercepted or turned back, and the extent to which the operations are effective in reducing, and not just displacing, illegal immigration. The United Kingdom should participate fully in any such evaluation.**

Commitment of operational assets

160. We considered in Chapter 5 the problem of states not making available for operations the assets and resources which they had undertaken to make available, and for the short term we recommended that Member States

should be asked to pledge to make available only as many vessels and other equipment as they are actually able to make available when requested. We now look at what might be done in the longer term.

161. Major Mallia thought it unlikely that Member States would be coerced into committing resources in the near or medium term (Q 395). However we believe that something stronger is needed sooner rather than later. We referred in paragraph 130 to Article 4(3) of the RABITs Regulation which provides that "Member States shall make the border guards available for deployment at the request of the Agency unless they are faced with an exceptional situation substantially affecting the discharge of national tasks." Regulations are of course directly applicable law. A request from Frontex addressed to a Member State to make border guards available to another Member State thus imposes on the first State a legal obligation to which there is only a very limited exception.

162. This provision could not be transposed directly into the Frontex Regulation; border guards by definition are always at land or air borders, whereas in a case of urgency assets such as ships and helicopters would only coincidentally happen to be where they were wanted. But in the case of operations planned some time ahead it should be possible for Frontex to stipulate in advance which of the assets pledged should be available where and when. The only excuse for a Member State not complying should similarly be "an exceptional situation substantially affecting the discharge of national tasks." If the consequence was that insufficient assets were pledged, that could be resolved only at the political level.

163. For Frontex to operate successfully, Member States must meet their obligations. **Consideration should be given to introducing into the Frontex Regulation a provision requiring, subject to strictly limited exceptions, compulsory deployment of vessels and equipment in joint operations and other Frontex activities.**

Widening the mandate of Frontex

164. We have stressed that Frontex is an organisation set up to promote cooperation at national borders, primarily against illegal immigration. Inevitably this involves consideration of the organised crime which promotes and facilitates much of this immigration. We received evidence from Major Mallia about the involvement of traffickers in illegal maritime immigration (Q 385), and during our visit to Dorohusk we heard about the part played by organised crime in immigration by land.[79]

165. Some of our witnesses seem to assume that it is only a matter of time before the mandate of Frontex is enlarged specifically to include fighting serious organised crime, or even counter-terrorism. This was the view of the National Coordinator Ports Policing in both his written (p 2) and his oral evidence: "It is quite clear that there is a unique potential within Frontex in our collective fight against terrorism and for purposes of national security ... I think the addition of counter-terrorism as an element of Frontex would be beneficial, and specifically beneficial to us" (QQ 27, 30).

166. However most of our witnesses disagreed. Mr Dodd's view was that an explicit counter-terrorism role would be "a considerable extension of its

---

[79] Paragraphs 26–29 above.

current capacity and ability". Such a remit might be considered in the future, but would take Frontex much further than its current capacity to deliver. He thought that the issue would certainly be raised during the Commission review to which we referred in Chapter 4 (Q 192). When he gave evidence to us in October 2007 Jonathan Faull told us that he thought that for the time being the mandate was the right one (Q 49). He was understandably unwilling to pre-empt the results of the Commission review, but he pointed out that there were many other systems in place for cooperation between police and counter-terrorism agencies, and duplication was the last thing that was needed (Q 66).

167. Organised immigration crime[80] is quite another matter. Mr Byrne told us that he would be interested in the Committee's view on whether Frontex should concern itself with dismantling the syndicates of organised crime which are responsible for much of the pressure on illegal immigration; this was a question he had not answered in his own mind.

168. The reason this work does not feature in the list of tasks in Article 2(1) of the Regulation is that Frontex is created by a Regulation under the first pillar, while cooperation in criminal matters falls under the third pillar.[81] Even so, the two cannot be divorced. General Laitinen put the matter in this way: "… border control is a cross-pillar phenomenon which serves all three pillars … this is quite a persistent question and dilemma for us to find an appropriate way between these more or less artificial pillars within the Community. Fighting organised crime is one thing we come across with these issues and it can be stated it is not a function or task of Frontex, but in practice in the Member States and also at the European level we have to work towards that objective. It is not a task but it is an objective" (Q 246).[82]

169. It is clear to us that combating illegal immigration must mean combating it by all available means. If, as appears, one of the main causes of illegal immigration, and one of the main reasons why it is often successful, is the involvement of organised crime, this is something in which Frontex should be closely involved. It cannot be right to attempt to divorce the cause from the effect. Our reply to Mr Byrne's question is therefore that Frontex should indeed be closely concerned with fighting the syndicates of organised crime which, as he says, are responsible for much of the pressure on illegal immigration.

170. **We agree with the majority of our witnesses that, for the present at least, it would be an unacceptable enlargement of the mandate of Frontex for it to concern itself specifically with counter-terrorism or serious cross-border crime which is not directly linked to illegal immigration.**

171. **Nevertheless Frontex must be involved in combating any organised crime whose aim is to facilitate and profit from illegal immigration. It**

---

[80] The Serious Organised Crime Agency (SOCA) uses this expression to mean both the organised facilitation of immigrants to the United Kingdom ("people smuggling") and the trafficking of people for criminal exploitation, for example as prostitutes or forced labour ("human trafficking").

[81] Immigration falls within Title IV of the TEC, while Police and Judicial Cooperation in Criminal Matters falls within Title VI of the TEU.

[82] General Laitinen was giving evidence before the signature of the Treaty of Lisbon, which would merge the first and third pillars.

is right that this should already be an objective of Frontex. Technicalities should not be allowed to stand in the way of this.

Cooperation with other agencies in combating organised crime

172. Frontex does not currently produce a collective intelligence product for dissemination to Member States. Each state is responsible for recording intelligence for its own use. The National Coordinator Ports Policing saw "significant scope for more action to be taken to effectively capture and disseminate intelligence that would be of use in combating crime and terrorism impacting on the United Kingdom." He would "potentially have some serious use of Frontex for intelligence-gathering purposes". (p 2, Q32).

173. While we do not think the mandate of Frontex should be extended to intelligence gathering specifically for purposes other than combating illegal immigration, inevitably, during its work on risk analysis and in the course of the operations it coordinates, Frontex will acquire intelligence and information which is not directly concerned with its own work, but which might be of great value to the agencies of the Member States and the international agencies whose aim is to combat terrorism and serious organised crime generally. **It is essential that there should be a mechanism enabling Frontex to transfer key intelligence to those who can best make use of it.**

174. This is precisely the task of Europol. It is currently a body established by a Convention between the Member States, but the Council is considering a Commission proposal to set Europol up as an EU agency with a rather wider objective. From the planned date of entry into force of the Treaty of Lisbon (1 January 2009) the "mission" of Europol, set out in Article 88 of the Treaty on the Functioning of the European Union, would be wider still: "to support and strengthen action by the Member States' police authorities and other law enforcement services and their mutual cooperation in preventing and combating serious crime affecting two or more Member States, terrorism and forms of crime which affect a common interest covered by a Union policy".[83]

175. Article 13 of the Frontex Regulation allows Frontex to cooperate with Europol and other international organisations. Mr Dowdall told us that "There is not currently a formal memorandum of understanding with Europol but Frontex and Europol do work closely together; they share their agenda and there is interchange of staff ... That has manifested itself in, for example, Operation Hera which took place at European airports focusing attention on illegal Chinese migration, and Europol contributed to that work with the provision of information and intelligence." He and Mr Dodd both advocated strengthening links with Europol (QQ 192, 200). Article 22(2) of the latest draft of the Council Decision provides that Europol "shall"—not "may"—conclude an agreement or working arrangement with Frontex.[84] This is a welcome development.

---

[83] Under Article 3 of the draft Proposal for a Council Decision establishing the European Police Office (Document 10327/07 of 4 June 2007) the objectives are "to support and strengthen action by the competent authorities of the Member States and their mutual cooperation in preventing and combating organised crime, terrorism and other forms of serious crime affecting two or more Member States". However there must be some doubt as to whether this draft will be adopted and come into force before1 January 2009.

[84] Document 16452/07 of 21 December 2007.

176. **We welcome the cooperation between Frontex and Europol, which in our view will benefit from being formalised in an agreement between the parties.**

177. **Intelligence and information coming to the knowledge of Frontex in the course of its work should be passed not only to Europol but also to other agencies which are well placed to make good use of it, and with which similar agreements can be concluded.**

An operational organisation?

178. The Regulation allows Frontex to become an agency with its own operational resources and assets. We received conflicting evidence on the desirability of this. General Laitinen himself, who might have been expected to favour this, left a decision on the issue "to those to whom it belongs", but thought it would be helpful if Frontex could be certain of having something to deploy in the most important operations, even if the main assets still came from the Member States (Q 256).

179. The Commission, in its evaluation of Frontex published last month, looked at possibilities for future development. It pointed out that the deployment of a RABITs team can be combined with technical assistance, and recommended that "this provision be made more operational by Frontex acquiring its own equipment for border control and surveillance, to be used by the RABIT teams, in order to ensure the availability of equipment at short notice". Another suggestion is that, in the longer term, Frontex might lease or even acquire equipment for permanent operations.[85] Two Members of the European Parliament would go further. Mr Moreno Sanchez, asked how he saw the future evolution of Frontex, replied that "in the end we have to try to get integrated control of the borders in cooperation, and Frontex is one of the tools for doing that" (Q 123). Mr Simon Busuttil went further still: "I do think that Frontex should develop further, should become operational in its development and should become the agency responsible for the protection and strengthening of the external borders, not just of the Member States but also of the Union itself" (Q 126).

180. However Major Mallia's view was that "from a technical point of view, I do not think Frontex as an agency is equipped to be operating aircraft, patrol vessels, helicopters, et cetera. It is quite a complicated task which requires a high level of skill and a high level of infrastructure." There was also the problem that "if Frontex decides to operate ships and aircraft, they will have to carry someone's registration and someone's flag, so someone will be responsible for them and therefore you cannot remove their national nature" (QQ 373, 399).

181. We prefer this view. **We believe that it would be wiser for Frontex not to acquire its own operational assets until the implications of this have been considered more fully by Frontex itself and by the Member States.**

182. Looking ahead still further, Jonathan Faull told us that he would be "very surprised" ever to see Frontex having its own forces in its own uniform. However he added: "I would never say never." This proved wise, since the

---

[85] Commission Communication of 13 February 2008: Report on the evaluation and future development of the FRONTEX Agency, doc. 6664/08, COM(2008)67 final, paragraphs 24 and 39.

Commission's forward look now suggests assessing whether Frontex should employ border guards itself.[86] This brings us back to the proposals for a European Border Guard. As we have explained, these proposals are for the present defunct, and in our view rightly so. The Commission states that it "intends to return to the question of a fully fledged European Border Guard system when experiences have been gathered on the functioning of those [RABITs] teams".[87] A discussion of this can perhaps do no harm, but it should not in our view lead to Frontex adopting any role similar to a European Border Guard.

183. **Suggestions that Frontex should become, in effect, a European Border Guard are in our view ill-conceived, and should not even be considered for the present.**

Our own assessment

184. After considering all the written and oral evidence we have received, not least on our visit to the Frontex headquarters in Warsaw, we think it right to summarise our own assessment.

185. **We believe that, in the short time it has been operational, Frontex has made an excellent start in its important role of coordinating action on the external borders of the EU. We congratulate those involved.**

186. **We nevertheless caution against too much being demanded of it. A new agency cannot be expected to double its size, its work and its budget every year. The time has come for a period of consolidation: somewhat slower growth, and concentration on improvement in the quality of operations rather than in their number.**

187. **It is not in the interests of the European Union as a whole or of the Member States individually that the United Kingdom should be excluded from full participation in the development and operation of Frontex. We recommend that the Government should persevere in negotiations in the Council of Ministers to end this exclusion.**

188. **The States which are full members of Schengen took the view that freedom of movement should take priority over border security. The United Kingdom takes the opposite view, and its geographical situation puts it in a better position to safeguard its borders outside Schengen. However this argument is undermined by the inadequate and unacceptable way in which the United Kingdom's borders are at present safeguarded. We therefore believe that the highest priority should be given to remedying this.**

---

[86] *Ibid*, paragraph 39.

[87] *Ibid*, paragraph 36.

CHAPTER 9: SUMMARY OF CONCLUSIONS AND RECOMMENDATIONS

Borders

189. The migratory pressure on Europe's borders will grow because there are a growing number of failed states where a combination of economic incompetence, uncertainty of property rights, corruption, internal conflicts, political anarchy and repressive regimes has created intolerable conditions for the local population. Conditions may also be intolerable in states where poverty is endemic, or in those which, though once prosperous, are now ravaged by war. It is therefore inevitable and predictable that people will attempt to escape to countries which they see as offering a chance of a better life. (paragraph 11)

The position on Schengen

190. Given the views of successive Governments on the comparative strengths of the United Kingdom and Schengen borders, it seems to us that "Possibly, but not yet" will for many years to come be the reply to the question of the United Kingdom becoming a full Schengen State. (paragraph 45)

The United Kingdom's borders

191. We recommend that more effective fencing should be put in place near the ferry berths at Calais as a matter of urgency. (paragraph 33)

192. We believe the work on e-Borders should be brought forward as a matter of urgency to protect Britain's territorial integrity. (paragraph 48)

Frontex

The position of the United Kingdom

193. For the present the United Kingdom has to accept that, not being a full Schengen State, it cannot play a full role in Frontex. Subject to that legal limitation, the Government should ensure that the United Kingdom participates effectively in the development and operation of Frontex. (paragraph 60)

Joint return operations

194. For the present we would not encourage Frontex to put any more assets into organising compulsory return operations. (paragraph 65)

Resources

195. We believe that before the European Parliament considers withholding part of the budget of Frontex, it should bear in mind the importance of Frontex being seen as a secure and responsible employer. Nothing should be done to undermine its operational effectiveness or put at risk the accumulated expertise of its permanent staff. (paragraph 79)

196. We believe the increased resources may usefully lead to a modest increase in the number of operations in 2008, but should be concentrated on further increasing the quality of those operations, and of the intelligence-gathering and sharing leading up to them. (paragraph 81)

Accountability

197. We believe that the current arrangements for financial accountability are adequate. (paragraph 89)

198. Frontex should raise its public profile by ensuring that information which is or should be in the public domain is easily accessible to the public, in particular on its website. (paragraph 90)

199. Frontex should be more formally accountable to the European Parliament. The Chairman of the Management Board and the Executive Director should, if so requested, appear before the Parliament or its Committees to discuss the activities of Frontex. (paragraph 91)

Joint operations organised by Frontex

Reports of operations

200. We believe that the host country, and other countries taking part if they wish, should be involved in drawing up a report after each operation from which lessons can be learned. Frontex should be responsible for coordinating such reports. (paragraph 96)

201. Frontex should formulate rules for data collection which will allow a better evaluation of the results and impact of operations. This evaluation should show in particular the kinds of people intercepted or turned back, and the extent to which the operations are effective in reducing, and not just displacing, illegal immigration. The United Kingdom should participate fully in any such evaluation. (paragraph 159)

Commitment of operational assets

202. We recommend that Member States should be asked to pledge to make available for Frontex operations only as many vessels and other equipment as they are actually able to make available when requested. (paragraph 106)

203. In the longer term, consideration should be given to introducing into the Frontex Regulation a provision requiring, subject to strictly limited exceptions, compulsory deployment of vessels and equipment in joint operations and other Frontex activities. (paragraph 163)

Disembarkation

204. It should not be the responsibility of those planning individual Frontex operations to decide the rules on disembarkation for those operations. Rules must be formulated which will apply to all Frontex maritime operations. This question must be addressed by the working group developing general guidelines about the law of the sea as it relates to EU States and illegal migration. (paragraph 112)

205. We believe that a fairer method must be found of calculating and granting financial assistance to those states which bear a disproportionate share of the burden of illegal immigration. (paragraph 113)

206. We believe that the fairness and effectiveness of the Dublin II system is something which must be addressed in the second stage of the work on a Common European Asylum System. (paragraph 119)

Operational cooperation by the United Kingdom

207. The United Kingdom has great experience of controlling sea and air borders, and recent experience of controlling the land border with the Irish Republic. This country has much to offer Frontex and the Schengen States. We hope that the Government will share their experience with them, and that they will make full use of it. (paragraph 125)

208. Improved coordination of border management of the Schengen States will be of direct benefit to the United Kingdom. The Government should make clear to the other Member States that they wish to play as full a part as possible in operations, and should commit resources to them for this purpose. The Management Board should not just allow, but should encourage, United Kingdom participation. (paragraph 126)

The right to bear arms

209. The liabilities of guest border guards, particularly those which arise from the use of weapons, need to be clarified in amending legislation. The particular position of participating United Kingdom border guards should also be addressed. (paragraph 135)

Other issues

The applicable law

210. Given the complexity of the law governing operations on the high seas involving illegal immigration, we think it essential that the Member States taking part in operations coordinated by Frontex should follow clear guidelines clarifying their powers and obligations in the different sea areas. (paragraph 145)

Agreements with third countries

211. We believe that working arrangements between Frontex and the authorities of third countries in the Mediterranean could play a valuable part in controlling illegal immigration to the EU. We hope that Frontex will carry forward the negotiation of such arrangements. (paragraph 152)

212. Member States, including the United Kingdom, should however be concerned to ensure that any such arrangements with a third country include meaningful guarantees for the treatment of would-be immigrants repatriated to that country. (paragraph 153)

Links with UNHCR and other bodies

213. We welcome the cooperation between Frontex and UNHCR, and would like to see this extended to other bodies with responsibilities for immigration, asylum and refugees. (paragraph 155)

Looking to the future

Widening the mandate of Frontex

214. We agree with the majority of our witnesses that, for the present at least, it would be an unacceptable enlargement of the mandate of Frontex for it to concern itself specifically with counter-terrorism or serious cross-border crime which is not directly linked to illegal immigration. (paragraph 170)

215. Nevertheless Frontex must be involved in combating any organised crime whose aim is to facilitate and profit from illegal immigration. It is right that this should already be an objective of Frontex. Technicalities should not be allowed to stand in the way of this. (paragraph 171)

Cooperation with other agencies in the fight against organised crime

216. It is essential that there should be a mechanism enabling Frontex to transfer key intelligence to those who can best make use of it. (paragraph 173)

217. We welcome the cooperation between Frontex and Europol, which in our view will benefit from being formalised in an agreement between the parties. (paragraph 176)

218. Intelligence and information coming to the knowledge of Frontex in the course of its work should be passed not only to Europol but also to other agencies which are well placed to make good use of it, and with which similar agreements can be concluded. (paragraph 177)

An operational organisation?

219. We believe that it would be wiser for Frontex not to acquire its own operational assets until the implications of this have been considered more fully by Frontex itself and by the Member States. (paragraph 181)

220. Suggestions that Frontex should become, in effect, a European Border Guard are in our view ill-conceived, and should not even be considered for the present. (paragraph 183)

Our own assessment

221. We believe that, in the short time it has been operational, Frontex has made an excellent start in its important role of coordinating action on the external borders of the EU. We congratulate those involved. (paragraph 185)

222. We nevertheless caution against too much being demanded of it. A new agency cannot be expected to double its size, its work and its budget every year. The time has come for a period of consolidation: somewhat slower growth, and concentration on improvement in the quality of operations rather than in their number. (paragraph 186)

223. It is not in the interests of the European Union as a whole or of the Member States individually that the United Kingdom should be excluded from full participation in the development and operation of Frontex. We recommend that the Government should persevere in negotiations in the Council of Ministers to end this exclusion. (paragraph 187)

224. The States which are full members of Schengen took the view that freedom of movement should take priority over border security. The United Kingdom takes the opposite view, and its geographical situation puts it in a better position to safeguard its borders outside Schengen. However this argument is undermined by the inadequate and unacceptable way in which the United Kingdom's borders are at present safeguarded. We therefore believe that the highest priority should be given to remedying this. (paragraph 188)

225. We recommend this report to the House for debate. (paragraph 8)

APPENDIX 1: SUB-COMMITTEE F (HOME AFFAIRS)

The members of the Sub-Committee which conducted this inquiry were:

†	Lord Dear
	Lord Harrison
	Baroness Henig
†	Lord Hodgson of Astley Abbotts
	Lord Jopling (Chairman)
	Lord Marlesford
†	Lord Mawson
	Lord Teverson
	Baroness Tonge
	Lord Young of Norwood Green

†   from 13 November 2007

The following former members of the Sub-Committee were members from the start of the inquiry until the end of the Session 2006–07.

Earl of Caithness
Baroness D'Souza
Earl of Listowel
Lord Wright of Richmond (Chairman)

Dr Valsamis Mitsilegas, Reader in Law, School of Law, Queen Mary College, University of London, and Major-General Adrian Freer were appointed Specialist Advisers for this inquiry.

Declarations of Interests:

A full list of Members' interests can be found in the Register of Lords Interests:

http://www.publications.parliament.uk/pa/ld/ldreg.htm

Interests declared by Members relevant to this inquiry

Baroness Henig
Chair of the Security Industry Authority
President of the Association of Police Authorities

Lord Wright of Richmond
Former Chairman, Joint Intelligence Committee

APPENDIX 2: CALL FOR EVIDENCE

Sub-Committee F (Home Affairs) of the House of Lords Select Committee on the European Union is conducting an inquiry into Frontex, the European Agency for the Management of Operational Cooperation at the External Borders of the EU Member States.

Frontex was established on 1 May 2005 by Council Regulation (EC) 2007/2004 and started work in October 2005. One of its main tasks is to co-ordinate joint operations by Member States at the external sea, land and air borders of the EU. To date, Frontex has managed several such operations on the main land and sea routes of irregular migration to the EU, and at key EU transit and destination airports. The UK is excluded from the Frontex Regulation (although it is challenging this exclusion before the European Court of Justice) but participates in joint operations on a case-by-case basis.

The management of the EU's external borders, particularly the Southern maritime border, has become a high priority for the Union with the continuous flow of irregular migrants from West Africa to the Canary Islands and from North Africa to Italy and Malta, and the countless deaths from attempting these journeys on unseaworthy boats. Although responsibility for the control and surveillance of external borders lies with the Member States, Frontex is increasingly coming under pressure to act comprehensively in all border management matters. Accordingly, the Agency's mandate and powers are expanding fast, as are its economic and personnel resources, and its operational means. The Regulation establishing Rapid Border Intervention Teams (RABITs) is only one example.

The Commission first advocated the setting up of an external borders agency in 2002, and this proposal was the subject of an earlier report of the Committee. The aim of the present inquiry is to examine where and how Frontex operates at a practical level, its decision-making structure and lines of accountability, and whether it has made any impact in reducing irregular migration; and to make recommendations on the future development of the Agency so that it can fulfil its mandate more effectively.

Written evidence is invited on all aspects of the subject. The Sub-Committee would particularly welcome comments on:

- whether Frontex staffing and funding are adequate to enable it to carry out its tasks;

- whether the institutional and legal framework ensures adequate accountability of Frontex activities;

- the legal framework for border guards' exercise of control and surveillance powers in the course of Frontex operations;

- whether and how international obligations with regard to search and rescue at sea affect the Agency;

- whether it is practical to retain a distinction at operational level between preventing irregular immigration and preventing crime;

- the number and nature of working agreements Frontex has in place with Member States, third countries, EU agencies and international bodies;

- whether there is sufficient cooperation from Member States in terms of personnel and equipment for joint operations;

- how Frontex pools information from the Member States to carry out risk analyses;

- the extent of Frontex involvement in surveillance operations;

- how Frontex joint operations are planned and mounted;

- how Frontex joint operations are monitored and the outcomes evaluated;

- whether there is, or should be, any involvement of, or assistance from, the military in Frontex operations;

- the disadvantages, if any, to the UK in not participating in Frontex, and how the Advocate-General's Opinion in the case challenging its exclusion from Frontex affects its current position;

- how the Agency's role should develop in the future.

APPENDIX 3: LIST OF WITNESSES

The following witnesses gave evidence. Those marked * gave oral evidence

* Mr Simon Busuttil, MEP
* Mr Gérard Deprez, MEP
* European Commission
* European Council on Refugees and Exiles (ECRE)
* Frontex (European Agency for the Management of Operational Cooperation at the External Borders of the Member States of the European Union)

  Government of Gibraltar
* Home Office, Border and Immigration Agency
* Home Office, Minister for Immigration

  Home Office, Heathrow Border Control

  Home Office, Coquelles and Calais Juxtaposed Border Controls

  Immigration Advisory Service (IAS)
* Immigration Law Practitioners' Association (ILPA)

  Meijers Committee (Standing Committee of Experts on International Immigration, Refugee and Criminal Law)
* Malta: Armed Forces
* Mr Javier Moreno Sanchez, MEP
* National Coordinator Ports Policing
* Polish Border Guard
* Polish Ministry of the Interior and Administration
* Refugee Council

  Spanish Embassy, London
* United Nations High Commissioner for Refugees (UNHCR)

APPENDIX 4: LIST OF OPERATIONS

Description of the operation	States involved
Agelaus (February 2006): an operation focusing on minors smuggled or trafficked to the EU by air, in particular those unaccompanied or travelling with other than close relatives, to develop procedures for identification, reception, shelter and protection of victims.	AT, BE, CZ, DE, EE, ES, FI, FR, HU, IT, LV, NL, PL, PT, SE, SK, SL, **UK**, and Europol
Agios (July-September 2006): an operation concentrating on intensifying passport controls in the Mediterranean Spanish Ports to identify falsified documents. 27 airports were involved.	DE, ES, FR, IT, NL, PT
Amazon: a three stage air operation taking place in November 2006, February 2007 and November 2007-January 2008, aimed at preventing illegal immigration by persons arriving at EU airports from central and South America. In addition, AT, BG, HU and RO participated in the third stage.	DE, ES, FR, IT, NL, PT, **UK**
Ariadne (April-May 2007): a land operation targeting illegal migrants from Ukraine and Belarus into Poland. The operation was extended to the Polish-German border to target the use of forged documents by facilitators.	AT, CZ, DE, EE, ES, HU, IT, LV, LT, PL, PT
Drive In (August-September 2007): a land operation targeting illegal migration across the West Balkans to Slovenia.	AT, BG, DE, IT, LV, RO, SL
Extended Family: the operation, in October and November 2007, focused on illegal immigration and human trafficking from Nigeria through airports including Madrid, Amsterdam and Malpensa.	ES, FI, IT, HU, NL, **UK**
FIFA 2006: an operation to cooperate with Germany in combating illegal immigration through EU airports, in preparation for the FIFA World Cup 2006.	AT, CZ, DE, EL, ES, FR, HU, IT, PL, SI, SK, **UK**
Gordius (April 2007): an operation to analyse routes and false travel documents used mainly by Ukrainian and Moldavian nationals for entry into Eastern European States.	AT, BG, CZ, DE, ES, FI, FR, HU, LV, PL, PT, RO, SK, SL, **UK**
Hera This succession of major operations was aimed at assisting Spain in dealing with illegal migration to the Canary Islands by carrying out extensive border controls, identifying immigrants and establishing patrols on the open sea near Senegal and Mauretania to reduce the number of vessels from African countries in Mauritanian, Senegalese and Cape Verde territorial waters. **Hera I and II** took place between July and December 2006, and **Hera III**, which had a budget of €2.75m, from February to April 2007. They were followed by **Hera 2007**, with a budget of €5.4m, itself a two-stage operation from April to June and July to November 2007. The UK took part in Hera I and in the second stage of Hera 2007.	DE, ES, FI, FR, IT, NL, PT, **UK** and Norway took part in Hera I and II. DE, ES, FR, LU, IT, NL, PT, SE and **UK** took part in the second stage of Hera 2007.

Herakles (August and October 2007): a two-stage land operation on the Hungary/Serbia border.	AT, BG, DE, HU, IT, LV, PO, PT, RO, **UK**
Hermes (September 2007): an operation targeting illegal migration across the Mediterranean from North Africa to Italy and Spain.	DE, ES, FR, EL, IT, PT, RO, **UK**
Hydra (April-May 2007): an operation aimed at the detection of illegal Chinese migrants arriving at EU airports.	AT, BG, CZ, DE, ES, FI, FR, HU, IT, NL, PL, SL, RO, **UK**
Indalo 2007 (November 2007): a maritime operation targeting illegal migration through the Western Mediterranean, from the North African coast to Southern Spain.	DE, ES, FR, IT, MT, PT, RO
Kras (September 2007): a land operation targeting illegal migration from Croatia to Slovenia.	AT, BG, DE, IT, RO, SL, **UK**
Long Stop (November-December 2007): an operation to detect Pakistani, Bangladeshi and Sri Lankan citizens arriving at EU airports in breach of immigration controls.	AT, CZ, DE, EE, EL, FI, FR, IT, NE, PL, PT, SL, **UK**
Minerva (August-September 2007): a maritime operation targeting illegal migration through the Western Mediterranean, from the North African coast to Southern Spain.	AT, BE, ES, DE, FR, IT, NL, PL, PT, RO, **UK**
Nautilus 2006: a maritime operation in October 2006 in the Southern Mediterranean aimed at combating illegal immigration to Malta and Lampedusa.	DE, EL, FR, IT, MT
Nautilus 2007: a further major two-stage maritime operation (June-July 2007 and September-October 2007) with a budget of €5.1m, targeting illegal migration from Libya across the central Mediterranean to Malta and Lampedusa.	DE, EL, FR, IT, MT and (for Stage II) PT, RO, **UK**
Niris: an operation to combat illegal migration flows through Baltic sea ports, especially flows organised by criminal networks from India and China.	States with borders on the Baltic Sea, including Norway
Poseidon 2006: a joint land and sea operation in June-July 2006 in the Greek islands and on the Greek land border with Albania and Turkey.	AT, DE, EL, FR, IT, MT, PL, **UK**
Poseidon 2007: a major three-stage joint land and sea operation with a budget of €2.25m, targeting illegal immigration to Greece and SE Europe from Albania, FYROM and Turkey. The three stages ran from May to October 2007.	AT, BG, CY, DE, FR, EL, IT, MT, NL, PT, RO, **UK**, Europol
Torino 2006: border checks at 24 airports of persons travelling to the Winter Olympic Games in Turin in February 2006.	15 Member States including **UK**
Ursus I and II: two operations at the Eastern EU external land borders, the first focusing on the Slovakian border with Ukraine, the second on the Polish border with Ukraine.	AT, BG, DE, EE, FI, HU, LT, LV, PL, RO, SK and Ukraine
Zeus (October 2007): joint air and sea operations to identify irregular migrants posing as seamen.	BE, CY, DE, ES, FI, FR, IT, LV, MT, NL, PL, PT, RO, SE, **UK**

APPENDIX 5: LIST OF ACRONYMS AND ABBREVIATIONS

ACPO	Association of Chief Police Officers
ALO	Airline Liaison Officer
BIA	Border and Immigration Agency
CRATE	Central Register of Available Technical Equipment
DATV	Direct Airline Transit Visa
DG JLS	Directorate-General Justice Freedom and Security of the Commission
Dublin II	Council Regulation (EC) 343/2003 of 18 February 2003 establishing the criteria and mechanisms for determining the Member State responsible for examining an asylum application lodged in one of the Member States by a third-country national (OJ 2003 L 50/1)
e-Borders	The Home Office programme for the electronic screening of all passengers entering and leaving the United Kingdom
EC	European Community
ECJ	European Court of Justice
ECRE	European Council on Refugees and Exiles
EU	European Union
Europol	European Police Office, set up under a Convention between Member States, likely to become an Agency under a proposed Council Decision
Frontex	European Agency for the Management of Operational Cooperation at the External Borders of the Member States
Frontex Regulation	Council Regulation (EC) 2007/2004 of 26 October 2004 establishing a European Agency for the Management of Operational Cooperation at the External Borders of the Member States of the European Union (OJ L349 of 25 November 2004, p.1)
FYROM	Former Yugoslav Republic of Macedonia
G5	The G6 before they were joined by Poland in March 2006
G6	The six largest Member States: Germany, France, United Kingdom, Italy, Spain and Poland
G6 meetings	The regular six-monthly meetings of the G6 ministers
G6 ministers	The ministers of the interior of the G6
HMRC	Her Majesty's Revenue and Customs
IAS	Immigration Advisory Service
ICC	International Coordination Centre (of an operation)
IDA	Inadequately Documented Arrival
ILPA	Immigration Law Practitioners' Association
IMO	International Maritime Organisation
IOM	International Organization for Migration

IRIS	Iris Recognition Immigration System
JHA	Justice and Home Affairs
LIBE Committee	Committee on Civil Liberties, Justice and Home Affairs of the European Parliament
Meijers Committee	Standing Committee of Experts on International Immigration, Refugee and Criminal Law
NCPO	National Coordinator Ports Policing
PNR	Passenger Name Record
QMV	Qualified Majority Voting
RABIT	Rapid Border Intervention Team
RABITs Regulation	Regulation (EC) 863/2007 of the European Parliament and of the Council of 11 July 2007 establishing a mechanism for the creation of Rapid Border Intervention Teams and amending [the Frontex Regulation] (OJ L199 of 31 July 2007, p.30)
RAU	Risk Analysis Unit of Frontex
SAR	Search and Rescue
Schengen *acquis*	The Schengen Agreement, the Schengen Convention, and all the instruments adopted under them (published in OJ L 239 of 22 September 2000)
Schengen Agreement	The 1985 Agreement between Belgium, Germany, France, Luxembourg and the Netherlands on the gradual abolition of checks at their common borders
Schengen Convention	the 1990 Convention implementing the Schengen Agreement
SIS II	Second generation Schengen Information System
SOCA	Serious Organised Crime Agency
TEC	Treaty establishing the European Community
TEU	Treaty establishing the European Union
Treaty of Lisbon	The Treaty between the Member States, signed in Lisbon on 13 December 2007, amending the TEU and amending and re-naming the TEC
UNCLOS	United Nations Convention on the Law of the Sea
UNHCR	United Nations High Commissioner for Refugees

APPENDIX 6: LIST OF RELEVANT REPORTS

Recent Reports from the Select Committee

Annual Report 2007(36th Report, Session 2006–07, HL Paper 181)

Relevant Reports prepared by Sub-Committee F

Session 1998–99

Schengen and the United Kingdom's Border Controls (7th Report, HL Paper 37)

Session 1999–2000

Enlargement and EU External Frontier Controls (17th Report, HL Paper 110)

Session 2001–02

A Common Policy on Illegal Immigration (37th Report, HL Paper 187)

Session 2002–03

Europol's role in fighting crime (5th Report, HL Paper 43)

Proposals for a European Border Guard (29th Report, HL Paper 133)

Session 2004–05

After Madrid: the EU's response to terrorism (5th Report, HL Paper 53)

Session 2005–06

Illegal Migrants: proposals for a common EU returns policy (32nd Report, HL Paper 166)

Behind Closed Doors: the meeting of the G6 Interior Ministers at Heiligendamm (40th Report, HL Paper 221)

Session 2006–07

After Heiligendamm: doors ajar at Stratford-upon-Avon (5th Report, HL Paper 32)

Schengen Information System II (SIS II) (9th Report, HL Paper 49)

Minutes of Evidence

TAKEN BEFORE THE SELECT COMMITTEE ON THE EUROPEAN UNION (SUB-COMMITTEE F)

WEDNESDAY 10 OCTOBER 2007

Present	Harrison, L	Teverson, L
	Henig, B	Tonge, B
	Listowel, E	Wright of Richmond, L (Chairman)
	Marlesford, L	Young of Norwood Green, L

Memorandum by National Co-ordinator Ports Policing

1. With reference to an invitation, dated 11 July 2007, to submit evidence and comments to the above mentioned sub-committee, I would ask for the following points to be considered. I am submitting these comments on behalf of the Association of Chief Police Officers [Terrorism and Allied Matters] (ACPO (TAM)) where, in my capacity as National Co-ordinator Ports Policing (NCPP).

2. The Office of the NCPP was formed in 1987 under the authority and control of the Home Office, where it formed part of the Terrorism and Protection Unit (now the Office of Security and Counter Terrorism—OSCT). There has been a National Co-ordinator since its inception, developing the police response at ports and borders and joint working with the other border agencies. In 2003, following the HMIC Thematic Inspection "A Need to Know", the NCPP moved under the Governance of ACPO (TAM).

3. The NCPP supports the Government's CONTEST strategy and the ACPO (TAM) Three Year Delivery Plan (2006–09), into which specific objectives for ports policing have been incorporated. Under the vision statement "Working together to secure UK ports and borders from the threat of terrorism and crime thereby reducing harm to the UK", we aim to achieve the following objectives:

    — More effective border controls.
    — The collection and development of intelligence.
    — Support to investigations.
    — Providing a hostile environment for terrorists and criminals.

4. Policing at the border and ports can be described as falling into three broad categories: Intelligence, Protective Security, and General Policing (including the management of major and critical incidents). The intelligence function at the border and ports is the role of Special Branch officers whose responsibilities are set out in the Home Office "Guidelines" for Special Branch. They cover: Counter Terrorism; Serious Organised Crime; and Child Abduction.

5. The current terrorist threat level within the UK necessitates that positive action is taken to prevent terrorists from entering the UK and, in the case of suspected "home-grown" terrorists that a sufficient capability exists to monitor their movements. The police work in close partnership with other border agencies; HM Revenue & Customs (HMRC) and the Border & Immigration Agency (BIA) as well as the Security Service. This border agency partnership approach has been shaped through the Border Management Programme (BMP).

6. SB officers at ports primarily rely on powers contained in Schedule 7 of the Terrorism Act 2000 (TA2000) to examine passengers and goods. This legislation allows a constable or designated officer to examine a person to determine any involvement in the commission, preparation or instigation of acts of terrorism. This examination may or may not lead to reasonable grounds for arrest being established.

7. The Serious Organised Crime Agency (SOCA) was established in April 2006 as a new law enforcement agency with a remit for reducing the harm caused to citizens of the UK by serious organised crime. The current top two priorities are combating Class A drugs and organised immigration crime. SOCA does not have a direct frontline presence at ports. Police work closely with SOCA in providing expert operational support, particularly in relation to tackling organised immigration crime.

8. In terms of the wider police responsibility related to combating less serious criminality (Level 1 and 2 crimes) that may penetrate the border, officers at ports also deal with such matters. With the development of e-Borders it is anticipated that the number of suspected criminals coming to police notice at ports will significantly increase. Early indications from Project Semaphore (the pilot of e-Borders) forecast that 38 arrests are made per million passengers that have passed through this system. Expected passenger numbers for 2014, when e-Borders is expected to reach 95% capacity, is 200 million. Potentially this could result in up to 8,000 arrests being made per annum at ports (although this figure must carry the caveat that it is based only on preliminary data).

9. In partnership with BIA (Enforcement and Compliance) police officers provide considerable expert practical assistance in the investigation and detention/removal of [inland] immigration offenders. A number of senior police officers have been seconded to BIA Enforcement. Their role is to co-ordinate teams of police and immigration officers through a network of police inspectors organised on the ACPO geographical regions. Within London over the past three to four years there have been a number of police officers co-located with BIA staff within Joint Intelligence Units. These officers mainly assist with the conduct of risk assessments prior to any operations being carried out. Additionally, for the past two years around 30 police officers have been assisting in visits and with the removal of Failed Asylum Seekers. Following the publication of the Enforcement Strategy an additional 65 police officers have been assisting BIA staff with the investigation of immigration crime—this includes both the investigation and charging of individuals under the current legislation via the courts, leading to either removal or formal deportation. Outside London the picture is similar, however the third strand mentioned above (ie assisting BIA staff with the investigation of immigration crime—this includes both the investigation and charging of individuals under the current legislation via the courts, leading to either removal or formal deportation) is planned to commence later this year.

10. The UK Human Trafficking Centre (UKHTC)—based in Sheffield—is led by ACPO and is responsible for ensuring that police and partner agencies maintain a joined up and strategic approach to tackling human trafficking. Their main aim is to increase knowledge and understanding of human trafficking amongst police and partner agencies. I am aware that the UKHTC have very limited interaction with Frontex.

11. At present the UK Police Service is not represented within Frontex. Should the scope of Frontex be expanded then I consider that the current arrangement, whereby BIA is the sole UK border agency present on the Frontex Management Board [indirectly representing other UK border agencies] as being insufficient. It is reasonable to assume that Frontex will widen its remit in the future. I consider that representation of the UK Police Service within this Agency would significantly improve upon the existing situation; by fully representing the interests of the UK in relation to any Counter Terrorism (CT) effort and combating criminality, particularly around operational activity and gathering intelligence.

12. Given the necessity to tackle terrorism and crime beyond our physical borders I would welcome any opportunity to discuss the possibility of increasing UK Police Service activity in the European arena, in order to secure links with other EU police and government agencies that are specifically responsible for monitoring European land and sea borders. It would be beneficial for UK police to gain a better understanding of [and influence] the EU Integrated Border Management (IBM) approach that has been adopted.

13. In relation to intelligence products, Frontex does not currently produce a collective intelligence product for dissemination to member states. Each state is responsible for recording intelligence for its own use. There is significant scope for more action to be taken to effectively capture and disseminate intelligence that would be of use in combating crime and terrorism impacting on the UK.

14. One of the Agency's main tasks is to co-ordinate joint operations at the external sea, land and air borders of the EU. Given the UK's current level of engagement with Frontex, even if SB officers were to take part in specific operations in a supplementary capacity it would at least create opportunities for gathering CT and crime intelligence around irregular migration. For example, where there might be a tacit connection between a human smuggling ring and a terrorist organisation then the opportunity to extrapolate and develop intelligence on that connection is not currently apparent (ie a structured approach to gathering and disseminating intelligence). As Frontex develops its operational capability and influence beyond irregular migration then the UK Police Service should be represented. Such representation would be of benefit to the UK in contributing to reducing harm to its citizens and the economy by increasing our intelligence gathering capability within the EU. Furthermore, I believe that the UK Police Service could offer much needed expert support in planning and managing operations to combat criminality.

15. In its current form Frontex is limited in what it can achieve; it employs 82 personnel and has a budget of €35 million. In order to become more efficacious in dealing with matters beyond irregular migration (eg criminality, CT) a significant increase in [specialist] resources would be required.

16. As Frontex comes under increasing pressure to act comprehensively in all border management matters I would look forward to engaging in discussion around the UK Police Service being singularly represented on the Management Board; in relation to CT and mainstream criminal matters. I am aware that two Border and Immigration officers are permanently based in Frontex, undertaking specific roles. I would see real benefit in initially placing a UK SB officer within the Agency to assist with operational planning and intelligence sharing.

John Donlon
Assistant Chief Constable
National Co-ordinator Ports Policing

4 September 2007

Examination of Witness

Witness: DETECTIVE CHIEF INSPECTOR TONY McCARTHY, National Co-ordinator Ports Policing, examined.

Q1 *Chairman:* Detective Chief Inspector, thank you very much for coming, and I would also like to thank you for the very useful written evidence which we received from the Assistant Chief Constable. Before we start, would you like to make any sort of opening statement?
Detective Chief Inspector McCarthy: No, not at all. I am happy to start.

Q2 *Chairman:* Then I think I would like you to give this Committee a brief overview, first of all, of your own position in this subject, where you stand in it and perhaps a brief summary of your past. I do not want a full curriculum vitae, but really what I would be very interested in is a brief overview of the current system of border controls in the UK and port controls, focusing in particular on the role between the various agencies involved, including of course the local police authorities, so could I throw that rather general question at you to start with.
Detective Chief Inspector McCarthy: I like general questions actually.

Q3 *Chairman:* I should have explained that a full record is being taken and you will be sent the transcript of the meeting for your agreement or comment.
Detective Chief Inspector McCarthy: There are three main border agencies operating at this point, the Border and Immigration Agency, formerly known as the United Kingdom Immigration Service, the police at borders, who are Special Branch officers primarily with support from Protective Security and general policing elements that are mainly uniformed officers, but also backed up by civilian staff and CID officers, et cetera, from the host force, and HMRC, Her Majesty's Revenue and Customs, are the third main border agency and they mainly deal with revenue-collection and customs-enforcement. On the police side of the business, our priorities are divided up into three areas. The first is intelligence where Special Branch officers operate mainly in a non-uniformed capacity in order to gain intelligence on persons of interest as they pass through the border, working very closely with other agencies, such as the Security

Service. The Special Branch officers are also responsible for child abduction matters and serious organised crime matters that are not being dealt with, in partnership with the Serious Organised Crime Agency.

Q4 *Chairman:* That includes people-smuggling, does it?
Detective Chief Inspector McCarthy: It does, yes. The lead on people-smuggling would be with SOCA, the Serious Organised Crime Agency, and obviously on the trafficking side that would be of interest to the United Kingdom Human Trafficking Centre which is in Sheffield. The police are also responsible at ports for protective security and that could be in two ways. That could be your armed officers or unarmed officers and both overt and covert in that respect as well. The third element of the policing effort at ports and borders is general policing whereby normal crime, which it would generally be tagged as, would be dealt with by police officers in uniform and again with CID back-up and civilian support staff as well. Currently, the three agencies work separately. I am sure you are probably aware that there is a Cabinet Office review currently under way to look at how the agencies could work even closer towards forming a unified border force.

Q5 *Chairman:* Is there Cabinet Office machinery already in place?
Detective Chief Inspector McCarthy: Yes, there is. It is under Sir Gus O'Donnell. He leads the review for the Prime Minister and a report is due back with findings, conclusions and recommendations by the end of October this year. That review team is looking at primarily the formation of a unified border force which looks this time to be made up of Border and Immigration Agency staff, HMRC front-line detection officers and will include also the full integration of UK visas into the Border and Immigration Agency. At the moment, it is still being discussed as to where indeed Special Branch officers fit within that and the wider police package, where that sits, and the general policing and protective security elements. There is some discussion as to

whether the police role within any unified border force would be a border security role or a border control role and we have really got our own definitions for the two within the police which I can give you now, if that is of any help. The police definition of border control is the facilitation of the legal, and the prevention of the illegal, movement of people or goods across the border, and our definition of border security encompasses that definition of border control and goes a bit further than that to include the protection of the border and ports from terrorism, crime and other threats to public safety. We see the police remit across the board if you take into account the three elements, the intelligence-gathering, the protective security and the general police element, as being primarily protective security and border security, but also with some element of border control, especially where SB are concerned. The fiscal make-up of the border controls means that Special Branch officers work immediately in the vicinity of immigration officers and also very closely with revenue and customs officers at the border, so geographically within the border in the arrivals and departures lounges the police are working quite closely, but separately in terms of their objectives with their partner agencies at the border.

Q6 *Chairman:* Could you say a word about your enforcement powers, speaking of the ports policing.
Detective Chief Inspector McCarthy: If we look at the general policing and protective security side first, they are general police powers and they are powers that are available to all police officers within the UK. Within Special Branch, the border control/border security element split, there is a specific piece of legislation which is used by SB officers which is Schedule 7 of the Terrorism Act 2000 which gives a power to officers to examine persons of interest or potential interest in order to confirm any involvement they might have in acts of terrorism or to render that person not of interest to police or the security services, but our chief role as SB officers at ports is to gather intelligence, to feed into security services for our own use and other agencies' use as is relevant.

Q7 *Chairman:* Have you personally actually taken part in Frontex operations?
Detective Chief Inspector McCarthy: No, there is absolutely no UK police involvement in Frontex operations, to my knowledge, at this point in time or previously.

Q8 *Lord Marlesford:* The post that you hold is a co-ordinating post.

Detective Chief Inspector McCarthy: Yes.

Q9 *Lord Marlesford:* How long have you yourself done it for or how long have people been doing it?
Detective Chief Inspector McCarthy: I am not actually the National Co-ordinator Ports Policing. An ACC, John Donlon, is the actual Co-ordinator Ports Policing. As to how long has he been in that role, I think he has been roughly there for about two years now. It would be a role that is untenured, so there is not a fixed term on it, as far as I am aware, but I can confirm that for you after this meeting, and I am not sure when John Donlon is due to leave his post.

Q10 *Lord Marlesford:* And you yourself?
Detective Chief Inspector McCarthy: I am a Sussex police officer. I am here for two years within the National Co-ordinator's office. I have been here a year already, so I am due to leave next July.

Q11 *Lord Marlesford:* The thing which comes out of your very useful note you sent us is the reference to e-Borders, and the obvious linkage between the police and e-Borders is the police national computer. In the e-Borders system whereby there is a checking of passports which, as most of us have experienced, is underway in a lot of ports, does that have an on-line link so that anyone who is on the PNC would show up?
Detective Chief Inspector McCarthy: The current system is HOWI, the Home Office warning index, and that is where your passport is swiped when you enter or leave the country into a WICU machine, a warning index machine, so if you hand your passport over to an immigration officer, they will swipe the passport and it will be fed into the database, be checked against that database and it will come back. The HOWI/WICU database at this time, if we wanted to make an entry on it for police concerns where somebody had been flagged up for police interest or there might be a security services interest, that would come up on the screen of the immigration officer who would then follow a pattern in order to notify the appropriate person or persons of that person coming to notice or passing through the port either for immediate action or action at a later time. As far as the PNC is concerned, that would be dealt with as a separate check. If the person was referred to the police, then it would be a standard check which would be undertaken. As far as e-Borders is concerned, it would be a standard check which would be undertaken once e-Borders is fully up and running.

Q12 *Lord Marlesford:* Do you have the capability or practice indeed with the appropriate people from the PNC record of noting where they are? Do you have the capability of putting them on the, did you call it, a warning list?

Detective Chief Inspector McCarthy: Yes, on the warning index. We do have access to that and we do that via the National Ports Office which is based at Heathrow.

Q13 *Lord Marlesford:* So that is happening now?

Detective Chief Inspector McCarthy: That happens now, yes, but e-Borders is an extension of that where we get passenger information in advance of the actual flight or voyage taking place, in which case we can run information against several databases which allows us to be aware of people in advance of them arriving in the UK.

Q14 *Baroness Henig:* This is in clarification of the question which you asked, Chairman, which was whether we had been involved in any Frontex operations and the reply was in the negative, but I gather we do have officers actually stationed at Frontex.

Detective Chief Inspector McCarthy: They are border and immigration officers.

Q15 *Baroness Henig:* So what do they do then? What is their job?

Detective Chief Inspector McCarthy: I think you probably need to speak to the Border and Immigration Agency, the border control representatives, to find out exactly what those officers do.

Q16 *Baroness Henig:* But they are based in Warsaw?

Detective Chief Inspector McCarthy: To my knowledge, there are two members that are permanently placed within Frontex at Warsaw, the headquarters, but they are not there in a liaison capacity, as far as I am aware, but more undertaking a specific role as part of Frontex itself. Then there is one member of the board of Frontex in representation of the Border and Immigration Agency, but that is not as a voting member, but as an invitee.

Chairman: I think we will have an opportunity to question them directly.

Q17 *Baroness Tonge:* I have a number of questions I want to ask you, but, first of all, can I just comment that I am awfully glad to hear that there is a review going on as to how these agencies interact and you are clearly in the thick of it.

Detective Chief Inspector McCarthy: Yes.

Q18 *Baroness Tonge:* So the first thing I would like to ask you is: do you think there is a danger in having these different organisations? My background is health and social services and everyone is always

buck-passing, "Oh, that's not us, that's him", another day saved, another day wasted. Does that go on? Secondly, I am not quite clear about the difference between organised immigration crime, which seems to be dealt with by SOCA, and smuggling and people-trafficking.

Detective Chief Inspector McCarthy: The review is formed by, and directed from, the Prime Minister's speech on 25 July which said that there will be a visible presence at ports for people arriving into the UK within the next several weeks. A lot of that work focuses on the primary line work, that first point of contact that the travelling public have with officialdom when they land or arrive in a country. Previously, there have been three lines of checks. The first is immigration officer checks, the second is potentially police and Special Branch officers interdicting members of the travelling public, and the third is an Her Majesty's Revenue and Customs officer obviously looking for revenue and illegal goods entering the country, so there is a three-tier approach to managing the border controls. What is happening now is that we are looking towards a single tier, a single primary line approach, which has meant that BIA and HMRC in particular are working more closely together and there is discussion as to whether the police, the SB element of the police, should be working at this primary line also. Our view within Special Branch and within the National Co-ordinator's office is that the work of the police is so unique here and so focused on counter-terrorism measures that it would be dangerous to put this into a primary line because it might mean diluting the skills of the officers having to deal with counter-terrorism issues. As far as buck-passing is concerned, I think there is potential for that if a single agency occurred where there was not a single governance chain of command. If there was a coming together potentially of the police, the Border and Immigration Agency and Her Majesty's Revenue and Customs at the border into a single agency and they retained three separate governance chains of command, then yes, of course there probably would be buck-passing that would take place in the future, but, as it stands at the moment, there are very clear distinctions and delineations between each of the agencies' responsibilities.

Q19 *Baroness Tonge:* And the difference between organised immigration crime and the smuggling and trafficking?

Detective Chief Inspector McCarthy: I have actually got a definition taken from the Serious Organised Crime Agency site that says exactly what organised immigration crime is. Serious organised immigration crime really looks at both parts of what you have described. It looks at smuggling and it looks at trafficking. Smuggling is the facilitation of people into the country who are coming in mainly to take economic benefit out of the country. Trafficking is the exploitation of people being brought into the country either to work as prostitutes or as some other form of exploitation. The two are regarded as being under the same label, so it is a split definition of that serious organised immigration crime.

Q20 Baroness Tonge: So they are one and the same thing?

Detective Chief Inspector McCarthy: Yes, they are one and the same thing in terms of that terminology, but they are two separate elements obviously. In particular, the trafficking element of that is of a particular concern because it obviously involves the exploitation of people, and the smuggling would be normally paid for to enter the UK in order to take advantage of potential benefits within the UK.

Q21 Lord Harrison: Chief Inspector, you may feel that you have answered these questions, especially in your very helpful definition of the difference between border security and border control, but to what extent does ports policing work involve the gathering and/or exchange of intelligence over the use of surveillance? The counter-terrorism concerns about which you have already spoken, how are they integrated, if they are, into your work and how deeply and what form does that take?

Detective Chief Inspector McCarthy: Our chief objective at ports and at borders is the combating of terrorism. Our obligation there is to gather intelligence, to monitor and to prevent the entry or the exit of persons suspected of being involved in terrorism, so our chief goal is to monitor terrorists and gather as much intelligence as possible, and that will be done in relation to security services and other agencies and interests as well to do with terrorism and counter-terrorism in particular. As far as surveillance of these people is concerned or any sort of police surveillance that takes place, if it is to do with serious organised crime, most of the time the surveillance would take place by the Serious Organised Crime Agency and if it is to do with a national security matter, it might be undertaken by the security services or it can be undertaken by the police, one of the counter-terrorism units or counter-terrorism intelligence units that exists in the UK under the SB auspices. As well as other potential agencies that could be involved in the surveillance of people outside of the ones I have just mentioned, we would help to facilitate their surveillance of people of interest to them and obviously we would want to know why they were doing it at a port and what the nature of the surveillance was in order to comply with the law.

Q22 Earl of Listowel: Detective Chief Inspector, please can you tell me what the legal framework is governing those apprehended at the border and refused entry and what remedies they have under UK law. Is there a different framework in England, Scotland and Northern Ireland?

Detective Chief Inspector McCarthy: That is certainly not my area of expertise. That would be a question that would probably best be aimed at a Border and Immigration Agency official to answer, but I do have some notes if you would like me to refer to them that I have gained in liaison with the Border and Immigration Agency. As I say, it is a Border and Immigration Agency area of responsibility, chiefly governed by the legislation under the Immigration Act 1971 which governs the entry into the UK of foreign and Commonwealth citizens and provides for their refusal of entry if they do not meet the standards or requirements contained for admission under that legislation. Individuals who hold a visa or prior entry clearance for the purpose of which they are seeking to gain entry or who already hold a continuing leave to enter in such a capacity are afforded a right of appeal before removal from the UK, unless the purpose for which they are seeking entry is different from that which was detailed in their original visa or entry clearance application. Other individuals either have no right of appeal against refusal of entry, for example, visitors, or a right of appeal only after they have been removed from the UK. Asylum claimants have a suspensive right of appeal against refusal for asylum and may not be removed from the UK while any such appeal is outstanding. Regardless of any statutory appeal rights or the absence thereof, any individual may seek to challenge their removal from the UK by means of judicial review. I can go into some more detail, if it would interest you, but again you might prefer to get this information from a Border and Immigration Agency officer.

Q23 Earl of Listowel: What is the extent of current bilateral or multilateral co-operation with equivalent authorities of other Member States on border management issues, what form does this co-operation take and what does it involve in practice? For instance, how far are there placements from one Member State to another of senior officials shadowing and so on?

Detective Chief Inspector McCarthy: As I have previously said, they are not involved within Frontex on the police side. It is wholly, I understand, the Border and Immigration Agency that are involved in Frontex. We would like very much to become involved with Frontex because we can see a clear potential to gather intelligence that would be of real benefit to national security and in our efforts to counter terrorism. Currently, there are police officers who are engaged through the Home Office and through the Foreign and Commonwealth Office in various posts abroad. I myself have been seconded to the Foreign and Commonwealth Office and I served in Bosnia and Kosovo, giving assistance to the local police. From an intelligence sense, it is very limited as to what our involvement is abroad in gathering intelligence. Of course we do have counter-terrorist liaison officers abroad in Europol and in Interpol which cover a number of countries, 75 countries worldwide, and the total number of officers at the moment is 17, so it is fairly limited in that respect, soon to be 18, I am informed, but they are not there primarily for an intelligence-gathering role, they are there to liaise. If there was an incident, for example, a serious or major crime abroad that involved potentially witnesses or victims or suspects even from the UK, then these officers would liaise with the host nation force in order to expedite the investigation. As I say, from our side on the National Co-ordinator's side and certainly ACPO, we would like more involvement in Frontex at this time just to see how useful it would be to us rather than jumping in fully. We would like to gauge the benefits that Frontex could offer us in terms of intelligence and operations linked to secure borders.

Q24 *Lord Harrison:* Those 17, soon to be 18, are they all linguists?

Detective Chief Inspector McCarthy: I cannot answer that, I do not know.

Q25 *Earl of Listowel:* How difficult is it to free an officer to go and work elsewhere? How much capacity is there, and obviously it is a question of resources to a degree, but is it your sense that there is a recognition of necessity for this and that there is a clear commitment to doing so or is it something which you find, as an organisation, quite difficult to do, but strive to achieve?
Detective Chief Inspector McCarthy: I think there is a general willingness to have officers based overseas, but it is for the national good rather than for a single constabulary's benefit. For example, you have 52 police officers within the UK and if they send an officer abroad to undertake a national role, the benefit to the individual constabulary might be seen by that constabulary to be limited, although the officer will gain additional skills from the placement, but generally the benefit is to the UK Police Service as a whole and not to that constabulary. Certainly from a counter-terrorism perspective, there are obviously fundamental benefits in sending officers abroad to gain contacts with officers abroad in the same positions, particularly on border control, which would allow us to gain a better picture of the movements of people across Europe in particular, which is our first line of defence.

Q26 *Lord Teverson:* Perhaps I could ask a very simple question in a way in terms of multilateral or bilateral co-operation. At ports, when one of your officers is at one of these ports, clearly a vessel that is coming in or a plane or a train, I suppose, in terms of Eurostar, which started somewhere else, do they ever speak on the phone to the police officer of the other EU State or the other EEA State at the other end? Does it work on an informal human level as well as a bureaucratic level, which I do not mean in the pejorative sense, but going around via national headquarters or whatever?
Detective Chief Inspector McCarthy: There perhaps has not been enough previously informing formal structures for making enquiries. As I say, the main hubs for those are Europol and Interpol which have been set up on a multinational basis, but there is certainly innovation and initiative shown at local ports whereby they build up a relationship by visiting opposing ports in order to gain a relationship and a line of communication so that if there is a query, they know who to contact immediately and enquiries can be made on a very efficacious basis in order to produce information which would be of use, so yes, it is done more on an informal basis outside of those organisations I have named, yes. Perhaps there could be some more work done on a local basis that is prescribed centrally in order for local forces in particular or local ports to maintain and to initiate even a good line of communication with their opposite numbers in ports that frequently use the same lines.

Q27 *Lord Marlesford:* It is helpful to have your expression of desire at least to get involved in Frontex and indeed the Home Office have said the same thing. Have you had the opportunity of forming any impression about how Frontex is going about its business which you could enlighten us with or maybe you could say if you have not?
Detective Chief Inspector McCarthy: I do, yes, have an opinion of Frontex. It is quite clear that there is a unique potential within Frontex in our collective fight against terrorism and for purposes of national security, to assist us with that. On the other hand, the feedback that we get, which is mainly by the Border and Immigration Agency, is that Frontex is not really performing to a standard that is currently beneficial. Certainly from our perspective, we view Frontex as an agency that deals primarily with what they refer to as "irregular immigration" or migration which we would probably term as "illegal immigration", and there is no focus on crime, serious organised crime, and no potential really for gathering intelligence that might assist in combating terrorism. If we were to become involved in Frontex, we would certainly hope that by that time or certainly without influence we could promote an increased awareness of the

possibilities concerning counter-terrorism for the whole of Europe, not just for the UK, and also serious organised crime. I do not think we are getting out of Frontex at the moment what we could and if we were involved in it, through my own experience of working abroad, our participation, I am very sure, would be much appreciated by the other Member States.

Q28 Chairman: The very obvious interest which you have shown in more police involvement in Frontex, have you actually made your case in Whitehall? Is this a particular question which Sir Gus O'Donnell's review is going to take on board, namely the extent to which the police should be involved in Frontex?
Detective Chief Inspector McCarthy: I personally have brought the subject of Frontex into the review debate and discussion, so I am sure that it will get a mention.

Q29 Chairman: Do you attend this group?
Detective Chief Inspector McCarthy: I am a member of the Cabinet Office review team, yes, on behalf of the police.

Q30 Lord Marlesford: I can see your point obviously, but, on the other hand, as I understand it, and you have just started this study really, Frontex is purely intended as a means of handling the very difficult problem of migration and the potential problem, so per se it is not actually concerned with terrorism or serious crime or anything else and, therefore, I suppose it could be argued that it has a clear remit to set itself up as a means of handling, almost physically handling, migration problems which might be a diversion or a digression or whatever if you start bringing in all the police stuff.
Detective Chief Inspector McCarthy: I am sure it would and again the same argument could be used, that to bring more activity into Frontex would dilute it and distract it from its original goal and, yes, that is a very good argument. I think though, to balance that out, that perhaps another argument could be that we are not doing enough in terms of policing serious organised crime outside of Interpol and Europol when looking specifically at borders. Frontex deals specifically with the borders and the integrated border management for the Eastern European States, et cetera, and we have got a vested interest in that as our first line potentially of defence in the future and if we are in the future going to fully sign up to Schengen perhaps and become full members of Frontex, then I think we need to set out our stall as to what we expect from Frontex in terms of national security measures as well, as I say, although it would possibly distract away from the current goal of dealing with these very complex migration matters. I think there is a need to prioritise within Frontex and I think the addition of CT or

counter-terrorism as an element of Frontex would be beneficial and specifically beneficial to us.

Q31 Lord Young of Norwood Green: I am not sure how relevant my question is in the light of your previous answer. According to us, the UK has participated in a number of Frontex operations, including Operation Torino at Heathrow. Has the NCPP been involved in any of these and could you give us more details about how they were conducted, their goals and outcomes?
Detective Chief Inspector McCarthy: Operation Torino was back in February 2006. I had to make some enquiries about this because I had no knowledge of it myself and indeed when we made communications with other police partners, they had no knowledge either, and that is because we were not involved. We made enquiries with the Border and Immigration Agency to find out that Operation Torino was a joint air operation co-ordinated by Frontex which ran from 3 to 26 February to counter illegal migration under the premise of attending the Winter Olympics in Turin. The UK had an Italian liaison officer present at London Heathrow for part of the operation and that officer's task was to target onward flights to Italy and advise on Italian documentation. There was no police involvement as it was an immigration-based operation and, as I have said to other questions, the Border and Immigration Agency would probably be best to provide you with more details of those operations.

Q32 Baroness Henig: I am very interested in the whole area of intelligence, obviously our own intelligence and also using, or having access to, other European countries' intelligence. You mention in paragraph 13 that there is currently no collective intelligence produced by Frontex for dissemination to Member States, and I wondered whether you knew what informed Frontex risk analysis which forms the basis of their operational working.
Detective Chief Inspector McCarthy: Again this is information that has been received via our contacts within the Border and Immigration Agency because we have got no one in place at Frontex, so our enquiries so far have been, "What could Frontex possibly offer us in the Police Service?", so we specifically ask questions around what they produce in terms of intelligence reports for dissemination to the Member States. I was basically informed that every State goes in and takes out what they feel is relevant, but there is no joint or collective intelligence product. Frontex is risk-led, so I am informed, and operations are planned and initiated on the basis of either internal risk analysis, a Member State proposing a joint operation or a Member State requesting assistance with a particular problem. I have already gone over the fact that we would

potentially have some serious use of Frontex for intelligence-gathering purposes and if we were to be members of Frontex in a voting capacity and being singularly represented as the UK Police Service, then our aim would be primarily to gain intelligence on national security matters.

Q33 Baroness Henig: So I suppose my follow-up on this then is: what more needs to be done to capture and disseminate effectively Frontex intelligence or intelligence relating to their operations? Presumably you operate within the national intelligence model.
Detective Chief Inspector McCarthy: Yes, we do.

Q34 Baroness Henig: So how could that model incorporate some sort of European intelligence which it does not at the moment? Is there any way of capturing European intelligence?
Detective Chief Inspector McCarthy: Certainly within Europol and Interpol there would be links with SO-15, which is part of the Metropolitan Police Force Counter-Terrorism Command, in terms of pumping intelligence into the UK system as a single point of contact. If there was any police representation within Frontex, ideally, from a ports and border perspective, we would look for that information and intelligence to be fed into the National Ports Analysis Centre which is based in Merseyside. That is how we would view the intelligence flow coming out of Frontex specifically.

Q35 Baroness Henig: But at the moment it does not?
Detective Chief Inspector McCarthy: At the moment, to my knowledge, we receive very little in the way of any intelligence from Frontex and if we do, it is via the Border and Immigration Agency who, as you can appreciate, focus on migration-related matters and not CT-related matters and certainly not to the extent that we are.

Q36 Lord Teverson: You have made it very clear in terms of UK police that have been involved in Frontex and, I must admit, certainly when I first looked at this brief, it seemed to me that it was almost entirely really a migration issue, but clearly these demarcations are not always useful because while you are doing one thing, you might as well do something else that is equally useful. Do you feel that the legal framework really leads to a demarcation that is very difficult in that area at the minute or how would you like to see things move forward?
Detective Chief Inspector McCarthy: Obviously there would have to be agreement amongst Member States as to what the objectives or the goals of Frontex were in the future and whether they were to draw any delineation between crime, terrorism and counter-terrorism and migration matters. If there were, I would see that Frontex would need to be invested in

significantly in order to achieve this and have a clear governance structure and make-up in order for it to concentrate efforts on a list of priorities other than just the single priority. It would be very difficult and need to be obviously marked out and discussed at length, but I think it could be achieved and it is certainly in our interests to become involved in that.

Q37 Lord Teverson: Do you like particularly the Frontex side because it actually has an operational element to it as opposed to Europol which is sort of information-swapping because one of the things we have discussed ourselves in a slightly different context is that Europol, a great idea, but actually the amount of data that there is there is not particularly great or particularly useful, so do you see it that way?
Detective Chief Inspector McCarthy: There is potential certainly and I suppose the thing which is exciting and different about Frontex is, one, that it concentrates on borders and obviously there is a great deal of discussion around borders at the moment, especially with the Prime Minister's announcement on 25 July towards a unified border force and there is a great deal of public anxiety regarding immigration matters in particular, but also, second to that, national security in terms of terrorism and terrorists entering and leaving the country, whether they be home-grown or not. If we could engage in operations beyond our physical borders, that must be of benefit to us in order to prevent the problem from coming into the UK in the first instance, so there are clear benefits to be had, but obviously in the scale of the operations and how much information was fed into the operations in order to inform the operations in the first place.

Q38 Lord Teverson: If you could choose, say, around our own borders an area where co-operation with another European Member State, say, France, the Netherlands or perhaps Spain, could be a lot better within a Frontex context operationally, what sort of instance would it be where you would say, "Yes, that would be a good solution for us in our border area"?
Detective Chief Inspector McCarthy: Well, currently we do have juxtaposed controls with France and Belgium where you have officers from Revenue and Customs, from the Border and Immigration Agency and the police working in France and in Belgium and vice versa with their officers working in the UK. That works well. Really, any operations would be an extension of that, but in order to do operations in another country using officers in a liaison or executive capacity would need the consent of that government for obvious jurisdictional reasons, but I would see it as an extension of that current co-operation which takes place in order to be more proactive rather than reactive, so yes, it would be

beneficial in that respect. Again, it would potentially be a marked effort in preventing the problem from reaching the shores of the UK and having dealt with it in a more combined and unified way amongst European partners.

Q39 Lord Teverson: What are your own views on the UK's position on Schengen? We only very slightly participate in Schengen. Do you think that border security would actually be easier if we were full members of Schengen and had all the things that go with it or would it actually create a border-free European Union with us as part of that and would that cause insurmountable problems? How do you see that?
Detective Chief Inspector McCarthy: There are obviously big concerns regarding free passage through Europe, especially if you consider the possibilities of a future where you have former communist Eastern European States being the first line of defence into Europe and where potentially once a malefactor, a wrongdoer passed that line of defence, they had free movement in Europe, and obviously that would cause us some serious concerns. However, there are benefits to be gained out of being full members of Schengen at the same time. In the interests of national security, it would be to the UK's advantage to be in a position to join EU colleagues in collectively combating illegal activity across the spectrum and, in that respect, we view Frontex as having great potential. We are aware that the UK has sought to become full members of Frontex, but was precluded from doing so because the UK is not a full member of Schengen. By not being a full participating element of Frontex, we believe that the UK is missing an opportunity to engage with EU partners and specifically, even on the police side, the police partners and border agencies and border controls in consolidating our efforts to more effectively tackle terrorism and immigration-based crime.

Q40 Lord Teverson: In terms of the problem with borders in Eastern Europe when those countries actually become full members of the Schengen system itself, yes, I understand that entirely, but why do you think it is any more difficult for us than it would be for the Netherlands or Sweden that would have similar issues?
Detective Chief Inspector McCarthy: I think the initial thought that comes to mind would be that our involvement politically as a nation abroad in various circumstances, Iraq and Afghanistan, makes us a particular target.

Q41 Chairman: I think in a sense you have answered the last question I wanted to put to you which really relates to Schengen in a different context and the

Schengen Information System II, SIS II, on which this Committee has produced a report and incidentally we are about to have a debate in the House of Lords on Friday on the subject, but we are a bit concerned, I think, that ministers have told us that the United Kingdom will not be ready to connect to SIS II until April 2010 which is rather a long way away. Are you worried at all about the effect that this delay might have on policing and border control enforcement?
Detective Chief Inspector McCarthy: I do not have a great deal of knowledge in this area, to be honest, but I would say that obviously any delay in our signing up to a database which would provide additional means for gathering intelligence or information that might help in the fight against terrorism of course would be to our detriment and it could not otherwise be.
Chairman: I think we are all familiar with the hideous problems that concern any large database, some of them caused by fires in an entirely unrelated neighbouring property, but I think we merely note that.

Q42 Lord Marlesford: In your paper, paragraph 12, you say, "It would be beneficial for UK police to gain a better understanding of (and influence) the EU Integrated Border Management (IBM) approach that has been adopted". I wonder if I could draw you out a bit on that because that is not directly Frontex, is it, or is it something else?
Detective Chief Inspector McCarthy: It is an element of Frontex and it is something that I had some involvement in while working with the border services in Bosnia and Herzegovina and it was basically the integration of border controls, working in a unified way across the region within the EU in order to be able to connect, connectivity in particular to connect to each other and maintain good communication systems to prevent wrongdoers from entering the EU as this first line of defence.

Q43 Lord Marlesford: That sounds very sensible, so what is happening as a result of the view that it is desirable?
Detective Chief Inspector McCarthy: Again, it is more based on immigration rather than counter-terrorism which means that it is more the Border and Immigration Agency's area of responsibility. However, it is something very obviously that we have a keen interest in and want to become more involved in and we see the portal for doing that as being Frontex.

Q44 Chairman: Chief Inspector, it remains for me to thank you very much. You have been extremely helpful. If, on consideration, you think there is anything that you could usefully add in writing, please feel free to write to us, but otherwise thank you very much for the very comprehensive and extremely useful replies to our questions and thank you for coming. We wish you all the best.

Detective Chief Inspector McCarthy: Thank you, my Lord.

TUESDAY 16 OCTOBER 2007

Present	Henig, B.	Teverson, L.
	Jopling, L.	Tonge, B.
	Listowel, E.	Wright of Richmond, L. (Chairman)
	Marlesford, L.	Young of Norwood Green, L.

Examination of Witnesses

Witnesses: MR JONATHAN FAULL, Director-General, Justice, Freedom and Security, and MR HENRIK NIELSEN, Deputy Head of Unit Borders and Visas, European Commission, gave evidence.

Q45 *Chairman:* Director-General, welcome. It has become almost a matter of routine, receiving you in this room. We are extremely grateful to you for agreeing to come and give evidence to us and the regularity with which we have the pleasure of seeing you. Thank you also, Mr Nielsen, for coming here. I will not introduce our team, most of whom I think you know from previous sessions, and all of whom, I think, myself excepted, have their names in front of them, but you probably remember by now who I am.

Mr Faull: I certainly do.

Q46 *Chairman:* Director-General, as you know and as usual, this is on the record. A transcript will be taken of the meeting and you will be sent the transcript, but, as before, if at any point you decide to go off the record we will ask Christine to lay her pen down and then you can say when you want to go on the record again.

Mr Faull: I can even say that Henrik was just telling me that there is nothing secret in the very fine briefing he has prepared for me, which gives no-holds-barred answers to all your questions, and if it would be helpful we can leave it with you.

Q47 *Chairman:* That, I think, would be extremely helpful; thank you very much, but if at any point you decide to go into ultimate secrecy and depart from your brief we will respect you. Director-General, can I start by asking you to give us your assessment of the work of Frontex so far? I think the Commission are intending to do a Frontex review early next year so it may be a bit premature to ask you for your conclusions, but anything you can tell us about how Frontex has performed and whether it has come up to your expectations would be very helpful. Moving on to the next question, what do you think the role of Frontex should be in controlling borders? Should it, for instance, extend to rescue at sea? Anything you can tell us of your assessment so far would be extremely helpful. I should just mention that we are going to Warsaw next week to visit Frontex and we are hoping to get to the Ukraine border to see how it is operating in practice.

Mr Faull: Good. Thank you very much and good afternoon to you all. We will indeed carry out a full review next year and we will know a lot more then, of course. What can we say now? We can say that, bearing in mind that Frontex really got going only two years ago, these are early days but I think we can say with considerable confidence that it is meeting the expectations that we had for it when it was created and that it is even continuing to meet expectations, which have grown considerably since that time and are continuing to grow. Frontex has taken forward activities in all the areas of its mandate and has become an important player in the implementation of Schengen rules on the management of the European Union's external borders. Those expectations were high and I think now are even higher, and those expectations are not only ours but also those of the Member States; they are those of public opinion generally, particularly in the countries most immediately exposed to migratory pressure. This has all meant that the agency has had to adapt to changing circumstances and has had to implement operations at short notice while being fully dependent on the willingness of Member States to co-operate with it, with each other and to provide equipment because Frontex is ultimately only an agency co-ordinating the work of the Member States, their border guard services and so on. There has obviously been considerable pressure on and interest in its activities at the Union's southern borders on the Mediterranean because that is where migratory pressure has been highest and where media and political attention have therefore been most closely focused. Your second question was what should the role of the agency be in controlling borders and should it extend to rescue at sea. These are all issues that we will look into next year when, on the basis of a thorough review, we will look at whether the current mandate given to Frontex could be extended.

Q48 *Chairman:* When do you expect your review to take place?

Mr Nielsen: February.

Mr Faull: I should have introduced Henrik, by the way; I am sorry. Henrik Nielsen is the Deputy Head of our unit dealing with borders and visas. He was previously my personal assistant and is an expert on these and many other matters and I may, if you agree, ask him from time to time to help me out with one or other of the answers.

Q49 Chairman: Of course, whenever you wish.

Mr Faull: For the time being we believe that the mandate is the right one. Risk analysis must be the basis for priority setting by Frontex. That is the case at the moment. That risk analysis is almost a daily one as things develop, as things change, as migratory pressure moves, but Frontex has proved within the legal framework set for it sufficiently adaptable and flexible to deal with issues as they evolve. Turning to search and rescue, search and rescue first of all are not simply a matter of border control or migration policy. They are part of a coherent framework (or at least a framework which should be coherent) set by the law of the sea with its own institutional framework. We have no EU legislation on search and rescue aspects of the law of the sea. They are governed by international rules. Article 98 of the UN Convention on the Law of the Sea, the Safety of Life at Sea Convention and the Search and Rescue Convention as well as international customary law all provide essentially that masters of ships are required to assist any person found in distress at sea. This obligation, of course, applies to Member State vessels participating in Frontex joint operations when a distress situation is encountered during such an operation.

Q50 Baroness Henig: Director-General, thank you for meeting us here yet again. Some witnesses in their written evidence to us have highlighted a general reluctance on the part of Member States to commit national assets for Frontex operations because there are not clear rules as to where people intercepted by EU joint operations at sea are to be disembarked, and I wondered what your views were on this and what proposals the Commission might put forward to address this problem.

Mr Faull: All Member States are subject to the same international legal framework but it is certainly true that differences in practical application and interpretation of that framework can be different from one country to another and those differences may have an impact on the effectiveness of operations, particularly when vessels from different Member States are acting within the framework of the same operation. You are right in pointing out that the issue of where persons rescued at sea should be landed is an extremely complex one on which different views are held. It is at this stage not possible,

and certainly it would be premature, to conclude that these differences are deterring Member States when considering whether or not to participate in joint operations. We are not aware of any example where a Member State has decided not to take part in a joint operation for this specific reason. We are discussing this very important issue with the Member States as part of the follow-up to a study which we recently published on the law of the sea.

Q51 Lord Teverson: Coming back to how the Commission reckons Frontex has done, what does it use as the criteria to assess the performance of Frontex? What do you do to give it five stars or two or one? Is there a formal way of doing it?

Mr Faull: There is and that will be spelt out in the evaluation with a proper methodology when it is carried out next year, so everything I say at this stage is preliminary. What Frontex does is, and, Henrik, do not hesitate to come in and complete or correct this if necessary, is risk assessment based, based on its own understanding of where its intervention is most needed and, of course, very largely from what Member States tell it about where they think its intervention is needed. It then sets up joint operations. The joint operations are only as good as the equipment and the resources and the men and women made available to it by Member States. We talk generally about its "toolbox", what is in its toolbox at any time, and then its operations take place, and its operations, which have been taking place very largely in the Mediterranean Sea in the recent period, are measured by how effective they are, first of all in dealing with the specific circumstances which called the operation into existence, and more generally (but this gets much more difficult) into any deterrent effect on illegal immigration that it might be having in the countries of transit and origin in respect of north and sub-Saharan Africa. That becomes much more difficult to assess but each operation is the subject of report and analysis. There are always areas of improvement and the adaptation process, as I said, is an eternal one, but the general assessment by Frontex itself, by us, by Frontex's management board and by the Member States is that it has made a difference and is doing a good job given the resources made available to it so far. It may sound vague to you but this is all at this stage rather preliminary because we will carry out this very full evaluation in the next few months.

Mr Nielsen: Also, of course, Frontex has published its annual report in which it describes overall its accomplishments, and I would stress once again, as Jonathan has done, that the individual reports on each joint operation describe exactly what has been done and to what extent the objectives have been achieved.

Q52 *Lord Teverson:* So there is quite an emphasis on the individual operations?
Mr Faull: Yes.

Q53 *Lord Teverson:* Because the macro side is very difficult to assess?
Mr Faull: The macro side is difficult to assess. We will try to develop a methodology for doing that. In an area like this it is always difficult first of all to say what would have happened if Frontex had not been there and the main focus of its activities so far in mounting joint operations has been because of the events in the Mediterranean, so yes, the focus is on that.

Q54 *Lord Jopling:* Reverting to the international law of the sea, could you tell us what your impressions are of the Commission's recent work on this, particularly so far as illegal immigration is concerned? Do you think it is just a study which will go into a pigeonhole and nobody will do much about it or do you see any signs of activity to follow it up?
Mr Faull: We have no illusions about the difficulties involved. The law of the sea is a matter of enormous complexity. These conventions took decades to negotiate and we are dealing here with extremely complicated issues. Nevertheless, the facts are these. We published a study in May 2007 on international law in relation to illegal immigration by sea in response to a request from the European Council in December 2005. The study looks at the current legal framework for the exercise of control and surveillance powers at the sea borders and the main obstacles to the effective exercise of that surveillance, and looks for solutions such as completion of the existing legal framework by bilateral or regional agreements and the establishment of guidelines for Frontex joint operations defining criteria for the sharing of responsibilities between Member States which participate in such operations. It also looks at the obligations of third countries under international maritime law (for example, with regard to search and rescue and safety of navigation) and the Palermo Protocol on the smuggling of migrants, and, of course, the Geneva Convention on refugees. Among the key issues is the one already alluded to of the appropriate place of disembarkation in a search and rescue situation, knowing that the way the Mediterranean Sea is divided into search and rescue areas does not tally with political geography. For example the Maltese search and rescue area is a very large and extensive one; it goes all the way to Crete in the east, the Sicilian island of Lampedusa is in the middle of it, and therefore the issue of where illegal immigrants are to be landed when rescued is a very acute one and one which arises between those two Member States. Another example is the question of who is responsible for the processing of an asylum application made following a rescue at sea. These are all issues which are not conclusively to everybody's satisfaction settled by the law of the sea texts as they stand at the moment. We looked into all of this and a meeting was held on 8 June with Member States and experts from Frontex but also from the International Maritime Organisation, the UN High Commissioner for Refugees' office and the International Organisation on Migration. It was agreed to set up an informal working group to look at what guidelines could be used by Member States in the context of Frontex joint operations. It would not be legislative and could, for example, be part of the operational plan, which is prepared in advance, of each joint operation. The United Kingdom is part of a group which is trying to draft such guidelines. It has met twice already on 19 July and 24 September. The next meeting will be held in the middle of November, so this is a way in which we could go which would mean not trying (because that would be a task of enormous proportions) to settle the law of the sea issue for ourselves, or indeed for the whole of the international community, but to deal with the specific case of what happens in a joint operation under Frontex's aegis, and there we would have, if you like, rules of engagement which would determine in advance what would happen in a particular operation in the event of rescuing putative illegal immigrants at sea, particularly with regard to the question of disembarkation and of asylum applications.

Q55 *Lord Jopling:* If there is an argument over who carries out a search and rescue, particularly a rescue at sea, because nobody particularly wants to be saddled with whoever is there, what role does the Norwegian Centre at Stavanger have in organising these rescues? I was there in May and a case came in when I was there of a ship drifting 200 miles east of Djibouti with no fuel and no food, and they were organising the rescue of that. Do they have a role in this within the waters around the EU?
Mr Nielsen: I am afraid I am not familiar with that particular centre unless it operates under the framework of the International Maritime Organisation.

Q56 *Lord Jopling:* Yes, it does.
Mr Faull: I do not know either. We will look into that and I will reply to you in writing. The general trend, therefore, as I said, is to try to craft rules which would apply in Frontex operations, no doubt meaning, therefore, that everybody would be able to say that that was without prejudice to their general view on the interpretation of international law. Perhaps I will go off the record here for a few minutes.

(There followed a short discussion off the record)

Q57 Baroness Henig: What is the international institution that can resolve the problem of which country should take illegal immigrants, because obviously you need a clear legal framework within which to operate?

Mr Faull: You do. We are in a way instigating reflection on this because people's minds are focused on it because of the events. Not only because of us but also because of our study and what will follow this is now on the agenda. How will it be settled? I do not know. There is an International Court of Justice which is the ultimate arbiter of international law if someone takes a case there. As far as I know there is no such case pending.

Q58 Baroness Henig: Yet.

Mr Faull: Also, the world community can reconsider the conventions in the UN Framework, but I do not see that happening either. It is probable that the best we can do as Europeans faced with a particular European problem is to sort it out for ourselves within the particular context of Frontex operations. If that works and is seen to work between countries of very different sizes and resource levels, perhaps that will shine out to the rest of the world as something which will be followed and will either harden into customary international law or will be taken up in an international convention one day. At the moment I think the best solution for us is to be pragmatic and solve the particular problem. After all, it is a problem of human tragedy as well; it is a life or death problem in the Mediterranean. We have to sort it out the best we can.

Q59 Baroness Tonge: Given that Frontex was only established in 2005 and started operations a year ago --- am I right?

Mr Faull: A bit more than a year ago.

Q60 Baroness Tonge: And after what you have been saying for the last half an hour, which comes over to me as if people have not really evaluated yet fully what Frontex is doing and how useful it is, nor been able to take stock of their achievements or their development needs, how are you expanding the role in the form of the RABITs Regulation? You are being a bit hasty, surely?

Mr Faull: No, with respect, I do not think we are being too hasty. I think that we have to prepare for the reaction to events which we know are taking place and are likely to continue to take place, particularly in the Mediterranean. The RABITs, as they are called, are now in legal existence as a possibility. No Member State has yet asked for the deployment of the RABIT team so the system is there ready to be used if needed and we thought (and it is not just we in the Commission, because after all the legislation was adopted by the Council ultimately) that it would be a mistake to wait for the full evaluation before taking any next steps because the events, often tragic ones, continue to occur. Obviously, we would not do anything which prejudged the outcome of the evaluation process but we do not believe that that is what we have done. We believe that this was a necessary next logical step in the protection of our borders and that it would have been wrong therefore to deny Member States the facility of the RABITs for a further period of time.

Q61 Baroness Tonge: Following on from that, the RABITs Regulation also says that the border guard teams should be able to carry weapons. Are we really sure that this is necessary and that it is even safe to do so? Do impoverished illegal migrants want to shoot their way into Europe? What is the reason for those border guard teams to have weapons, first of all, and how will it change the nature of Frontex, because I am sure it will, and is it compatible with the different character of the different Member States, some of whom have the military guarding their borders while others have unarmed police? Has this really been thought through properly?

Mr Faull: Yes, it has, and it is safe and it is compatible with the requirements of the countries concerned. The rules now provide that border guards participating in a RABITs team or in joint operations can carry weapons under the same conditions as the border guards of the host Member State. That means that they can be fully operational in supporting that Member State in which they are deployed. Nevertheless, with the exception of self-defence, the use of force remains subject to the consent of both the home and the host Member State in accordance with their law and only in the presence of the border guards of the host Member State, so we believe that the necessary safeguards are in place. It would only be in a situation in which the host country's border guards would be armed and on the same conditions of their being armed that the guest border guards who were there to help them would be able to be in the same situation as they are. This was adopted unanimously by the Council. Although qualified majority voting would have sufficed it was adopted unanimously.

Q62 Baroness Tonge: If someone is killed as a result of them carrying weapons whose responsibility is that? Is that the Member State's responsibility or is it the responsibility of Frontex?

Mr Faull: They are not employees of Frontex in any way. They are officials of their Member State which would take responsibility.

Mr Nielsen: Yes, but during the deployment it would be the laws of the host Member State that applied with regard to any criminal liability.

Q63 *Baroness Tonge:* And that applies to any Frontex operation?
Mr Nielsen: Yes.

Q64 *Baroness Tonge:* It is under the law of the Member State?
Mr Nielsen: Yes.

Q65 *Baroness Tonge:* Weapons or not?
Mr Nielsen: Yes.

Q66 *Lord Marlesford:* The stage that Frontex has reached from your description, Director-General, sounds very like, if one can use a military analogy, joint planning staff. Do you see it perhaps evolving into an operational capability with its own personnel and, secondly, it has been suggested to us that it could have an anti-terrorist and anti-crime role. Would you favour that or do you think that would be a diversion from its primary purpose?
Mr Faull: Its primary purpose today is very clearly guarding our borders. I do not know what the evaluation will come up with and I do not know where the political debate will go after that evaluation has been made public. At this stage one can only speculate and I am reluctant to do that. At the moment Frontex has a very clear mandate. It has proved flexible enough to meet the border control challenges facing it so far reasonably satisfactorily. We will know more when the evaluation is carried out. There are many other systems of co-operation in place regarding the police and counter-terrorism agencies and duplication is the last thing we need in a complicated field. If that has given a little bit away of my thinking, so be it, but let us wait for the evaluation. Frontex is today a co-ordinating body. It is not an operational body in its own right. It brings together the operational agencies and forces and bodies of our Member States. It is—we sometimes use this analogy—a phone number so that the Spanish, facing a problem in the Canaries, say, do not have to ring around 26 countries; they have one number in Warsaw, they ring the number in Warsaw and Warsaw knows what the other 26 countries can and cannot do, have available, do not have available, and can provide an answer.

Q67 *Lord Marlesford:* So you do not see it ever having its own forces in its own Frontex uniform?
Mr Faull: I would be very surprised. I would never say never to anything. There will be a full evaluation. The European Union has in its Member States 27 differently constituted organisations responsible for border control in these other areas. They are not

going to disappear. Look at the experience we have had in the customs field. We have had a Customs Union in Europe now for 40-odd years, I suppose, but the national customs officials are still there doing their national jobs alongside their EU responsibility. We are not looking for symbols here; we are looking for pragmatic responses to real life and death situations.

Q68 *Earl of Listowel:* I have a supplementary which very much relates to what you have just been saying, Director-General, and it is about the concerns expressed earlier about how to manage the expectation on this organisation, which I think has been a theme of the afternoon's discussion. If one thinks of something like CEPOL, that is a small organisation which has been working for a while and is well recognised as being effective in what it does. These evaluations will be helpful to that, I suppose, but is there anything that should be done now to keep states which are under a great deal of pressure from immigrant flows from perhaps raising their expectations too high about what it can achieve?
Mr Faull: I am sure we should and I recognise that perhaps we are not doing it fully successfully. Frontex is not and cannot be the magic wand which will solve this problem for 27 countries. Illegal immigration is a multi-faceted phenomenon. Our border with Africa is a very narrow stretch of sea. Illegal immigrants are often the subject of trafficking by extremely sophisticated organised criminal gangs and they are very able to switch routes at short notice. When one route is policed successfully we find another one opening up. I have no doubt that this is a complex issue. I think it is a very welcome development that all European Union Member States have understood that it is a common endeavour, that our border is at the south of Italy, in Malta and in Spain just as it is in Finland and at Heathrow Airport and all these other places. That is true, I would even say, moving on to more controversial grounds, beyond the distinction of who is in Schengen and who is not because of movement within the European Union. That is understood. Frontex is a small, modestly resourced agency which is really no more than a clearing organisation for assets, ideas and risk assessment made at each Member State's level and then trying to organise a co-ordinated response to that. It is obviously not the only answer. There are many other answers needed, both at our level and at the level of each individual Member State, but, knowing that Member States face different challenges because of their size, because of their geographical location, because of their resources, I agree with those who say that we should not allow expectations to rise too high because that can only be followed by disappointment. Frontex has an important role to play. We should try to make sure

that it has the resources needed to do its job. Member States should provide it with the resources and assets that it needs to do its job. That I think everybody agrees with, but there are many other things that need to be done as well.

Q69 *Chairman:* You referred to non-Schengen states. Do you want to make any comment on the position of Gibraltar?
Mr Faull: No.

Q70 *Baroness Tonge:* Director-General, I am so sorry but I want to get this absolutely clear and you may think this stupid woman keeps on going on about this. You say that Frontex does not have a uniform; you do not employ border guards yourself, so when a Member State calls Frontex for help on a particular problem who decides whether they will carry weapons or not, and if the states that come in to help that state normally carry weapons will they rule what goes on or will the Member State who does the calling in rule what goes on? I just want to get the weapons thing clear.
Mr Faull: The calling-in Member State, the host Member State, if you like, has to give consent, so if the host Member State does not want weapons to be carried they will not be carried. Is that right, Henrik?
Mr Nielsen: They have a right to carry their weapons, with certain exceptions of types of weapons that can be prohibited by the host Member State. That is for the carrying of the weapons, but for the actual use of the weapons there is a need for the consent of both the Member State of the border guard where he is employed and of the Member State where he will go.
Mr Faull: Except in cases of self-defence, presumably *force majeure*.
Mr Nielsen: Yes. As an example, if a UK border guard goes to Spain and the UK border guard authority decides, "No, we do not want you to use your weapon in this operation", they will say so and then he cannot. He can still carry it, he can use it for self-defence, but he will be prohibited from using it in terms of the use of force.

Q71 *Lord Teverson:* Does Frontex ever operate on a Schengen border as opposed to the EU external border?
Mr Faull: An internal Schengen border?

Q72 *Lord Teverson:* No. Would there ever be a situation where it operated on a Schengen border as opposed to the EU external border?
Mr Faull: I think I see what you mean. We have three categories at the moment. We have the fully fledged Schengen countries like Belgium with no external border except ports and airports.

Q73 *Lord Teverson:* I suppose I am talking about, say, the east German border.
Mr Faull: You mean between Germany and Poland today?

Q74 *Lord Teverson:* Yes. Say between the 15 and the Visegrad. It never operates on that border?
Mr Faull: No, it does not, but it does operate already at the external border of the new Member States about to join Schengen, and you may see them at the Poland/Ukraine border, for example, because Poland is already in the external bit of Schengen. The only thing that has not happened yet, and we hope it will happen soon, is that the internal borders between Poland and other Schengen countries will be dismantled. As for the United Kingdom and Ireland, you and the Irish have your own external borders for which you are responsible and there is still a border between you and the rest of the European Union, but Frontex does not operate in Calais, for example, let alone Dover.

Q75 *Earl of Listowel:* Does the Commission believe that the current legal framework ensures adequate transparency and accountability of this agency?
Mr Faull: Broadly speaking, yes. The agency's work, including its priorities, its annual work programme, its annual report, is subject to its management board. The annual report is sent to the European Parliament and to the Council and is published, and the agency, usually through its Director, frequently appears before the Justice and Home Affairs Council of Ministers and before the relevant committee in the European Parliament. The general Regulation 1049/ 2001 regarding public access to European Parliament Council and Commission documents applies to the agency. The executive powers of the agency, its staff and Member State border guards, when operating under its aegis, are regulated by European law. For example, the regulation creating the Rapid Border Intervention Team, the RABIT, and regulating the task and powers of guest officers, regulates the issue which we have just discussed about whether the national law of the home or the host state applies. It is true that in the preparatory phase of joint operations the impact and efficiency of the operations can be influenced by the extent to which they are made known in detail in advance. As is the case in an individual country, major operations to intercept illegal immigrants and those who organise movements of illegal immigrants have to be implemented with a certain amount of discretion, at least in their preparatory phase, before they are put into operation. The fundamental basis of the activities of Frontex risk analysis is based on intelligence information from Member States which is necessarily treated as confidential so that the interests of the Union as a whole and its Member

States are not imperilled. As a European agency, and certainly within the terms of its current mandate, Frontex is not a decision-making body. Its role is simply to support Member States in their efforts to control their borders, their part of the external borders of the Schengen area. Consequently, all decisions that may need to be taken during a joint operation, such as denial of entry, interception of vessels suspected of carrying illegal immigrants, search and rescue, grant of access to international protection, are taken by a Member State, not by Frontex itself, and those decisions are subject, of course, to all relevant provisions of European and international law. Frontex is a European agency financed by the Community co-ordinating operations involving border guards from different Member States and therefore issues of accountability and monitoring do arise; we are aware of that, and that will form part of the review of the existing legal framework in the evaluation report and its follow-up under Article 33 of the Regulation.

Q76 Lord Young of Norwood Green: Director-General, I think you have probably touched on a bit of my question but I will expand it. What is the role of the Commission in facilitating co-operation between Frontex and third countries, and is there a wide variation in the response of these countries—and I am sure I know part of the answer to that—and can you give some examples, either on or off the record? *Mr Faull:* First of all I will tell you what is on the record. The agency is given the task of facilitating operational co-operation with countries, including developing its own co-operation with the relevant authorities of foreign countries (we tend to say third countries; it is our jargon) under existing working arrangements and in compliance with the European Union's general external relations policy. The agency receives a mandate from its management board, and we have two representatives on that management board alongside the Member States and the United Kingdom and Ireland have observers, and therefore any arrangements to be concluded with a foreign country are approved by the board both initially before negotiations start and when they are ready for conclusion. We are happy to provide assistance and guidance to the agency both here domestically in Europe and through the use of our delegations in foreign countries where appropriate. I would now like to go off the record for a minute.

(There followed a short discussion off the record)

Q77 Lord Teverson: What does the Russian agreement allow you to do? What does it accomplish? *Mr Nielsen:* One thing is just, as I say, an exchange of expertise and best practice and supports training of border guards in a third country. A next step could be

the exchange of intelligence information for the purpose of the risk analysis, so classified information from the Russian border guards, for instance. A third level would be the actual involvement of a third country in a joint operation in relation to a specific border crossing point. That is at least the ambition.

Q78 Lord Teverson: To what extent is the Schengen Borders Code applicable to Frontex operations outside the EU external border? *Mr Faull:* First of all, the Schengen Borders Code applies to Member States and to Norway and Iceland as participants in the Schengen area, and soon Switzerland, I suppose,— *Mr Nielsen:* Yes, within a year. *Mr Faull:* --- and Lichtenstein shortly thereafter as regards the control of the external border, including border surveillance, to prevent the unauthorised crossing of the border. Border surveillance can also be carried out on the high seas, of course, in order to detect people seeking to circumvent entry via authorised border crossing points into the European Union. However, provisions relating to measures taken after detection, such as interception and disembarkation, are not covered by the surveillance rules of the Schengen Borders Code. They are governed by the law of the sea which binds all Member States and in turn is based on the jurisdiction and national legislation of the flag state of each vessel. Activities on the territory of a third country can be carried out only on the basis of an agreement with that third country and that agreement would have to decide what the applicable law to any specific activity would be.

Q79 Lord Jopling: We understand that the Council of Ministers has adopted conclusions on the EU's southern maritime borders which we understand are meant to encourage an integrated approach to border control and surveillance operations. This is, as we understand it, a joint effort between Member States, the Commission and Frontex, but also involving the International Organisation for Migration and the UN Refugee Commissioner. Could you tell us how you think this is going and do you think much will happen in practice, and what in particular might be the role of the IOM and the UNHCR? *Mr Faull:* This is an important step forward. The Council conclusions referring to an integrated approach want us to look beyond interception to the protection needs, repatriation possibilities and rights of migrants to dignified treatment and to seek international protection. As a result of this wider scope we are promoting co-operation between Frontex on the one hand and the IOM and the UNHCR on the other so that arrangements can be found to co-ordinate support from UNHCR and

IOM to migrants intercepted in the course of joint operations and disembarked in a Member State, or indeed in a foreign country. UNHCR has appointed a representative to Frontex in Warsaw and the Frontex management board has given Frontex a mandate to negotiate formal working arrangements with the IOM and the UNHCR. Both of these organisations participate in the meetings of the expert group created to follow up the study on the law of the sea and to draft the practical guidelines for Frontex joint operations I referred to earlier. IOM and UNHCR could make a significant contribution to our understanding of migratory flows, the course they take and the reasons for them. They have a vast network of offices and relations with non-governmental organisations in most of the foreign countries in which we are particularly interested. Frontex for its part can provide both organisations with general updates of operational activities and the main results of its risk analyses, thereby establishing a two-way information flow. Training is organised by Frontex for EU border guards. That training should cover principles of international protection and refugee law and could also cover such practical questions as how to deal with interception of immigrants and how to deal with would-be asylum seekers and UNHCR and IOM could have a role to play in helping with the training of border guard staff in these areas.

Q80 *Chairman:* Do either of them send observers to the operations?
Mr Faull: Not that I am aware of.
Mr Nielsen: No, I do not think that has occurred yet. That would, to start with, be subject to the approval of the Member State that is hosting the operation.

Q81 *Chairman:* And is the representative of UNHCR, for instance, in Warsaw somebody who would anyway be there as a UNHCR representative or as somebody specifically attached to Frontex?
Mr Faull: I think specifically attached.
Mr Nielsen: Yes.
Mr Faull: I think it is a new position.

Q82 *Chairman:* On a resident basis?
Mr Faull: Yes. You may meet him or her there.

Q83 *Lord Jopling:* Does Frontex have any role at all in seeking to find intelligence as to when illegal immigration is about to happen, ships sailing, movements of that sort? Have they an intelligence role, because one would have thought that if they could have it would be a very valuable part of their activities?

Mr Faull: No. My understanding is that they are entirely dependent on Member States for that sort of information. They do not have networks of intelligence operatives.
Mr Nielsen: No, but we are trying to put them together with the ILO network, the immigration liaison officers of Member States that are active in third countries, which could feed into at least Frontex risk analysis with their knowledge and their intelligence from specific third countries.

Q84 *Lord Marlesford:* During our recent study of the Schengen information system we learned that the British Government much regretted the refusal to share information on Schengen with the United Kingdom Government even though the United Kingdom Government paid its full whack of the cost of the Schengen Information System. I personally would deplore it as an appallingly non-*communautaire*, dog-in-the-manger attitude. Do you intend that attitude to continue in the development of Frontex or will you try and improve that?
Mr Faull: We work with the legal situation as it is, trying to do what is best for all Member States, whatever legal arrangements they may have decided to have. The integrated border management system that we have is Schengen-related, quite obviously, and is based on the Schengen rules in which the United Kingdom does not participate. Schengen Member States assess and develop responses to their integrated border management challenges according to their needs. The United Kingdom, no doubt, individually faces very similar but not necessarily identical challenges and it may be regretted that unless the necessary conversations are able to take place full account is not taken on the Schengen side of British concerns and full account is not taken on the British side of Schengen concerns, both, after all, being extremely close neighbours and bound together in all sorts of economic and other ways in the European Union, so there is a risk of loss of useful experience and sharing of best and worst practice, what works and what does not, across the Channel. I think everybody is aware of that and everybody tries with the best possible will to make sure that there are bridges between the two systems, but there are two systems and as time goes by and as the integrated border management system of the Schengen area becomes more integrated it is likely to grow in ways which are different from what the United Kingdom is doing, facing its own specific national challenges, which again are extremely similar to those that the Schengen countries face but not necessarily always the same, and certainly the United Kingdom is not involved in devising the common solutions which the Schengen countries are.

Q85 *Chairman:* Director-General, you have dealt admirably with our questions, if I may say so, as always. We are very grateful to you and we are very grateful for your offer to let us have your brief. Can I thank you both very much for coming, and again for your courtesy in coming *chez nous* as opposed to *chez vous*.

Mr Faull: Indeed. We are on Her Majesty's territory here.

Chairman: Yes indeed. Thank you again.

TUESDAY 16 OCTOBER 2007

Present	Henig, B.	Teverson, L.
	Jopling, L.	Tonge, B.
	Listowel, E.	Wright of Richmond, L. (Chairman)
	Marlesford, L.	Young of Norwood Green, L.

Examination of Witnesses

Witnesses: MR SIMON BUSUTTIL, Member of the European Parliament, MR GÉRARD DEPREZ, Member of the European Parliament, MR JAVIER MORENO SANCHEZ, Member of the European Parliament, and Ms HÉLÈNE CALERS, LIBE Committee Secretariat, European Parliament, gave evidence.

Q86 Chairman: Welcome to all of you. Thank you very much for coming to give evidence to us. I am Lord Wright of Richmond. I am Chairman of a House of Lords European Sub-Committee and the purpose of this meeting, as you know, is to collect evidence for an inquiry which we have just started into Frontex, and we will in fact be visiting Warsaw next week to talk to Frontex themselves. The purpose of this occasion is to seek your views as Members of the European Parliament on Frontex. We have allocated the questions among ourselves, of which you have had notice, but perhaps I may leave it to you to decide which of you want to answer the particular question. The meeting is on the record. A record is being taken and you will be sent transcripts of the evidence for you to agree or not agree in due course. I wonder if I could start by asking any or all of you to give us your assessment of how Frontex is working so far and whether it has met the European Parliament's expectations, but first of all could you quickly introduce yourselves?

Mr Busuttil: Good afternoon. On behalf of my colleague, Mr Moreno Sanchez, I would like to welcome you to the European Parliament. My name is Simon Busuttil. I am a Member of the European Parliament for Malta. I come from the EPP-ED Group, which is the largest political group in this Parliament. It is the political group in which the British Conservatives are aggregated; at least, they were till this morning. I would like to start by answering your question on my assessment of Frontex so far. It is a negative assessment so far but it is also a hopeful assessment. It is negative to the extent that I do not think that Frontex is doing enough, in particular to stem the immense wave of immigration that is coming northwards from Africa at the moment, hitting in particular southern Mediterranean Member States, such as Malta, Italy and Spain, but also Greece. It is hopeful also, but at the same time I appreciate that Frontex is a very young agency. It has been established for only two years, operational for less than two years, and therefore I am hopeful because I hope that in the future Frontex will become even more effective than

it has been so far. I can go into a great deal of detail as to why I think Frontex should be more effective than it is and how this could be done, but I suppose at this introductory stage I should stop there because perhaps there will be supplementary questions and also to give my colleagues the opportunity to introduce themselves and to intervene.

Q87 Chairman: Thank you very much.
Mr Moreno Sanchez: I am Javier Moreno from Spain. I am a member of the Socialist Group here in the European Parliament. As you may know, it is very important for countries in the south to get Frontex. I was the European Parliament Rapporteur on policy priorities in the fight against illegal immigration of third-country nationals. We adopted two reports two weeks ago in Strasbourg, one about the fight against legal migration and another about illegal migration. I used to say that Frontex is a baby which was born just two years ago and it is a baby which needs the support of its parents. Its parents are the Member States and the Member States have to give it the tools, the financial and human resources, to implement its actions. As Simon said, it has started, it is not enough, but I think it is important because it is based on one principle, which is obligatory solidarity between the states. It is very important that we share the responsibility on migration and the fight against illegal migration. I think the basic principle is very good, but, as always in the European Union, we are starting and we are very slowly working on that, but the problem is that migration goes faster than our responses and that is why from the Parliament we are asking for more money and more people so that Frontex can help everyone. It will not be a panacea in the fight against illegal migration but it is one tool, one instrument, which is very important.
Mr Deprez: In my opinion, it is too early to assess the personality of Frontex. It is a very young agency, only two years old. Frontex has to work in a very difficult situation because the territory it has to protect is very large, as it is the ocean. It has nothing to do with the borders of Belgium, with the Netherlands or with Luxembourg. I would like to

add that Frontex is not an operational agency. It only has to manage co-operation between Member States. It does not have its own agents but only depends on the voluntary co-operation of the various Member States and, as you can appreciate, this makes the operation of Frontex very difficult. Indeed, one must make a distinction between Frontex as such and the Member States, which have to put the human and tactical means at the disposal of Frontex.

Q88 Chairman: How do you assess the contribution that Member States have made so far? Do you think Frontex is adequately understood within the European Union? Are Member States adequately aware of the contribution they could and should be making to it?
Mr Deprez: It is difficult to answer your question. I think that there are some Member States which are well aware that they have to do something but not all members are currently aware that they have to put people or technical means at the disposal of the agency. This is the reason why I think that RABIT is a new stage in the operation of Frontex, offering a new kind of non-mandatory co-operation between Member States.
Mr Busuttil: Frontex has created what we call a "CRATE", or "toolbox", if you like, which is a register of assets, typically boats, helicopters and planes, belonging, of course, to the individual Member States—because Frontex, as Mr Deprez has just said, does not have its own army, it does not have its own coastguard, it does not have its own assets—but registered in the central Frontex register in the form of a pledge, that is to say, when Frontex needs to embark on a mission it will call upon the assets in this register in order to use them in its different missions. The problem is two-fold there. The first problem is that I do not think that the Member States were very generous in the assets that they pledged, and there is a list, and I suppose you can get access to the table I have here which shows which Member States actually registered assets in this toolbox. The second problem, which is even worse, is that the Member States were even less generous in honouring their pledges. To give you one instance, in the Frontex mission in the Mediterranean in July there was not even one Italian boat and yet this list tells me that Italy pledged as many as 32 boats to Frontex, so there is a huge discrepancy between the pledges and their fulfilment. These are commitments. We are not talking about all the army or all the assets of an individual country. These are assets pledged to Frontex. There is still a huge discrepancy between the pledges and the promises that have been fulfilled.

Q89 Chairman: Whose job is it to follow up these pledges and remind Member States of their pledges?

Mr Deprez: That is not specified.

Q90 Chairman: It is not a Frontex responsibility?
Mr Deprez: No. Frontex is only prepared to co-ordinate the assistance that the different Member States are offering to a country which has problems with illegal immigration. The Regulation does not specify who is in charge of reminding Member States that they have to send personnel and equipment to the countries which need them.
Mr Moreno Sanchez: From the Parliament we asked the Commission to ask the Member States but we had no response. In order to convince the states there is one important argument: the excellent results of Frontex's operations. The Vice President of Spain, Maria Teresa Fernandez de la Vega, said just a few weeks ago that with Frontex's four joint operations in the Canary Islands during the first eights months of 2007, the number of illegal immigrants who have arrived in Spain has been reduced by 75%

Q91 Chairman: Compared with last year?
Mr Moreno Sanchez: Yes. Where it works it works, so we have to convince the other states that we mean it and that they have to deliver.
Mr Busuttil: I think you have really put your finger on the button, as it were, because this is the point of the whole thing: who is responsible for making sure that the pledges that have been made are honoured. This is the great loophole. Mr Deprez next to us here is historic in this sense because he recently was responsible for a new law, the RABITs legislation, which introduced a novel concept, which is what he calls "compulsory solidarity", and he put it into law. This means that Member States are obliged to participate in this RABITs scheme, and this is not about assets now; this is a different notion. The RABITs, as you are aware, are the Rapid Border Intervention Teams, but in that respect legislation was introduced and the notion of compulsory solidarity was introduced. We have nothing of the sort with respect to the pledging of assets, and maybe we ought to introduce that.

Q92 Baroness Henig: Can I first of all thank you all very much for giving us your time. It is a very valuable opportunity for us to hear different perceptions of how you think things are going. Taking account of aspiration as against reality, which we have just been looking at, what do you think the role of Frontex should be in controlling borders? Should its role, for instance, extend to rescue at sea, and I am mindful that many of you are from southern European areas?
Mr Moreno Sanchez: We have put exactly this point in our report from the Parliament. We believe that steps should be taken to introduce within the

mandate of Frontex operations of the rescue of migrants and asylum seekers at risk. Frontex has to rescue and save people, and to stop illegal migration. Commissioner Frattini told us two weeks ago that last year 400 people were arrested, people who were trafficking human beings. We do believe that the first thing Member States and third countries have to do is to respect international law and international obligations on the rescue of persons at sea. If they have people dying they have to rescue them.

Mr Deprez: According to the Council Regulation of 26 October 2004 establishing a European agency, rescue does not count amongst the tasks of the agency. However, there are international laws in this field to protect people who are in danger at sea and give them assistance: when you are doing an operation and you see there are people in a boat and they are in danger you have to intervene and give assistance to those people, even if it is not a task or an obligation foreseen by the regulation; but it is an international obligation. The next problem is what to do with those people? But this is another matter. So it was not necessary to add rescue as a task of this agency because there are international laws to protect people who are in danger at sea.

Mr Busuttil: I just want to place emphasis on the last point made by Mr Deprez. I strongly feel that rescue at sea is just one side of the coin. The other side of the coin—and it is the same coin, believe me—is who is going to take responsibility for the lives of those that are rescued at sea? This difficulty has been played out at sea this summer with countries arguing with each other over who is going to take the people who are saved at sea. There was never any difficulty over who should save them. Of course we should all save them. Wherever you are you have to save lives at sea. The difficulty is who should take them after they are saved and this in turn may perhaps affect the readiness, if you like, of Member States to participate in Frontex missions, to offer assets or to honour their pledges.

Mr Moreno Sanchez: What we cannot do is what we are doing month after month, and yesterday we had another example, which is to delegate the responsibility to the boat's captain. Yesterday it was a Spanish captain who saved people and afterwards he had a problem going back to Libya to give them back. Frontex and the states have to take the responsibility to rescue and to assume this responsibility. We cannot delegate it because it is happening day after day. Yesterday there was a Spanish captain who had to save the people and afterwards he had the problem, "What do I do with all these people on my boat?", because Libya did not want to have them and I think it took was one or two days to find a solution and at the end the Libyan authorities said okay because the Spanish Foreign Minister called Tripoli and said, "You have to do

something". We cannot leave this problem to the boat's captain.

Q93 *Lord Jopling:* The evidence that you have given to us underlines evidence we already have, the point that states are reluctant to fulfil their obligations because there are no clear rules as to where people rescued at sea should be disembarked. I wonder if I could ask you—and, my Lord Chairman, I do not know whether you think the answer to this question might be better off the record—if you could tell us why, the Italians having committed 32 ships, there was none available as there should have been? What is their response to this? Also, what I would like to ask particularly is what is your solution to this very serious problem which clearly undermines the whole concept of Frontex? How do we get out of this? What is the way? Is it politically possible?

Mr Deprez: It is a very difficult question. When you read the regulation, it is clear that, at the moment, responsibility for the control of external borders lies with Member States. Frontex is only offering support in cases of emergency. In my opinion, it is necessary to make a new regulation establishing compulsory assistance to some Member States in cases of emergency, especially to some very small states facing great influxes which they are not able to control, as Malta, for example. I do not say anything against Malta, which is facing a totally new situation as a recent member of the European Union. It is a kind of new airport and they are totally unable to control that. I think it will be necessary to make a new regulation saying that in cases of emergency if Member States receive a solicitation from Frontex they are obliged to give some support. There must be in some cases compulsory assistance to some Member States. If there is no compulsory assistance, there will always be difficulties. It is in this sense that we have to make some kind of progress. That is my opinion.

Mr Busuttil: What did the Italians say? Off the record, did you say? No, the Italians said on the record—

Q94 *Chairman:* Just to be clear, do you want to go off the record?
Mr Busuttil: No, I was joking.

Q95 *Chairman:* I would prefer you to stay on the record.
Mr Busuttil: I have absolutely no difficulty in doing that. The Italians in the summer when this happened simply said that they thought that Frontex missions would never be sufficiently effective without the participation of Libya because, as you know, Libya has refused to participate in these missions although it was repeatedly invited to do so. The Italians

clearly have a point, but if we have to wait for the Libyans to join us in participating in this mission we will never be able to do anything. We could not have been held at ransom, if you like, by the Libyans until we got some action in place. The Italians put forward that argument in July but subsequently changed their mind and when the mission resumed in the month of September—because it stopped in August; for some incredibly strange reason it stopped at the peak of summer, but that is beside the point—the Italians were there in relatively full force. As to the solution, I will just make one note. The European Parliament, because here you are talking to parliamentarians, have very limited powers in this respect but perhaps our strongest powers here are our budgetary powers. Since we are part of the budgetary authority of the European Union we are trying to make sure that we use that power, if you like, as a leverage to get what we want in terms of the greater effectiveness of this agency. We have done two things recently in the Budgets Committee and we shall be voting on this in plenary at first reading for the 2008 budget next week. First of all, we have voted to double the budget of the agency for next year. Secondly, we have voted to put in reserve, to freeze effectively, up to 30% of the administrative budget of the agency and only to release it if we are satisfied that Frontex has improved its accountability towards us and its effectiveness on the ground.

Q96 Chairman: Do your proposals in the Budget Committee reflect the ambitions and applications of Frontex themselves? In other words, are you talking about roughly similar sums?
Mr Busuttil: You will be surprised to hear that we are not, not at all. We have actually voted a budget which is far greater, it is plus 30 million over and above what the Commission and Frontex originally requested from us, the reason being, of course, not that Frontex does not want to work or does not want to have the budget to work, but because it is very conscious of the fact that it is a young agency and therefore it should learn how to walk before starting to run. But, of course, we have no interest in seeing Frontex walk. We want it to run at great speed and this explains why we have done this. Incidentally, this is the second year running that we are giving more money to Frontex than it requested at the beginning of the budget proposals. Last year we increased their budget unilaterally by €15 million and, sure enough, this year, because the missions grew in number, they came for an additional €7 million, so over and above their original request for the 2007 budget they now have in hand plus €22 million, so I think we are not far

off the mark when we give them plus €30 million this year.
Mr Moreno Sanchez: I just want to add one thing about the solution. It is a key issue to control our borders and I think we have to do that inside the European Union but also in co-operation with the third countries. I think we have taken important steps with the creation of RABIT's teams, and with the Rabat and Tripoli ministerial conferences in 2006 and the UN Global Migration Forum, in Brussels. I do believe it is important that third countries get involved and that we help them to control their own borders. As I have said Frontex is one tool, but also close co-operation and dialogue with all third countries concerned is very important.

Q97 Earl of Listowel: You referred earlier to the expectations on Frontex but do you feel that the expectations on Frontex are being managed well? Is the Commission sending out clear messages about what Frontex can do and what it cannot do?
Mr Busuttil: My reaction to that question would be that this is not about expectations. This is about events and we have already been overtaken by events, so yes, it could be that people have a lot of expectations, not least in my own country, that Frontex will work miracles and solve everything. Clearly it will not, but we have to act fast simply because we have been overtaken by events.

Q98 Lord Jopling: Following my original question, you talked about the solution being to introduce a degree of compulsion. Has anyone drafted a form of words yet which would give those new powers and, if so, could we see them?
Mr Deprez: To some extent, yes. If you read, for example, the regulation creating the RABIT teams, Article 4 says: "Member States shall contribute to the Rapid Pool via a national expert pool on the basis of the various defined profiles by nominating border guards corresponding to the required profiles". "Shall contribute" implies a kind of compulsory determination, but there is no sanction and no juridical control if a Member State does not act accordingly. It is a kind of political compulsory mechanism but is not a juridical one.

Q99 Baroness Tonge: I just wanted to be quite clear how the money works. You said there had been an increase in the budget this year. Is that money for Frontex administration or is that to pay Member States for their contribution? That money goes to Member States governments, does it?
Mr Deprez: That is the operation of credits. It is not for the personnel of the agency.

Q100 *Baroness Tonge:* No; I just want to know exactly where it goes.
Mr Deprez: It goes for the operations.

Q101 *Baroness Tonge:* Does it go into the Member States' government?
Mr Deprez: Yes, for the operations.
Mr Busuttil: The money is divided, to put it briefly, into two sections. You have the budget allocation for the administration of the agency and you have the budget allocation for operational purposes, the operational budget. Clearly, missions would be paid out of the operational budget whereas the staff salaries and administration would be paid out of the administrative budget. If I can give you the numbers, you have around €15 million for the 2008 administrative budget, and it is 30% of this budget that we have frozen, and then you have another €53.5 million for the operational budget.

Q102 *Baroness Tonge:* I cannot understand why the Member States are paid for the cost of their contribution to the operation, why a country such as Italy is not providing what they pledged, because it is no financial loss to them if they do, presumably, because Frontex pays them.
Mr Busuttil: Of course this question is very much open to interpretation. I will give you my own and I am sure my colleagues will have their own too. I think it is back to the link as to who will take responsibility for the people who are saved. It all boils down to that. The general reluctance, I think, boils down to that. It is not about who is going to save the lives; it is about who is going to host them as a country after they are saved.

Q103 *Baroness Tonge:* We were also concerned that, given the short life that Frontex has had so far, not only should the RABITs regulation come into force so quickly but that they should be allowed to carry arms, that the teams should be armed. We wondered what the responsibility is again between Member States and Frontex for the carrying of those arms and who ensures that people are properly trained and use them properly.
Mr Deprez: According to the regulation, members of the RABIT teams have the opportunity to carry arms if their home country gives them the right to do so. They are not forced to carry arms, but they have the right to do so, should they be in the same situation in their country of origin and in the country where they have to work. However, in the absence of an agreement between the sending country and the country which hosts the RABIT members, they will not be allowed to carry their arms. In other words, if the same regulation on the carrying of arms applies to the country of origin and to the country where they have to work, RABIT agents will automatically have the right to carry arms. In the case of a disagreement, both countries will have to reach an agreement. I do not see any problem.

Q104 *Baroness Tonge:* So you could have a Frontex operation where some of the guards contributed by one country would be armed and the others were not?
Mr Deprez: Yes, indeed, it can be the case if the country of origin, for example, decides that the agents sent to the territory of another Member State are not authorised to carry arms. According to Article 6(5) "While performing their task and exercising their powers, members of the teams may"—"may"—"carry service weapons, ammunition and equipment as authorised according to the home Member State's national law. However, the host Member State may prohibit the carrying of certain service weapons, ammunition and equipment, provided that its own legislation applies the same prohibition to its own border guards. The host Member State shall, in advance of the deployment of the teams, inform the Agency of the permissible service weapons, ammunition and equipment and of the conditions for their use". You may have a totally different situation if there is no agreement between the Member State of origin and the Member State of the territory where they have to work.

Q105 *Chairman:* Has this in practice become an issue yet?
Mr Deprez: I don't know. I don't think so.
Mr Moreno Sanchez: Yesterday they started the first practice exercises.
Mr Deprez: It was one of the points on which we had the most difficult discussion with the Council about this regulation, but we reached an agreement and all Member States agreed.
Mr Moreno Sanchez: It is very important to underline, as Simon has said, that we do not have many competences in this subject in the Parliament, but this regulation was under the co-decision process and we worked hard and fast in the Parliament and we passed it on the first reading. We had a very intensive dialogue and co-operation with the Council and we all agreed that it was very important to adopt this regulation, and we managed, with the Council and the Commission and the Parliament, to get it. If there is the political will I think we can go on.

Q106 *Baroness Tonge:* Just to come back on that, would it not be more important then, with this difficulty of countries not delivering what they have pledged, to sort out this problem of who takes the people who are rescued before you go into the RABITs regulation and have lots of arguments about arms? Surely that is the key to the Frontex operation, to decide that. Surely this is absolutely basic to the operation and it is something that has not been decided yet.

Mr Deprez: There was a situation of emergency though. Considering the situation at sea, the only people whose lives are saved are those who have the chance to find the boat of border guards. That is the reason why the RABIT system is also protecting the lives of those people. It does not provide for an organised system of rescue, but only for border control. That is the point of this regulation. However, during this border control, RABIT agents save people when recognising their boats, because if the boats are not recognised on the sea those people will die. That is a fact.

Mr Busuttil: I would like to add something to that. First of all, we must make a clear distinction here. Being obliged to contribute to RABITs is regulated by law and that is very clear and, as Mr Deprez has said, there is the notion of compulsory solidarity there. It could be political/quasi-judicial, but let us hope. The other issue is on pledging and honouring the pledges with respect to assets. That is not yet regulated by law. Maybe you could propose that we have such a law. It would be splendid for us to co-operate with you in that respect. I will just make one point in this respect. Towards the end of May there were three incidents in the Mediterranean Sea involving a number of countries quarrelling amongst themselves as to who was going to save and take people. Basically, these incidents—and this is why the quarrelling started—took place in Libyan waters, as happened yesterday. Following those incidents my country, Malta, made a proposal to the EU Council of Ministers which basically went as follows. It is clearly up to all of us to have the responsibility to save lives, but if lives are saved in third country waters, for example, Libya, and this third country refuses to take on its own responsibilities under international law, for example Libya, in that specific case the people whose lives are saved will be apportioned among all 27 Member States on the basis of proportionality. This is the proposal that my country made, referring only to people saved in third country waters, and the reply that it got was a deafening silence.

Mr Moreno Sanchez: We have it in our report.

Q107 Lord Marlesford: I want to focus my question on the Mediterranean again which is such an important area in this respect. We have had extremely good evidence from the Armed Forces of Malta sent to us from the High Commission of Malta in London, which gives us a lot of information, but I would like to take advantage of having a representative from Spain here to ask if he would like to tell us a little bit about how at the moment Spain is organising its relationship with Frontex, first of all which government department in Madrid is responsible and, secondly, which units of the various Spanish forces would normally be responsible for Frontex operations when called upon, and also any information we could have as examples. Presumably one of the major areas from which people are coming into Spanish waters or into Spain is Morocco.

Mr Moreno Sanchez: First of all, as I said before, Frontex is a tool; it is not a panacea. In the Spanish Government we are starting several measures to fight against illegal migration, and the one of the measures is based on the co-operation with the third countries. For example, we have just started a pilot project to have a centre of information for people in third countries. We have started an information campaign in Senegal in order to inform the people the risks they would take if they came to Spain illegally. The crucial point with Morocco, with Senegal, with all these countries, is the co-operation.

(There followed a short discussion off the record)

In Spain it was shocking, all these pictures on the television day by day showing thousands of immigrants trying to reach our continent, but this is a very small part of our problem because most illegal immigrants come through the airports. We have begun special measures for people who come from Latin America because they come to live in Spain but they never go back; they stay. We have a real problem with this kind of illegal immigration and also the *cariocos* arriving to our coasts

Q108 Chairman: And over-stayers, people who have stayed longer than they should have done?

Mr Moreno Sanchez: Of course.

Q109 Lord Marlesford: Which government department in Madrid has overall responsibility?

Mr Moreno Sanchez: Home Affairs, just for the control of the borders. But also Employment and Social Affairs Ministry because we are trying to make an integrated policy *on* immigration and we are trying to stimulate legal migration because we need it in Spain.

Mr Deprez: Not only in Spain.

Mr Moreno Sanchez: Not only in Spain, but we need it economically and demographically, so we are trying to stimulate the channels for legal migration through cooperation with third countries. We are trying to run a pilot projects to offer legal contracts to possibly workers from countries of origin. This is not new. I am the son of immigrants. My parents went to Switzerland a long time ago and they went to Switzerland with a contract. They had a contract signed in Spain and they went to Switzerland. We are trying to do the same in Spain proposing contracts to workers from Senegal or Morocco. We need these workers. There is another very important point on the fight against illegal immigration: the fight against illegal employment. That is the most difficult thing because there is a lot of money and a lot of interests in that field and we haven't had the political determination to fight against that now. There is also a psychological dimension. . If the illegal immigrants know that in Spain we pursue illegal employment, in the end they will not come. They will not take the risk of dying in trying to reach Europe if they have to go back home because there is no work. Control of the borders is very important but it is not the only tool. We have to make an integrated policy at the European level.

Q110 *Lord Jopling:* But is not one of the problems in Spain that once an illegal immigrant is within the confines of Spain you can only hold them for 30 days and if they are still there after 30 days they have to go and they are free to go anywhere within the EU? Is there any move to try to change that rule, which does make Spain a huge magnet for illegal immigration?

Mr Moreno Sanchez: Last year we sent back more than 99,000 illegal immigrants. Readmission policy is an important pillar of our policy. We have developed an awareness campaign explaining that if they arrive to our country, we will treat them with dignity, respecting their human rights, but afterwards we will send them back home. You can ask yourselves: "As Socialists you could do that?" Yes, nevertheless this is only one instrument of our integrated policy. When we approved our masse regularisation process of illegal immigrants it was criticised by several Member States. However, in November 2005 we had more than one million illegal people working and living in Spain. There were three solutions in order to resolve the problem. First, send back one million people. Second, leave the people as they were without any rights or any obligations. Third, which is what we have done, put in place an integrated plan for migration. But before setting off this integrated approach we had to resolve the situation, so we proposed this regularisation linked to an employment contract. That was the main difference in comparison with other countries actions. By giving a contract to these migrants we gave them the opportunity to participate in the economic and social system. At the end we had 600,000 people who had rights, who paid taxes, and we created 600,000 jobs. I would like to underline one thing. We always explained that it was a one-time event, if not, everybody would have come. We just have elaborated a Strategic Plan for Citizenship and Integration 2007–10 with €2.005 millions in order to integrate the immigrants into our society, to ensure

the immigrant population's access to public services, particularly education, employment, social services, health, and housing, in equal conditions to those of the autochthonous population.

Q111 *Chairman:* We are moving some way away from Frontex. I do not mean that rudely, but to what extent can Frontex provide any sort of help or co-operation for this problem?

Mr Moreno Sanchez: In Spain we defend that Frontex must be more and more efficient. Therefore FRONTEX must have the resources that are necessary for its actions and more powers, because the fight against illegal immigrations does not affect only Spain.

Q112 *Chairman:* It is already the case?

Mr Moreno Sanchez: Yes. The European Union's Eastern countries are starting to face the same problem that we have in the Mediterranean area.

Q113 *Chairman:* We are going to visit the Ukraine border next week.

Mr Moreno Sanchez: For Spain it is crucial that all Frontex's tools get to be implemented. Our Government have also asked for permanent operations in all high-risk areas. We defend the necessity of permanent joint monitoring patrols, operating throughout the whole year and coordinated by Frontex in all these areas.

Mr Deprez: At the moment, the problem of illegal immigration in Spain is not a problem for Europe because the majority of the immigrants stay in Spain. Why do they stay in Spain? Because the majority of them come from Latin America, so they speak the same language. They stay in Spain and they find jobs in Spain because there are a lot of sectors providing them with legal and illegal jobs, such as the agriculture, construction and other fields, except for the industry.. So as I said and as far as my experience is concerned—but I do not say that your experience is the same as mine—illegal immigration in Spain is particularly the problem of Spain and not of the rest of Europe.

Q114 *Lord Jopling:* Yes, but there are a huge number of people who go from Africa to the Canaries and from the Canaries they are taken then to Spain, and if they stay 30 days they are then free to stay, and they are not South Americans at all.

Mr Deprez: Yes, but if you compare the number of people who come from Latin America with the people who come from Africa, I think the percentage is 90/10, perhaps less, according to statistics.

Q115 *Lord Teverson:* Again, my thanks for the time you are giving to this and the depth of information you have given us. I am particularly interested in whether you think the current legal framework is adequate for accountability. Clearly, you do not think it is adequate in terms of forcing every Member State to do their bit but in terms of accountability is it good enough, and in terms of yourselves as parliamentarians do you feel that the European Parliament and your committee have sufficient power to make Frontex accountable? What would you like? What is your preference in terms of reporting?

Mr Busuttil: If I may I will start but I am sure my colleagues will continue. I do not think there is sufficient accountability and I think we ought to improve the accountability of Frontex. The reason that there is such little accountability to the European Parliament is in a way understandable. Frontex was conceived as an agency that reports to Member States. It is a Member State agency, if you like, and therefore for a long time after it was set up the European Parliament was out of the picture except once a year when it had to sign the budgetary cheque. This time around we signed the cheque, a good cheque, as it were, but we made clear conditions on the cheque. This we did in order to increase accountability. I do not think that even this will be sufficient. There is increasing pressure now from the European Parliament to have an overall review of the mandate and the tasks of Frontex and I think this is one of the things we will be doing over the coming year. We are going to have a much closer look not just at what Frontex is doing but also at what it should be doing and whether what it should be doing is in line with its mandate in the relevant regulation.

Q116 *Chairman:* Can I just interrupt you there because I think we all know that the Commission are due to produce a review on Frontex in the spring, I think in February next year. How far do you see yourselves as European parliamentarians involved in that review?

Mr Busuttil: As a matter of procedure the European Commission comes to us with its proposals so we will be debating its proposals and therefore we will be actively involved. I would like also to take this opportunity to invite you to send us your views once you are through with this inquiry on how you see the mandate of Frontex in the future because I am certain that this will have a very significant input in our work next year.

Q117 *Chairman:* You will, of course, all be sent copies of our report when it emerges, and your contribution today is an extremely helpful contribution towards that.

Mr Deprez: It must be clear that Frontex is a European agency and not an inter-governmental agency. It is part of the European system, the Community system, even if its board members are sometimes also members of national governments. Its budget is part of the budget of the European Union. Its financial regulation belongs to the financial regulation of the Community system. The status of its agents is regulated by European law. We all have the opportunity to control Frontex to some extent, except for specific operations. We cannot control specific operations as the agency responds to the demands of the various Member States which are facing an urgent situation. But apart from that, we may control everything if we want to, and we are beginning to do it. As my colleague said, we put some credits in the reserve and we asked the Director of Frontex to come to us in order to discuss their work programme for next year. I am going to meet him tomorrow with the President of my committee and we will have a first discussion.

Mr Moreno Sanchez: At the beginning they did not come, but now they do.

Mr Deprez: No, at the beginning they did not come but now they do because they understand that they have to present their programme to the committee in the Parliament.

Q118 *Lord Young of Norwood Green:* Frontex has a number of working agreements with third countries and there are more being negotiated. Do you think these agreements take sufficiently into account European Union action in other fields, such as foreign policy and development co-operation, or the human rights record of the third countries concerned?

Mr Deprez: I am not able to answer this question.

Mr Busuttil: I would like to come in on that question to tell you one country with which Frontex does not have an agreement. It is Libya, and this explains why we have such major difficulties, whereas, on the contrary, ever since the European Union and Frontex started engaging with countries such as Mauritania and Senegal we have seen incredibly positive results in that area. As Mr Moreno Sanchez has said, there has been this year a huge reduction in the number of immigrants arriving in the Canary Islands and therefore Spain, so clearly the co-operation of third countries is crucial.

Mr Deprez: I have read your question. I think it is very strange, if I may express my feeling, because it says, "Frontex has a number of working agreements with third countries", but it is not the task of Frontex to take into account the fields of foreign policy, development co-operation or human rights. It is not the task of Frontex to say anything on those fields. I do not understand the question. Foreign policy, development co-operation, human rights policy are the responsibility of the European Union as such. They do not belong to working agreements between Frontex and other countries. You say Frontex has a number of working agreements with third countries. Are you sure of that?

Mr Moreno Sanchez: Maybe it is the Commission which—

Mr Deprez: The Commission, but are you sure Frontex has working agreements with third countries?

Q119 *Lord Young of Norwood Green:* Maybe it is the way this question has been framed. You said you had had co-operation from Mauritania and Senegal.

Mr Deprez: Yes, between Spain and those countries, not Frontex. There are agreements between some Member States and countries of origin of illegal immigrants and there are some agreements between the European Union as such and countries of origin but I do not know if there are working agreements between Frontex and --- I do not know.

Ms Calers: If I may, I know that, for example, there is a working agreement with Ukraine, but it is a working agreement for co-operation between Frontex and the border guards department of Ukraine.

Q120 *Chairman:* And I think we were similarly told by the Commission.

Ms Calers: Yes, Frontex itself. It is in the regulation of Frontex that they can negotiate such agreements with third countries.

Q121 *Chairman:* We were told by the Commission this afternoon that there is also an agreement between Frontex and Russia.

Ms Calers: That I would not know.

Mr Deprez: But only in the specific fields of competence of Frontex, not in foreign policy and development co-operation.

Chairman: That might well be. Lord Teverson?

Lord Teverson: All I was going to say, my Lord Chairman, is that we think it is particularly within the powers of Frontex to do that, but I had interpreted this question as, in a way, should not trying to get co-operation from third parties be a part of this? You use other bits of EU foreign and development policy to get leverage on third countries to make these agreements. Surely, like us in the world of politics, in the world that you live in you use your leverage on budgets to get the Director of Frontex sitting here talking to you, and then you get Libya in front of Frontex to do a third party agreement by some other pressure that is put on through the neighbourhood agreements or whatever. That is surely how it works, is it not?

Q122 *Chairman:* But by individual states or by Europe?

Mr Busuttil: By the European Union itself as well. If I may, that is already being done. To take one example, the African, Caribbean and Pacific countries with which the European Union has one comprehensive agreement known as the Lomé Convention, now the Cotonou Agreement, has in Article 13 a provision which specifically states that any national of either party who is illegally staying on the territory of the other party has to be repatriated and therefore there is an obligation of re-admission, of accepting back this person. This is found in Article 13 of the Cotonou Agreement, the new agreement with the ACP countries. It is already there, but does it mean that it is enforced? The answer is probably no, it is not.

Q123 *Chairman:* We now come to a question which I think to some extent has been dealt with by Mr Moreno Sanchez and also by Mr Deprez, looking at the future of Frontex. From the point of view of the European Union Parliament do you see it evolving into a more operational organisation as opposed to a sort of co-operative and facilitating organisation, and do you think it should evolve into co-ordination of action against terrorism or other serious crime as opposed to purely illegal immigration? Would one of you like to answer that? The broader you can make it the better. How do you see the future evolution of Frontex?

Mr Moreno Sanchez: I do believe in the necessity of a common approach based on an integrated control of the borders in co-operation with Frontex

Mr Deprez: Except for the United Kingdom, I think.

Mr Moreno Sanchez: Frontex is not the only tool but it is an important one together with the exchange of information, in order to ensure the borders are under control

Chairman: I really cannot allow your comment to go unanswered. The United Kingdom is actually making a very significant contribution to Frontex—

Mr Deprez: Yes, I know.

Q124 *Chairman:* — both in terms of operations and in terms of finance. I just thought it might be worth making that comment.

Mr Deprez: But my comment was about the integrated system of border control. It concerned a very specific situation. I did not say that you were a bad payer in the European system.

Q125 *Chairman:* Has anybody any additional points?

Mr Busuttil: I was going to support what Mr Moreno Sanchez said. I do think that Frontex should develop further, should become operational in its development and should become the agency responsible for the protection and strengthening of the external borders, not just of the Member States but also of the Union itself. I think there is also an increasingly important link to make between Frontex and the Schengen zone in particular, so that once one person enters the Schengen zone there is absolute free movement within that zone. That zone today has 15 countries, unfortunately not including the United Kingdom, but come next year it is going to enlarge with another nine countries, so there is a huge territory there, and in that territory, once you have penetrated the external border, you can move freely throughout it without any passport checks whatsoever. However, what this means is that it is no longer true to state that the responsibility of our external borders resides solely with the individual Member States. What is true is that that responsibility should as a minimum be shared with the European Union.

Q126 *Lord Young of Norwood Green:* What sort of timescale do you envisage for the development of Frontex in the way you have described?

Mr Deprez: Ten years?

Mr Busuttil: If there is unanimity voting on that one it is going to be a long haul.

Mr Deprez: In Article 14 of the regulation on the European Agency for the Management of Operational Co-operation, there is an article about the "operational co-operation" between Member States and Frontex.

Chairman: I would like to thank our visitors from the European Parliament very much indeed for their contribution. As I said at the beginning, this meeting has been on the record and you will be sent a transcript of our discussion. I really would like to thank you all very much indeed for an extremely helpful meeting and I wish you all the best. We will in due course, not, sadly under my chairmanship, be producing a report and you will, of course, receive copies of it. Thank you very much.

WEDNESDAY 17 OCTOBER 2007

Present	Harrison, L	Marlesford, L
	Henig, B	Teverson, L
	Jopling, L	Tonge, B
	Listowel, E	Wright of Richmond, L (Chairman)

Memorandum by Border and Immigration Agency, Home Office

Whether Frontex staffing and funding are adequate to enable it to carry out its tasks

1. Frontex received a substantial budget increase in 2007 to increase its capacity to deliver. The 2007 work programme was allocated €35.3 million of which €20.7 million is for operations, €9.4 million for staff and €5.2 million for administration. We believe this is sufficient, once the new staffing is in place by the end of the year, for Frontex to carry out its tasks as envisaged by the Frontex Regulation. It now needs the necessary time to embed and train staff, and to focus on improving the quality of operations before further expansion.

Whether the institutional and legal framework ensures adequate accountability of Frontex activities

2. Frontex is accountable for its activities through the Executive Director to the Frontex Management Board, the European Commission and the European Parliament. Articles 3.3 and 20(2)(b) of the Frontex Regulation (2007/2004) set out its evaluation and reporting procedures, which include an Annual Report which is made public.

3. Responsibility for operations, within the framework of the Schengen Borders Code, is first agreed by the Member States involved as part of the operational plan. The host Member State leads on the operation itself. Individual operations make provision for evaluation which is considered within the Agency to inform further action, and the annual report.

4. European and national parliamentary scrutiny take place when legislation is being negotiated and adopted. Both the European and national Parliaments also routinely call Ministers and EU and national officials to give general evidence on EU organisation activities. Our view is that all the above processes, and the review mechanisms built into both Regulations, which the UK has the opportunity to feed into, ensure accountability proportionate to Frontex's current remit.

Comments on the legal framework for border guards' exercise of control and surveillance powers in the course of Frontex operations

5. Member State border guards taking part in Frontex operations until recently acted only as observers. The amendments to the Frontex Regulation by the RABITs Regulation clarify and strengthen the powers of Member State officers participating in Frontex operations (including RABITs), enabling them now to carry out tasks and exercise powers of border control and border surveillance. This includes, for example, examining documents and stamping passports. The legal framework for the border guards to apply is the Schengen Borders Code as this is the law which governs the crossing of the border where the guards are operating.

6. In respect of UK participation, the legal position is more complex. Subject to the forthcoming decision of the ECJ on the issue, neither the Frontex Regulation nor the RABITs regulation apply to, or bind, the UK. However, under Article 20(5) of the Frontex Regulation, the UK may take part in joint operations or pilot projects with the agreement of Frontex. Where UK immigration officers do so, they will be "guest officers" under the new Article 1(9) of the Frontex Regulation (as amended by the RABITs regulation). Were we to choose to do so, UK immigration officers could be able to exercise executive powers as part of the law of the host Member State (through the directly applicable Regulation). However, as UK immigration officers are appointed under the Immigration Act 1971, and their powers and duties derive from statute, it is likely that primary legislation will be needed to enable UK immigration officers to exercise executive powers as a matter of UK domestic law. In the meantime, UK immigration officers will continue to participate in joint operations and pilot projects as observers/advisors.

7. In respect of RABITs, it may be the case that, as a matter of European law, UK immigration officers cannot take part in RABITs under the RABITs and Frontex Regulations as members of teams exercising executive powers because the text of the RABITs Regulation does not contain provision allowing UK participation by agreement. We are exploring with Frontex and its Management Board ways in which the UK could participate in RABITs in an observing/advisory capacity.

Whether and how international obligations with regard to search and rescue at sea affect the Agency

8. Those Member States who take part in operations in the territorial waters of Member States, in international waters or in the territorial waters of third countries, will have to do so in accordance with their obligations under the international law of the sea, including those obligations concerning search and rescue. The UK has not yet participated in such operations. Our position is that responsibility and the legal framework which applies to the particular circumstances of the operation should be determined by the Member States involved as part of the operational plan, taking account (as they must) of international law.

9. We welcome the Commission's recent publication of a working paper calling for clarification of the international law of the sea as it relates to illegal migration. A working group has been established, in which the UK participates, to discuss general guidelines on the application of the law of the sea specifically to Frontex maritime operations. The UK supports the Commission's view that we need clear guidelines for the interception of ships suspected of carrying illegal migrants. The UK is keen to have guidelines that provide greater clarity on obligations regarding the disembarkation of migrants. The next meeting of this working group is on 24 September in Brussels.

Whether it is practical to retain a distinction at operational level between preventing irregular immigration and preventing crime

10. Irregular migration can involve criminal acts by individuals ranging from low level facilitation to organised crime. The exercise of immigration control can have an impact on other crime so close co-operation between the different authorities is needed. There is currently a distinction at operational level. However, wider Government organisation to ensure border security is being reviewed by Sir Gus O'Donnell as announced by the Prime Minister on 25 July.

The number and nature of working agreements Frontex has in place with Member States, third countries, EU agencies and international bodies

11. The Frontex and RABITs Regulations provide the legal framework for co-operation with EU Member States and Framework Partnership Agreements set out administrative detail such as reimbursement procedures. Separate agreements exist for the UK and Ireland. The Management Board authorises all mandates for the Executive Director to negotiate Working Arrangements between Frontex, third countries and other international organisations. These arrangements agree terms for facilitating operational co-operation between Frontex and the country/organisation concerned including capacity building assistance and support for joint operations. Working Arrangements have been agreed with three countries and mandates agreed to negotiate with a further 10. Progress is being made on a Working Arrangement with Europol but close co-operation already exists. Dialogue continues on co-operation with other international organisations and countries. Feedback on the progress or outcome of negotiations is provided at Management Board meetings.

Whether there is sufficient cooperation from Member States in terms of personnel and equipment for joint operations

12. In our view, Frontex does not generally face difficulties in obtaining personnel and equipment for joint operations. It has built up a significant Central Register Technical Equipment (CRATE) that Member States have made available for operations (in accordance with Article 7 of the Frontex Regulation). This includes helicopters, aircraft and ships. Member States have signed MoUs to provide the equipment that they have pledged and this should assist Frontex with better operational planning.

How Frontex pools information from Member States to carry out risk analysis

13. Currently Frontex collects information by sending out questionnaires to central points of contact in each Member State. This data is collated and informs both tailored risk assessments on particular issues throughout the year and the annual risk assessment, in addition to drawing on other existing data sources, for example CIREFI reports. The compiled reports are discussed at quarterly Frontex Risk Analysis Network (FRAN) meetings and issued for onward distribution within relevant Member State departments. Frontex continues to examine whether it should use Iconet, a web-based database, as its primary tool for receiving information from Member States.

The extent of Frontex involvement in surveillance operations

14. Frontex is involved in surveillance operations at both sea and land borders. Surveillance at sea is carried out by ships and aircraft as part of joint maritime operational plans and through the pilot European Patrols Network (EPN), which co-ordinates and harmonises existing southern Member State patrolling and surveillance activity. Subject to review, the EPN is due to become permanent in 2009. On land, surveillance is a component of existing Member State practice so is built into individual Frontex operational plans.

How Frontex joint operations are planned and mounted

15. Frontex publish a work plan at the beginning of each year which sets out in very broad terms the number of the different types of operation (sea, air, maritime) they plan to mount in the course of the year. Frontex provides an outline of each operation to Member States and calls for expressions of interest. Interested parties are invited to a planning meeting at which further details of the operations are discussed and agreed. The operational plan is then issued to participants and Frontex appoints a co-ordinator. The host Member State retains the lead for the operation. Participants travel to the location of the operation on the agreed date and the operation begins and runs according to the operational plan.

How Frontex joint operations are monitored and the outcomes evaluated

16. All Frontex operations are organised by a project manager who is responsible for all aspects of the operation, including finance. Project managers hold evaluation meetings after every operation for participants to provide feedback prior to the completion of the final report, produced for all operations. This is only circulated to the Member States that have participated.

Whether there is, or should be, any involvement of, or assistance from, the military in Frontex operations

17. On the whole, Frontex operations are not focussed on military activities. Although we do not object to EU Member States assisting Frontex with military assets where this is part of their normal procedures (which some do), we believe that the first port of call for such operations should be civilian agencies or commercial options which are likely to be more readily available and cheaper. Where Frontex calls for the use of specific UK military assistance we will treat each request on a case-by-case basis.

The disadvantages, if any, to the UK in not participating in Frontex

18. We are leaders in strengthening border control in Europe by creating a new offshore line of defence, by checking individuals as far from the UK as possible and through each stage of their journey, using new technology particularly biometrics and new approaches to managing risk and intelligence. While we have sought to parallel and co-operate with Schengen in so far as possible, as an island, we have seen the maintenance of checks at points of entry as the best means of securing our border.

19. Nevertheless, an effectively managed and secure EU border is in the interest of all Member States, including the UK, not just in terms of combating illegal migration, and cross-border crime but also as part of the EU-wide counter-terrorism effort. The UK values the role played by the agency in providing a co-ordinating link between the various border and immigration agencies to contribute to this goal.

20. Although we are excluded from full participation, we believe we can and do make a valuable contribution by exchanging experience, knowledge, best practice and technology, and are keen to continue working closely with our partners to ensure more structured and effective management of the EU external borders. Were the UK not able to participate in Frontex, we would lose a significant opportunity to demonstrate a tangible UK commitment to supporting EU efforts to strengthen external frontier security and respond to illegal migration.

21. In addition, we know that irregular migrants often travel through other European states on their way to the UK so non-participation would reduce our opportunities to share and develop intelligence, identify needs, plan disruption and assist in building capacity both in Member States at the external EU borders and in the third countries from which migrants embark.

22. We also recognise that Member States are responsible for the operational control of their own borders and want Frontex to develop as an adjunct to Member State border control activity. If we did not participate, the UK position on its development and our desire as a matter of principle to have access to Schengen building measures for migration purposes may not be given appropriate weight.

How the Advocate-General's Opinion in the case challenging its exclusion from Frontex affects its current position

23. The Advocate-General's Opinion is that the UK cannot participate in the Frontex Regulation in the sense that the Regulation applies to and binds the UK. If the ECJ also reaches this conclusion, then the position of the UK in relation to Frontex will be as at present, that is: the Frontex Regulation does not bind nor apply to the UK, but the UK may take part in operations on a case-by-case basis, with the agreement of the Frontex Management Board under Article 20(5) of the Frontex operation.

How the Agency's role should develop in the future

24. Frontex has met its objectives in a number of ways. It has demonstrated an ability to coordinate the efforts of the Member States in operations at the external Schengen borders. Those operations have demonstrated that they are not capable, by themselves, of preventing irregular migration, but a drop in illegal migration across the Mediterranean this summer suggests Frontex activities are having some effect on stemming the flow. Malta experienced a 20% fall in seaborne migration by 13 July this year compared to the same period of 2006 (967 to 769). 12,419 migrants have landed on Italy between January to August 2007, compared to 14,511 in 2006. Illegal immigrants arriving at Spain in boats have decreased 55% to 6,306 in the first six months of 2007 compared with the same period last year.

25. Frontex also performs a useful role in raising the level of expertise in European border management and promoting a consistent application of the Schengen Borders Code. Other developments this year include the pooling of technical equipment, operational co-ordination with third countries and the introduction of Rapid Border Intervention Teams to further strengthen its work.

26. We are particularly keen that Frontex makes progress with operational co-ordination with third countries from which illegal migrants originate and transit. This is in line with the EU's Global Approach to Migration. Third countries of origin and transit may themselves lack the expertise, legislation or capacity for national border management. We see an increasing role for Frontex in providing scoping studies for improvement to border crossing points and port security, as well as the provision of advice and assistance to allow these countries to manage their own migration flows or to mount effective search and rescue operations.

27. The European Parliament considers that Frontex should take responsibility for maritime search and rescue (SAR) missions in the Mediterranean. Frontex's aim is to improve the integrated management of the external borders of the EU, with the co-operation of third countries. It has no specific search and rescue remit. It is inevitable that a maritime operation to control the external borders has a SAR dimension, hence our keenness for clear guidelines on these in the context of international obligations. We consider, however, that the strengthening of external border security should remain the priority for Frontex, and Member States retain responsibility for search and rescue. The European Patrols Network will continue this effort but securing engagement from third countries in maritime operations is imperative, both for increasing effectiveness of the operations and in humanitarian terms by reducing the number of migrants attempting hazardous crossings from Africa to the EU.

28. Frontex has also come under pressure to expand its remit in joint EU returns. While Frontex clearly has an important role to play, its resources should be targeted where they can add real value ie assisting those Member States with less experience. Joint charter flights should remain a Member State responsibility and the lead Member State should continue to be responsible for its own joint operations. Were Frontex to adopt a role whereby they were to ensure details of spare capacity on any Member State flight to a specific destination gets well advertised, this could work well.

29. We want to see Frontex develop in a sustainable manner. The agency is still relatively young and we are concerned about overstretch. It is already under pressure to deliver in areas that might be considered to be beyond its original remit. The UK believes there is a continuing need to refine the Agency's approach both to planning, based on the effect the operation is expected to achieve, and to evaluation of operations to further increase effectiveness. Following recent staffing and budget increases, it needs time to embed and train staff,

and focus on improving the quality of operations before further expansion of its role. We look forward to contributing to the Commission Frontex review in early 2008. This will be a chance to take stock of Frontex's achievements and development needs.

Development of training/skills for border guards

30. The Frontex Training Unit runs specific training courses and seminars and cascades common training tools to Member States via training co-ordination points. This includes Common Core Curriculum training on key facts and procedures in each Member State and includes a specialist training topic each year, this year document forgery detection. Mid-level officer training on leadership, management styles and operational activities, including application of the Schengen Borders Code, has also recently been set up. In addition, each country offers training in their particular specialisms to other Member States. The UK makes a significant contribution to production and delivery of Frontex training, offering expertise in document forgery detection and use of detection technology and has sent one delegate to attend the September mid-level officer course.

2012 Olympics Co-operation

31. We are committed to making sure that Olympic security planning is robust. We recognise that the 2012 Cultural Olympiad and the Games will attract a large number of visitors from overseas and that some individuals may seek to use the 2012 Cultural Olympiad and the Games as an opportunity to enter the territory of the EU Member States for purposes which may pose a security, criminal or immigration threat.

32. Whilst we want to welcome visitors, it will be necessary for us to undertake comprehensive and rigorous immigration and security checks on all those working, participating or watching the Games, to prevent anyone planning to exploit or disrupt the London Games from doing so.

33. We intend to discuss with Frontex the potential for a joint operation of the type mounted for both the last Winter Olympics in Italy and World Cup 2006 in Germany. These operations were mounted at major continental European hub airports in the Schengen area. The provision of information from the UK to the control authorities in the participating states on the issue of visas and the accreditation of members of the Olympic family and the deployment of UK officials to the hub airports would be likely to form a central part of such an operation.

UK CONTRIBUTION TO FRONTEX

1. The UK's contribution to Frontex is subject to a complex legal framework arising from our exclusion from the Frontex Regulation. Regulation 2007/2004 of 26 October 2004 (the Frontex Regulation) does not apply to, nor bind, the United Kingdom (Paragraph 25 of the preamble to the Regulation). This is subject to the forthcoming decision of the European Court of Justice on this issue. However, the UK is able to participate in joint operations and pilot projects on a case-by-case basis with the agreement of the Frontex Management Board (Article 20(5) of the Frontex Regulation). Under Article 12 of the Frontex Regulation, the Agency shall facilitate the operational cooperation of the Member States with the UK in matters covered by its activities and to the extent required for the fulfilment of its tasks under Article 2(1).

2. We have demonstrated our commitment to Frontex by negotiating the amendment to the Frontex Regulation and through an annual financial contribution to Frontex which, with the agreement of the management board, enables us to participate in joint operations and wider Frontex activities on a case-by-case basis wherever we see benefit to the UK and the EU. The UK's contribution to the Agency can be broken down into three categories: finance, staffing and equipment.

Finance

3. In 2006 the UK contributed €226,300.00. In 2007, the UK increased its contribution to €570,300 in line with Frontex's increased budget, based on intention to participate in: up to 17 joint operations, pilot projects, at least one return operation, training activities and at least five research and development studies. We receive up to 80% reimbursement for joint operation travel and subsistence costs and up to 100% reimbursement for other Frontex activities.

Staffing

4. In staffing terms, the UK contributes in three ways, through attendance at the Management Board, seconding staff to the Agency HQ and participating in joint operations and Frontex activities in an observing/advisory capacity.

5. In line with Article 23 (4) of the Frontex Regulation the UK is invited to attend meetings of the Management Board and does so on all occasions, as well as actively contributing to discussions. Tom Dowdall, Border Control Director of European Operations, is the official UK delegate and John Fothergill is his alternate.

6. The UK has seconded two staff to the Agency's headquarters in Warsaw; one Airport Operations Officer who plans and co-ordinates joint airport operations; the other having initially been seconded as Head of the Risk Analysis Unit is now a special adviser to the Executive Director of Frontex with particular responsibility for third country relations. We are considering increasing the number of UK secondees to the Agency, subject to suitable posts and qualified UK candidates being available.

7. In 2006 the UK participated in seven joint operations at the EU external borders. So far in 2007 we have participated in 11 joint operations with plans for at least a further two (see Annex A). This includes support for tackling illegal seaborne migration from Senegal and Mauritania and enhancing border checks and surveillance on the land and sea borders of the Mediterranean. We have contributed experts who advise on debriefing and maritime intelligence techniques and experience and new detection technology experts who can advise on the use of equipment and techniques for searching vehicles and freight. The UK will continue to support projects that are intelligence-led, cost effective and aim to strengthen vulnerable points on the EU external border.

8. We have participated in several training, research and pilot project activities. February 2007 saw UK participation in a project focusing on detecting minors being trafficked by air. Training experts have contributed to developing both the Common Core Curriculum for EU border guards and common standards on forgery detection and use of detection technology, in addition to delivering courses. The UK is participating in a research and development project on developing new technologies to enhance border security and controls.

Equipment

9. The UK has provided the loan of Border and Immigration Agency equipment, including New Detection Technology, to the agency's Central Register of Available Technical Equipment (CRATE/"toolbox"), to assist with border checks in joint operations. So far we have loaned six CO_2 probes and three Heartbeat units in response to two joint operations. All are still on loan except for two CO_2 probes which have proved unsuitable for the type of freight being examined during one operation.

14 September 2007

Annex A

FRONTEX OPERATIONS 2006

Torino (3–26 February 2006)
Counter illegal migration via the Winter Olympics in Turin.
UK hosted Italian Border guard at Heathrow. Staff completed daily returns forms.

Medsea and Bortec Support Groups (March–November 2006)
Determine whether a network of national contact points could enhance control and surveillance of EU Southern and Maritime borders.
UK sent maritime security experts to provide guidance at the meetings.

Fifa 06 (9 June–9 July 2006)
Counter illegal migration via the World Cup (held in Germany).
UK took part in information gathering and exchange.

Poseidon I (25 June–5 July 2006)
Focus on irregular migration towards Greek ports of Patras and Igoumenitsa.
The UK provided debriefing and maritime intelligence experts.

Gate of Africa (17 July 2006–3 September 2006)
To enhance the detection of false and falsified documents used to enter EU via Spain.

UK provided two intelligence and immigration experts.

Hera I (19 July 2006–30 October 2006)
Identify nationalities of migrants and the routes taken to travel to Canary Islands.
UK provided two document experts.

Support to Malta (September 2006)
To provide support to Malta to counter influxes of irregular migrants.
UK provided senior officer to assist the Maltese.

Amazon I (1–22 November 2006)
Focus on document abuse by South/Central American Nationals arriving in eight European airports.
UK provided an intelligence officer to the Frontex co-ordination centre in Warsaw.

FRONTEX OPERATIONS 2007

Agelaus (February 2007)
Raise awareness of minors illegally entering EU MS. Aim to establish intelligence sharing between member states and, where appropriate, third countries.
Three UK airports participated; LGW, LHR, MAN.

Amazon II (19 February 2007–9 March 2007)
Target the abuse of documents relevant to entrance into EU MS by South/Central American Nationals.
UK provided coordinator to work alongside officers from Germany and Spain.

Hydra (11 April 2007–11 May 2007)
Tackle illegal Chinese migration arriving at EU external borders by air.
The UK filled in the daily incidents sheets, and deployed three border guards to Vienna, Prague and Bucharest.

Gordius (16 April 2007–29 April 2007)
Analysis of routes and false documents that are used to enter the EU via the external border countries of Eastern Europe.
The UK provided two experts and technical equipment.

Poseidon 2007 Stage II (26 June 2007–15 July 2007)
Provide support for local authorities in the Aegean Sea and land borders between Greece, Albania, Bulgaria and Turkey.
The UK provided seven experts and technical equipment.

Herakles I (8 August–17 August 2007)
Focus on illegal migration over EU external land border between Hungary and Serbia.
The UK provided two experts to work simultaneously for seven days.

Five further operations are ongoing involving UK detection technology experts and equipment and debriefing experts.

Examination of Witnesses

Witnesses: MR TOM DODD, Director, Border and Visa Policy, and MR TOM DOWDALL, Director of EU Operations, Home Office, examined.

Q128 Chairman: Good morning, everybody, and a particular welcome to the two Toms sitting at the table. Thank you very much for coming. As you know, this is a witness session on the record. It is being recorded and you will be sent a transcript in due course to check. This is part of this Committee's inquiry into Frontex. I am very grateful to you for coming and also for the extremely helpful written evidence which the Home Office sent us, for which, no doubt, at least one of you must be responsible. Before we start, could I warn you the acoustics in this room are almost as bad as my hearing, so could I please ask everybody to speak up. I wonder whether we could start. Mr Dowdall, I think you are the UK delegate to the Frontex Management Board, am I right?

Mr Dowdall: Yes, I am indeed.

Q129 Chairman: With that in mind, and there will be later questions related to that, could I ask you both— and, please, come in as you wish, either of you—to give this Committee a brief overview of the current system of border controls in the UK, focusing in particular on the roles of the different agencies and co-operation between them.
Mr Dowdall: Thank you very much, my Lord Chairman. Just as a brief introduction from me, my name is Tom Dowdall, Director within the Border Control Directorate of the Border and Immigration Agency. I have specific responsibilities for the border control operations that take place at the frontier

between the UK, France and Belgium, which we know internally as "juxtaposed controls", and that is the border control operation which takes place at Calais, Dunkirk, the Eurotunnel and also the Eurostar services between Paris, Brussels, Lille and the UK.

Q130 Chairman: Do your responsibilities go back to the days of Sangatte?
Mr Dowdall: No, they do not in terms of that area. I have been a senior manager within border control for five years. During the difficulties that we had at the time of Sangatte, which was at a peak in 2002, my responsibility was for the airport side in effect, thank goodness.
Mr Dodd: If I could just come in there, my Lord Chairman.

Q131 Chairman: I should have welcomed you back.
Mr Dodd: Yes, thank you. It is a great pleasure to be here again. I am Tom Dodd, Head of Border and Visa Policy, and I am responsible for the policy relationship with Frontex. Could I also say we very much welcome this inquiry into Frontex, particularly in advance of the Commission review of Frontex next year. We are here to try and assist the Committee in any way that we can this morning.
Mr Dowdall: My Lord Chairman, to answer your specific question about the UK borders, the UK borders currently are managed principally by three agencies, the Border and Immigration Agency, HM Revenue & Customs and the police in the form of Special Branch. The responsibilities of border control extend to the admissibility of people into the UK. For those who are non-EU passengers, it is working, indeed, with our UKvisas colleagues in granting of leave to enter and determining the admissibility of passengers to the UK. For EU and UK passengers, it is ensuring that those passengers who cross our frontiers have a right to do so and are the rightful holder of the documents they provide in order to cross the border.

Q132 Chairman: Have the new arrangements, which I think most of us have now witnessed at the airports, changed the tripartite relationship that you referred to?
Mr Dowdall: The new relationships—Sorry, in terms of what?

Q133 Chairman: I mean the new arrangements for arriving at Heathrow, which most of us have witnessed over the last month or two, have they changed this relationship that you referred to between the three organisations?
Mr Dowdall: No, it has not. Obviously there is the work going on that has been commissioned by the Prime Minister and is being carried forward by Sir Gus O'Donnell in looking at the relationship between the three agencies through the Unified Border Force. The specific relations in terms of the checks and controls that we have in place at our airports and seaports, I guess it is certainly to deal with both the immigration threat but also our concerns about the terrorism threat to the UK.

Q134 Chairman: Your reference to Sir Gus O'Donnell really takes me on to the next question. Is there something either of you or both of you can tell us about the O'Donnell Review and quite how it fits in with the UK attitude generally to Frontex and immigration?
Mr Dodd: Yes. As you know, the Prime Minister announced in July the decision to integrate the work of BIA, Customs and UKvisas and to establish a Unified Border Force. He asked Sir Gus O'Donnell to look at this and he is doing so at the moment and he is due to report at the end of October. Obviously I cannot prejudge what he is going to say and what ministers decide to say on the basis of his report. I do know that report is considering our wider border relations, so it is not just looking at the UK frontier but also beyond the frontier and things like Frontex, our relationship with key EU partners and so on. Separate from that, we are doing some pilot work, particularly with Customs, in six key ports around the UK to see how we can bring together a single check for both customs and immigration purposes and that work we are going to pursue, in a sense, in parallel to the review as part of our step to improve integration with the other border agencies.

Q135 Chairman: I realise you cannot pre-empt the outcome of it, but is Sir Gus O'Donnell's review taking Frontex as part of its agenda?
Mr Dodd: I think it will include references to Frontex, yes. It is clearly looking at the UK border and one of the guiding lights of our philosophy of border control generally is to export the border as far away from the UK as possible and hence Frontex is part of that process, so it will include references to Frontex.

Q136 Lord Marlesford: Could I ask a supplementary on that, Lord Chairman. This review, what is the genesis of it? Was it a suggestion from the Home Office? It was announced by the Prime Minister, I know. Was it the Home Office that wanted it or the former Home Secretary who wanted it? How did it come about that we are suddenly having it?
Mr Dodd: I think I said the Government wanted the review rather than any particular minister. Possibly, it came in in a particular context of the terrorist incidents over the summer and those, I think, inspired a fresh look at our border arrangements. It was generated by Government as a whole rather than by any specific individual.

17 October 2007   Mr Tom Dodd and Mr Tom Dowdall

Q137 Lord Marlesford: Not by the Home Office?
Mr Dodd: Clearly the Home Office was party to that decision, but Number 10—

Q138 Lord Marlesford: It was not your idea?
Mr Dodd: We have been working on ways to improve the integrity of border co-operation with other border agencies over a number of years, so I would see this as very much consistent with that approach of integrating agencies.

Q139 Baroness Tonge: Could I just ask, of the three branches of our current system of border controls, who carries arms and what sort of arms do they carry? Do any of them carry arms, the Special Branch of the police, you said, Customs and the immigration service?
Mr Dowdall: Neither the Border and Immigration Agency nor HM Revenue & Customs are armed officers. As I understand, it is not usual for Special Branch officers to be armed. However, the other elements of policing in airports in terms of dealing with both criminal threats and the wider physical security, including counter-terrorism, means that those officers are armed and visibly so.

Q140 Lord Jopling: We understand from your Department's border strategy that you tell us the UK Government is an enthusiastic supporter of Frontex, but evidence we have had from the National Co-ordinator Ports Policing tells us that your view is: "The UK is not getting enough out of Frontex". Is that a true reflection of the Department's attitude and, whether it is or not, what changes would you like to see in Frontex so that it was more useful to the European Union as a whole, but the UK in particular, so that we all get maximum benefit from it?
Mr Dodd: If I may answer that. Obviously I think it is worth re-stating our legal connection with Frontex. We are formally excluded from Frontex and we participate on an *ad hoc*, case-by-case basis with the agreement of the Frontex Management Board so, in a sense, we already start off two steps back in our relationship with Frontex. In terms of what we get out of Frontex, I think we do get a great deal out of Frontex in terms of the opportunity to exchange experience and intelligence and to develop new technologies. We think that Frontex has a valuable role in co-ordinating and strengthening activity at the EU external border and also has done valuable work in improving the capacity of European border guards. Frontex has only been going for about two years or so, it is quite a small and very young organisation. We think it could do more to improve its performance. In areas, for example, like improving the planning of operations, which would be valuable, in terms of more work it could do with

third countries beyond the EU external border and more work it might do to co-ordinate returns of flights, this sort of thing. We had some of these ideas which we will be feeding into the Commission review that is taking place next year.

Q141 Lord Jopling: I wonder if you could enlarge on what you said, and I wrote it down, that there was a role in the exchange of intelligence. I ask this question because when we were in Brussels yesterday talking to the Director General of the Commission I particularly asked him what the role of Frontex was in terms of gathering intelligence. I was more or less told there was not one, so what did you mean?
Mr Dowdall: Effectively Frontex has to collect intelligence in order to be able to inform the operations that it commits to and it commits the Members States to, so it does gather information and intelligence into its Risk Analysis Unit. It does that in a number of ways from the Member States in terms of questionnaires and information that are provided by the Member States. It is fair to say that relationship, and certainly what we have seen, between the intelligence we gather and provide to Frontex and then what is done next is a process which is evolving and needs to improve. When Frontex gather that information, they then conduct some analysis of that, which they will discuss at various levels. They have a Risk Analysis Network meeting which brings together representatives of the Member States on a quarterly basis and that information is then disseminated back to the Member States also. Within my own operations and border control we will also consider that information to determine our own priorities and how we understand the risks facing the UK. What I would say, my Lord, is that, whilst that process I have outlined is what we have in principle, we have certainly seen over the course of the lifetime of Frontex so far that has improved but needs to continue improving and there is a number of areas that we can see that needs to happen in.

Q142 Chairman: Could I ask you to put that into the context of planning operations? I am grateful for the quite detailed description of which operations we have been involved in. Does Country A say to Frontex, "Look, we happen to know that there are boats coming towards us with a lot of illegal immigrants, would you please plan an operation to try to deter them?" Does it work like that?
Mr Dowdall: It can happen in a number of ways and that is certainly one of the ways that it can happen. Certainly I think there is evidence, particularly in the Mediterranean, of those countries identifying the particular pressures that they have experienced because of illegal migration across the Mediterranean. Of course, you then have to enhance what could simply be a request for help into

something more tangible that we can very effectively say, "This is the problem and this is how we would need to counter that particular problem". It is partly countries identifying a problem and it needs to be more sophisticated than that, certainly in the longer term, whereby we can understand what the risks overall are to the external border and that we can quantify those risks. Of course, just simply saying, "We have got a problem", may well be a problem for a Member State, but we have to understand and weight that across the risk to the whole of the EU. That is the purpose of the Risk Analysis Unit, that it needs to make some sense of that information, to analyse it, to weight it and consequently then to identify a course of action which should be the kind of operations that we have provided you with, so those operations should be very much geared towards countering those very specific risks.

Q143 *Chairman:* That analysis takes place in Warsaw, does it?
Mr Dowdall: Indeed, yes.
Chairman: Where incidentally we are visiting next week.

Q144 *Lord Jopling:* Because we are not members of Frontex, would you like to talk to us about what influence we have over executive decisions and operational matters because we are a rather semi-detached member of the whole outfit?
Mr Dowdall: We have associate membership of Frontex and I sit on the board. Whilst we do not have a vote on the board, what I can do is to provide input into the discussion and debate that takes place at the Management Board. In reality, although decisions are subject to a vote so far, the only decisions that have been subject to a vote were the appointment of the executive director and the chair. Therefore, we do have an ability to influence the decisions that are taken by the board. The UK operations are well respected and, therefore, our view is sought and we are listened to. Some decisions are taken by written procedure and we are informed of that, but we do not have a say in that particular procedure.

Q145 *Lord Jopling:* You mentioned the executive director and the chairman, would you have voted in favour of those two individuals if you had had a vote? Secondly, would you speculate as to what is coming up over the next year or so which could either come to a vote or find the UK in conflict with potential decisions which might be proposed to Frontex for agreement?
Mr Dowdall: In terms of the appointment of the two people currently, I cannot say what the view of the UK was at that time because I was not involved there. What I can say is that they have both been, and are, very effective in their roles and are people who,

certainly, we have a tremendous amount of respect for from the UK. In terms of the look ahead, the areas where there will be a vote will be in the appointment of a new chair, because a new chair will be appointed next spring, and the vote for that will be at the next Management Board that takes place in Lisbon in November. There is also some selection of people to be involved in both the review and audit of accounts and also in terms of the Frontex involvement in the review that the Commission will be embarking on next year, so there will be votes for members of the Board to be involved in those particular groups. The UK will be excluded from those votes. Those are the main areas that I see coming up over the next year.

Q146 *Lord Jopling:* Those only refer to individuals, do they not?
Mr Dowdall: Yes.

Q147 *Lord Jopling:* What I also want to know is with regard to management and policy decisions which must be under discussion now, over which, as a member of the board, you have been expressing, perhaps, a minority view or a sole view. Could you just help us with what is in the offing which you have been expressing a view about that could find us either in the minority of one or a perfectly normal minority?
Mr Dowdall: The key issues for next year will be the plan to increase the funding to Frontex, a significant increase in funding, and the decisions then on how that funding will be best spent. The UK view is that it should not fund simply a major increase in operations but should be focused on increasing the quality of the operations that are undertaken, also the quality of the intelligence-gathering machinery and the intelligence itself that is produced and shared with Member States. Those are key areas next year in relation to how that money is spent.
Chairman: Lord Listowel has a supplementary question on this.

Q148 *Earl of Listowel:* I think that Lord Jopling, if I may say so, has helpfully teased out the difficulties that are presented by the semi-detached status of the UK. Looking at it from a pragmatic point of view, would membership of Schengen enable the UK to make a very significantly greater contribution to the success of Frontex; if you can speak about that?
Mr Dodd: I think it is probably for me to answer. As you know we have actually challenged our exclusion from Frontex before the ECJ—there is a case at the moment, which is current, and clearly we feel that we should have the right to be full members of Frontex. Whether membership of Schengen would improve our position or not—and that is the moot point really—clearly we have good operational relationships with European Member States, we have

a world influencing development of European border management policy, and it comes back to the bigger question about Schengen, whether the disadvantages of being members of the Schengen border zone outweigh the advantages, and I think from our view governments have been pretty consistent that Schengen border zone membership would actually reduce our border security. We have the fortune, or misfortune, to be an island and that generates very strong advantages from the border control perspective which would be lost were we to be a party of the Schengen border zones. I think that would remain the case.

Q149 *Lord Jopling:* We were told yesterday by the European Parliament that they are proposing an increase in the budget, I think from 21 or 22 million euros from memory. Do you welcome that and do you think it could be usefully embraced in improving the work of Frontex?

Mr Dowdall: We welcome the increase. As I indicated earlier, we would certainly welcome the increase as long as that money is wisely spent, obviously. We understand that some of that increase is dependent upon various measures being taken to improve issues of accountability within Frontex and therefore there will be reports that have to be presented by the Executive Director to the Commission, and we clearly welcome anything that brings with it additional accountability. The important thing is how that money is spent and that it is spent on improving the quality rather than the quantity within what takes place within Frontex. The work has evolved effectively since 2005. We have engaged this year in a number of operations and it is important now that we properly analyse the benefits of those operations. Not only analyse the immediate benefits of the operations but understand whether or not those operations have had some form of displacement effect, for example to other parts of Europe. Therefore, we would support anything that would focus attention on improving that analytical capability and also focus attention on developing the right relations between Frontex and other institutions both within Europe but also with third countries and neighbouring countries of Europe as well. The answer is not simply having operation after operation which certainly has an immediate impact, but the most effective operations that we have had in place have involved some very good cooperation with third countries.

Chairman: I think that in effect really answers question five, does it not?

Lord Jopling: Yes, I think it probably does; I do not think we need bother with that.

Chairman: Lord Marlesford.

Q150 *Lord Marlesford:* I would like, if I may, to go on to discuss with you the linkage between e-borders and Frontex, but first of all perhaps I could get from you some understanding of how far you have got with e-borders?

Mr Dodd: How far have we got with e-borders? We have an e-borders programme; we have in place a pilot, which is called Operation Semaphore, which from memory is covering about 10% of the routes to and from the UK in terms of taking passenger information on those routes, analysing and assessing it and then authorising or commissioning actions from the border agency against passengers who are suspect or are otherwise of concern. We aim to cover 65% of movements by 2009 and 90% of movements by 2011. At the moment we are in the final stages of negotiating a contract with a supplier to transform Semaphore into a properly functioning programme. So I think that is where we are with e-borders at the moment.

Q151 *Lord Marlesford:* At the present time you do have electronic scanning and reading of passports already operational—

Mr Dodd: At the borders.

Q152 *Lord Marlesford:* At the borders. And these are used fairly universally on entry?

Mr Dodd: Every control now has a scanner.

Q153 *Lord Marlesford:* What about on exit from the UK?

Mr Dodd: We have not had for some time full embarkation controls from the UK. We can introduce embarkation controls in an emergency and we do so on an intelligence-led basis; so where we suspect that there is illegal activity taking place then we will put in place embarkation controls.

Q154 *Lord Marlesford:* But you do not plan, even now, to introduce embarkation controls on the basis of swiping passports electronically? You do not even plan it at the moment?

Mr Dowdall: The intention under e-borders is that that is a key component whereby we will have that audit trail of electronically being able to count all of those entering the UK and all of those leaving the UK and being able to reconcile that. So that will be done electronically. The physical kind of control that we have had traditionally in terms of embarkation control will be a supplementary control and will be something that is targeted as opposed to universally in place. So passengers leaving the UK would not ordinarily expect to have their passports to be subject to a physical control by an immigration officer when leaving the country, unless it was targeted, and it would be done in a different electronic way through the e-borders work.

Q155 *Chairman:* Can I break in on this and remind you that the Prime Minister's statement on 25 July appeared to be significantly moving forward the e-borders programme; is that right? Has the programme been accelerated as a result?

Mr Dodd: The programme is being progressed as quickly as it can be. I am afraid I do not have the Prime Minister's statement in front of me so it is difficult for me to comment on what was said at the time. We are looking to take forward the e-borders programme as quickly we can and as part of the work on the unified border force to make it as relevant to the needs of all the border agencies as possible.

Q156 *Lord Marlesford:* Can I take it a little further? In the 12 months to April 2007 you cancelled 288,000 UK passports which had been reported lost or stolen. When you cancel a passport it presumably means the passport can no longer be used?

Mr Dowdall: That is correct.

Q157 *Lord Marlesford:* So somebody attempting to enter the country with one of those passports and the passport being swiped it would reveal the fact that it had been cancelled; would it or would it not?

Mr Dowdall: It would reveal a concern to the immigration officer—

Q158 *Lord Marlesford:* Immediately?

Mr Dowdall: Yes, who would conduct a further inquiry, and would make inquiries with the passport service.

Q159 *Lord Marlesford:* So in other words, somebody coming into the country at the present time and their passport being swiped, had that passport been stolen and reported as stolen and cancelled by you that would instantly be revealed on the screen?

Mr Dowdall: It would not be instantly revealed on the screen, it would register as a concern to the immigration officer and then to get the detail behind that he or she would then conduct a further check. But that is what officers must routinely do at any time that they would get any kind of concern registered on our watch list.

Chairman: I am sorry to interrupt you, but can we bring this back to Frontex?

Lord Marlesford: Can I just follow this up?

Chairman: Quickly, please.

Q160 *Lord Marlesford:* What I do not understand is if these passports have been cancelled there is no way at the present and apparently no plan to know if they have been used to get out of the country because they are not been swiped and will not be swiped; is that correct?

Mr Dowdall: The controls on leaving the country at the moment for embarkation are targeted controls, so they are not universal in the same way as those arriving in the UK; that is correct.

Q161 *Lord Marlesford:* So they would not be picked up if they were being used to leave the country?

Mr Dowdall: Not by an immigration officer unless they came to a targeted immigration control.

Q162 *Lord Marlesford:* Do you see that as a serious gap in your frontier control?

Mr Dowdall: The question really is in terms of determining where we have to put our effort into dealing with the greatest risks and the greatest risks that we have determined are for those arriving into the UK.

Q163 *Lord Marlesford:* On what basis?

Mr Dowdall: On the basis of having to manage an effective immigration control for those arriving into the UK.

Mr Dodd: I think it is worth saying that if there was somebody of particular concern to UK authorities in respect of leaving the country then we would put in place measures to try and detect that person with the other border agencies. So if somebody was trying to use a forged passport to do so we would could look into that.

Q164 *Lord Marlesford:* I am not talking about a forged passport but a passport that has been cancelled by you but is somewhere around.

Mr Dodd: We would be looking for that individual along with our other sister border agencies if that person were of concern to the UK.

Chairman: Back to Frontex, please.

Q165 *Lord Marlesford:* How does this fit in with Frontex? Frontex is meant to be some method of dealing with irregular immigration, so how does your e-borders fit in there?

Mr Dodd: I spoke earlier about our philosophy of trying to export the border as much as possible. E-borders is a key component of that; our work with Frontex is also a component of that. In terms of information that intelligence discloses, the exchanges my colleague talked about, those will be fed into e-borders. At the heart of e-borders is, in a sense, an intelligence, information and fusion cell where we are bringing information together to assess and analyse passenger movements. So information from Frontex about passengers, about illegal migration will be fed into that process to improve our picture of immigration and passenger flows to and from the UK.

Q166 Lord Marlesford: Did I hear you use the phrase "export the border"?
Mr Dodd: Yes.

Q167 Lord Marlesford: Could you explain that because I did not understand it?
Mr Dodd: If somebody who risks harm to the UK actually enters the UK then that is something which we try and prevent; we are trying to stop people who would cause harm or could risk causing harm as far as possible, away from our shores, from coming here.

Q168 Lord Marlesford: The principle that you earlier enunciated is that the advantage of having our own border control is one of the reasons, or perhaps the main reason why we are not part of Schengen.
Mr Dodd: Yes.

Q169 Lord Marlesford: And that there are problems, as we have discussed, in being part of Frontex because they are not part of Schengen. If your borders are not properly controlled, as you have made clear they are not—
Mr Dodd: No, I did not say that. I did not say our borders are not properly controlled.

Q170 Lord Marlesford: I interpreted you as having done that, but that of course is my opinion. What, then, is the advantage of not being in Schengen if you are not introducing or even planning to introduce full electronic border controls for people leaving and entering the UK?
Mr Dodd: If I may say, that is precisely what we are doing; we are planning to introduce a system which will count individuals in and out of the country.

Q171 Lord Marlesford: I am not talking about counting.
Mr Dodd: It will enumerate the name of the individual, and the information on the travel document and other information will be assessed and counted in and out of the country. So by 2014 we aim to have a full picture of all passenger movements in and out of the UK.
Chairman: We must move on. Baroness Henig.

Q172 Baroness Henig: We have heard that we operate on a case-by-case basis in participation with Frontex, and you told us that there have been a number of Frontex operations, including Operation Torino and Operation Agelaus at UK airports, in which you have participated. I wondered whether these had been devised and requested by the United Kingdom and really how such requests operate within the terms of the arrangements for the UK's participation in Frontex operations? So some idea of how that has worked in the past and whether we plan to host other operations in the future?

Mr Dowdall: I can answer that one. On the specific operations that you have raised, Operation Torino was a Frontex operation directly in response to the Winter Olympics in Torino, in Italy in 2006. That related to conducting document checks and also ensuring that we effectively hosted the Olympic family into the Winter Olympics. That took place at a number of hub airports around Europe. We hosted one Italian document adviser who, as in all these operations, did not exercise executive controls but effectively provided us with any useful advice on Italian documents, Italian visas and also the specific visas in relation to the Olympics. Operation Agelaus was actually promoted by one of our officers who is based full-time in Frontex. That involved the collection of information across a number of airports within Europe and dealt with the arrival of unaccompanied children into Europe. We collected intelligence from three UK airports but that did not involve hosting any officers at all, and was indeed the same at other hub airports within Europe. We get involved in a number of operations, as we have said. First of all, we consider requests that will come to the UK, as indeed those requests come to other Member States as well, and we make a determination on whether we should get involved in those operations based on the risks that it is seeking to address, based upon the skills that our own people have and therefore the benefits that we can bring to an operation. But also, because often the requests that come through are not necessarily to deal just with people but also to deal with the provision of the equipment, we will provide some equipment to support those operations. We have certainly identified particular risk areas that we would like Frontex to give consideration to, and that includes operations that are particularly focused upon illegal Chinese migration by air into Europe and there was an operation that took place earlier in 2007 and we continue to make the case for further operations next year also.

Q173 Chairman: Can I just interrupt? You referred to our associate membership of Frontex.
Mr Dowdall: Yes.

Q174 Chairman: Does the fact that we are not full members of Frontex become an issue when we are talking about hosting Frontex operations in this country?
Mr Dowdall: In terms of hosting operations, principally the operations are in relation to the external Schengen border, so it would be unlikely for us to host an operation. Torino was a very specific issue and certainly we would consider any requests on a case-by-case basis to allow officers to operate within the UK. It is unlikely.

Q175 *Baroness Henig:* Presumably now the 2012 Olympics is going to come on to the radar and that is going to be a major operation not just for the UK but presumably for Frontex as well and I wondered what the planning was in connection to that?

Mr Dowdall: I think you will find in most recent history that there have been good levels of cooperation not only for the Winter Olympics but also the World Cup in Germany in 2006 where host countries work together particularly effectively. We want to take that forward and certainly be able to translate them into 2012, so that not only are all the controls that we need to have in place in the UK but also the controls that we will be discussing with Frontex, how we can be supported in dealing with the 2012 Olympics, and that cooperation is not just simply around what happens within Europe but also in terms of our relations outside of Europe and obviously from where athletes, participants and others originate, who will naturally be travelling to the UK.

Q176 *Lord Jopling:* Going into the future to 2012, the Olympics, which concerns me enormously. As an aside I previously said that if this circus has to come here then we should realise that it is a recipe for bombs, bullets, bloodshed, blackmail, boycott and bogus budgets, and bogus budgets is already well proved. What are you doing specifically already to arrange for a Frontex participation in all of this for 2012? At the Athens Olympics NATO were fairly heavily involved with AWACs and various other things, but when I was last at NATO not terribly long ago I was told that no discussions have taken place at all. What discussions have you had with Frontex about this and have you now had discussions with NATO over this and what in fact positively have you been doing to prepare proper security for the 2012 Olympics?

Mr Dodd: Clearly we do intend to discuss with Frontex the assistance that Frontex and through Frontex we are able to gain with border security around the Olympics, and it is our intention to do so. Dare I say it, the Olympics are in 2012 and it is 2007 so, without being complacent, there are a few years to get these operations going. In terms of the Olympics security more generally, there is a considerable effort going into Olympics security planning across government. Within the BIA itself we recently set up an Olympics group headed by a the Senior Regional Director for the southeast, who is going to take forward the work internally to ensure that we are in a position to both facilitate legitimate visitors and athletes and also prevent people who would cause harm from exploiting the Games.

Q177 *Chairman:* Is this a subject for the O'Donnell Review?

Mr Dodd: Olympics security?

Q178 *Chairman:* Yes.

Mr Dodd: I think the O'Donnell Review is not focused on Olympics security; it is focused more on generally enhancing border security, which thereby will improve Olympics security.

Baroness Henig: It is a good job that the budget is increasing because I would have thought that planning for the Olympics is going to be a major operation for the whole network.

Q179 *Lord Jopling:* The answer, as I get from what you have said, that really nothing much, apart from one or two thoughts for the future, has been done so far about the 2012 Olympics.

Mr Dodd: I am sorry; I did not actually say that, if I may say. We are doing some Olympics planning, we have set up a proper coordination group and we are taking steps to get ready for the Olympics; we are taking it seriously. It is five years from now and we feel that by starting now we will be in a position to be prepared for those Games.

Chairman: Baroness Tonge.

Q180 *Baroness Tonge:* Could one of you put in a nutshell what you think Frontex's role should be in controlling borders, and should it, for instance, include things like rescue at sea?

Mr Dodd: The explicit role of Frontex at the moment is to coordinate activity at the external border to improve border management and border security and to work with third countries. It does not have an explicit operational role in terms of actually protecting the border itself. It would be our view the fact that that is correct, it is the duty of individual Member States to protect their own border.

Q181 *Baroness Tonge:* After all that has been said— and you have said a lot already, both of you—you think that it is a useful role, and do you think Britain ought to be part of it?

Mr Dodd: Of Frontex?

Q182 *Baroness Tonge:* Yes.

Mr Dodd: Clearly we are at the moment challenging our exclusion from Frontex before the European Court of Justice and so we feel we have a right to be part of Frontex. We do see it playing a valuable role. It is worth saying that Frontex is a new organisation, it has a small number of staff, and I think that often a lot of commentators and certainly some Member States load a lot of expectation on what Frontex can actually do. Frontex is doing things, it can do more in the future, but it is in a sense a bit of a toddler and we should not have too many expectations of what it can do.

Q183 *Baroness Tonge:* Extending to things like rescue at sea?

Mr Dodd: As I said, because Frontex does not have an operational responsibility it does not have a specific SAR remit at the moment. It is quite clear that Frontex operations inevitably do get involved in search and rescue because there is a humanitarian duty at least to deal with people who are found at sea. This is an area which is being studied; there is a Commission-led working group which is working at guidelines around Frontex operations, to which we are a party, and I am sure as we go into the Commission review of Frontex this will also feature as an important issue which will be discussed.

Baroness Tonge: My Lord Chairman, can we raise the problem of Malta that we heard about yesterday, or is it covered in the other questions?

Chairman: By all means ask it.

Q184 *Baroness Tonge:* It would be good to know our country's view on this. The Maltese MEP that we met yesterday said that they had a great problem because they are just in the right place for having a lot of people coming into Malta and if they are rescued at sea they tend to dump them in Malta, or that was the impression he gave. We were told that there was a great deal of trouble in Member States of Frontex not supplying the facilities that they had pledged to Frontex because there was this issue of who took the people once they had been apprehended or rescued. I wondered if we have a view on that? It is clearly a big problem for Frontex because they are not getting the resources because nobody can deal with this basic problem of how they deal with the people.

Mr Dodd: If I may say, I am not sure that is our view. Certainly from what we have seen we have not seen Frontex facing difficulties in getting the equipment that it actually wants to use for its operations.

Q185 *Baroness Tonge:* That is what we were told.

Mr Dodd: I think there were one or two occasions when the timings changed and the participants had to withdraw their equipment earlier because they had to use it for domestic purposes. As you say, certainly there may be some reluctance on behalf of States to volunteer equipment because of concerns over search and rescue, but I do not think that Frontex, in our view, has had problems in obtaining equipment or the necessary equipment for those operations.

Baroness Tonge: Is it possible to follow that up because we were told quite clearly that this was a very big problem?

Q186 *Chairman:* You will of course in due course be able to see the evidence that we were given yesterday. Baroness Tonge is quite right. It was the Maltese MEP in particular who certainly gave us the impression that pledges had not been fulfilled and that there were serious delays in providing the equipment and assistance requested.

Mr Dowdall: Could I say here that it is not something certainly I have been aware that has been raised at the management board.

Chairman: Thank you very much. Lord Listowel.

Q187 *Earl of Listowel:* Following that with a brief supplementary, which is does this case not perhaps illustrate the danger of raising expectations, of which you have just spoken, that already there is disappointment about one nation in the Mediterranean and the performance of Frontex, and we need to see what the background behind that is. Is enough being done to actively downplay expectations? One further reflection is, if the UK was a full member of Frontex it might be playing a part now and it might be able to play a more effective part in downplaying expectations in what Frontex can achieve, and indeed being more effective in highlighting the quality of input rather than the quantity of input. Perhaps the question to answer is, could more be done now to downplay expectations?

Mr Dodd: We are not in the business of downplaying expectations and we use our position in Frontex to argue for an organic and sustainable development of Frontex. As I have said, it is the toddler analogy—we move to the next stage, we want it to do more but have to do it in a gradual way. I think that is our view and I think a view shared by a number of Frontex Member States and we work collectively with others of like mind to put forward that view within the organisation.

Baroness Tonge: Just on that because Lord Jopling has just reminded me that we were given the specific example that on one operation the Italians had pledged 32 ships, I think it was, and they did not turn up for that particular operation and the Maltese had to take over and subsequently had to take the people into Malta. I am surprised if that has not actually been raised at the board; it seems extraordinary.

Q188 *Chairman:* I have already pointed out that you will have a chance to see the evidence given yesterday. It would be very helpful if you could make a note of this point and write to us when you have seen what the MEPs said to us. Would you be happy to do that?

Mr Dowdall: Yes, I shall do that.

Chairman: That would be very helpful. Lord Listowel.

Q189 *Earl of Listowel:* May I ask you about the RABITs, please? What is the added value of the RABITs Regulation to the work of Frontex? What is the UK's position in relation to participation in RABITs' operations?

Mr Dodd: We welcome the RABITs Regulation and the creation of RABITs; I think we see this as strengthening the capacity of Frontex. As you know, hitherto border guards working within Frontex have had to only work as observers whereas now they are allowed to exercise executive powers. In terms of our role, obviously the Regulation does not bind or apply to us and we are currently in discussion with Frontex to see how we might participate in an observer role in RABITs as they develop.

Q190 *Baroness Tonge:* We understand that Frontex is planning to carry out the first RABITs operation in Portugal probably going on at the moment, and I wondered if the UK knew about this exercise and whether there has been enough time really to train people for a RABITs operation in such a short time since the setting up of Frontex? Can I add, as an addition to that, my particular obsession is that there is a regulation that RABITs can be armed RABITs if required on particular operations, and I wondered if we had a view on that, as to whether they should be armed?

Mr Dowdall: We are aware of the planned RABITs operation, which is due to take place in early November. Principally this particular operation is part of that learning and development of the creation of RABITs and so in scale it is relatively modest. It is seeking to identify what the administrative barriers and hurdles are that have to be crossed in terms of bringing together a pool of officers in another country, and so therefore the key benefits are around identifying what those hurdles are and seeking ways to overcome from, and very much the operational benefits on this occasion will be taking second place. The UK is involved with others in delivering quite a comprehensive training programme not only to the RABITs officers but also much more widely to all of those involved in Frontex operations, and that is everything from the development of forgery skills, the development of leadership skills that need to be deployed in this particular kind of activity and also in ensuring that those officers operating are completely familiar with the Schengen codes also. So that has to be an important element of this. So if we were to say is this going to be an operation that is up and running and delivering immediate operational benefits, I would say that that is setting the standard too high at this stage. It has to be part of, if you like, taking the practices and the theory into properly identifying and learning and making mistakes, I

guess in order to be able to put in place a much more effective operation for the future. So I think the timescales, therefore, with those aims in mind, are realistic.

Q191 *Baroness Tonge:* And arms?

Mr Dodd: On the issue of arms the RABITs Regulation does set down some very strict rules on the use of arms. Arms can only be borne if that is consistent with the law of the host State. The host State has to give explicit permission for the use of arms. There are rules about how those weapons can be used; they can only be used if the guards from the host State are actually present. The rules are very strict of course. For our organisation, our officers do not carry arms so they would not be in the position of using them in that context.

Chairman: Lord Jopling.

Q192 *Lord Jopling:* Continuing this theme of future activities, the National Coordinator Ports Policing has suggested to us that Frontex might think in the future of covering coordination of counter-terrorism and serious crime. What do you think of that? Do you think that is a serious possibility or not?

Mr Dodd: As I said before, Frontex is quite a new organisation; its focus is on immigration and border management. It is a developing organisation and its remit could expand in the future. I am sure that this issue will be raised as part of the Commission Review. I think an explicit CT role will be a considerable extension of its current capacity and ability. In terms of serious crime there are already increasing operational links with Europol, for example, in terms of analysis and I think there was a joint operation at one point. So in terms of going forward I think we would probably advocate strengthening links with Europol as a first step and clearly a CT remit might be considered in the future, but it would be something that would be taking Frontex much further than its current capacity to deliver the mandate.

Q193 *Lord Jopling:* Do you think that Frontex will be likely to be more secure in being able to hold within it very sensitive information than some of the other bodies we have around? Interpol is not the most secure organisation in the world. The government has been telling me recently that they are passionately opposed to the European Union's proposal to put together a list of critical infrastructure in each of the countries of the Union because this will be a gift for terrorism, to have a list of the key points to strike. Going to NATO, for instance, it is common knowledge that both Britain and the United States are very wary of putting sensitive intelligence into NATO and are very selective what they feed into NATO because it too leaks like a sieve. Have you any optimism that Frontex would not also leak like a sieve if they were given the sort of information about counter-terrorism and serious crime?

Mr Dodd: It depends on the nature of that information. Clearly highly classified material requires very strenuous handling arrangements and I can say that those are not in place in Frontex. Obviously there are ways of making CT information usable by the frontline; we ourselves have a system for transmitting information to our frontline to deal with suspects of concern and so on and so forth. So there are ways of making it work and reducing things for classification where they can be distributed. Going back to my earlier remarks, I think that imagining Frontex to be some sort of security service for Europe for the future at the border would be taking it a bit too far for the time being.

Chairman: I think the next question on the hymn sheet has been adequately dealt with, so Baroness Henig.

Q194 *Baroness Henig:* In September the council adopted conclusions on the EU's Southern Maritime Borders which encourage Member States, the Commission and Frontex to further develop in cooperation with international organisations such as IOM and UNHCR, the integrated approach to border control and surveillance operations, and I wondered what that involved in practice and what role was envisaged for the IOM and UNHCR.

Mr Dowdall: The UK welcomed the conclusions that were reached and there are four tiers involved in the integrated border management and it is a reflection really not just simply of what control authorities can do but the fact that it has to work with others in order to be able to effect an effective border control. So the integrated border focus is on measures in third countries and cooperation with those countries as well as ensuring within the area of free movement that there are controls that are in place, and that there is effective cooperation between Member States and between the institutions in Europe as well, and that there is also seen to be coordination and coherence in the decisions that Member States take with the institutions. That is all to be welcomed. We recognise that in order to effect returns, for example that capacity has to be built in those host countries and the way often to be able to build those is through organisations such as the IOM, who have the confidence of the host countries and are trusted by those third countries. Therefore, in practice that means that certainly we are keen to work with institutions such as the IOM in that kind of activity. We also have an UNHCR representative in Warsaw, who is the UNHCR Frontex representative and they are involved and are aware of operations and able to add a dimension in terms of international protection of human rights as well. So it is important that there

is that recognition there; it is important that there is recognition in terms of that capacity building, and certainly our own evidence, for example last year in Operation Hera I and indeed this year in Operation Hera II—that was in relation to illegal migration to the Canary Islands—that was a successful operation. It reduced illegal migration into the Canaries, comparing 2006–07 by about 55%. But it worked principally because of the measures and the relationships that were built with those countries on the coast of Africa.

Q195 *Chairman:* Does the British Embassy in Warsaw have a watching brief over Frontex? When you are not there, for instance, do they have a reporting responsibility or a liaison responsibility?

Mr Dowdall: In terms of the management board it can only be me or my deputy who can sit on the management board; we are the only people that are designated. The Foreign Office will naturally have an interest in terms of the fact that Frontex is based in Warsaw. But most of the direct relations take place between Frontex and our point of contact that we have within the board of immigration agency headquarters in the UK.

Q196 *Baroness Henig:* I have a supplementary. I just want some comment from you, is everybody working to the same interpretation of international maritime law or are there different perceptions of the international legal obligations?

Mr Dodd: We certainly have our view of our international legal obligations but I am not sure that I can speak for other Member States.

Q197 *Baroness Henig:* In Frontex as against the United Nations, for instance.

Mr Dodd: In terms of what, I am sorry?

Q198 *Baroness Henig:* Everybody is interpreting international maritime law in the same way, are they? So there is no obvious problem there. This whole issue of international maritime law I understand is something that the European Commission is looking at.

Mr Dodd: There has been a European Commission report, I think, on the law of the sea and how it applies. I could give you more information on that[1].

Q199 *Baroness Henig:* I just wanted assurance that there was consistency in the way that that would be interpreted.

Mr Dodd: I have never come across a law which has been interpreted consistently, I have to say.

---

[1] (See further supplementary evidence, page 51)

Q200 Baroness Henig: I will move on to my next question, which is also about cooperation and in this case to what extent does Frontex cooperate with other EU agencies, such as Europol? What are the terms of such cooperation and whether cooperation is envisaged with other organisations, such as NATO?

Mr Dowdall: There is not currently a formal memorandum of understanding with Europol but Frontex and Europol do work closely together; they share their agenda and there is interchange of staff between Frontex and Europol also. That has manifested itself in, for example, Operation Hydra which took place at European airports focusing attention on illegal Chinese migration, and Europol contributed to that work with the provision of information and intelligence. It is fair to say that since Frontex has started it has been working to establish cooperation in connection with institutions within Europe and beyond. Europol is a good example of that. My understanding is that Frontex has held meetings with a range of other European organisations including Eurojust, European Police Academy and European Maritime Safety Agency, so it has worked with a range of those European agencies. Also with European missions dealing with border assistance, for example EU BAM, which is the work going on between the Ukraine and Moldova. Also more widely on the international organisations, as I referred to you in an earlier question, with UNHCR and IOM and others. As I understand it, you are visiting Warsaw later this week and they will be able to provide some further information on that. I think it is important from our perspective that we see and encourage Frontex to be engaged very actively at senior levels with these various agencies, particularly where there is common interest, but also in making sure that we do not have agendas that are going in opposite directions. It is important for me as a member of the management board that I get assurance that the Frontex Executive Director is making those connections, and so far they have been very active in that area.

Q201 Baroness Henig: NATO has not been mentioned.

Mr Dowdall: I am not aware of any direct discussions that have taken place with NATO at this stage.

Chairman: Thank you very much. Lord Teverson.

Q202 Lord Teverson: First of all, can I apologise for not having been here for the earlier part of your submission. You have said that Frontex has working arrangements with three countries and you have mentioned Switzerland, which actually is going to be a member of Schengen, I think, next year, or certainly agreed to, and Russia and Ukraine, and we heard a little bit about the Ukraine in agreement yesterday

when we were in Brussels; and with a mandate to negotiate with a further ten countries. I would be interested to know what those are and what the framework for such cooperation is, particularly whether it includes the obligations under the International and Human Rights law, so it is that broader international area and where it moves forward.

Mr Dowdall: The Frontex Executive Director has been mandated by the board to develop the working agreements that are in place, so the three that you have referred to already, which also includes Russia and the Ukraine as well as Switzerland. The mandates have also been agreed with ten others, and if I may refer to my notes on the ten? Those mandates have been agreed with Croatia, Turkey, the Former Yugoslav Republic of Macedonia, Morocco, Libya and Egypt, Mauritania, Senegal, Cape Verde and also the CIS coordination centre, so not a country as such but the coordination for what was the former Soviet Union. The legal framework for those arrangements is provided through the Frontex and the RABITs regulation, and the working agreements set out a number of elements which we expect to include financial arrangements.

Q203 Lord Teverson: What sort of financial arrangements for these agreements? Does money change hands?

Mr Dowdall: In terms of setting up the operations would be any reimbursement procedures that involved any payments that had been made. I think Frontex would be able to provide you with some further detail on that later this week; unfortunately I do not have that detailed knowledge for that. You mentioned humanitarian legislation. Tom?

Mr Dodd: Again, I am not actually clear whether that is included in the agreements or not; I think that is for the Frontex management board to respond to.

Q204 Chairman: Can I just say at this point that in our discussions today, when you consider the transcript if you think that there is anything that would be helpful for you to let us have in writing, please feel free to do so.

Mr Dodd: I think we might come back and elucidate on the agreements.

Q205 Earl of Listowel: Just before we move on, just a tentative question. Given its consideration and contribution to migration flows in the Mediterranean has any thought been given to approaching Libya in the context of this sort of agreement? If so, might the UK have a particular role in those arrangements?

Mr Dodd: I do not cover Libya any more but I used to cover it, and obviously there have been a number of efforts to improve migration cooperation with Libya both bilaterally and also through the

European Union. We are working particularly with Italy on something called the East African Migration Routes Initiative, which is an effort to enhance migration and the capacity on that eastern route, which does include Libya.

Q206 Chairman: Libya was one of the countries that you mentioned.
Mr Dowdall: Yes, it was.
Earl of Listowel: I apologise, I missed that.

Q207 Lord Teverson: One final follow up on the question. When we were talking to some of the MEPs yesterday they were almost unaware—or one of them was—that Frontex had its own remit for negotiation and I am interested in understanding whether Frontex feels that its negotiating mandate is satisfactory or strong enough or is it that it can do what it needs to do with the mandate it has? Is it satisfied with that?
Mr Dodd: I think we will have to come back to you on that point. I think it is worth stressing that these are very much technical operational agreements about the common working of border guards and those sorts of issues; they are not intended to be high-level political agreements.
Chairman: Lord Marlesford.

Q208 Lord Marlesford: The United Kingdom is challenging its exclusion from full participation in Frontex before the European Court. What are your views on the Advocate General's recently published opinion, and when do you expect the decision of the court? Will the Reform Treaty, currently being negotiated in Lisbon, change the interpretation of what is a Schengen-building measure?
Mr Dodd: As you know, we are challenging our exclusion from the Frontex regulation as a matter of principle and as a matter of law and the Advocate General has given an opinion. We are very glad that he has said that the UK can participate in Schengen building measures where they are autonomous of the underlying Schengen measure, and we are a bit disappointed that he has found that Frontex is not such a case. Obviously we look forward to seeing the full written report, which we expect in the first quarter of next year. If we win the case then we will have an opportunity to opt in both to the Frontex and the RABITs regulations and become full members of Frontex. If we lose then our position will remain as it is currently and involvement on a case-by-case basis. In terms of the new Treaty, that does not make any difference, I think, to our Schengen position and to our relationship with Frontex.

Q209 Lord Marlesford: Have you attempted to see that it does make a difference?

Mr Dodd: The draft Treaty makes some significant changes to consideration of JHA matters. It does preserve our opt in; we have the capacity to opt in to immigration and asylum issues. We believe that we have the legal basis to be full parties to Frontex, so I am not sure that there are any changes that can be made in the Treaty that would make that any different.

Q210 Chairman: The last question I have is the rather difficult question about Gibraltar. I should tell you that we asked the Director General yesterday if he had any comments to make on Gibraltar's exclusion or inclusion, to which he said no. But I hope that perhaps you can be a little fuller.
Mr Dodd: My Lord, I am very happy to say that the lead on Gibraltar belongs to the Foreign Office, as you know, rather than the Home Office. Obviously we were not a full party to the negotiation of the original Frontex regulation so we could not affect the wording that is in it. Should we win our case in the ECJ then we would seek to ensure that Gibraltar is able to play a full part in Frontex. I understand that the Gibraltarian government made a number of representations to you, including on a number of matters of law, and I think we would have to look at what they have said in more detail and then come back to you with a rather fuller response as to how we would see handling the issue of Gibraltar in the future.

Q211 Chairman: I understand that the government of Gibraltar is worried that increased participation by the United Kingdom would be at their expense and they would be excluded and I wondered whether—and I accept that this is a Foreign Office question rather than a Home Office question—you think those fears are justified?
Mr Dodd: Obviously I cannot speak on behalf of the government of Gibraltar but clearly we are trying to improve European border security and that includes improving the security of Gibraltar, and that is our objective.

Q212 Lord Marlesford: Is the government of Gibraltar wholly responsible for the control of its borders both for Spain and land borders and sea borders?
Mr Dodd: Again I am not an expert on Gibraltar and border control. I understand that they are responsible for their land borders but whether they are responsible for their air borders, I am not quite sure but I am sure we could find out.
Chairman: Thank you very much.

Q213 Lord Jopling: I did not quite follow your earlier answer. I thought you implied that if the UK won at the European Court of Justice then that would put right the situation of Gibraltar. I may have misheard you but if I have you right why does it follow that Gibraltar's problems would be removed when I think you said that the original rules of Frontex eliminated Gibraltar.

Mr Dodd: I did not actually say that; what I said was if we win the case we would seek to put beyond doubt the ability of Gibraltar to participate in Frontex operations and it would therefore participate, through us, in Frontex. There is a lot of legal ambiguity around this issue and, as I said, the Gibraltarian government has made some representations to you on matters of law which we need to look at and consider, and we can come back with a fuller view having seen what they have said.[2]

Q214 *Lord Jopling:* In those circumstances how would a decision be taken—by a straight majority or does it need unanimity? What would be the basis of changing the rules at this late stage?

Mr Dodd: Should we win our case then the regulation would need to be amended to change the wording on our position and that of Ireland as well. Therefore there will be an opportunity to re-discuss

---

[2] (See supplementary evidence, 10 December 2007)

the regulation. I assume it would then be subject to QMV as to whether changes could be made at that point.

Q215 *Chairman:* If you have further points on that, after consultation with the Foreign Office, please let us know.

Mr Dodd: Yes.

Q216 *Chairman:* Can I thank you both very much indeed for extremely helpful answers to our questions. The two Toms have really been extremely effective in helping us find our way towards this inquiry in this context and I thank you both very much indeed for the time you have given us.

Mr Dodd: We of course cause confusion in our own organisation as well by being the two Toms. I understand that this is your last session of Chairman of this Committee.

Q217 *Chairman:* It is indeed.

Mr Dodd: I really wanted to thank you on my behalf and on behalf of my colleagues for your chairmanship over the last few years and what a great pleasure it has been to appear before you as Chairman of this Committee.

Chairman: That is very kind of you; thank you very much indeed.

Supplementary written evidence by the Border & Immigration Agency, Home Office

During the evidence session on 17 October, I promised the Committee an update on Gibraltar's position *vis-à-vis* Frontex.

Gibraltar's interest relates to Article 12 of the Frontex Regulation. This provision was drafted against the background of the UK having been prevented from participating in the adoption and application of the Frontex Regulation, the point that we are challenging before the European Court of Justice. As the UK was prevented from participating in the Regulation it does not apply to us or, therefore, to Gibraltar.

It was nevertheless recognised that the UK (and Ireland) has expertise in the area of border control and that provision should be made in the Regulation to allow the Schengen member States and Frontex to avail themselves of this expertise. This is addressed by Articles 12(1) and (2) of the Frontex Regulation, which provides for Frontex to facilitate operational co-operation between the Schengen States and the UK and Ireland. The mechanism for this co-operation is set out in Article 20(5) of the Regulation. Under that Article the UK can make requests to participate in the Agency's activities. The Regulation provides for such requests to be dealt with by Frontex's management board, and to be decided by an absolute majority of its members. In practice, the UK requests to participate on a case by case basis and Member States have the opportunity to object if they wish, by written procedure. We have made a number of such requests without any objections and participated in a number of the Agency's operations.

Gibraltar cannot submit its own requests to the Frontex management board—it is for the UK to submit requests—but we do not consider that there is any legal bar to Gibraltar personnel participating in Frontex operations as part of the UK's participation in such operations following a successful request under Article 20(5).

Article 12(3) of the Frontex Regulation is the only provision in the Regulation that mentions Gibraltar. This provision is not concerned with Gibraltar's role in the UK's operational co-operation under Articles 12(1) and (2). It is concerned with the remit of Frontex. Article 1(1) of the Regulation provides that Frontex is established with a view to improving the integrated management of the external borders of the Member States. Under Article 1(4) the reference to the external borders of the Member States is to be construed as a reference to the Schengen external border. As such it excludes the borders of mainland UK (and Ireland) but includes the external borders of the Schengen States, including those of Spain. But for Article 12(3) this would have included that part of the Spanish external border that runs between Spain and Gibraltar. As Spain disputes the line of that border, however, it pushed for the inclusion of Article 12(3) to suspend Frontex's remit in relation to that part of the Schengen external border until the dispute is resolved.

Our position is that Article 12(3) does not exclude Gibraltar personnel from participation in the operational co-operation provided for under Article 12(1) and (2), where the UK co-operates with other member States under the auspices of Frontex to improve the management of the (remaining part of the) Schengen external border.

We believe Gibraltar has a Treaty right to participate in this Schengen-building measure, alongside the UK. Therefore, if our challenge in the ECJ is successful and consequently UK involvement in Frontex is subject to renegotiation, we will wish to assert Gibraltar's participation under the Regulation at the same time. Any decision on this issue would, however, be subject to QMV.

Finally, whilst the UK is responsible for representing Gibraltar in the EU, under the Constitution of Gibraltar, the administration and operation of immigration and border controls in Gibraltar are the responsibility of the Government of Gibraltar.

Tom Dodd, Director
Border & Visa Policy

10 December 2007

Further supplementary written evidence by the Home Office on the European Commission report International Maritime Law in response to Q198 from Baroness Henig, 17 October 2007

— International law of the sea consists of a substantial body of legal rules comprising both customary international law and several treaties. Inevitably, as with any body of law, there may be differences in opinion on how the law is interpreted between different States. It is clear that States participating in Frontex operations will have to do so compatibly with their obligations under international law. These obligations will be considered carefully when any operation is planned, with any differences in interpretation examined and resolved to the satisfaction of the participating States. The UK will not act in a way which it considers to be contrary to its international obligations.

— We welcome the Commission's recent working paper calling for clarification of the international law of the sea as it relates to illegal migration. We support the Commission's view that clear guidelines are needed for the interception of ships suspected of carrying illegal migrants, particularly on obligations regarding the disembarkation of migrants.

— The responsibility for migrants rescued/intercepted during the course of Frontex operations and the legal framework which applies is determined by the Member States involved as part of operational plan, taking account of international law.

— This system appears to work for joint operations but we support the Commission's initiative which has led to a working group to agree general guidelines for Frontex operations, including who is responsible for migrants intercepted/rescued during Frontex operations. The UK participates in this ongoing working group which met on 24 September in Brussels and discussed the detail of the guidelines. Some progress was made but its clear significant further discussion is required prior to agreement. The next meeting is scheduled for 29 November.

14 November 2007

TUESDAY 23 OCTOBER 2007

Present   Harrison, L.   Teverson, L.
                      Henig, B.   Wright of Richmond, L. (Chairman)
                      Jopling, L.   Young of Norwood Green, L.
                      Listowel, E.

Examination of Witnesses

Witnesses: GENERAL ILKKA LAITINEN, Executive Director, MR JOZSEF BALI, Head of Land Sector, Operations Unit, MS MARI KALLIALA, Head of Analysis and Planning Sector, Risk Analysis Unit, MR RICHARD ARES, Strategic Development Office, MR SAKARI VUORENSOLA, Legal Adviser, and MR GRAHAM LEESE, Special Adviser, examined.

Q218 *Chairman:* Again, I really want to thank our hosts very much indeed for the presentations this morning, they were extremely useful. Thank you very much for giving us copies of the slides. We have given you quite a long list of questions that we want to ask this afternoon, some of which are probably duplicated by the discussions we had this morning. Can I start off with the first question?
General Laitinen: Certainly.

Q219 *Chairman:* This is really a general question about the assessment of the work of Frontex so far. I think this gets on to evaluation. I would like your answer to whether Frontex is actually keeping up with your expectations. I think Lord Jopling will later come in with a question about your tasks but there is one particular task that I am interested in and that is people smuggling. Could you give us some assessment of how far you have been able to help control and catch people smugglers? Really it is your assessment of where you have got to so far. This is all on the record but if at any point you want to go off the record that is perfectly acceptable, although I like to keep that as limited as possible.
General Laitinen: Certainly. Thank you very much, my Lord Chairman, for the questions you have provided. First of all, I have to say I found them appropriate and straight to the point. If I may start with a basic assessment of the activities of Frontex so far. We have to bear in mind that we are still at an initial stage. We have only been in existence for two years, a little bit more, which is a relatively short period of time for a European agency. More particularly on the achievements, the basic structures, the basic procedures, the modus operandi of the operational co-ordinator at the European level, which is called Frontex, is in place. We have created the structure and we know what to do. My assessment is we are doing the things that the Regulation stipulates that Frontex should do in a balanced and appropriate way. We have arranged almost 40 joint operations so far. If I may assess the results of these operations they can be put in three

categories. The first one is excellent, the second is satisfactory and the third is promising. On the Canary Islands' operations between 2006 and 2007 we have witnessed a decrease of almost 70% and I consider that is an excellent result.

Q220 *Chairman:* That is over the year, is it?
General Laitinen: Yes, comparing the same period of time in 2006 that we have now gone through in 2007. There has been a slight decrease in the central Mediterranean and I consider that to be a satisfactory result but there are some other areas, particularly eastern Mediterranean, where we have witnessed an increasing trend and that is not good news but the good thing is we know what it is all about, so we know the phenomenon as such and, therefore, we have been able to illustrate the overall picture. This perhaps could serve as a basic assessment of the work of Frontex so far. There are a lot of basic things to be completed, a lot of ongoing incomplete projects in place but we know the view is clear and we know what to do. It is a matter of prioritising and allocating the resources in an appropriate way to find the best possible solutions.

Q221 *Chairman:* Thank you very much. People smuggling?
General Laitinen: People smuggling is an issue that, unfortunately, we do have some figures on.
Mr Bali: Yes, I have some figures. You mentioned Poseidon 2007 and in the third phase in September/October the figures were 40 facilitators, which means that in 40 cases the national authority started with an investigation. We have some results from Hera. The number of facilitators is less but it is really very difficult because it is different country-by-country based on national law. In a lot of cases we are facing the problem that on the boat there are 20 migrants plus the facilitators, but based on national law after three days they start their investigation and it is in the detention centre that it is not possible to identify the facilitator or to prove the crime. This statistic is very different. In some countries, for example on the

Greek-Turkish land border, the facilitators do not cross the border, they only escort the immigrants to the border line and then send them. We know that it is organised crime and there is a facilitator but you cannot do anything against him. It is a main objective of the operation but case-by-case the figures are very different.

Q222 Chairman: Can I remind you, I am sure unnecessarily, this is a British parliamentary inquiry and, therefore, I would like to ask a question, and I hope you will bear this question in mind in all your answers, about UK participation. How far is the UK participating in risk analysis, in operations, and have you got any comments to make on the British participation?

General Laitinen: If I may say some general words. We have the legal background for setting up links between UK colleagues and Frontex. I consider this machinery relatively cumbersome but it is something we have been able to do. This means that practically speaking, in terms of risk analysis and also the joint operations, we do not see any difference between our UK colleagues and the others, if we just exclude the administrative or the legal preparation for that. It is also visible here in our staff. There is no difference between the UK and other colleagues here but it requires considerable effort to meet all of these practical and administrative issues. If I may come back to the previous question for clarification. It was said that human smuggling and arrest and investigation of traffickers is the key objective but it is not the key function of Frontex. It is not our function but, on the other hand, it is the key objective to bring these perpetrators to justice and suffer the consequences. This makes it somewhat, I would not say schizophrenic but it is an interesting pattern that we have to apply at the border.

Chairman: I think that is a natural lead-in for Lord Jopling to ask his question about tasks.

Lord Jopling: I am afraid that the list of questions that I understand we have given you and the excellent presentation this morning did not very fully cover, if I might say so, two of the six tasks which Frontex is saddled with under the Regulation. Let me just read them both out. One is 1(b) under Article 2: "assist Member States on training of national border guards, including the establishment of common training standards". Training kept coming up as part of the wider discussion this morning but I think it is important for us to know how big the training function is in Frontex, how many people are involved, how much you spend on it, how far you have got in establishing common training standards and what you are doing over the whole of EU on training national borders. For our inquiry it is very important we hear the answer to that. The second

task which you are provided with is, and again I quote: "(f) provide Member States with the necessary support in organising joint return operations". I think I am right in saying the word "return" only appeared once in the very last of the slides this morning and the matter does not appear in the questions. This is obviously a very important part of your work and it is one of the six tasks. Where are you getting to on that? What are you doing about organising joint return operations? I think some of us would regard this as a hugely important part of your work and we would like to have an assessment. I am afraid the answer to this single question, which is really two questions, could keep us going for most of an hour but I am sure you will make it a bit less.

Q223 Chairman: Can I just interrupt to say that if on this or any other point you wanted to follow up with a written comment to us we would be very happy to receive any written comments if, for instance, statistics are not immediately available and you are able to give us something in supplementary form.

General Laitinen: Thank you very much. I am very pleased to answer both of these questions. I have to apologise that we did not manage to get a representative from the Training Unit for this event. As far as the training is concerned, it is the other core element in the entity that we call capacity building. One is research and development and training is the other. How we are performing these duties are two-fold. On the one hand, we have created a training programme which is called the Common Core Curriculum, and that is something the Regulation refers to. We are happy to publish the revised version of this Common Core Curriculum in December this year. It is a product which has been carried out, or compiled, with the close co-operation of international organisations and, of course, the Member States. It has been made under the control of two universities to ensure compatibility with the Bologna and Copenhagen processes. It is for the quality management side. This is something that already exists but will be revised. It is a basic training programme where the Member States to a certain level are committed. They do not have a legal obligation to apply that Regulation but there is only a handful of Member States that does not apply this Common Core Curriculum yet. This is for the border guard training. It is applied partly but not entirely. An additional element here is the mid-level training. We are seeking to have a Common Core Curriculum for mid-level training and we have launched periodical four-week courses for mid-level officers, so at the lieutenant/captain level, those who are in charge of one unit at the border and so on. These are the type of people who will be participating in these courses. I think the fifth or sixth course is ongoing.

The duration is four weeks. Based on that experience we complement the curricula series offered to the Member States. This is one part. The other part is more risk-analysis based training activities where we arrange courses for the Member States, mainly border control authorities, on different subjects: land border related training, aeronautical training, helicopter pilot training, travel document detection training, pedagogical training for trainers and so on, and linguistic skills. There are different areas. In 2006 we established a network of partnership academies where for the time being there are nine national academies belonging to border control authorities which are together and there is common management organised by Frontex for doing these things jointly, and each of these academies are specialised in one particular topic: one for training for land border related issues, one for linguistic training, and so on. This is our instrument to promote these training activities. We are using these two issues. I am very glad to be able to inform you that for training projects for 2006 we committed almost €500,000 for that purpose and for the time being for 2007 the commitment for training purposes is almost €2 million. It is quite an active field of our functions and training. This is very important bearing in mind capacity building for the longer term investment in operational co-operation. May I now turn to—

Q224 *Lord Jopling:* How many of the projected 198 personnel next year will be involved on the training side?
General Laitinen: For the time being I think the staff number of training units—I will have to double-check—is eight, nine, 10 people. I will have to check it and give you a precise answer.
Lord Jopling: Thank you.
Chairman: I think Lord Listowel may have a quick question.
Earl of Listowel: It is not a quick one. I am afraid following from both of your questions there is something I would like to ask.

Q225 *Chairman:* Let us go on to answer the second question and then we will come back to that.
General Laitinen: As far as the return operations are concerned, it is stipulated in a slightly different way in the Regulation to provide necessary support or assistance to the Member States, which means that we have not adopted that active role in this particular area. Our main objective and guideline for performing these functions is we focus more on the capacity building and the longer term investment in that, compiling best practices for the acquisition of travel documents, best practices for carrying out joint return operations and those kinds of things. We have created the Core Country Group where for the time

being there are seven such European Member States who have been the most active in arranging return operations, mainly by air, where they are planning and implementing these rules and guidelines. Our role is to spread this news to all the other Member States as to what could be available for their needs in that way. Another feature which is worth mentioning is we have conveyed the other financial possibilities of the European Community to this operational field knowing that the return operations are extremely expensive and it is not possible to allocate money sufficiently from Frontex's budget. We convey this money from the so-called Return Fund, which is a future instrument, and its predecessor, which is this kind of temporary financial instrument, to those countries that can use it for their purposes. We do have limits operationally speaking in performing return operations and we focus more on capacity building, gathering best practices and promoting the Member States to carry out these duties by themselves.

Q226 *Earl of Listowel:* May I ask a brief question. You may feel that perhaps you can attach your answer to it to some of our later questions but maybe a brief answer now as well. My Lord Chairman referred to your expectations of Frontex, but the expectations placed on Frontex by others seem to me increasingly to be unrealistic. It seems to me that your work depends very much on the goodwill of different states, both within the European Union and outside, and that goodwill depends on the quality of the work that you do. It seems to me the danger is that as expectations are raised on what you can deliver, the very quality of what you can provide may be undermined and you may not be able to add the value to the border services that you wish to. There is a danger also that you might begin to seem to be superseding the role of certain Member States rather than supporting the role that they have, their responsibility for their own national border guard service. I do not know if you feel that is a realistic concern but certainly it is something that has come through to me in the course of this inquiry. Perhaps, as I say, you can attach your answer to that in later questions.
General Laitinen: Yes.
Earl of Listowel: Thank you.

Q227 *Chairman:* Do you want to respond to that?
General Laitinen: It may be a good idea to tackle this issue. Your conclusion on the expectations is right. We have been struggling with the more or less realistic or unrealistic expectations from different sectors towards Frontex. The common denominator in this case is that the role and the remit of Frontex has not been entirely understood, either by accident

or deliberately. Very often we have felt that Frontex is considered to be a European panacea for all border related issues and if there are some problems at the external borders it is Frontex who is in charge of that instead of considering Frontex to be a co-ordinator to co-ordinate such co-operation where the Member States participate of their own volition. That is the difference and it is a very persistent challenge for us to spread the news on that. When it comes to our assets I would put it into three corners of a triangle. The first one is our financial resources, the second one, which to a certain extent is related to the first, is our human resources, and in the third corner is the willingness of the Member States to participate in joint operations. This means that the budget and human resources sides are only two corners of the triangle which cannot be the only successful factor for these challenges. For the time being, and more in the future, the Member States play a critical role in this regard. If we have finances, if we have capable, sufficient and professional staff, that is not enough if there is nobody to participate in this co-operation where we act as the co-ordinator. If we think of it more from the management point of view, the development of Frontex and how the budget and human resources have been developed during these two years of our existence, it is a soaring threat, it is a drastic increase and it is anticipated to continue in the future. This is a challenge for such a new organisation which is still building the basic procedure, the sound financial management, the human resources management, quality management, evaluation or indicators of performance. All of these kinds of things would have to be postponed because of this urgent need and expectation of the need for these operational things. I have to be honest and say this is really a dilemma for Frontex. It seems quite seldom that we are thinking about a period of two years and what is normal for a European agency when it is established and what can happen in two years. Normally the first two years is only for taking the curtain down and saying, "Here is the agency" and we have to start running immediately, but this is slightly different. On the other hand, I have to say that it has somehow developed the nature of my staff here which has a very strongly pioneer-oriented spirit. Everyone feels that it is our mission to do it in the current circumstances and also in the future when the expectations will be even higher.

Q228 Chairman: Can I move to our second question which is probably implicitly answered by your organisational chart. Who do you report to? Can you explain a little more the relationship between you and the Management Board? Who takes the operational decisions? Who is responsible for giving you

operational directions? Who decides on the Annual Work Programme?

General Laitinen: The functions and the powers of the Management Board are clearly stipulated in Article 20 of the Regulation. Generally speaking, the Management Board takes the strategic decisions, which is adopting the Work Programme, the organisational structure of the agency and the budget. It is linked more to the time span of one year which belongs to the Management Board. When it comes to deciding on the particular operations, whether to launch them and how to finance them, the allocation of money to particular operations, that belongs to the Executive Director. It is clear that there is not a mixture in that. There is one individual case where the Management Board is entitled to intervene in the operational issues and that is of an advisory nature. It is entitled to advise on the issues directly related to the technical development of border control and so on. The share of responsibilities is very clear. The other part is the reporting chain. I report directly to the Management Board as an entity. Whenever there is a meeting, which is on average five times a year, I give a thorough report of all the activities, both orally but also in written form, as to what is the state of play, what are our plans and so on. It is a very important part knowing that the input of the Management Board on operational issues is somewhat limited which means I consider it appropriate to maintain very thorough reporting towards the Management Board.

Chairman: Thank you very much. That is very clear.

Q229 Baroness Henig: I would like to move on to assessment of performance, which is an interesting area and I am sure one that you are very involved in and concerned to undertake. I wondered how the performance of Frontex was measured, how often and by whom? I am very mindful of the fact that presumably you will have internal assessment of performance but also your Management Board will have expectations of performance and hold you to account against those. I imagine also that Member States might have ideas about performance. Are you all working to the same kind of performance assessment mechanisms? Could you shed some light on this whole area of performance assessment.

General Laitinen: Thank you very much for that excellent question. It is very important. Evaluating an operational agency like Frontex is a very challenging task. There are difficulties in finding appropriate indicators on operational output to determine the level of performance. We are working very hard on that. We have an idea how to do it but we need to develop it. I am afraid that it is not only a one year project, it takes time to achieve the prototype at least and to establish this kind of quality management system for the operationally tuned actors it is often possible only by applying the rule called trial and error. That is one side. We have an idea of how it could go, which is a compilation of a series of different indicators for which we need some reference. We need to have a certain history in order to evaluate the existing situation and also to predict the future. That is for the operational side. As far as the management and administration is concerned, it is somewhat easier to do. There are some standardised criteria for all European agencies and Community bodies, which are called the internal control standards, and we apply these control standards already which is one of the preconditions to achieving financial independence. This is already in place. For the evaluation of our administrative performance there are different bodies that take care of that. We do have an internal auditor within this agency who mainly provides me and my Deputy Executive Director with the findings of how the procedures are ongoing. We do have input from the European Court of Auditors, which has already paid one audit to Frontex and the next one is anticipated to take place very soon. We have a third auditing body, which is the Internal Audit Service of the European Commission, which has also visited Frontex. From my point of view there is sufficient coverage of different aspects of auditing and there are quite frequent visitors here. What is the good news is that the findings of the recent audits, both by the European Court of Auditors and the Internal Audit Service, were very positive. They concluded that the basic management in terms of human resources and finance is in place and that the system is sound, let us put it that way.

Q230 *Chairman:* I think, given the reluctance of the Court of Auditors to sign off accounts, you deserve our congratulations.
General Laitinen: This is now the state of the play. The operational side is more complicated and requires more perspective and more effort, but when it comes to the administrative side it is much easier to do and is further developed for the time being.

Q231 *Baroness Henig:* Thank you very much. In a sense, I would like to turn the thing around now. Given that Frontex is a facilitator, and we keep hearing that, to some degree your success or failure in your performance is going to be tied to the performance of your individual Member States because of the way you operate. I wondered, therefore, whether there were some states that were very active members as against others that were not, and that would therefore affect things because you would obviously want to operate with those that were

active because you would have more chance of success, although the need might not be in that area. My second supplementary to that would be do Member States divide up into consumers of your services and providers of your services? Is that a pattern that you can see as well?
General Laitinen: This is a very fundamental question, for a co-ordinator to have something to co-ordinate. First of all, I have to say that there is still a lot of room for increasing the activeness of Member States to participate in our operation by deploying technical means and experts for the joint operations that we have. That is one corner. The other fact is if we compare the situation of 2005 with 2006 and now with 2007 the trend is continuously increasing. For instance, in 2006 at sea borders the overall number of Member States which participated in joint operations was 15 compared with the existing figure in 2007 which is 22. This is an increasing trend. As for land borders, in 2006 we had eight Member States participating in different operations whereas the figure in 2007 is 23. Also, at the air borders in 2006 it was 18 compared with 2007 which is 26. This means that we can say that all the Member States participate in at least some of the operations but what is needed and what is my desire is to have more active participation of all Member States in the different operations. The trend is promising and what is needed is to have some patience to see how the Member States become more active in that. On the other hand, we have to take into consideration the fact that Member States are in charge of controlling their external borders and that is the priority for them and the European co-operation which is co-ordinated by Frontex is an additional element in that. They need to consider where to put their limited resources, whether on the domestic side or the European side. The trend is promising and it is increasing considerably. I am very satisfied with that but there is still a lot of room for improving their activeness.

Q232 *Chairman:* Can I ask you a specifically British question on this point. We were shown in evidence we have already been given what was to me quite an impressive list of operations in which there has been British participation. Have you got any general comment you would like to give us on British operational participation?
General Laitinen: I think we have a summary of the UK's participation. Generally speaking, I have to say that the UK has been active in participating in joint operations, no matter if the practical and administrative side is somewhat complicated and requires a case-by-case decision for each particular operation by the Management Board, which is carried out by a written procedure and it is

customary. If you think about operations where the UK has participated in 2006 and 2007, the UK has participated in four pilot projects. Three of them were the Border Management Conferences aiming to promote third country co-operation where the UK has played a very important role. The fourth pilot project where we had UK participation was the Focal Point Office pilot project which is a system along the external borders where there are joint offices where experts from different Member States come together and assist their host country colleagues to perform their duties and act like a liaison officer in this regard. The UK has been active in creating this concept. They have participated in joint operations, Gordius, Herakles and Kras, both land borders but also airport and maritime operations. Those three that I mentioned are land border operations. As far as the sea border sector is concerned, there are six joint operations where the UK has participated and I can say that in all the main operations in the Canary Islands, in Malta and in the eastern Mediterranean the UK has participated either by deploying technical assets or experts to the joint operations. When it comes to air border operations, altogether there are four air border operations where we have seen UK participation. This brings me to the conclusion that we do have active participation from the UK, no matter if the procedure is relatively heavy to apply. This indicates the activeness of our British colleagues in this. There are also some activities on the return operations side, the best practices compilation and the training for the return officers in this regard where the UK has been very, very active.

Q233 Lord Young of Norwood Green: What is the framework for the review of Frontex which is to be carried out by the Commission? I noticed there was a reference to this in the Management Board Programme of Work where it says: "As mentioned in the Hague Programme, the Commission will carry out an evaluation of Frontex tasks. As a result of this evaluation, new tasks will be assigned to Frontex". Perhaps you can capture that in your answer.
General Laitinen: Yes, certainly. I think that the Commission would be the more appropriate body to respond to that.

Q234 Chairman: I should tell you that they have already.
General Laitinen: Okay. That is good. From my point of view and from Frontex's point of view it is like stocktaking where we are now: have we met the expectations which were in place when the Regulation was adopted; have we carried out right and appropriate duties; is the role of Frontex as a co-ordinator a sufficient one or would there be deeper involvement of this entire integrated border management in that sense; or perhaps find some new areas of co-operation which could be addressed to Frontex. This kind of more politically oriented assessment is now in question. This is somewhat different from the assessment which is based on Article 33 of the Regulation which is the Management Board driven assessment for the overall internal functioning of the agency which belongs to the Management Board. These two assessments, in addition to the third assessment which is for the top managers of this agency based on the staff regulations, are ongoing in the same way. Coming back to the Hague Programme based evaluation, that is more about paving the way for the future on integrated border management and what would be the role of Frontex within this framework.

Q235 Lord Young of Norwood Green: I think you probably touched on this in your presentation but, nevertheless, are you satisfied with the involvement of EU institutions in setting the budget of Frontex? Is it right that some of the budget should be made conditional on future developments which are not within your control?
General Laitinen: Generally speaking, I have been very satisfied with the budget authority and the Commission's involvement in the financial management of this agency. What is somewhat exceptional is the rate of growth of this agency. This is a unique situation where a European agency has been developed so rapidly and with such a drastic increase from the first year of its existence. On the other hand, I found it was a clear signal from the Council and the Parliament to address and indicate the importance of Frontex by allocating more money to this agency than was proposed. Normally the trend is just the opposite, to cut off some expenditure. I found it a very positive signal. Now that the budget side is in place it requires adequate human resources. The third point, coming back to the most critical factor, which is the Member States, has to be in balance. That is the main challenge for us in order to digest the increased financial resources of Frontex. Another thing I have to say is that focusing only on the operational expenditure is not enough for a co-ordinator. This is simply due to the fact that our success relies very much on the added-value that we are able to prove. If the human resources and the administrative side are not in balance with the soaring resources and financial resources for the operational element the results can be counterproductive. It could even reduce the level of the quality of our products. There could be more pressure and more tasks to do with less human resources to be allocated to that.

Chairman: I think that leads immediately to a factual question from Lord Listowel. I beg your pardon, I interrupted you.

Q236 Lord Young of Norwood Green: This is really a supplementary briefly, if I may. I am a bit puzzled that they do not understand the importance of the point that you make. The success of the operation depends on your risk analysis model and your R&D as well needs to feed into that, so I am puzzled they cannot see the importance of that connection. The only other point I would make is that when I looked through your budgetary allocation it did seem that the staffing you have allowed for training seems small in comparison to the size of the task, but it may be that is a question you are building on.

General Laitinen: Thank you very much. Another issue which I think is worth mentioning here is that the Management Board established an objective which would be the optimal division line between the administrative and operational expenditure and this rate is 33/65. In other words, one-third for administration and two-thirds for operations, knowing that the operational work my staff is doing here is part of the administrative budget. In 2008, as was discussed previously, our operational budget is due to be increased by 140%. For that purpose I have made a proposal to increase the administrative budget and also the human resources staff number of this agency by 19% which leads to the final figure of 25/75 which is much more at the optimal level established by the Management Board. This is a very important point in this regard. As far as the training staff are concerned, the Training Unit applies a somewhat different modus operandi when performing their duties. They have gathered an expert pool that they use for shorter term projects which means that the co-ordinating role is within the Training Unit and where the actual planning and implementing work is carried out by these qualified training assistant officers, if I can use that phrase. Very often these guest officers come from the partnership academies, so they are the teachers at these national academies, who come together, draft a project and implement that project. In that time they serve the agency for a shorter period of time which reduces the permanent staff figure to that relatively low figure. I do agree that if we compare 89 staff members to the existing 125 it is not that much bearing in mind the importance of the capacity building factor and the training being a part of that.

Q237 Chairman: I think it is my fault for interrupting. I am not sure we have given you a chance yet to answer the second part of Lord Young's question, which was is it right that some of the budget should be made conditional on future developments which are not within your control? I will just make a comment. As a former accounting officer of the British Diplomatic Service I am well used to situations where a lot of things happen that are not under your control. Perhaps you would like to comment.

General Laitinen: Thank you very much. We have now experienced enough to have a budget reserve and conditional budgets. It might sound attractive but we have to keep in mind the heavy procedure which is very much out of the hands of the actor itself, it is for the budget authority under the duration of this procedure, but it does not provide us with sufficient flexibility to adapt our operational activities for that. This means that I would prefer to have certainty in relation to the budget and, if needs be, an additional element for that instead of starting planning for the operations which are the subject of the reserve. I consider budget reserve as an undesirable exception. If the only option is to earmark this money and put it into reserve then that is the case but it is not the best possible solution for to continuity and consistent management and planning taking into account all of these procedures that have to be put in place.

Q238 Earl of Listowel: Do you consider that Frontex staffing and funding are adequate to enable it to carry out its present tasks? Will they be for the future? We have already dwelt on those questions to some degree but, please, if you have further comments we would be grateful for them. Also, just a point of detail and perhaps you can write to the Committee on this if you have this information, have you information on the retention of staff and on their levels of sickness absence? I ask this because that can be an indication of the state of morale of staff. If Frontex is being asked to do too much in too short a time that might be a helpful indicator as to whether that is the case or not.

General Laitinen: Thank you very much for that question. During the two years of the agency's existence we have been at the edge all the time when it comes to human resources and the operational and other types of expectations. There are some challenges that we have had and we will have in the future in recruiting staff. One is of an administrative nature and others are related to the seat and the Community salary system that we apply. Generally speaking, we have been in a permanent emergency situation for two years and if we did not have this pioneer spirit from the entire staff and very high morale in relation to work, very strong commitment to the work, this would not be the case. I can say openly and loud that this would not be the case. I do have some strong concerns in relation to 2008, but in the situation where the operational budget is due to be increased by 140% we have a plan with the budget authority to put 30% of the previous budget's administrative expenditure into reserve which means that we are not able to commit the salaries for the entire year for the whole staff and that is not a good message for the staff that a European agency is not able to guarantee the salary payments for the entire fiscal year. That is one issue in relation to that. We need to work hard to meet all the conditions to release the budget reserve but in addition, in this new situation which is anticipated, we need a 19% increase in our staff, and that is the minimum, and adequate new allocations for the administrative budget which would take the staff up to 189 by the end of 2008. I would like to mention another factor which is related to recruitment and also in relation to the existing staff, and that is what is called the correction coefficient which means different places within the European Union are rated at different levels when it comes to salary levels. Here in Warsaw it is one of the lowest figures in Europe, it is 77.6% of the salary level from the level of 100 which is applied in Brussels and Luxembourg. These ratings change annually, so they can go up and down one year after another. Last year was the first time in my career, and I think it was the first time in my colleagues' careers, when our net incomes decreased because of the change in the correction coefficient at the same time as when in absolute terms the cost of living standard in Warsaw and Poland increased by a certain per cent. This is a de-motivating and discouraging factor for recruitment. The difference is so drastic, 100 compared to 77.6. We have had a lot of cases in our recruitment where even at the stage of short-listed candidates, when they learn and understand what the correction coefficient means they have withdrawn their applications. It is a matter of almost one-quarter of the income that they have calculated.

Q239 Chairman: Who sets the coefficient?
General Laitinen: It is the Community. The final decision is that of the Council. It is based mainly on the statistics by the National Statistic Services and Eurostat.
Earl of Listowel: My Lord Chairman, is there time for one very quick question?
Chairman: Extremely quick. We are half way through and we are by no means half way through the questions, so we have got to get a move on.

Q240 Earl of Listowel: Briefly, in terms of staff support, does this "permanent emergency" that you have described in any way undermine the amount of support staff you receive in terms of supervision, in mentoring, in management? If you would not mind being very brief in your answer, or perhaps writing to

the Committee on that point, that would be helpful. Then I would like to go on to the next question.
General Laitinen: I can provide some written evidence for you.
Chairman: That would be very helpful.

Q241 Earl of Listowel: Thank you very much. How many regional centres does Frontex have? How are they staffed and where are they located, please?
General Laitinen: For the time being we do not have any specialised branches anywhere. The entire staff of Frontex are at the headquarters here in Warsaw. We have a plan to deploy an official to Brussels to serve our interests vis-à-vis the European institutions in the near future but he or she will be the only ex-pat of the agency.

Q242 Baroness Henig: Hypothetically, if there was somebody based in Brussels their salary then should be determined by the cost of living in Brussels, not the cost of living in Warsaw. Would that happen or not?
General Laitinen: That would be the case.

Q243 Baroness Henig: So you could have people in regional operational centres earning more because of where they are based than in the headquarters of Frontex?
General Laitinen: Yes, that is a fact.
Chairman: A familiar situation to some of us!

Q244 Lord Harrison: General Laitinen, a point of clarification and then a question. I know that you will give me a full answer and not a three-quarters one according to the coefficient rule you were talking about earlier. You said that the United Kingdom is an active participant in the work that is being done in joint operations but you said it increased bureaucracy in terms of the single applications that have to be made to the Management Board. So, on the one hand, it is doing well in terms of co-operating and working despite being outside or of a semi-detached status but, on the other hand, it is increasing bureaucracy which is wasteful of resources. That is a yes or no really.
General Laitinen: This is the will of the lawmakers.

Q245 Lord Harrison: Thank you.
General Laitinen: The reason is that the UK does not fully implement the Schengen acquis and we can see the consequences in the Regulation establishing Frontex, which is a subject for the Schengen System. What I have to say in addition to what I said on the UK's participation is that the Management Board has stretched its flexibility to find as smooth and flexible a procedure to meet the requirement of case-by-case decisions on each particular joint operation

where UK participation is desired, including the justification that is also desired.

Q246 *Lord Harrison:* That was the full answer that I was inviting. I would like to ask you this question: in response to the Chairman earlier when he asked about trafficking you said that was an objective but not a function of Frontex, and we thoroughly understood that, but inevitably in the work that you do in co-ordinating the 27 Member States there must be times when you feel you want to trespass beyond the established role of Frontex. I had in mind, for instance, when you are doing sea operations, that if there is a disastrous situation at sea which you come across you cannot be like the commercial cameraman or journalist who simply takes the photo, you would feel you would have to intervene and effect a sea rescue. Is that the case? What are the guidelines for you in stretching beyond what might be understood to be the established role of Frontex?
General Laitinen: I have a reference to the maritime operations, certain maritime search and rescue operations, vis-à-vis the border surveillance on that. We consider border control as an instrument which can be used for different purposes. Managing migration flows is one of those, promoting bona fide travel, making it as difficult as possible for the facilitators and irregular migrants to cross borders is one objective. This is not entirely aligned with the existing structure within the European Union by defining different pillars. I would say that border control is a cross-pillar phenomenon which serves all three pillars whereas the legal basis of the Frontex Regulation is within the first pillar. This is quite a persistent question and dilemma for us to find an appropriate way between these more or less artificial pillars within the Community. Fighting organised crime is one thing we come across with these issues and it can be stated it is not a function or task of Frontex but in practice in the Member States and also at the European level we have to work towards that objective. It is not a task but it is an objective. The same applies to the maritime operations. We cannot label our operation to be a maritime search and rescue operation because that is beyond our remit. It is not even a remit of the European Union, it is part of the international maritime law. Everybody knows a coastguard vessel or a Navy vessel, whoever navigates in the sea for whatever purpose, has to take action if people are in distress. Unfortunately, particularly in the central Mediterranean, this is the main modus operandi of the human smugglers and the facilitators, to make the journey become a search and rescue operation which guarantees reception and a way to the closest safe haven. This is a hard game. This is a very dramatic game which is going on. We feel obliged to perform these duties even if when

reading the Regulation and implementing the law it is not clearly written and could be controversial. It belongs to the performance.

Q247 *Lord Jopling:* Can I just follow that last point up before I move on. I went to an extraordinary place in Stavanger in Norway in May where they co-ordinate rescue at sea and other maritime and terrestrial problems. The day before I was there, there had been a local problem in Norway and when we were there they got a message that there was a ship 200 miles off Djibouti in the Indian Ocean drifting with no fuel and no food and they organised a rescue operation. They do that worldwide, it is the most extraordinary place. Do you have any relations with that organisation?
General Laitinen: No, we do not.

Q248 *Lord Jopling:* The next question is with regard to co-ordinating joint operations. You have said a good deal about this, particularly the problem of making sure that all of the states concerned want to co-operate. You have said a good deal on that but do you want to add anything?
General Laitinen: No, I think we have covered and returned to this issue many times.

Q249 *Lord Jopling:* Okay. The next one is that we have been told that Frontex operations respond to an International Co-ordination Centre which is established for the particular joint operations and manned by a Joint Co-ordination Board with representatives of all national contingents participating in the operation and Frontex. Could you tell us more about this. What is the Board? Who is on it, who is the Chairman of it? How are decisions taken? Where is the ICC located and how is it funded? Just explain to us the structure of those two organisations.
General Laitinen: We should not speak about organisations in this regard. It is how we are arranging joint operations. If we take Warsaw first, it is a customary procedure in Warsaw that we activate our Frontex operational centre here where all the flows of information come, the daily reports and so on. That centre, which is still at the initial stage but functions, can serve different operations if they are going on at the same time. There is a channel and a flow of information to the operational theatre, if I may use that phrase, and each operation has a part of that structure in place which contains the Co-ordination Centre which has a direct link to the Frontex operational centre here. The leader of this centre is a representative of the host country as our joint operations are always led by a Member State and that role belongs to the officer of that Member State. Quite often those Member States, in particular

in the bigger operations, who have provided and deployed main assets to those operations also deploy an expert to this Co-ordination Centre where they jointly manage the performance of these operations. Quite often in these bigger operations one officer from Frontex is deployed to this Co-ordination Centre to safeguard our interests that the operational plan is fully respected and also the financial issues which might occur in the course of this operation. There is no fixed institution or organisation, it is just a way of managing joint operations where some different words have been used, "committees" or "boards" or whatever. It is a matter of managing joint operations.

Q250 *Baroness Henig:* This goes back to sea operations, a different aspect of sea rescue. Some witnesses who have given evidence to us highlighted a reluctance on the part of some Member States either to commit national assets for Frontex operations or to activate those assets that are already in play. The reason given to us, particularly by a Member of the European Parliament, was that there were not clear rules as to where the people intercepted by EU joint operations at sea were to be disembarked and the fear that the particular nation that intercepted these people then had to take these people back to their own country. I wonder whether you could comment on this and whether directions or guidelines have been given in relation to disembarkation in Frontex operations undertaken thus far.

General Laitinen: Thank you very much for that question. I have witnessed discussions on this issue at different levels but when it comes to the planning and implementation of a joint operation I have not come across an issue which is a critical point for the Member States to determine whether to deploy an asset or not. It is more a question about a Member State finding an appropriate allocation for their own limited resources. Can they afford to give an aircraft, helicopter or vessel for an operation for this period of time. I do agree that at a certain level there have been some political tensions in determining who is in charge and some criticism of whether existing laws and rules are fair. I am not the person who can say this or that on this issue. What I can say is it has not been a major factor for a Member State in determining whether to participate with technical equipment in an operation or not.

Q251 *Baroness Henig:* Are you then saying that formally no directions or guidelines have been given but that possibly informally this might be an issue? Is that what you are saying?

General Laitinen: To my understanding the rules are quite clear. Another question is who considers them to be fair or appropriate. For us, the rules are clear: not only determining what is the state of play if we are acting in territorial waters or international waters but is it a real border control situation or a maritime search and rescue operation. The rules are clear. There is room for clarifying some application of these rules but in general terms the rules exist. It is a matter of a difference of interpretation.

Q252 *Baroness Henig:* Are you saying the Member States, or some of them, may be deliberately looking at this from a particular viewpoint or misunderstanding the law of the sea?
General Laitinen: I am not going to say that. I have to limit my answers to the role that I have.

Q253 *Lord Young of Norwood Green:* I think, again, you touched on this in your presentation but perhaps you could develop it. Some witnesses have told us that while there is no lack of registered assets for Frontex operations in the Centralised Record of Available Technical Equipment—that delightful acronym, CRATE—Member States do not always honour their pledges. Could you give some examples of this, diplomatically of course? Is there a mechanism for ensuring that pledges are honoured and assets pledged are made available for operations?
General Laitinen: Thank you very much. When speaking about this Centralised Record of Available Technical Equipment, sometimes called by the forbidden nickname "toolbox", it is one of the means of Frontex. We do have 27 helicopters in this Centralised Record at the moment, 21 fixed-wing aircraft and 116 different types of vessels. In addition, we have almost 400 items for border surveillance, equipment for land borders and maritime borders. This is a compilation of the Member States' assets which, if the conditions are met, could be deployed to a joint operation if the contributor considers it is possible. It is an instrument to facilitate, on the one hand, the bilateral assistance from one Member State to another in which the only involvement of Frontex is to provide a list of equipment which could be available but having no financial contribution to that. This Centralised Record serves as a planning instrument for Frontex when planning and preparing the joint operations, what would be the assets that we would desire to have in the joint operation, but it is not an entirely Frontex controlled armada which simply depends on the will and management of this agency to deploy or not.

Q254 *Chairman:* That possibly deals with my next question which is the command relationship with Member States' assets. The specific question is who,

for instance, would be in charge of an Italian ship used for an operation hosted by Spain or Malta?
General Laitinen: These rules are clearly stated in the operational plans. One of the rules is that there is no other captain on the ship than the captain. Every time it is the captain of the ship who makes the final decision. That is the purpose of having a joint planning session, which is a customary event in Frontex to gather all of the participating Member States together to draft the joint operation and then agree on the joint operation. From our point of view there is another aspect for the operational plan, which is the Community funding aspect. The issues which are listed in the operational plan are the conditions to have a Community fund involved. If there is a case where the rules are not respected then the financial conditions are not met. It is one of the core issues in a joint operation to make clear who reports to whom, what is the reporting system, who gives alerts to whom and who makes these decisions.

Q255 *Chairman:* It would be specified in each case?
General Laitinen: Certainly.

Q256 *Lord Teverson:* Moving on from CRATE, would you ever see that Frontex has its own operational assets or is this a bridge too far?
General Laitinen: Thank you very much for that interesting question! Many people tend to think that we already have those. We can split that question into two parts. We can have a legal approach and a political realistic approach to that. If we speak about the Regulation, in principle the Frontex Regulation already establishes the possibility for Frontex to have its own assets. If we start thinking about the cost and how it would fit into the existing budget of Frontex, which in 2008 would be about €70 million, and we all know what one helicopter, fixed-wing aircraft or coastguard vessel would cost, it is a matter of making a decision in that sense. In an optimal situation I would find it helpful if to a certain extent Frontex could have certainty to have something to deploy to the most important operations whereas the main assets could still come from the Member States. There are different ways to do that and purchasing equipment is not necessarily the only way to do that. We would like to have a higher level of certainty, to have some assets even more rapidly than the state of play today but I leave that to those to whom it belongs to determine what is the line to take, whether in the future we could have our own assets and so on.

Q257 *Lord Teverson:* I thought you would say, "No, I don't want anything to do with that" and I am interested that you did not say that. Perhaps you could tell me which sorts of assets would be useful and by not having them at the moment, and I

presume you do not mean particularly battleships or things like that but the smaller things maybe, it does not work properly now because you have to take time in assembling things which perhaps you could have.
General Laitinen: I think the contribution of the Member States is two-fold. It is either in the form of human resources, experts, or tangible assets, technical equipment. When we speak about the deployment of experts to our land border, maritime, airport or other types of operations, pilot projects, we have not witnessed considerable difficulties in having these experts for these joint operations. That is one side. What we have seen is that it is a continuous challenge for us to encourage the Member States to deploy technical equipment and we are speaking more about helicopters, fixed-wing aircraft for surveillance purposes and different types of vessels for both controlling and surveillance purposes. To a certain extent that is quite understandable because they are the visible means for that particular country to demonstrate their capability to control their own borders and if we make a move from these assets to another area it could be interpreted in a different way.

Q258 *Chairman:* Lord Jopling has just drawn my attention to Article 3 which actually refers to your technical equipment. What does that mean? It says "It", ie the agency, "may also decide to put its technical equipment at the disposal of Member States".
General Laitinen: I consider that to be more—

Q259 *Chairman:* For the future.
General Laitinen: --- of an optional nature. That is aligned with the possibility to purchase such material.

Q260 *Chairman:* General Laitinen, you are being extremely generous with your time. Our programme says that we finish at 4.15, are you happy to go on to 4.15?
General Laitinen: I think we had planned to have this session finish at 4.00 so we still have some time.
Chairman: Good. On that plan could we please frame our questions accordingly?
Lord Teverson: I have another 13 questions which are not on this list actually but we obviously will not get on to those! In terms of planning, perhaps you could just take us through the practicalities of the moment that a Member State suggests, or you suggest to a Member State, that an operation gets underway. What happens in terms of the planning of that in a practical sense?

Q261 *Chairman:* Including the risk analysis aspects.
General Laitinen: The starting point is with the risk analysis and all the Member States, our stakeholders or clients, receive all these risk analyses so they are aware what ideas we have in mind for these eventual joint operations. Also, when they look at the Work Programme they say, "There could be this number of joint operations in the maritime area depending on the risk analysis and so on", so they have this idea in their mind, as we have here, as to what could be the state of play. Then when it comes to the stage of further elaborating these recommendations in the Joint Operation Initiative, as we call it, we put it into formal consultations with the Member States via designated points of contact. Each Member State in a Schengen country has designated a point of contact for Frontex and that is the channel through which we go. Normally it is in the form of a fixed letter where we give a deadline, a proposal on what would be desired from that particular country, and then respecting this deadline we receive their response to our request. Hopefully it is a positive response but in some cases it is a negative which gives us the possibility to consider the appropriateness of the operation and whether we have reasons to go to the next stage which is finalising it in the operational plan and giving a decision on financing that, which requires a planning meeting and briefing with all participating countries together. This is how it goes. We are going to launch a more systematic planning round for the Member States which relates to the Work Programme. Acknowledging that there are a lot of conditional and dependent issues in the Work Programme, we would like to have annual consultations with all the Member States to look at the fact that it could be the case that next year we will have these kinds of operations, some of them of a more permanent nature, and according to the Centralised Record of Available Technical Equipment it could be our desire that they deploy these vessels at the beginning of the year for these operations and aircraft and helicopters this year, so we could have more certainty and promote the readiness of the Member States to be prepared for forthcoming requests for particular operations.

Q262 *Lord Teverson:* For an operation that is not necessarily one that you have planned in the Work Programme a year ahead, say, but one that is more reactive, what sort of timescale does it take, and I know it depends on the size of the operation or whatever? Can you do this quickly or is anything going to take three months?
General Laitinen: As a rule, and if it is the first time ever we learn there is a reason for launching a joint operation, if we do it very quickly then an operation can be in place in two weeks.

Lord Teverson: Two weeks, that is very good. Thank you.
Chairman: I do not know whether you think high seas has been adequately dealt with?
Lord Teverson: No, we have not really got on to that. Did you want me to do that one, my Lord Chairman?
Chairman: Please do.

Q263 *Lord Teverson:* In terms of the high seas our question is one about what happens when there is this issue of migrants in distress. I know you have talked about it to some degree but how is that actually handled and on something like a drug trafficking operation how does that work? I think one of the things we have come across is that there is some tension, particularly in the Mediterranean, between different Member States on how you deal with that sort of difficulty.
General Laitinen: Our focus is fighting illegal immigration, that is the main objective for this instrument that we are using, but it does not exclude the other objectives on drug trafficking or other types of organised crime. It is for the Member States and the participating countries to think about what their action would be if they came across a boat or a ship loaded with drugs instead of human beings. I imagine they know how to act but we have not strongly taken into account that co-ordinating role because in that case we come across certain difficulties that give room for different interpretations of the Regulation. It is a fact that we acknowledge and trust that the participating countries and the host country will give instructions on how to handle these kinds of cases and convey that to the competent authority. In some cases it could be the same authority. It is a kind of dual role which is quite often the case. This brings us to the question of the need to further promote integrated border management when in the future we should not be in a situation where there are some legal hindrances to a rational performance of their duties but to a certain extent, unfortunately, this is not the case at the moment.

Q264 *Lord Jopling:* This morning one of your final presentations drew our attention to your partners, in particular international organisations and NGOs, including organisations like UNHCR and OSCE, and at the bottom it said, "et cetera". Could you mention any other organisations with which you have an active participation? I am thinking particularly as to whether you have had, or can conceive of the possibility of having, an involvement with NATO? I ask that because you mentioned your participation in the Winter Olympics and a football tournament somewhere and I recall that NATO had a major role at the Athens Olympics. As I understand it, on the 2012 Olympics in London they have had no discussions whatsoever with NATO. Have the London Olympics had any discussions with you? Are you in any way involved in that and do you envisage having any association with NATO in the future?

General Laitinen: That is an interesting issue, once again. We all know that in the areas where Frontex are concentrating our operational activities there are NATO activities going on in the same regions. When we speak about the overall concept of security where there is not a clear dividing line between the internal and eternal security we are more or less dealing in the same areas. On some general occasions we have been in touch with NATO officers in relation to informing each other as to the appropriate level of what kinds of activities we have in an area and what kinds of activities they have in an area, so in very general terms we are aware of what each other is doing in this sense. I consider the determination of having formal co-operation between NATO units or bodies at the external borders of the EU and Frontex to be of a political nature and I leave it for others. For the time being, having awareness of each other's activities at a general level is sufficient for us.

Q265 *Lord Jopling:* The London Olympics 2012, has there been any discussion with you on that?

General Laitinen: Not directly. I think the common denominator would be the host country of this event, as was the case with the Turin Olympic Games and the Football Championships. The Member State normally establishes a task for the overall security features where the different actors come across instead of having horizontal connections. It could be the case that both bodies will meet each other in this framework.

Q266 *Baroness Henig:* This is for clarification, please. You gave us a slide this morning that was entitled "Overview of Co-operation with Third Countries" and I think as part of that you were talking about working arrangements that were being put in place with third countries. I think I understood you to say, and correct me if I am wrong, that you had not yet established working arrangements with Senegal or Mauritania, is that correct?

General Laitinen: Yes.

Q267 *Baroness Henig:* Yet when you were talking about the Hera operation that did involve those countries. If you have not got working arrangements with them, how did this operation work?

General Laitinen: That is a very good question. Our first priority is to have a bilateral agreement with the particular third country and Frontex, which is the more desirable solution, but this is not the only option for arranging a joint operation where third countries can be involved. The other option is to have

a bilateral agreement with a third country and an EU Member State as the basis for running these operations, which has been the case with Senegal and Mauritania. Our activities in that area are based on the bilateral agreements between Spain and Mauritania and Spain and Senegal. That is the legal basis for us to have the possibility to have operational activities co-ordinated by Frontex in the territorial waters of these two aforementioned countries.

Q268 *Baroness Henig:* It is an ad hoc more complex relationship until you can establish that?

General Laitinen: That is right. Our priority is to seek a more consistent and permanent solution, which means that we would like to have a bilateral agreement. I have to stress that we do not establish a partnership with a country or a government but the border control authority of that third country and Frontex. That is the priority for us, but not the only way out.

Q269 *Lord Young of Norwood Green:* Is that what you meant by the "local authorities"?

General Laitinen: Excuse me?

Q270 *Lord Young of Norwood Green:* In your report you said: "For the first time such an operation was carried out in the territorial waters of Senegal and Mauritania in close co-operation with the local authorities".

General Laitinen: Those authorities of those third countries, that is right.

Chairman: Lord Harrison, I think you have a sort of trinity of questions about RABITs.

Q271 *Lord Harrison:* I do. General Laitinen, we move on to another delightful acronym, the RABITs—Regulation on Rabid Border Intervention Teams. Could you say how it will change the nature of Frontex operations? Could you tell us whether it extends the powers of the border guard teams allowing them to carry weapons, will they be armed, and perhaps you can give us a scenario which would illustrate that to the Committee? We understand that next month, in November, the first of the RABIT operations is going to take place in Portugal. How are you getting on preparing for that with your staff and so on? Just to make a quadruple question: when Lord Teverson mentioned assets, would this be an appropriate area where it might be useful to have assets to help the work of Frontex ready, there and waiting?

General Laitinen: Thank you for this excellent question, once again. RABITs, or the Rapid Border Intervention Teams, are in addition to the Centralised Record of Available Technical Equipment. It is another means related to Frontex.

What I have to say is that it is not a permanent asset of Frontex which can be deployed on any occasion in any situation to the joint operation but the Rapid Border Intervention Teams, the so-called RABITs, is an emergency instrument which can only be deployed if certain conditions are met. The basic requirement for having the possibility to deploy these units is that the situation should be urgent and exceptional, so this is the starting point, which means the level of commitment of the Member State has been raised to a higher level. If there is an emergency situation, an exceptional situation, the Member States are more committed to providing their experts being a part of the RABIT teams.

Q272 Lord Teverson: I am sorry to intervene but could I just ask for a real example of what that circumstance might be so we can practically get it in our minds as to what might cause a RABIT intervention.
General Laitinen: Our interpretation is somehow turning it around. If such an event has been mentioned in our risk analysis that this kind of thing is going on, our interpretation is we do not have the basis for considering that event to be urgent and exceptional. That makes sense because the normal operations that are systematically running are based on the risk analysis which gives us reason to believe that those needs are covered by so-called "normal" operations.

Q273 Lord Teverson: I am sorry, I probably did not make myself clear, my apologies. I was trying to understand what might physically happen that would cause one of these things. Is it football hooligans invading France?
General Laitinen: I was about to come to the point.

Q274 Lord Teverson: I am sorry, I apologise.
General Laitinen: It is very difficult to present a scenario. We have had a scenario for determining the numbers but that is not a tangible example. Let us imagine the situation in 2006 in Lebanon when a lot of people left their homes. In that case finally it was in a somewhat controlled manner but this could have been an event where these Rapid Border Intervention Teams were deployed. If we think about another event a little bit further back in history, some continuous assaults in Ceuta and Melilla, this kind of very hard and urgent phenomenon could be a reason to deploy this unit which just comes out of the blue. It was an exceptional situation that we did not have any pre-warning of. My interpretation is that the Rapid Border Intervention Teams could have been deployed in that case.

Q275 Lord Harrison: Could you just say about Portugal, for instance, in November?
General Laitinen: Yes, certainly. Frontex's role is of course to maintain this emergency instrument called Rapid Border Intervention Teams. We have compiled experts from the Member States based on certain criteria, certain profiles and what kind of expertise is needed. There is an organogram with organisations for that purpose. Now we are at the stage where we have to test that the procedure that is written both in the so-called Rapid Border Intervention Teams Regulation and also Frontex's Regulation, that we have understood it in the same way and test that the system goes as planned. Another element is the practical exercise. It has been prepared for a couple of events before but the first time when the experts meet teach other will take place in early November in Portugal when we will see how these practical things, identification issues and the different kinds of practical things which relate to the deployment on that will be tested. Perhaps Sakari Vuorensola, our Legal Adviser, could say an additional word because this is really his favourite topic.
Mr Vuorensola: Thank you very much. Since you asked how RABIT activities would change the nature of Frontex operations, there is one very important aspect which has now changed because of the new Regulation and that is the use of executive powers. Until the RABIT Regulation came into force all the powers that our guest officers in joint operations had were based on the national law of the host Member State and the possibility of that national law to delegate executive powers to foreigners doing the job, which is usually reserved only to their own national border guards: checking persons, asking for identification and doing other border controlling tasks.

Q276 Chairman: And carrying arms.
Mr Vuorensola: And carrying arms, for example, and using force. The RABIT Regulation makes a considerable change here because, as you know, the Community Regulation has direct effect; it is directly binding and supersedes national law. This Regulation now says that RABIT team members as well as guest officers in our normal joint operations on the basis of this Community piece of legislation now have executive powers, all executive powers that are necessary to fulfil the so-called Schengen borders code, which is the codification of the actions done by the border control activities. It also gives the right to carry a service weapon and to use it in the case of self-defence or certain limited other cases in the use of force, but in this last case the national law is also involved. This is a very important development in Community law that for the first time we have

Community Regulation saying that foreign officers have certain powers in another country.

Q277 *Lord Harrison:* This is such an important point, my Lord Chairman, perhaps I could just come back on it briefly. This is something that would excite the eurosceptic press enormously back in the United Kingdom, the idea of foreigners toting guns and so on and so forth. Has it been an anxiety expressed by other countries? Is it something that you are dealing with?

General Laitinen: Bear in mind it was only in July when this particular Regulation and amendment came into force and there have not been too many operations so far where we have applied these European executive power rules. So far we have received no negative feedback on these issues. From the co-ordinator's point of view it is a very good thing that we can train and practise with our staff and experts in a very similar way instead of learning 27 different national rules of what is possible in one country and what is strictly forbidden, what you must do and must not do and things like that. This amendment was very warmly welcomed by us as co-ordinator.

Q278 *Lord Jopling:* How many people are going to be involved in the Portuguese exercise? How long will it last? Will it just be a desk operation or will you deploy them on a scenario which you have manufactured in order to have the exercise?

General Laitinen: I would prefer to give a written contribution.

Lord Jopling: I would be very grateful if you would.

Q279 *Chairman:* General Laitinen, we are fast approaching four o'clock. Can I ask you the last question which is of considerable importance to us, and that is the British position, the rather anomalous British position if I can put it that way? What disadvantages for you come from this rather special position of Britain's relationship with Frontex, leaving aside the fact that we do not have voting rights? Does it create problems for you and, if so, what sort of problems? As a supplementary to that, could I just mention the word Gibraltar.

General Laitinen: I am not going to start with Gibraltar. I would prefer to start with the issues. To be honest, there are two types of challenges with the specific role of the United Kingdom vis-à-vis

Frontex. They are both operational and financial. We do not have certainty on the UK contribution for the forthcoming years as to what will be their financial contribution. There are no clear rules upon which these financial contributions can be based. There is agreement on that but no clear rules, so there is a question mark. There are a lot of legal issues in different stages of planning and implementing joint operations where we have to use a tailor made instrument for having a way out. Involvement of the Management Board for the particular operations is certainly somewhat different with the overall level of decisions of the Management Board. It has to take a decision on a case-by-case basis on a particular country's participation in a particular operation. This requires not only an additional administrative burden for the agency but also for the Member States who have to respond to these issues. We have to apply a lot of these exceptions and keep them in mind. We come across these kinds of issues with the particular and specific role of the United Kingdom vis-à-vis Schengen and Frontex too. I do not have any particular points to say about Gibraltar.

Chairman: I quite understand.

Lord Young of Norwood Green: Very wise.

Lord Teverson: My Lord Chairman, if I can just make a request. I think there is a number of other issues that have come up from this morning and I just wondered whether it might be possible that if there were other questions of a sensible length we could write to Frontex and ask for written replies.

Chairman: Certainly, through the Chairman.

Lord Teverson: Indeed, absolutely.

Chairman: Related to that, there are one or two points which you very kindly said you would follow up in writing. We will send you a full record of this session and, when looking at that, you are free to suggest amendments or corrections, but most particularly could you have a look at it and consider whether there is anything supplementary which would be useful for us to have in writing. May I thank you very warmly for your reception today. You have been extremely helpful, and it was also a very nice lunch. I thank you and your colleagues very much for the time you have spared for us and for the very helpful evidence you have given us which will, I hope, in due course, sadly not under my chairmanship— sadly for me—but under my successor chairman, be extremely valuable for the report which I hope will emerge sometime in the spring when the sun is shining. Thank you very much indeed.

Supplementary written evidence by Frontex

1. STAFFING QUESTION

The Earl of Listowel asked whether the staffing difficulties referred to by the Executive Director in oral evidence had had a knock-on effect within Frontex headquarters in terms of the quality of management, mentoring and supervision. The short answer is that there has been no perceived diminution in the management functions of the Agency due to a large extent to the excellent quality and pioneering spirit of the original staff, including managers, posted to Warsaw in October 2005. This pioneering spirit of the staff was a positive aspect referred to by the Executive Director in his oral evidence.

The Earl of Listowel also asked for details of retention and sick rates as possible indicators of motivation and morale of the Frontex staff. The following statistics are available:

(i) *No of resignations from offered positions (interviewed and offered jobs)*

During the period 2006–2007, 28% of candidates offered a job in Frontex resigned. Among them 8% were Poles and 20% were foreigners. The high percentage of resignations among Contract Agents (CAs) in 2007 (50%) may be due to the fact that employees working under this type of contract are not well paid compared to Temporary Agents (TAs). Moreover, the contracts for TAs are of 3 years duration with 9 months probationary period, whilst TAs are offered 5 year contracts with a 6 months probationary period.

Year	No of posts to be occupied	Resignations Polish nationalities	Resignations expats
2006 Resignations from offered posts	8%	4%	4%
2007 Resignations from offered CA posts	50%	19%	31%
Resignations from offered TA posts	13%	0%	13%
Resignations from offered posts (TA and CA) in 2007	28%	8%	20%

(ii) *Frontex staff—average number of days on sick leave per person*

Average number of days on sick leave per person for the last two years did not exceed 1.7 day per person. Excluded are two persons who were seriously sick during that period.

	Average Number of Days on Sick Leave per Person
X–XII 2005	0.32
2006	1.63
I–IX 2007	1.05

(iii) *Retention of Frontex staff*

For the period of 2006 and 2007 the retention rate was always higher than 92% (table prepared for Seconded National Experts and other staff separately)

Type of agent	Retention rate
TA, CA, AUX 2006	97%
TA, CA, AUX 2007	98%
SNE 2006	92%
SNE 2007	97%
Total	96%

TA = temporary agent; CA = contract agent; AUX = auxiliary staff; SNE = seconded national expert

2. RABIT QUESTION

Lord Jopling sought details of the first RABIT exercise. The first RABIT exercise took place between 5 and 9 November 2007 at Sa Carneiro airport, Porto, Portugal comprising a total of 16 border guards from 16 Member States divided into three teams. The main objectives of the exercise were:

— to test the new mechanism in real circumstances;

— to test the administrative procedures necessary for deployment within the time limits mentioned in the RABIT Regulation (in close cooperation with host and all other participating Member States);

— to deal with operational challenges (national expert pools, list of permissible weapons, databases, etc.) and open questions in advance of real missions; and

— to further develop the management of RABITs within Frontex.

3. NUMBER OF STAFF EMPLOYED IN THE TRAINING UNIT

The Executive Director undertook to provide the exact number of staff currently working in the Training Unit at Frontex Headquarters. The figure is 9.

4. UK POSITION IN RELATION TO ITS PARTICIPATION IN FRONTEX ACTIVITIES

A number of members of the Committee indicated that they would welcome further written details concerning the current UK position in general and comments on possible Frontex participation in the Olympics 2012 in particular.

In respect of the UK position, the Advocate General (AG) in Case C-77/05, *UK v. Council*, has concluded on 10 July 2007 that the Frontex Regulation is a measure relating to the external borders and closely linked to the abolition of internal borders, an area in which the UK does not participate. Therefore, the UK cannot have a right to fully participate in the Frontex Regulation and in the activities of Frontex. The Advocate General advises the Court to dismiss the UK application and to conclude that the Frontex Regulation does not apply to the UK in the way that the UK argues.

There is no legal obligation for the Court to follow the advice of the Advocate General. The Court, nevertheless, often follows the advice of the Advocate General, but this is not automatic. The final Court ruling is still likely to take another couple of months.

Frontex has received signals from the UK that a Court ruling following the AG's opinion could have implication for the way in which that Member State wishes to participate within the framework of Frontex activities.

As an important consequence, a Court ruling upholding the UK's exclusion from Frontex would confirm also the UK's exclusion from Regulation (EC) No 863/2007 (the RABIT Regulation).

The amendments to the Frontex Regulation by Regulation (EC) No 863/2007 also have importance consequences for the UK's participation in Frontex activities. Both RABIT team members and guest officers in Frontex activities have now been endowed with certain tasks and executive powers, which would not be available to participating UK border guards. Furthermore, the questions related to possible liabilities of the UK border guards participating in Frontex operations, both in RABIT teams and in joint operations/pilot projects, would be unclear.

The main practical implication of the UK not being able to participate fully in the Frontex Regulation and in its activities is that operations and projects mounted by the Agency cannot, as a rule, take place within UK territory. Operations that do take place within the UK, therefore, must be construed as separate UK operations, albeit it is possible for them to be planned, organised and executed in parallel with the respective Frontex operations. In this case, Frontex can facilitate cooperation and coordination of two such different operations. Frontex cannot, however, finance and reimburse the costs of activities that take place within the territory of the UK or Ireland and which are part of such separate operations.

It is open to Frontex to propose the participation of the UK in Frontex operations, ie operations where UK officers or assets would be deployed in Frontex operations taking place within the Schengen territory or at its borders. For each operation where UK participation is proposed, the operational plan must set out justification as to how such participation would contribute to the success of the activity concerned, and the Management Board of Frontex must give its acceptance on a case-by-case basis by simplified written procedure under Article 20(5) of the Regulation. Where the proposed participation is approved, the UK has the right to be reimbursed for its costs in accordance with normal Frontex rules and practices.

In respect of the specific question as to whether Frontex could become involved in the Olympics 2012 being hosted in London, on the assumption that available intelligence nearer the time shows a need for such an EU-wide operation and given that the current UK position remains the same, it is probable that the type of parallel joint operations, mounted in both Schengen and non-Schengen territory/borders (described above), would be an appropriate solution.

It is desirable that the UK would be willing to continue supporting Frontex activities in different forms. Over the last two years it has played an active role in Frontex' activities and has contributed financially to these activities. It has also committed various items of technical equipment—three heartbeat detectors, 12 CO_2 probes and one Passive Millimeter Wave Imager (PMMWI)—to the Central Record of Available Technical Equipment (CRATE), which are at the disposal of Frontex for its joint operations.

In view of Article 12 of the Frontex regulation, which states that the Agency shall facilitate operational cooperation of the Member States with Ireland and the United Kingdom, and in view of the Council declaration inviting Frontex to explore ways in which the United Kingdom can practically support the operations of Rapid Border Intervention Teams, Frontex remains ready to accommodate any possible participation of the UK as well as Ireland.

Compiled by Graham Leese and approved by Ilkka Laitinen, Executive Director

12 November 2007

TUESDAY 23 OCTOBER 2007

Present   Harrison, L.   Teverson, L.
               Henig, B.   Wright of Richmond, L. (Chairman)
               Jopling, L.   Young of Norwood Green, L.
               Listowel, E.

Examination of Witness

Witness: Mr Soufiane Adjali, Senior Liaison Officer to Frontex, UNHCR, examined.

Q280 *Chairman:* Can I open the meeting by thanking you very much indeed for receiving us at rather short notice. We have spent much of today with Frontex, with the Director and his colleagues. There was not very much discussion about UNHCR, so it is very helpful for us if you can give us as much detail as you can about your relationship with Frontex, where the respective responsibilities fall, how far you are involved in risk analysis, the other parts of Frontex's operations, and really anything you want to tell us. This is part of a House of Lords Committee inquiry into Frontex. As we have just said between us, this conversation will be recorded but if at any point you want to go off the record please feel free to do so. As I explained to you, it is helpful for us to have evidence on the record for the purpose of our inquiry. We will send you any transcript of this meeting for you to comment on, correct or amend as you wish.
Mr Adjali: Thank you. First of all, I would like to introduce myself. I am Soufiane Adjali. I have served the Office of the United Nations High Commissioner for Refugees (UNHCR) for many years and I have served in many part of in the world, in the Middle East, in Africa, in the Balkans, and now I am serving here as Senior Liaison Officer to Frontex since July 2007. The specificity of this position is to work toward the establishment of a formal co-operation agreement with Frontex. We are still at the initial phase of getting to know each other, as organisations. However, we have already a first draft Agreement for Co-operation on the desk of our Assistant High Commissioner for Protection and this week or next week, we will be sharing it with Frontex.

Q281 *Chairman:* This will be what, a formal agreement?
Mr Adjali: A Formal co-operation. In fact, we call it an Agreement for Co-operation.

Q282 *Chairman:* I see.
Mr Adjali: This will enable both Organisations, in particular UNHCR to include protection safeguards in border management. That is our key objective.

Q283 *Chairman:* As Liaison Officer do you attend Management Board meetings?

Mr Adjali: No. UNHCR does not attend and it is not even foreseen in the draft formal co-operation agreement. In the Regulation establishing Frontex, we are not mentioned except in Article 13 which authorises Frontex to establish formal relations with UNHCR and any other organisations, including third countries.

Q284 *Chairman:* Since you have taken up this position have there been any particular refugee problems affecting Frontex's operations?
Mr Adjali: It is complex because at the moment UNHCR does not have a formal co-operation. In the future, we will be sitting and discussing protection benchmarks and safeguards to be included in Frontex Operations. At this stage, I will always refer to the UNHCR Ten Point Plan of Action, which sets the right approach when there is a situation of mixed migratory flows. This is a working protection document, which is still being developed and which we use in situations of mixed migration flows.

Q285 *Chairman:* Thank you very much. Incidentally, any of you who want to weigh in please do if you can catch my eye. I see that item two is data collection and analysis. Again, I entirely accept what you say about being rather new to this role but so far how far have you been involved in the risk analysis operation?
Mr Adjali: (The answer was given off the record)

Q286 *Chairman:* Can we go back on the record and ask you to describe to us the respective relationships between you and Frontex and the IOM and Frontex?
Mr Adjali: Recently the European Commission has called for a meeting with Frontex, IOM and UNHCR. At this stage we are still talking about the way in which each organisation could have an input in the Frontex Sea Operations. Of course, UNHCR will have a protection input based on the Ten Point Plan of Action.

Q287 *Chairman:* Do IOM have a liaison officer like you in Warsaw?
Mr Adjali: At this stage, there is no-one in Warsaw from IOM.

Q288 Lord Teverson: Could I just ask how you came to be here? Did UNHCR see Frontex was operating, this was important and, therefore, you decided to come here and have a relationship with them, or did they consult with UNHCR and that meant you came here? How does it work?

Mr Adjali: There were several High Level Meetings between UNHCR and FRONTEX prior my deployment as a Liaison Officer. However, usually asylum seekers have to cross the borders of their country to seek asylum. Frontex which stands for Frontières Extérieures—External Borders, is in charge of EU Borders' Management, therefore, anything linked to the entry points and borders are relevant and important to UNHCR. Because a border is the first place where a person can express her or himself and indicate that s/he is seeking asylum. It is only after that their status will be determined accordingly as a Refugee or not.

Q289 Chairman: We had some discussion at Frontex about a rescue at sea and the difficulty of disembarkation. Again, these are early days but how far are you able to help Frontex decide who being disembarked is a refugee, who is an asylum seeker, although that is probably quite obvious when they seek asylum? Would you be involved in this sort of decision-making?

Mr Adjali: It is at too early a stage to speak about the decision-making. Clearly rescue at sea is an important issue. I do not think we could determine if a person at sea, is a refugee or not. There is a need to disembark them in safe port, where you may have a professional team, who will identify irregular migrants.

Q290 Chairman: And judge who they are.

Mr Adjali: It is an initial step and then after we get into the refugee status determination process. When you see the "vessels" people are using on the high seas, for people who are navigators—you come from a country of great navigators—there is a custom of solidarity at sea and when we see 200 people in a really small wooden boat on high seas, I believe that it is necessary to rescue them and disembark them.

Q291 Chairman: I am sorry, I will give the floor to anybody else in a moment. Have you yet been associated with a Frontex operation?

Mr Adjali: As UNHCR?

Q292 Chairman: Yes.

Mr Adjali: No, not yet. In the future, let us say, it will be on a case-by-case approach. Co-operation at this stage is very much to be formalised..

Chairman: I am sorry, I have been rather monopolising the discussion.

Q293 Baroness Henig: You have not been concerned with any particular operation but I notice in your ten point plan you say you are concerned about the strain on a number of Member States and you single out in particular Malta and Cyprus. Given that has been something we have been looking at, and we have certainly heard from a European Member of Parliament from Malta about the particular problems, is that something you will be talking to Frontex about? This is an area that we have been exploring today about the extent to which burden sharing is a reality and how Frontex can operate in that kind of area.

Mr Adjali: Without being specific on countries, we will be talking about everything.

Q294 Baroness Henig: But some things more than others.

Mr Adjali: Everything, on all the borders, sea, land and air borders. With borders like airports, land borders, initially it is always something that the media are not attracted to, but when it comes to the sea everybody is watching. There are countries that are on the way and, of course, these are entry points and protection is important. Countries are bound by international instruments and then by regional instruments. When you are bound by an international obligation, and Frontex is made by countries, Frontex is obliged, like the countries that have established it, to respect international law.

Q295 Lord Young of Norwood Green: I just want to make sure I understood you. When you talk about mixed migration I presume you mean what you refer to as asylum seekers or there might be refugees. Is that what embraces mixed migration?

Mr Adjali: Yes. Mixed migration includes persons who could be economic migrants but also asylum seekers, who could become refugees and other persons of concern to UNHCR. By Mixed flows, we mean that we cannot be 100% sure that they are all illegal migrants—economic migrants.

Q296 Lord Young of Norwood Green: You do not make any distinction between whether they might be legal or illegal?

Mr Adjali: (The answer was given off the record)

Q297 Chairman: Tomorrow we are visiting the Ukrainian border. While you have been here have you had experience of refugee movement from the Ukraine to Poland?

Mr Adjali: Recently in media reports and UNHCR Poland is working on this case. If I am correct it is about a family movement from the Ukraine through Poland to Slovakia, a Chechen lady and her 4 kids whom 3 died during the movement.

Q298 *Chairman:* Yes.
Mr Adjali: I am not working on Poland. My focus is Frontex.

Q299 *Earl of Listowel:* The proceedings today began by the leader of Frontex saying very clearly that human rights affects everything they do. I suppose that Frontex offers the opportunity to really raise the standards of border guards and particularly their understanding of what human rights are, so I imagine that is something that pleases you. I was certainly very concerned to learn that there are very high expectations on Frontex and there seems to be a tension between their delivering the high quality input and training, for instance, that they provide and getting involved in the nitty-gritty, getting involved in the operational work which is so important to small states. I wonder whether you have had time yet to think what the UNHCR position is on this. Is UNHCR keen to see that Frontex does the very important foundational work of raising standards across the board or is UNHCR keen to see Frontex getting very much involved in operational matters? You have only just recently started but do you see the tension there to a degree?
Mr Adjali: In fact, Frontex has invited UNHCR to work with their working group in charge of drafting the Common Core Curriculum for border guards. We have been invited and have had the right to provide relevant inputs in terms of international refugee law and international human rights standards. UNHCR has contributed and will continue to contribute. It is a process. Throughout life we learn and I hope that the border guards will continue in their career to learn relevant aspects of Refugee Law and Human Rights. Training is part of the co-operation. We want to establish appropriate training workshops for personnel involved in Frontex operations.

Q300 *Chairman:* Related to that, and perhaps this is going to be included in the agreement, do you see UNHCR as having a monitoring role, monitoring Frontex co-ordinated operations?
Mr Adjali: If you look at Article 35 of the 1951 Convention we do have a supervisory role in the implementation of the Convention. As I said, it is an EU agency created by different states so we still have a role in each member state to supervise the implementation of the 1951 Convention. Of course, we are not supervising Frontex but we are working on establishing a formal relationship which could help us contribute to bring higher protection standards in border management.

Q301 *Baroness Henig:* I just wondered whether UNHCR was concerned about migrants being intercepted in the Mediterranean and returned to

Libya, which I understand is one of the problem issues.
Mr Adjali: (The answer was given off the record)

Q302 *Baroness Henig:* I thought you might say that, particularly in view of what you have just said about your monitoring role.
Mr Adjali: (The answer was given off the record)

Q303 *Lord Jopling:* I used to be part of the OSCE years ago and as one who has admired your organisation over the years, coming from spending the day with Frontex here and seeing that they list the UNHCR among the very many groups with which they have co-operation, and looking through these papers, I find virtually no mention of Frontex. I have found Frontex mentioned twice, but there may be more. Listening to what you said earlier, and it will not be long before you have been here for six months, how often do you meet them? How often do you meet them officially? I am not talking about privately. How often do you have meetings with them and how often do you get involved in their decision taking? Forgive me, it does seem to me that you are somewhat detached from that and whether that is your policy or their policy I really would not know. It would be helpful to know a little more closely what the connection is.
Mr Adjali: I have been here two months precisely.

Q304 *Lord Jopling:* I thought you said you came in July.
Mr Adjali: Yes, July, two months. I prepared a meeting in September where Frontex participated which was a side event to the executive committee of UNHCR. We are meeting regularly. We are not involved in the decision-making process of Frontex. On the basis of Article 13 of the Regulation that established Frontex, we are going to formalise our co-operation. Clearly we are meeting on a regular basis to identify areas of cooperation. We are at the initial stage and we are trying to see where we could co-operate, what our inputs could be. We are contributing to the Core Curriculum for border guards, as I mentioned. These are strategic inputs and I hope this will continue in the sense it is always protection sensitive and in respect of the principle of *non-refoulement*.

Q305 *Chairman:* You are the first formal Liaison Officer with Frontex?
Mr Adjali: Yes.

Q306 *Earl of Listowel:* Do you recognise that Member States co-operate voluntarily with Frontex? Is that correct? I believe it is correct. Do you see the danger that if expectations are raised too high on what Frontex can deliver and disappointment arises from that then the possibilities that Frontex offers in terms of raising the quality of a border guard's performance and the humanity with which it is delivered are lost? Do you see that as a concern?

Mr Adjali: I cannot speak in the name of Frontex or the EU.

Q307 *Earl of Listowel:* That is fair enough.

Mr Adjali: One point that I did not answer was in relation to the fact that there is not much reference to Frontex in our documents. It is really a Protection working document that we are developing. As long as we do not have any formal relationships we do not put many references in but rather explore possible areas of cooperation, interlocutors and players.

Q308 *Lord Young of Norwood Green:* I was looking at point two of your ten point action plan on data collection and analysis, and there does seem to be a community of interest on one point where you say: "UNHCR will advocate for the creation of harmonised data collection systems so that reliable data on migration (including asylum, trafficking et cetera) are available and can facilitate analysis of and responses to migration trends". That is something that may not be exactly in those terms but in their risk analysis management that is the sort of information that Frontex will be using. Do you see any community of interest there?

Mr Adjali: (The answer was given off the record)

Q309 *Lord Young of Norwood Green:* Can you enlighten my ignorance here. Can you translate "*refoulement*"? What does it mean?

Mr Adjali: It means if you arrive at the border and you say, "I am not willing to return to my country of origin, I want to seek asylum" and the authority says, "You are denied access" you just go back" or, "You are not going to enter", they send you back to a country where this person might be at risk of being persecution.

Q310 *Lord Young of Norwood Green:* So sending them back is *refoulement*?

Mr Adjali: Yes. I am being very, very basic here. It is simply a person being denied access to all the legal procedures and sent back to his country of origin or place of habitual residence where he might face persecution. It is Article 33(1) of the 1951 Convention which defines the Principle of non-refoulement. This Article is known to all UNHCR protection officers.

Q311 *Chairman:* Mr Adjali, you have been extremely helpful. Thank you very much. I fully accept you are very new in the job but you have been very frank with us, both on and off the record. I really am very grateful to you for having received us because it is an important part of the Frontex picture.

Mr Adjali: We are in the process of building something and it is important when it is about borders that UNHCR is present, but it has to be present within a legal framework and we are working towards that.

Q312 *Chairman:* When do you expect that framework to be finished?

Mr Adjali: It has to be shared first with Frontex and then we will see.

Q313 *Chairman:* Of course. Thank you very much indeed.

Mr Adjali: You are welcome.

WEDNESDAY 24 OCTOBER 2007

Present   Harrison, L.   Teverson, L.
           Henig, B.   Wright of Richmond, L. (Chairman)
           Jopling, L.   Young of Norwood Green, L.

Examination of Witnesses

Witnesses: COLONEL ANDRZEJ MACKIEWICZ, DEPUTY COMMANDER WOJCIECH WOŁOCH, CAPTAIN MONIKA PARSZEWSKA, MAJOR STANISŁAW ZELENT, and CAPTAIN PIOTR SAWICKI, members of the Nadbużański Border Guard Regional Unit, examined.

Q314 Chairman: Good morning.

Mr Wołoch: (Through an interpreter) Good morning. I would like to welcome all of you here to the sector of the Nadbużański Border Guard Regional Unit based in Chelm. We are at the border guard post at Dorohusk. First, let me introduce myself and at the same time I would like to apologise on behalf of my Commander who could not be here to take part in this visit. Unfortunately, at this very moment a burial ceremony has just started. This is the burial of the Commander of this particular border guard post. He died last Sunday and it was a tragic death. I am Deputy Commander of the Nadbużański Border Guard Regional Unit. My name is Wojciech Wołoch. I have been the Deputy Commander for almost two years. I would like to propose the following timetable: the first part will take place here where there will be a multimedia presentation of the whole regional unit and then a presentation of the border guard post at Dorohusk. I hope that during the short presentations you will have a chance to become acquainted with some general information on our regional unit and our border guard post at Dorohusk. Of course, this is only a general description of the unit. If you have any questions do not hesitate to ask. After the first part I would like to suggest going out to do a sightseeing tour so you can become acquainted with the border crossing point at Dorohusk. You will become acquainted with the general organisation of duties and with the first and second lines of control. We will be in the Schengen area quite soon and the level of our preparation for accession to the Schengen countries is almost complete. It will be better to show you that and then answer all the questions you may possibly have. Then I would like to suggest going to lunch, which will be in Chelm, and the headquarters of our unit are also based in Chelm. Do you have any proposals or remarks of your own as far as this timetable is concerned?

Q315 Chairman: Deputy Commander, can I first of all thank you very much indeed for receiving us today. On behalf of all my Committee and my colleagues, can I express our condolences on the death of your Commander. Would you please convey our condolences to the General as well? I will not introduce all of my colleagues because you have already greeted them, but we are very pleased to be here. We are much looking forward to hearing what you have to tell us about the work of the frontier guard. As you probably know, we are here as a sub-committee of the House of Lords in London and our interest is an inquiry which we are doing into Frontex. We have also very recently completed an inquiry into the Schengen Information System SIS II so, apart from wanting to hear from you anything you have to say to us about Frontex and your relationship with Frontex and the impact that Frontex has on your work, we would be very interested also to hear what you expect to be the impact of joining Schengen. Our primary interest is Frontex so we would very much like to know what impact Frontex has on your work and, indeed, what advantages or even disadvantages Frontex might have on the work of the frontier guard. Having said that, your proposed programme sounds excellent to me, it is exactly what we want. I suggest if you are ready that we continue with the programme.

Mr Wołoch: We will start with the presentation because some of your questions may be answered. Later on we will talk about Frontex and answer your questions.

Q316 Chairman: Thank you very much.

Mr Wołoch: Before we start I would like to introduce some border guards who will participate in this visit. Of course, you know Mr Director, Colonel Mackiewicz. This is Major Zelent and he is Deputy Head of the Border Management Department. He is responsible for the border management of the whole border sector protected by our regional unit.

Ms Parszewska: I am Captain Monika Parszewska. I am a specialist in the presidential department and I will make you acquainted with the presentation. Today I also act in the capacity of interpreter, so forgive any possible mistakes, I only use English occasionally.

24 *October 2007*   Colonel Andrzej Mackiewicz, Deputy Commander Wojciech Wołoch,
Captain Monika Parszewska, Major Stanisław Zelent
and Captain Piotr Sawicki

Q317 *Chairman:* We congratulate you.

Ms Parszewska: Thank you.

Mr Wołoch: This is Captain Sawicki. He is the leader of the Border Duty Group and he is from the border guard post. We will start with the presentation on the regional unit.

Ms Parszewska: Some information on the Nadbużański Border Guard Regional Unit which is based in Chelm. As you know, Poland borders upon seven countries, as you can see from the map. The length of the whole border is more than 3,500km, including the external border of the European Union which is more than 1,500km. The border that is protected by our border guard regional unit is almost 500km long. This is something about our regional unit and the structure of the Polish Border Guard. We have 12 regional units in the Polish Border Guard. As you can see, unit headquarters is based in Chelm. We have training centres based in Koszalin and Ketrzyn for training border guards. We have a training centre for dogs in service and that is based in Luban.

Q318 *Chairman:* Can I ask a quick question because I noticed in the first slide you described the border guard as a division of the Home Army. Are you interchangeable with the Army or do you join the border guard and stay with the border guard for life?

Mr Wołoch: It is only a matter of tradition, of conferring names upon regional units. The 27th Volhynia Division of the Home Army took part in battles during the Second World War. It took part in battles in the framework of some underground activities and in the war in this particular area. As far as the organisation of the Polish Border Guard is concerned, we are a border police. It is only due to some historical memory that we remember such divisions.

Q319 *Chairman:* Thank you very much. I apologise for interfering.

Mr Mackiewicz: (Through an interpreter) One more bit of information I would like to add is that in case of war or the state of war, it is the Army that takes responsibility for the protection of the border.

Q320 *Chairman:* Thank you very much, that is very clear.

Ms Parszewska: As of 1 May 2004 we joined the European Union and at the same time the border protected by our unit became the European Union external border section. The length of the protected border section, as I have already mentioned, is almost 5,00km long, with Belarus 171km and with the Ukraine 296km. Most of it is the River Bug and it is almost 400km long. We have also the land border on the southern section and it is almost 70km long. As you can see, there are 17 border guard posts that are subordinated to our regional unit. The ones that are marked with a green square are responsible for both border surveillance and border traffic control. Those marked with a yellow circle are responsible for border surveillance. These are the border crossing points. On the Polish-Belarussian border sector and on the—route—to Brzesc there are border crossing points protected by the Border Guard Post in Terespol. In Terespol there are two border crossing points, one is for passenger traffic and there is also a railway border crossing point. There is also a car terminal at Koroszczyn for lorries, along with the border crossing point in Kukuryki. Moreover, at the Polish-Belarussian border there is the Sławatycze-Domaczewo border crossing point for passenger traffic.

Chairman: I am sorry, I do not want to ask questions which you are going to answer later but could I just be clear, are these crossing points the only places where you could actually cross the border or are there bridges which are not protected by the border guard?

Ms Parszewska: Only the border sector with Belarus?

Q321 *Chairman:* Between those points are there other bridges where a car could cross and which you have to patrol?

Mr Wołoch: As I have already mentioned, these are the only border crossing points on the border sector with Belarus. In-between the two border guard posts there are other border guard posts responsible only for border surveillance, so it is not possible to cross the border, there are no bridges, it is the green border.

Q322 *Chairman:* Thank you very much.

Ms Parszewska: Now we have the border sector between Poland and the Ukraine. Starting from the north, as you can see, there is the border crossing point where we are right now, Dorohusk. There is a crossing point for passenger cars and for lorries. There is also a railway border crossing point here. The next one is Hrubieszów. There is a railway border crossing point on the route to Włodzimierz-Wołynski. The last border crossing point subordinated to our Regional Unit is in Hrebenne. In Hrebenne there is a road border crossing point for lorries and passenger cars and there is a railway border crossing.

Q323 *Lord Jopling:* Can I ask a question now. Following my Lord Chairman's question, how many crossing points are there both over the river and over the land border further south which are not permanently manned?

Mr Wołoch: All border crossing points are open 24 hours so it is possible to cross at any time.

Lord Jopling: I did not mean that. Are there any other ways of crossing the river apart from here?

Lord Young of Norwood Green: Unofficial, illegal?

Q324 *Lord Harrison:* Unmanned.

Mr Mackiewicz: It is impossible.

Mr Wołoch: There are no such points. There are no temporary border crossings.

Q325 *Lord Harrison:* Are there not old roads and bridges which exist? Are there not old roads which existed before?

Mr Wołoch: As far as the border sector on the River Bug is concerned, in practice at each place where there is a border bridge there is a border crossing point at the same time, so there are no additional bridges that are unused. On the land border there are roads, roads leading directly to the border, but it is not possible to cross the border at such places, apart from some special situations when the chief border delegates may issue a permit to cross the border at some other place apart from the border crossing points, but special permission is required. Of course, the persons, who on the basis of such a permit, will cross the border at such a place, will undergo a routine border check and these are very rare situations, usually relating to some regional religious ceremonies.

Q326 *Chairman:* Do you have no problem with smugglers trying to get across the river at points where you do not have a frontier guard?

Mr Wołoch: Of course there is such a threat and there have been cases of attempts to smuggle goods. In further slides there will be some information relating to smuggling. There have been cases of illegal immigration and smuggling of contraband, not only at border crossing points but also in-between. For example, last month three illegal immigrants were apprehended when trying to cross the border from Ukraine to Poland. It was not at a border crossing point but at the green border. I would like to stop the presentation for a minute. The signal that you hear is to commemorate the Commander who has died. (One minute's silence was observed) Thank you. I would like to go back to the previous slide. The squares are used to mark the border crossing points and the circles are the border guard posts used for border surveillance, for protection of the green border. I would like to explain some things on illegal immigration and related things will be discussed later. Cross-border crime may be encountered both at the green border and at border crossing points. As far as illegal immigration is concerned, at border crossing points it is mainly forgery of documents and attempts to avoid border checks. I would like to add that as far as the checks of trucks and lorries are concerned, in previous years there were cases of people trying to cross the border illegally hiding in trucks, and not only trucks but in vans and smaller vehicles.

Q327 *Chairman:* Could I just ask, on the other side of the border are there Belarus and Ukrainian posts opposite all your frontier posts? Do you find co-operation with the Belarus and Ukrainian authorities is good?

Mr Wołoch: As far as co-operation is concerned, that will be discussed later on because there are some slides relating to that. Of course, there are some border guard posts on the opposite side and each border guard post has its counterpart on the other side.

Q328 *Chairman:* That was what I wanted to know.

Mr Wołoch: You must remember that in the past it used to be the border with the Soviet Union. It is worth mentioning here that the number of border guard posts on the opposite side is even bigger than here and this especially refers to the Belarussian sector.

Q329 *Chairman:* Thank you.

Mr Wołoch: Going back to the attempts of the smuggling of people, there are no such attempts in vehicles right now. At all border crossing points that are designed for cargo we have special equipment which is an x-ray and all the vehicles are checked. There is equipment such as Heimann, which is also a kind of x-ray. The Heimann is used to check all the lorries that have customs seals and you cannot open them. We have also heartbeat detectors for detection of heart beating in closed spaces. In practice, since the installation of such equipment at border crossing points, there have been no attempts at illegal immigration in vehicles but, of course, it sometimes happens at the green border. As an example, three immigrants were caught last time. As far as smuggling of goods is concerned, not long ago during a weekend we stopped cigarettes that were smuggled across the River Bug.

Q330 *Chairman:* What do you do if you find an illegal immigrant in a truck? Are they sent back?

Mr Wołoch: There is a procedure when an immigrant is caught and some papers have to be prepared. When the procedure is completed, they are sent back to the country they illegally came from.

Q331 *Chairman:* I am sorry, I keep interrupting, but if somebody applies for asylum at the border what do you do?

Mr Wołoch. If the apprehended immigrant does not apply for a refugee status, after having completed the procedure relating to illegal border crossing, they are sent back to the country they illegally came from. If such a person applies for a refugee status, the procedure is instituted concerning granting the refugee status. However, such cases are not numerous as far as people are concerned who have already crossed the border. It mostly refers to people who are not entitled to cross the border but they reach the border crossing point and at the crossing point itself they apply for refugee status before even crossing the border. These are mostly citizens of Russian Federation of Chechen origin.

Q332 *Lord Harrison:* Before we move on, could I ask about the trains. Do the trains stop and do you get on board to check them, or are they checked by passport control and border control whilst they are moving over the border?

Mr Wołoch: There is a border station used for such checks of trains and their passengers. There are special control teams and they search for cargo hidden in compartments. There are also some control teams to deal with passport checks.

Q333 *Chairman:* But the train has to stop?

Mr Wołoch: Yes. At each border crossing point. At the same time, when the train stops, passport control is carried out, and also customs control and radiometric control. At all border crossing points there are radiometric gates installed and that applies to the railway and road border crossing points. Apart from that, members of the control teams have special mobile equipment for detection of documents forgery and radioactive materials.

Q334 *Chairman:* Do you use dogs?

Mr Wołoch: Yes, of course. The dogs we have here on duty are specially trained to detect persons, drugs, weapons, ammunition and explosives. We also have some sniffer dogs and patrol and attack dogs.

Ms Parszewska: I will continue.

Q335 *Chairman:* I am sorry, we make your work very slow.

Ms Parszewska: That is not a problem. You have already asked about illegal immigration and here you can see some information on the main threats at the border section protected by our unit. As you can see, the first threat is the migration of nationals of Asian and ex-Soviet Union countries. There is also the smuggling of goods and these are mostly cigarettes.

Sometimes it is alcohol, but in a small amount. In terms of smuggling of works of art, narcotics and weapons—they are smuggled to Poland and to the West. Members of criminal groups come from the East to Poland. Smuggling of stolen vehicles—takes place from Western countries and Poland to the East.

Q336 *Chairman:* How much information do you have here about, for instance, stolen vehicles? Are you informed by someone that vehicles have been stolen and you are asked to look out for them?

Mr Wołoch: As far as stolen vehicles are concerned, the control of vehicles takes place at several different levels. This information is included on IT databases and we have access to all information concerning stolen vehicles that are searched for. The next stage is to verify the documentation for the vehicle in respect of forgery and control of identification features of a particular vehicle and, of course, operational materials we have at our disposal because we are entitled to carry out some operational activities. For example, I would like to tell you that in 2006 402 stolen vehicles were seized and in the first half of this year 146 vehicles.

Q337 *Chairman:* Were they all Polish vehicles or were some of them coming from elsewhere?

Mr Wołoch: These are vehicles that were stolen in the whole of Europe, but not only Europe. Sometimes these are vehicles stolen in the United States and they reach Europe on a ferry and in the framework of transit they go to the Ukraine.

Q338 *Chairman:* Thank you very much.

Ms Parszewska: I have some statistics and you can see the performance of statutory duties. This is some information about the refugees from Chechnya because they constitute a special problem at the border with Belarus. As you can see, in 2006 more than 3,000 persons of Chechen origin applied for refugee status and in 2005 more than 4,600.

Mr Wołoch: I would like to stop here for a moment. In the last four years we have observed a decrease in illegal immigration at the border sector with the Ukraine. In spite of the fact that it is still high, it is much lower than four years ago. This year we have started to note that there is an increase in illegal immigration at the border sector with Belarus. Of course, the general proportions are to the disadvantage of Ukraine, as there are bigger numbers of illegals at this border sector. However, this year, and in particular in the second half of this year, there has been a significant increase in illegal immigration at the Belarussian border sector.

Q339 Chairman: Can I ask, have you or the Ukrainian or Belarus authorities been able to identify any of the people smugglers, the people actually sending these illegal immigrants across the border?
Mr Wołoch: Of course we have. Speaking of illegal immigration, I think mostly of organised illegal immigration. There have been cases of individual border crossing but the main threat is the organised illegal immigration that is conducted by organised groups. We pay most attention to the detection of organisers of such illegal immigration and we want to send them to the prosecutor. I would like to show you an example which happened one and a half months ago when we managed to detect a smuggling channel. During a month we apprehended two groups and these were nationals of China. One group included ten persons and the other one 18. In the framework of the operational and investigation work we also apprehended 12 organisers and facilitators from different levels of cross-border criminal groups, not only at the border itself but also inside the country, those who, in a way, commissioned such illegal border crossings. They were at the top of the criminal hierarchy. At this moment there are some penal proceedings under way.

Q340 Lord Harrison: How did you do that, because you caught the ten and 18 coming through and then you caught 12 organisers? What are the mechanisms to trace it back to the real criminals who are organising these groups coming through? Did you interrogate them here? Did you interrogate them very hard?
Mr Wołoch: There are different methods. These are mostly reconnaissance activities. We try to get some information first on the criminal groups. The Polish Border Guard, just as the police, is statutorily entitled to carry out such reconnaissance activities and, of course, we interrogate witnesses, illegal immigrants and facilitators. You asked about the interrogation and it is not such hard interrogation, theses are routine activities. No physical impact is used because I understand that it is what you meant in your question.

Q341 Chairman: We congratulate you, this was obviously a very successful operation, but can you comment at all both on the co-operation you received from the Belarus or Ukrainian authorities and, secondly, and nearer to the subject of our inquiry, is Frontex involved in these operations? If so, how?
Mr Wołoch: As far as co-operation with neighbouring countries is concerned, we will talk about that later but I would like to tell you something about co-operation with Frontex. I would like to add one sentence concerning the co-operation with border authorities protecting the border on the opposite side. Such co-operation is conducted on an ongoing basis but at this moment it should be underlined that co-operation with the Ukraine is more open and dynamic in comparison with the co-operation with Belarus. One factor that may have an influence on this kind of co-operation is that the border authorities protecting the border sector on the Ukrainian side are more like a police formation and in Belarus it is more like the Army.

Q342 Chairman: And Frontex?
Mr Wołoch: Of course, the co-operation with Frontex keeps on evolving each month. One operation took place not long ago and soon another will take place here. During the last operation conducted with Frontex we had guests from other European Union Member States here, eight guest officers who stayed at this particular border guard post. In my opinion, co-operation with Frontex is a very good and positive aspect of border protection. We have been engaged in several common operations with Frontex. What is important as far as such co-operation with Frontex is concerned is that the exchange of information is very positive, it takes place fast and the information exchange is very precise.

Q343 Chairman: That is very helpful. Is it fair to ask if our friend, the Colonel, wants to add any comment on this?
Mr Mackiewicz: Yes, of course. As far as co-operation with Frontex is concerned, at the level of headquarters of the Polish Border Guard it is a more strategic one and as far as some operations are concerned, in order to decide which border guard unit shall participate, there is joint acceptance required from both the Border Management Department and the Bureau of International Co-operation. This concerns land, sea and air borders. This is directed at the countries where there is an increased level of risk. There is an exchange of officials from different authorities and they are interchanged between different authorities involved.
Chairman: Colonel, thank you very much. I apologise to the Deputy Commander.

Q344 Lord Jopling: Can I ask another question and it is a question which I understand it is impossible to give a precise answer to. Looking at those figures, about a quarter of the people you apprehended were on the green border and that presumably includes the terrestrial border south in the mountains. Could you make an estimate of how many illegals are coming across this border whom you do not apprehend because we have had a problem in Northern Ireland

24 October 2007   Colonel Andrzej Mackiewicz, Deputy Commander Wojciech Wołoch,
Captain Monika Parszewska, Major Stanisław Zelent
and Captain Piotr Sawicki

and we understand that it is impossible to stop migration across terrestrial borders in particular? Could you make an estimate of how heavy is the inflow of illegal immigrants into the EU across this border?

Mr Wołoch: Of course, as you have already said, it is very, very difficult to precisely estimate such figures but I would like to underline one thing: the border guard conducts checks and control activities at different levels and there are different stages involved and that is why we have some notion of the numbers of illegals who were not apprehended at the border. The first line of control is the border. The second line are activities in the border zone and also inside the country, so hotels and other places are checked where illegal immigrants may gather or may be kept. At the second stage we can make some estimate as far as numbers are concerned but, of course, this is not the full percentage because to the whole figure the numbers of illegals should be added, the illegals who are apprehended at the internal European Union border. In order to get such figures we must add the numbers of illegals who manage to cross the border and stay at hotels and other places, and the number of persons stopped at the border with Germany, the Czech Republic and Slovakia. At this moment it is difficult for me to say what the exact percentage is because such analyses are conducted here as far as the regional unit is concerned, so the information will not be complete because it is up to the HQ to make such analyses. At our border sector we estimate that it is between several and a dozen or so percentage.

Q345 *Chairman:* Deputy Commander, I am particularly guilty of having interrupted your presentation but I think it is time really to discipline myself and my colleagues to allow you to get on with the presentation. My apologies.

Mr Mackiewicz: I have something else to say about illegal immigration. Sometimes people cross the border to Poland legally and then they become illegal immigrants.

Q346 *Chairman:* Overstayers.

Mr Mackiewicz: Because they try to reach other countries of the European Union and Great Britain as well. We have had such cases of that. It happened in 2006 when illegals used Polish identity cards and travelled on a bus to Great Britain.

Mr Wołoch: It should be underlined that the exact percentage is impossible to be given, for example, because some channels of illegal immigration could have operated before. During several months of an investigation and elimination of the migration the percentage will vary, from a dozen or so percent to several percent, because in a given year we may not

know such a channel of illegal immigration existed so we do not take such figures into account. That is why it is really, really difficult to estimate such a percentage. On the examples I have already provided, for example at the border with Belarus, it is difficult to say whether these were the first cases of smuggling of people. During the preparatory proceedings we found evidence that there were at least two cases of illegal immigration that were successful for the organisers. That is why it is very difficult to tell you the exact percentage.

Ms Parszewska: We have talked about illegal immigration. If you are interested in the main nationalities, these are mainly nationals of Moldova, Georgia, Vietnam, Russia and Pakistan. This is data from 2006.

Q347 *Chairman:* Will you be able to let us have copies of these slides?

Mr Wołoch: Yes.

Ms Parszewska: These are graphs representing the numbers of persons apprehended for breaching the legal borders. Here you can see what happened in previous years at the border with Ukraine, which is the green colour, and the border with Belarus, which is the yellow colour. The numbers of the apprehended on the border with Belarus are much smaller. This is more information about the apprehended persons. 18% of them were apprehended for attempting to cross or crossing the state border illegally. The 82% remaining were apprehended for other crimes and offences. These are mostly for organising and assisting in illegal border crossing or attempting to leave Poland in a stolen vehicle or smuggling goods. This is information on passenger border traffic. As you can see, there was a decrease in numbers in 2004 when we joined the European Union. Of course, one of the reasons was the visa requirement that was introduced but then each year gradually the numbers have increased. In 2006 12 million passengers crossed the border. Here you can see some numbers as far as particular border crossing points are concerned. As you can see, the biggest number of travellers crossed the border in Terespol. At Dorohusk more than three million passengers were cleared last year. This is some information on the foreigners who were denied entry into the territory of Poland. There were more than 22,000 of them in 2006. They were mainly refused entry because they did not have the financial means to cover their stay here, they did not have a valid visa or their purpose for entry was other than their declared one. These are two slides about co-operation with the border protection services of Ukraine and Belarus. As you can see, the Commander of the Nadbużański Border Guard Regional Unit has his counterpart in Brest, this is the

Commander of the Brest Unit of the Belarussian Border Forces. In Ukraine there are two units, one is based in Luck and the other one is based in Lvov. Our Commander co-operates with the heads of the Luck and Lvov units of the Ukrainian State Border Service. In Dorohusk there is a consultation point and you will have a chance to see that later on. It started to operate in—December 2004 and there is a similar one in Krakowiec. This is mostly for the exchange of information.

Q348 *Chairman:* Can I just ask, at a personal level do you communicate in Russian with Ukraine and Belarus?

Ms Parszewska: Yes. The proposal now is to shorten the discussion. I will not present the whole of the presentation but only general information as you will have it on the CD, which I have got here. We need some time to go around and do some sightseeing, and lunch is waiting as well.

Q349 *Chairman:* I promise not to ask you another question!

Mr Wołoch: Unfortunately we have some technical problems but there are only a few slides left. They concern the equipment that we use for border checks and border surveillance but we will see such equipment outside. There is also a slide with service dogs, which we have already discussed. Just to supplement some information, I would like to say that we have 47 dogs in service. We also have aircraft. There is one plane and two helicopters. This is a short summary of what has been left in the presentation. They are used for border surveillance and equipped with infrared equipment. There is special equipment at the border guard posts, mobile equipment for border surveillance and infrared equipment. As far as the presentations are concerned you will have them on the CD. You can see the details later on. It is difficult to discuss all of that here because we are short of time and sometimes equipment can fail us.

Chairman: Human beings are much more reliable.

Lord Teverson: It is the Microsoft world conspiracy!

Chairman: Thank you very much.

THURSDAY 25 OCTOBER 2007

Present	Harrison, L.	Teverson, L.
	Henig, B.	Wright of Richmond, L. (Chairman)
	Jopling, L.	Young of Norwood Green, L.
	Listowel, E.	

Examination of Witnesses

Witnesses: MR WIESLAW TARKA, Under-Secretary of State, MS MALGORZATA KUTYLA, Director for International Co-operation and the EU, Ministry for the Interior and Administration, and BRIGADIER GENERAL MIROSLAW KUSMIERCZAK, Commander-in-Chief of the Polish Border Guard, examined.

Q351 Chairman: Good morning. Thank you for meeting us this morning.

Mr Tarka: Welcome to the Ministry of the Interior and Administration. As I understand we have a very limited period of time because today I am leaving for our German/Polish Commission in Wroclaw in the west of Poland, so unfortunately I can only offer you half an hour. I think that is sufficient time to touch on the most essential problems that may be of interest to you. I know that you visited the border crossing point at Dorohusk yesterday and I hope that was interesting as it is at the eastern border of Poland to the Ukraine and very soon it will be the outer border of the Schengen area, most probably from 21 December this year. I think it would be of interest if I give you a very brief introduction to the Ministry itself and then I will talk about our management of the external border, that is the external border of Poland, the European Union and, as I said, from 21 December the outer border of the Schengen area. As you know, the Ministry of the Interior and Administration is the largest ministry in Poland, being responsible for the border guard, police, government security, fire services, administration, computer development, informatics, registers, passports, ID cards and so on. I know that you do not have ID cards in England but we have a long tradition of ID cards. Everything is within the Ministry of the Interior. As we have the border guard, I would like to present the head of the Polish Border Guard, General Miroslaw Kusmierczak, who is responsible for the border guard that we are very proud of because it is a unit that is relatively young, more or less 15 years old. It is very modern and very well organised, providing security not only for Poland but in the future for the entire European Union being within the Schengen area. Our border became the external border of the European Union from 1 May 2004. The line of our external eastern border is 1,185km. It is one of the longest sections of land frontier guarded by a single Member State. As far as the eastern border, we compete with Finland. Finland has a long border but, as you know, their location on the map is slightly different, they are

further up on the map. In the central section of Europe this is definitely the longest border. We bear responsibility for providing all Member States with a high level of security against threats from unwanted persons or goods and in order to do so we have developed a clear and effective border management system. I have the honour to be the head of the inter-ministerial Group on the management of the state border because at the border we do not only have border guards responsible for border traffic but we have customs services as well under the Ministry of Finance, or the Chancellor of the Exchequer in your terms, and we have some services that are with the Ministry of Agriculture and Rural Development and so on. I will give you a short insight into the list of ministries represented on the inter-ministerial group and you will know who is participating in the border management and who is present at the border. It is our Ministry, of course, chairing this group, then we have the Ministries of Finance, Economy, Defence, Environment, Treasury, Foreign Affairs, Agriculture and Rural Development, Transport and Health. We have the secretary of the Committee for European Integration as we have many European funds that have been received by Poland in order to develop the infrastructure at the border. We have the head of the customs service, the chief commander of the border guards, the chief commander of police and head of the office of foreigners, or aliens' office, the office responsible for migratory affairs in Poland. The task of this group includes the preparation of state border management programmes, the principles for financing by the respective bodies, and providing opinion on the initiation of activities concerning the organisation and maintenance of border crossings and the conditions to perform effective operational border control, customs, sanitary, veterinary, phytosanitary, chemical and radiometric services, the co-ordination of co-operation of central and regional, national authorities within the scope of state border management, and providing opinion on the initiation of activities to improve the conditions of the border crossing service for persons, goods and vehicles. The main document for us is the so-called

25 October 2007   Mr Wieslaw Tarka, Ms Malgorzata Kutyla
                      and Brigadier General Miroslaw Kusmierczak

Integrated Border Management Programme that we have launched for 2007–13 developed by our Ministry headed in the Department by Ms Kutyla, who is here, who is the head of the Department for European Union and International Affairs. This document provides strategic goals and priorities for the new Financial Perspective 2007–13. It is no coincidence that those two terms overlap. It regards problems such as investment in border infrastructure and the enhancement of inter-agency co-operation systems. Priorities set out by the programme correspond with the priorities of both Polish and European strategic documents, especially such European programmes as the External Border Fund that you can find in the strategic guidelines. You probably heard of this at the border at Dorohusk, that the Polish law clearly identifies the administrative authorities responsible for maintenance and investment at the border crossing points. Two years ago we cleared a system and now the representative of the government's administration in the Voivod region is entirely responsible for all border crossing points on the river, land, railway and so on. The Voivod is responsible for the maintenance of border crossing points and conditions to perform all of those controls that are needed. It is responsible for planning and carrying out investments at border crossing points and is responsible for construction of new border crossing points. As I said, we have the Chief of the Polish Border Guard here. The border guard is an armed, uniformed and fully professional service that is responsible for border surveillance and control. The Polish Border Guard organisational and structural capabilities and equipment are entirely in line with the Schengen requirements and appropriate to the future task. Border control of goods that enter the international market is performed by several national services, like the customs service under the Ministry of Finance, veterinary inspection, the state plant and seed inspection service, the state sanitary inspection and agricultural and food safety inspection. The supportive role in all of those matters is carried out by the police in areas such as combating cross-border and organised crime. I have to add as well that approaching the date of entry of Poland into the Schengen area, some time ago we changed the law of the border guard so the border guard has the right to act not only within the border strip or close to the border but on the entire surface of the country, so it means that the border police are the second police service in Poland that can be active over the entire territory of the country. To leave some time for possible questions from your side, because I think that will be the most important and interesting part of our meeting, I will briefly mention the efforts that we have been making in order to improve the border

crossing point standards to facilitate and secure this movement. This year Voivod has spent approximately €43 million for the border infrastructure. Moreover, we have an ongoing Programme of modernisation of Police, Border Guard and State Fire Services and the Government Protection Bureau for 2007–09 that was passed by our parliament in January of this year and this programme allocates an additional €246 million for border guard infrastructure and equipment. We are raising money from several foreign funds as well to enhance border management, for example the Schengen facility, the Norwegian financial mechanism. At the present moment there are three new border crossing points that have been built. At the Polish-Russian border with the Kaliningrad district we have a very special border crossing point there at Grzechutki. It is next to the Augustuv channel where there is a river border crossing point at the border with Belarus, a very special tourist initiative. A similar project is Bialowieza, a road border crossing point, but it is only for pedestrians and bicycles. That is very important because it is in the middle of the forest and it has to meet the very high architectural and environmental criteria required in this national park. 14 border crossing points have been enlarged and modernised recently. At the border with the Ukraine we are planning four further new road crossing points: Dolnobyczow-Uhrynow, Zboreze-Adamczuki, that is for the Voivod Lublin region, Malhowice-Nizankowice and Budomierz-Hruszew, which is the Subcarpathian Voivod to the south-east of Poland. All of those projects I have mentioned are additional ones. We think the essential infrastructure as far as border crossing points are concerned is already there and we have to effectively use the infrastructure that is already in place but organised better. We will see how the flows of goods and persons will look after the entry of Poland to the Schengen area when the Polish outer border will be at the same time the outer border of the Schengen area. I have been talkative and used the majority of our time, but not too much so we have some minutes left for your questions. Please feel free to ask questions of me or my colleagues.

Q352 Chairman: Minister, thank you very much indeed. Given the shortage of time available to you, I will not introduce all my colleagues. We are all members of a House of Lords sub-committee and we are conducting an inquiry into Frontex. Can I thank you very much for receiving us in your busy life, for sparing us half an hour. Is it impertinent of me to greet you as another ex-diplomat? I think we are probably the only two ex-diplomats in the room. It is very nice to meet you, thank you very much for receiving us. If I may, I will start with a question or

25 October 2007 Mr Wieslaw Tarka, Ms Malgorzata Kutyla
and Brigadier General Miroslaw Kusmierczak

two, but I hope that the General will be happy to continue to answer our questions after you have to leave. That depends on the General's programme. Minister, could I ask you to tell us what you regard as the main threats across your border, both land, sea and air? In your priorities, where are the threats facing Poland?

Mr Tarka: I am participating in discussions within the European Union on the borders and at the present moment we have a very heavy accent put on the southern border where there are problems in the western part of the Mediterranean area between Italy and Libya. At the present time we do not have a threat to the eastern border of the European Union on the Polish section or Finnish or Baltic sections. The major threat is if we forget and we think it is given for all time and take it for granted that there will not be any threat in the future. The major threat is if we sleep now and do not think of possible scenarios in the future. The situation is under control now and the economic situation to the east of the Polish border in the entire area is improving, so it is diminishing the pressure on the external European border but it is not forever, not for all time. Even today we have to pay attention to possible medium and long-term risk analysis. We have to maintain the infrastructure and reserve funds for the eastern border as well, not only to think unilaterally of the southern border which is really in the short-term and a known problem. I would say that is the problem.

Q353 *Chairman:* That is very helpful. Can I ask a second question, and that is the subject of our inquiry is Frontex. Is there anything you can tell us about the relationship between your Ministry and Frontex and the extent to which you are finding Frontex helpful or unhelpful, but I hope helpful, in the frontier guard activities?

Mr Tarka: We are very proud to have Frontex here in Poland. Their location here, some 200km from the eastern border of the European Union and very soon from the eastern border of the Schengen area because Belarus is 200km from here, the Polish-Belarussian border, is symbolic and very important. It is the first agency that has been located in one of the new Member States and we are very proud of it. At the same time, from the beginning we have been very keen to preserve and respect the status of this agency because it is a European agency, not a Polish one. We have to support and create an environment for the good functioning of this agency but without interfering too much in internal problems. We have given a starting package to this agency, 18 months for the building, and we are paying for this. We have raised funds and bought about 35 working places, computers and equipment, furniture and so on, as a starting package. In the long-term we do not think

that we should contribute in a special way financially because we are a member of the European Union, so we are funding this via the European Union as a whole. Our philosophy was to create and support the agency but at the same time the agency is responsible for itself, it is an independent agency. They have to build their future on their own because they are adults, it is an adult institution, but we understand at the very beginning it can be difficult. The situation with Frontex was complicated because, on the one hand, it was a new agency in a period of organisation and growth and, on the other hand, there were tasks put on its shoulders from the very beginning. It was very difficult to start to work immediately while at the same time building up the structure. I hope the agency has got over this period. We have helped as much as possible, I have had good contact with General Laitinen, but at the same time we were very clear from the beginning that apart from the starting package it is a European agency that must regard itself as a European agency and find solutions within the European framework.

Q354 *Chairman:* Do you envisage concluding a long-term status agreement with them?

Mr Tarka: Yes. We have signed something called the Memorandum of Understanding because the protocol immunities between Poland the European Union are already in place that not every member country has. We think we should avoid duplication of many regulations. Even if we sign a first, second or third agreement but do not use it, it is not worth anything. From the very beginning our position has been that we wanted the agency to realise and use the law that is already in place. In the beginning there was a little bit of a misunderstanding because we felt that instead of creating new law you should first use the law that is in place. For us, the existing law, the protocol of immunities that we have signed with the European Union regulating practically all areas, was enough. As there was a repeated requested from Frontex to sign a possible Memorandum of Understanding we have done it but for us it is confirmation of rights that were already there.

Chairman: Thank you very much. Minister, if you have got a few minutes perhaps I could ask Lord Harrison to ask a question.

Q355 *Lord Harrison:* Minister, would you take our best wishes to the people of Wroclaw when you get there today. I was very pleased to meet the deputy mayor and minister for tourism earlier this year in London. Poland will soon be responsible for a large part of the external EU border to the east, how do you assess the level of trust that other EU countries invest in Poland accomplishing this task? Has the fact of Frontex coming into existence strengthened the level of trust that we place in you to do this job well?

Mr Tarka: Thank you very much for that question. The answer is quite complex. The security of the Polish section of the border is our national responsibility. I do not think that anyone in Europe can think that we value our own security less than European security, or the other way around. Polish security and European security, the security of the future enlarged Schengen area, is the same. We are protecting our external borders in the interests of Poland in particular but in the interests of Europe as well. Frontex is one of the elements and it is a European agency, so it is not only responsible for Poland but from our perspective it is responsible globally in European terms. We are very proud of our border guard because it was built from scratch. You probably know that the old Communist countries were guarding the western border because tourists came to the west, not to the east. According to this principle, the responsibility at our eastern border was on the Soviet side, not on our side. It was a disadvantage at the very beginning but after it was to our advantage because we could build it from scratch, from nothing. We think that we have done it very well. I hope you have seen the infrastructure at Dorohusk, which is not the largest and most modern of border crossing points. In March of this year we opened a newly modernised border crossing point at Hrebenne at the border with Ukraine and the international connection between Warsaw and Kiev. It is one of the major European transportation corridors. We have very good infrastructure in place. We have a very good service and very motivated border guards. We are not just proud of our border guard outside of Poland but at the same time it is a question of information and if you take the latest reports after the evaluation of our borders we are very proud of that.

Chairman: Minister, I should have said earlier, if I may, without being impertinent that I think you have every reason to be proud of your frontier guard. We were given an extremely good programme yesterday and visited the frontier guard at the border and we were very impressed by everything that we saw.

Q356 *Lord Jopling:* Minister, I hope you will allow me to be frank. The impression I have got from listening to you over the last half an hour is that you are justifiably proud of your existing border guards and you are glad to have Frontex based in Warsaw, but what I have not heard is how you believe that Frontex can make things better. Looking at the six tasks which are laid down in the Union's Regulation setting up Frontex, will you tell us over the next ten years or so how you think things could be made better for you in Poland as a result of the activities of

Frontex, because that is what we are inquiring into? With great respect to you, I have not really heard from you any specific things that you think you can benefit from by the activities of Frontex.

Mr Tarka: Thank you for that question. I thought that I had answered it indirectly but I will repeat it. As I understood our discussion here it was about the national responsibility prior to the enlargement of the Schengen area and our national responsibility for border security. Of course, the security of the Polish border as a part of the European external border is another question because it is another framework, it is the European perspective, not the national one. If you ask me, I would need an hour to approach the question in a general way. I would like just to signal two items here. I think it is a real value-added for us and especially for countries that are smaller than Poland, because Poland is a member of the G6 group, as is the UK, and we have already had our first presidency in this group and Jacqui Smith in support last week. For Poland, but especially for smaller countries where the ability for risk analysis, strength analysis, is limited it may be of real value-added, the competence and knowledge on a global scale that a separate state cannot do. That is one thing. The second thing is what is happening now on the southern border of the European Union where if it is needed you can act quickly. At the moment it is not needed at the Polish eastern border for the reasons I gave, because the situation is stabilised, but that may not be forever. If, in the future, there is a similar threat—we do not think it is immediate or medium-term but perhaps long-term—a similar situation to that in the Mediterranean area, there could be a need for quick action. That is the second thing. I will add a third, which is the strengthening co-operation between border guards and the training of personnel according to the same rules and standards, that we speak the same language and our way of thinking is becoming closer and closer. It remains a national responsibility but we have a platform so we can become even closer.

Chairman: Minister, that is very helpful. If you have got another minute or two can I give the last question to Lady Henig.

Q357 *Baroness Henig:* You have told us how Poland has taken steps to comply with Schengen, and I was very interested in all the preparations you have made and money you have spent, and that is extremely impressive. I wondered what broadly your views were on the Schengen System, ie seeing that developing with Poland as a member running that frontier.

Mr Tarka: In what terms?

Q358 *Baroness Henig:* What are your views on the Schengen System?

Mr Tarka: I am chairing a Polish-Lithuanian cross-border co-operation committee and two weeks ago we had a meeting in the north-eastern city of Augustuv and on that occasion I visited the border crossing point between Poland and Lithuania. Soon it will be the internal border but at present it is the outer border and the SISoneforall has functioned there from 12 September. I was impressed how the SIS System is working there. When they are checking the documents, it is a very practical and very simple thing to check ID cards or passports and it is reacting within one second. We are very grateful to Portugal for giving us this solution. The system is functioning well. We know that it is temporary and we are preparing for SIS II. Yesterday in our parliament I was discussing with our MPs the possible solution that will bridge if there are further delays to SIS II. You need a legal bridge for SIS NET. Everything is temporary. I am very grateful to Portugal, the system is working well and we have already had more than 1,000 hits on the system since 12 September, so it is evidence that the system is working well and it is bearing fruit for us.

Q359 *Chairman:* Minister, when I was head of the Foreign Office in London I once received an ambassador, who will be nameless, and I counted that he said "finally" five times. I wonder if I can just say "finally" for the last time. Have you got anything you want to say to us about the rather special position of Britain vis-à-vis Schengen? Does it impinge on your interests at all?
Mr Tarka: I would not like to in any way interfere in the United Kingdom's internal affairs.

Q360 *Chairman:* Oh, pity!
Mr Tarka: I think we live in a more and more globalised world and at the time of the Internet, of other electronic penetration and so on, the traditional ways of securing internal security are not enough and they are really out of date. On the security of Europe as a whole, speaking of Joe Scarborough, he used to say it is impossible to be pregnant 50%, half-way pregnant; you are pregnant or not. It is the same with Schengen. If you participate in the system entirely then you have the legal basis and can exchange documents, data and so on. You can find a halfway solution for the short-term but in the long-term you are in the system or you are not. Being in the system we hope that we will have a good experience as we have done so far with Schengen. In this co-operation we have already seen that the only way to actively and in an effective way combat organised crime and international criminality is to do it together and not separately. Thank you very much.

Q361 *Chairman:* Minister, thank you very much indeed.
Mr Tarka: Thank you. I wish you all the best for your stay in Warsaw.

Q362 *Chairman:* That is very kind of you. Thank you. General, can I repeat my thanks for the programme we were given yesterday. Also, can I repeat my condolences about the loss of your Commander in Dorohusk. If you are happy I wonder if you would answer a few questions, particularly about Frontex, because that is the subject of our inquiry. As the overall Commander of the frontier guard, could you just give us some idea of how far you regard Frontex as helpful, what are your relations with Frontex and anything you want to say about that aspect of your work.
Brigadier General Kusmierczak: (Through an interpreter) Thank you for your condolences on the death of the Commander in Dorohusk, which was an unexpected event and we were shocked by this.

Q363 *Chairman:* I am very sorry.
Brigadier General Kusmierczak: As far as our co-operation with Frontex is concerned, we are participating in the activity of Frontex on the external borders. We have already participated in more than ten such actions on external borders. We are preparing to do two such operations on the Ukrainian-Romanian border and Ukrainian-Hungarian border. As far as these two actions are concerned, they are going to take place at the end of October. The first action at the Ukrainian-Romanian border will concern traffic control. The other action on the Ukrainian-Hungarian border will concern illegal migration, so the green border crossing. We have appointed about 20 border guard officers to participate in the RABIT groups. Also we have search equipment and two helicopters, cameras and night visors, so if need be we are ready to delegate our specialists to participate in those operations where needed. Those who will be delegated speak English better than me so there will be no communication problems.

Q364 *Chairman:* Through your interpreter, if I may say so you speak English perfectly.
Brigadier General Kusmierczak: Of course, I can also communicate with the French or Germans in English; it is no problem!

Q365 *Chairman:* I think you can. Monsieur Giscard used to communicate with Helmut Schmidt in English and if Monsieur Giscard could do it I think you can.
Brigadier General Kusmierczak: But not on such serious matters.

Chairman: General, I wonder if I could ask Lord Teverson to ask a question.

Q366 *Lord Teverson:* General, can I congratulate you on what I thought was the extremely professional operation that we saw yesterday. What we were particularly interested in was the trust between your own border guard and those of neighbouring countries, in your instance particularly Belarus and Ukraine. We were pleased to meet a Ukrainian border guard who was stationed at Dorohusk. How does that work and does co-operation across the border work well? Are trust levels good? Is that continuing to develop successfully?

Brigadier General Kusmierczak: Under the last evaluation on the border with Ukraine our co-operation with Ukraine was satisfactory but those relations have become a little bit more difficult after some remarks made by an EU expert from Estonia about our co-operation with Ukraine. This expert said that as far as the two border crossings are concerned the co-operation is too close. There is an example of one border crossing in Zosin where we made some border checks on one side and Polish functionaries were making checks on the Ukrainian side and vice versa, which meant that Ukrainian functionaries made controls on the Polish side. There is no regulation as such either in the Schengen code or in other regulations indicating where these checks should be made, if they should be made on the one side or the other side of the border. As far as the Polish-German border is concerned, this is a good example where Polish Border Guards were realising checks on the German side and vice versa. It was not an obstacle for Germany to enter the Schengen area. We changed the checking rules in Zosin and began to realise checks only on our side which made the co-operation a little colder.

Q367 *Chairman:* The Minister said to us, quite understandably, that you regarded the checks on your frontier as being particularly in the interest of Poland but also in the interest of the whole Schengen area, and that will particularly apply when we become full members of Schengen. To what extent do your Ukrainian and Belarus colleagues see your frontier guard operations as in your mutual interest, as much in the interest of Ukraine and Belarus as they are in the interest of Poland?

Brigadier General Kusmierczak: The incident I cited had no influence on the overall security of the Schengen area and the Belarussian and Ukrainian services are aware of the fact that this is the security of the whole Schengen area and the third countries are also responsible for the control on counteracting illegal migration. Our co-operation with the Ukraine

as far as counteracting and fighting illegal migration is becoming better and better.

Ms Kutyla: (Through an interpreter) I would like to mention two important elements concerning our co-operation with Ukraine. It is good because for more than ten years we have been supporting Ukrainian efforts to gain EU funds and those funds will be transferred to finance border infrastructure on the Ukrainian side and the Ukraine will benefit from some programmes which will allow investment in the area of equipment for border guards. Also, Ukrainian border guards are involved in some twinning programmes which allow them to learn how Polish know-how could be used in their case.

Q368 *Chairman:* Is this an area where Frontex can be of help?

Ms Kutyla: From the financial point of view it is more complicated because there are some financial regulations which mean that we are working on programmes that were approved two or three years ago by the European Commission. This perspective allows us to think only of these programmes. As far as Belarus and Ukraine are concerned, we cannot compare the co-operation with those two countries because it is rather different. With Belarus we are taking into consideration the political situation, so political talks are not involved with this country. As far as Ukraine is concerned, the situation concerns the fact that after our accession to the Schengen area we had this problem of fees for visas to be paid. We are expecting the agreement between the EU and the Ukraine to be signed this year because it will have an impact on the fee which will not be €35 but €60.

Chairman: General, I know your time is very limited and you have to leave soon but could I ask Lord Jopling to ask our last question.

Q369 *Lord Jopling:* Coming back to Frontex, you have recently participated, as we understand, in Operation Ariadne. I wonder if you could tell us what lessons you have learnt from that and how, as a result of Ariandne, you would like to see Frontex developing their activities in the light of those lessons learnt?

Brigadier General Kusmierczak: This operation that was carried out on the Ukrainian-Polish-Belarussian border was aimed at detecting illegal migration, document counterfeiting and detecting people transported illegally. As far as the phenomenon observed on those borders we can say the phenomenon of illegal transportation of people is more frequent on the Polish western border than on the eastern border where illegal crossing is made with the help of false documents or with authentic documents but issued under another name. We would really like to exchange our experience concerning the fighting of illegal migration and document counterfeiting, so every opportunity for us to share this with other border guards is important. We are really interested in repeating this kind of operation on our borders because it can only help us to check our know-how, ability and skills.

Q370 *Chairman:* General, thank you very much indeed. I am very grateful to you for sparing time for us this morning. It has been a great experience for this Committee to see what the frontier guard are doing. Although the main topic of our inquiry is Frontex, nevertheless it has been very important for us both to see on the ground yesterday what you are doing and to hear from you today. On behalf of all my colleagues, can I thank you very much indeed.

Brigadier General Kusmierczak: It was a great pleasure for me to present our activities and methods of fighting the most important threats, and among those threats the illegal migration.

Chairman: I would also like to express, through you, our thanks to the Colonel for the help he has given us, and for his company which we have much enjoyed. Thank you very much indeed.

WEDNESDAY 28 NOVEMBER 2007

Present	Dear, L	Marlesford, L
	Harrison, L	Mawson, L
	Henig, B	Tonge, B
	Hodgson of Astley Abbotts, L	Teverson, L
	Jopling, L	

Memorandum by Malta High Commission

GENERAL

1. This document has been prepared by the Armed Forces of Malta (AFM) in response to the Call for Evidence issued by the Sub-Committee in caption in regard to an inquiry into Frontex, the European Agency for the Management of Operational Cooperation at the External Borders of the EU Member States. The views and opinions therein are derived from the institutional knowledge and experience of the AFM and are thus a fusion of the inputs from various individuals involved in operational and technical cooperation with Frontex.

AIM

2. The aim of this document is to provide responses to a number of questions raised in the said Call for Evidence. Only those questions which directiy regard areas of competence of the AFM have been addressed. The responses address matters at the operational and strategic level as it is deemed that responses at the political level are not within the purview of this organisation.

Responses are being provided to the following points:

— The legal framework for border guards' exercise of control and surveillance powers in the course of Frontex operations.

— Whether and how international obligations with regard to search and rescue at sea affect the Agency.

— Whether it is practical to retain a distinction at operational level between preventing irregular migration and preventing crime.

— Whether there is sufficient cooperation from Member States in terms of personnel and equipment for joint operations.

— The extent of Frontex involvement in surveillance operations.

— How Frontex joint operations are planned and mounted.

— How Frontex joint operations are mortitored and the outcomes evaluated.

— Whether there is, or should be, any involvement of, or assistance from, the military in Frontex operations.

— How the Agency's role should develop in the future.

INSTITUTIONAL BACKGROUND

3. In order to provide a deeper understanding of the responses given, it is appropriate to understand the character and roles of the AFM in regard to border control. The AFM is the national military force in Malta with an establishment of 2,050 personnel. In addition to the primary role of the maintenance of the security and integrity of Maltese territory in peace time and in crisis, the AFM also fulfils a number of "soft-security" roles which in many other States are undertaken by police or para-military organisations. Given that the AFM is also the sole national agency which disposes of significant coastal surveillance, maritime and air assets, many of these toles are associated with the maritime area.

4. Notable among these and relevant to the discussion in question are the following responsibilities:
— The AFM is the Competent Authority for Maritime and Aeronautical Search and Rescue (SAR).
— All surveillance of Malta's Blue Borders including a 12NM band of territorial sea and a 24NM Contiguous Zone.
— Providing maritime law enforcement services in regard to traffic safety, illegal trafficking, fisheries and anti- and counter-terrorism.
— The provision of coastal maritime traffic control and safety communications.

5. All these activities are underpinned by local legislation empowering members of the AFM to act in these roles. Most notable among this legislation is Subsidiary Legislation 220.06 which accords Police and Customs powers to members of the AFM in the fulfillment of their duties. It is of note, however, that eventual investigative and prosecution actions are taken by the Police. Thus the involvement of the AFM is very much limited to the operational aspects of preventing and controlling illegal migration. It is against this background that the responses to the points indicated in paragraph 2 above are provided.

RESPONSES

6. The legal framework for border guards' exercise of control and surveillance powers in the course of Frontex operations. When operating in the maritime arena, activities are limited by the constraints imposed by the applicable body of formal international law, international customary law and domestic legal provisions. Beginning from the innermost jurisdictional zone, the internal waters of a coastal state ie those waters enclosed by the baseline, these are deemed equivalent to the land territory of the state and thus the latter may assert full jurisdiction including arrest for illegal entry. Within the territorial seas which extend 12 nautical miles from the baseline, jurisdiction is limited by the doctrine of innocent passage which, however, is intended to prevent interference with legitimate coastal traffic and is not a right which must automatically be accorded to a stateless vessel transporting migrants. On the other hand no obligation exists to prevent the passage of such. Thus within this zone the coastal state can continue to exert substantial control and, should this be acceptable under its domestic law, may grant the exercise of such control to the assets of third states. It should be noted that the internal waters and territorial seas of a state are deemed to exist *ipso facto* and do not require any declaration on the part of the coastal state. Furthermore, surveillance within these zones may only be conducted by the coastal state or other authorised parties. The furthest reaching jurisdictional zone relevant to border control tasks that may exist, subject to declaration by the coastal state, is the contiguous zone that may extend up to 24NM from the baselines. Within this zone the coastal state may exercise the control necessary to prevent and punish infringement of *inter alia* immigration laws committed within its territory or territorial seas. Third parties may conduct surveillance activities within this zone without the consent of the coastal state.

7. Actions on the high seas present a more difficult legal scenario. While it is generally accepted that any vessel may exert jurisdiction *vis-a-vis* a stateless vessel, what is less clear is whether such actions are provided for in the national legislation of the state from which the enforcing vessel hails. Furthermore, it is also generally recognized that any actions are subject to the principle of proportionality and undertaken with the aim to arrest the vessel and its occupants. Thus actually using any level of force to constrain a migrant vessel to alter course or return to its port of departure has at best only a very tenuous legal basis.

8. Whether and how international obligations with regard to search and rescue at sea affect the Agency. Search and Rescue (SAR) does not fall within the competency of Frontex nor that of any of the Commission Agencies. The fundamental obligations regarding SAR are generated by various international law instruments most notably the UN Convention on the Law of the Sea (UNCLOS '82), the SAR Convention '79 and the Safety of Life at Sea Convention (SOLAS '74) together with various amendments that have been made to the latter two conventions. The obligations therein are generally imposed on States and the vessels that fly their flags. However, given that Frontex joint operations are conducted by warships or other state vessel provided by the various EUMS, it is clear that such obligations remain incumbent upon the masters of these vessels regardless of the type of operation in which they are involved. Thus, if in the course of Frontex operations the commanding officer of a state vessel becomes aware of a distress situation (distress being defined as a situation in which persons are in imminent danger and require immediate assistance) then there exists a duty to immediately provide assistance insofar as this does not unduly endanger the crew of the assisting vessel or the assisting vessel itself In practice, this obligation generally leads to vessels involved in Frontex joint operations being regularly tasked to undertake SAR operations with a corresponding reduction in the effort allocated to pure border-control operations. It should also be noted that at such time as SAR operations are initiated, such vessels would no longer respond to the coordination of the International Coordination Centre (ICC) established for the particular joint operation but receive operational instructions and guidance from the

Rescue Coordination Centre (RCC) responsible for the SAR Region (SRR) within which SAR activities are taking place.

9. A further aspect of SAR which impinges directly upon Frontex joint operations at sea is the question of where rescued persons are to be disembarked. Again, some amount of international law provides regulation in this regard. However, a number of challenges exist which have yet to be addressed. Amendments to the SAR and SOLAS Conventions promulgated in 2004 and which came into force in 2006 were designed to clearly delineate the manner in which disembarkations of rescued persons should occur. However, although accompanied by guidelines, the said amendments still contain points which remain debatable. In light of this, Malta together with Finland and Norway have declined to accept these amendments or in some cases parts thereof The situation is further complicated by assertions made by organisations such as the UN High Commission for Refugees (UNHCR) and the International Organisation for Migration (IOM) that third countries, as exemplified by Libya, do not represent a safe place to disembark rescued migrants. In fact the United Nations High Commissioner for Refugees (UNHCR) condemned the return by Italy of 180 people to Libya on 17 March 2005, saying that it was far from certain that Italy had taken the necessary precautions to ensure that it did not send genuine refugees back to Libya, which could not be regarded as a place of safe asylum which statement was also quoted in a European Parliament Resolution on Lampedusa of the same year. An additional layer of complexity is added by the fact that it is conceivable that rescued migrants are in a position to claim asylum in that State to whom a warship or state vessel belongs. This has resulted in the necessity for arrangements to be put into place prior to the commencement of a given joint operation, a process which may be somewhat contentious at times.

10. Whether it is practical to retain a distinction at operational level between preventing irregular migration and preventing crime. The act of irregular migration has, in the majority of EUMS, been decriminalised. That having been said, the facilitation and organisation of such voyages remains a criminal offence carrying significant penalties including incarceration. Thus, at the operational level there is inevitably a blurring of the dividing line between the two issues. What is more of an issue in this regard when considering Frontex joint operations is the question of jurisdiction. In the cases of operations which occur on the high seas, exercising jurisdiction is difficult as a jurisdictional nexus cannot always be established. Thus any distinction between irregular migration and preventing crime is academic given that no jurisdiction really exists to suppress either. This statement must obviously be qualified insofar as certain crimes do exist (piracy, slavery, illegal transmission) that attract universal jurisdiction on the high seas but these are of little relevance to the matter at hand.

11. In practice, when considering the type of Frontex joint operations that have been mounted in the central Mediterranean, operations are not occurring in a zone where jurisdiction can be exercised in respect to either irregular migration nor criminal activities unless the latter have been made subject to the provisions of a particular bi- or multi-lateral agreement or convention.

12. Whether there is sufficient cooperation from Member States in terms of personnel and equipment for joint operations. When one considers the first phase of Operation Nautilus II held between 25 June 07 and 27 July 07, it becomes immediately apparent that the said operation was under-resourced, especially in regard to surface assets. The force offering received for the five-week operation conducted in the offshore environment was as follows:

Surface assets:	Malta	3 vessels for the duration of the operation
	Greece	1 vessel for 2 weeks
	Spain	1 vessel for 10 days
Air Assets:	Malta:	2 aircraft for the duration of the operation.
	Germany:	2 medium helicopters for 3 weeks
	Italy	1 aircraft for 1 week
	France	1 aircraft for 1 week

With the notable exception of the German contribution, all assets were committed for relatively short periods and, especially in the case of the surface assets, their operational activity during the committed period was limited while the assets themselves were not suited to an operation occurring some 100 nautical miles from the available shore facilities. This is despite the existence of CRATE (Centralised Record of Available Technical Equipment), a database maintained by Frontex of those technical resources which EUMS may consider making available for joint operations. The weakness of CRATE is that the listed resources are only deployable subject to the approval of those EUMS making them available and sufficient financial resources being available to fund their deployment. In fact, Ilkka Laitinen, Director of Frontex, stated in a 11 June 07 press release that "At the same time one can hear voices from Member States inviting Frontex to use Rabits immediately for stopping the flow of illegal migrants from Africa. These voices would also like Frontex to deploy as much equipment as possible to the region. Why? Because Frontex has 21 airplanes, 27 helicopters and 116 boats. That's the fact I cannot deny, we have them . . . on paper."

13. It is the reasons behind this lack of participation that bear further examination. The general reluctance to provide surface assets is related to the fact that no clear solution exists as to where any rescued persons are to be disembarked. Thus a justifiable apprehension exists on the part of the donor nations that national military or police assets may become involved in complicated situations with substantial numbers of third country nationals aboard who may register asylum claims on board. Therefore further moves towards clarification of the legal framework and operational procedures under which such operations take place may serve to allay such fears and provide for a more robust participation by operational assets of the various EUMS.

14. The extent of Frontex involvement in surveillance operations. Frontex itself does not generally play an active operational role in operations. The role of the agency is more that of a coordinator which serves to pull together the various national resources and personnel provided by the respective EUMS. That having been said, Frontex retains an oversight role both during the planning phases of the operation as well as during the implementation. Support is also provided in the form of provision of intelligence as well as financial assistance that offsets up to 80% of the operational costs incurred by the individual EUMS.

15. During the operations, coordination of the activities is exercised from an International Coordination Centre (ICC) established for the particular joint operation. The ICC will be manned by representatives of all national contingents participating in the operation as well as Frontex representatives who together form the Joint Coordinating Board (JCB). All decisions regarding the manner in which operational resources are employed are taken in a collective manner by these persons with national representatives having the final say on how their assets are employed. Throughout this decision-making cycle the role of the Frontex representatives is to facilitate this process while ensuring that the activities decided upon are in line with the overarching operational, strategic and political objectives set out for the particular joint operation. The Director of Frontex has also been empowered to negotiate operational agreements with third States which may facilitate the conduct of such operations but whether such powers have been exercised to date is not known.

16. How Frontex joint operations are planned and mounted. Before the beginning of each new year, Frontex invites EUMS to submit proposals for border control operations for the ensuing year which proposals generally include the objectives, the area and duration of the joint operation. FRONTEX will then assess the proposals and decide which operations are viable subsequent to which the operational budget allotted by the Commission is divided amongst the approved operations. The amount of funds channelled to each operation is based on the proposed duration of the operation, the assets involved, and the estimated effectiveness of the operation.

17. Those EUMS which have had their proposals approved are then requested to forward a draft operational plan, which is in turn forwarded to the other Member States for their assessment. Frontex then invites EUMS to participate in the operations and initiates a series of planning meetings in Warsaw and the host countries. Meanwhile, the Member State which proposed the operation is tasked with preparing a detailed plan for the operation, whilst Frontex assists by coordinating all the operational details with the participating EUMS. If needs be, the original operation plan may be further modified until all participating EUMS are satisifed that the contents thereof conform with the parameters set by their respective politicians and service exigencies. A final operator's brief is held in the hosting country a few days prior to commencement during which advance parties discuss final logistical requirements and tactical information and procedured.

18. Once the operation commences, this is coordinated through the International Coordination Centre (ICC) that is based in the hosting Member State. This is manned by local personnel that are specialists in communications and operational planning. Meanwhile, the ICC is also equiped in accordance with the minimum Frontex requirements in regard to such items as PCs, faxes, telephones, etc. The ICC's primary tasks include:

    a. Implementing the operational schedule authorised by Frontex for participating units in coordination with the latter agency.

    b. Coordinating the development of maritime/air operations in respective operational areas.

    c. Receiving reports from assigned assets, collecting and evaluating all the data, and conveying relevant information to other National Coordination Centres.

    d. Once migrant vessels are sighted, the ICC will provide assets with recommended courses of actions in accordance with national and international law.

19. The ICC will report to the Joint Coordinating Board (JCB) which is responsible for running the joint operation. This Board is led by an official designated as the Coordinator who is generally a senior national officer of the leading Member State. Other members of the JCB include a representative from each Member State which provided air and/or maritime assets, who are designated as National Officials as well as a Frontex liaison officer and intelligence officer who maintain the flow of information to Frontex after analyzing information from debriefing teams. The latter are expert interviewers that are provided by participating Member States for the duration of the joint operation. The command and control of maritime and/or air assets participating in the operation remains under the authority of National Commands through the nominated National Officials on the JCB. The tactical command of maritime and air assets remains under the authority of the specific Commander of each asset. Patrolling is carried out by naval and air units in order to acquire a clear surface situation in the sectors, whilst information regarding contacts of interest is forwarded to the ICC via any communication means for guidance and action deemed necessary.

20. How Frontex joint operations are monitored and the outcomes evaluated. Frontex assesses joint operations through its Risk Analysis Unit (RAU) which prepares questionnaires in order to collect specific information during and after the EU joint operations for further analysis. Frontex staff attached to the ICC send daily reports which give a breakdown of all relevant information pertaining to the operation. These analytical questionnaires are analysed in order to provide a picture of difficulties or obstacles encountered by the forces deployed. All information received at Frontex is assessed and documented, and when appropriate, alerts are passed onto other EUMS. The latter are expected to give feedback to Frontex through their respective National Focal Points. of Contact (NFPOC) regarding migration trends in their respective countries so that Frontex will be able to ascertain whether the on-going operation could have induced a displacement effect. At the end of the operation, the RAU compiles an evaluation report, which is intended to indicate the success or otherwise of the operation. The said evaluation report generally includes the following topics:

— Analysis of Replies to the Analytical Questionnaire.

— Number of migrant cases including Asylum Seekers.

— Routes adopted.

— Entries refused (in case of airports).

— Migration trends.

— Other Irregularities which may include implications in the trafficking of drugs and human beings.

— International Criminal Networks.

— Comparison by statistics with previous operations.

— Operational Evaluation by the Deployed Experts.

21. The scope of the final evaluation report is also to make recommendations for the future. This may include the improvement of basic tools such as language skills, IT, or analytical questionnaires which need to be more target-specific. Another vital aspect is to ascertain whether the operation actually induced migrant traffickers to change their *modus operandi* by putting pressure on other illegal points of entry including major changes to the migratory routes. In this sense, the evaluation report makes recommendations to secure other weak and illegal access points which have emerged during the joint operation. The recommendations also include courses of action to target specific nationalities attempting to enter EU borders, including the possibility of improving international enforcement agencies such as Europol or Interpol which could be better exploited to enhance the investigation of cases related to the involvement of travel agencies, smuggling organizations, and other trans-border crime.

22. Whether there is, or should be, any involvement of, or assistance from, the military in Frontex operations. Military involvement in Frontex operations already occurs, with the AFM being a case in point. Furthermore, Operation Nautilus has involved military resources from both France and Italy at various stages. Such involvement generally takes place when the military is assigned full or partial responsibility for various aspects of border control in the State of Origin. This would usually imply that some form of national legislative framework supporting such an employment of the armed forces exists. Furthermore, especially in the case of maritime operations which generally take place on the high seas, the specific nature of a maritime or air unit bears little relevance given that activities are governed by international legal frameworks which generally accord the same rights to warships and other state vessels such as those operated by police or customs agencies.

23. A number of other considerations must be taken into account when considering the employment of military assets. On the one hand such assets are generally extremely capable in regard to their detection and tracking facilities and are usually far more deployable than police or customs assets which are designed for employment within areas of national jurisdiction. Such assets are also more interoperable as procedures are usually based on widely-accepted standards. That having been said, care must be exercised during operations where third countries may be hosting operational assets or allowing them to operate within their national jurisdictional zones. While it may be perfectly acceptable from a political point of view to permit such activities when undertaken by "non-belligerent" police and coastguard platforms, the presence of military platforms may lead to friction and weakened internal support for such activities given the spectre of colonialism.

24. How the Agency's role should develop in the future. There is a body of opinion that feels that Frontex should continue to evolve into an operational organisation in contrast to its present roles of coordination and facilitation. This view is supported by the Frontex Regulation which foresees the procurement by the Agency of its own operational assets. Thus, in theory, Frontex could evolve into a supranational "border guard", operating in support of the overarching interests of the Union. Such a view is, however, overly simplistic especially when applied to operations in the maritime field. All aircraft and vessels must perforce operate under the flag of a state, be they military or civilian. Thus a national connection is inevitable bringing with it all the considerations related to asylum claims, use of force, operational procedures, command and control and disciplinary structureS necessary within a uniformed force. It is hard to imagine any EUMS allowing use of its flag for the assets involved in such operations without retaining at least some level of control over the activities of those assets especially when one considers the eventual diplomatic implications which may arise.

25. Maintaining such a force also requires a substantial investment in all the support structures associated with such resources, be they technical, administrative or infrastructural. When one considers, for instance, the approach of NATO to the generation of a multinational force, it quickly becomes apparent that NATO itself operates very few resources (restricted mainly to support and research platforms) preferring instead to rely on the contributions of the member states operating under NATO command, control and coordination. Even this approach requires the promulgation of unanimously-approved procedures, rules of engagement, operating standards and equipment specifications.

26. Thus a more realistic way forward for Frontex seems to be to enhance its coordination and facilitation activities while continuing to rely on the individual EUMS for force offerings. This process can be encouraged by Frontex providing robust, consensus-based operating procedures under which to conduct such operations while also making efforts to provide clarity as regards the legal framework within which the operations must take place. The provision of support assets, such as unmanned surveillance platforms, may also represent an area where Frontex can make a further contribution to future joint operations. All this should occur against a background of expanded efforts by Frontex to provide intelligence support during both the planning and deployment phases of such operations as well as increased financial assistance to offset the substantial unplanned costs incurred by EUMS when deploying national assets out of area Increased financial resources would also allow an increase in the geographical and temporal scope of operations thus providing a more persistent deterrent to would-be migrants rather than a temporary stop-gap measure.

27. Efforts also need to be made by Frontex to assist in addressing the indirect costs and long-term financial and social aspects incurred as a result of such operations. Some EUMS may shy away from hosting such joint operations due to the fact that there is a strong possibility of these resulting in an elevated influx of would-be migrants which are intercepted or rescued by participating units. Establishing a framework by which this burden can be equitably and efficiently shared will further encourage the various EUMS to take a leading role in such operations by freeing them from the political and financial concerns that may be associated with such activities.

28. Finally the Agency must make more of its role as the Union's interlocutor with third states in regard to migration matters. The leverage available should be used to move transit and source countries towards operational agreements which see them not only allowing EUMS assets to operate in their jurisdictional areas but possibly even participate as partners in joint activities. While some progress has been made in certain regions in this regard, other areas are lagging far behind with no sustainable solution to the migration issues in sight without managing to obtain the cooperation of various non-EU partners.

7 September 2007

Examination of Witness

Witness: MAJOR ANDREW MALLIA, Staff Officer II, Maritime, Air and ADA Operations, Armed Forces of Malta, examined.

Q371 *Chairman:* Major, we are extremely grateful to you for coming from Malta in order to give evidence to this Committee. We are a sub-committee which deals with, among other things, immigration affairs. We are a sub-committee of the European Union Committee of the House of Lords. May I also welcome the High Commissioner who is sitting behind you. It is good to have you with us. We will send you a transcript of your evidence in case there are any corrections you feel you must make, and if there any questions that you feel you cannot answer precisely or if there is anything you want to supplement, you are very welcome to write to us in the course of the next week or so. Let us now proceed. Would you give the Committee an overview of the tasks of the Maltese border guards, their institutional structure and their powers, including what coercive powers they have and whether you have the right to use weapons. Also, could you tell us what national resources and capabilities Malta allocates towards dealing with both legal and illegal migration? I know you could probably talk to us for two hours on those questions but we have about an hour and a quarter before we must wind the session up, so if you could be reasonably brief we would appreciate that because we have, as you know, a lot of questions to ask you.
Major Mallia: My Lord Chairman, I will do my best. First of all, may I thank you for this invitation and pass to you the greetings of the Commander of the Armed Forces who has also thanked you for this opportunity to make ourselves heard. To begin with a general picture of how border control is organised in Malta: there are two agencies which are involved in border control, the Malta Police and the Armed Forces of Malta. The division of their duties is that the police deal more with the regulatory side of business—so visas, immigration control, et cetera—and to do that the police allocate about 150 people at the airport, in the seaports and within their headquarters. These include both uniformed officers as well as civilian employees working as immigration officers. On police establishment and exactly how they are organised, I do not have that available. That is not exactly our line of business; however, if that is of interest to you, I am sure I can make that available to you at reasonably short notice. In regard to the Armed Forces of Malta, our role is purely on the blue borders, on maritime borders. We are in that role purely due to the fact that we are the sole maritime forces in Malta. There is no maritime police, there is no maritime customs agency, there is no border guard as such, as there is in many other European countries, so we have taken upon us this role more as an automatic reaction to the fact that we are the sole maritime force. However, we are also legally empowered to do this role. The officers of the Armed Forces have the right to act as police officers and customs officers when conducting law-enforcement business, so it is covered by the appropriate legislation within Maltese law. What powers do we have to conduct the control and protection of the Maltese maritime borders? We have all those powers which are accorded to us, in most cases, by international law. Operations at sea generally tend to be governed by international legal instruments rather than purely national ones, and the National legal instruments that we have reflect very closely the international legal regime, so we will have a Territorial Seas and Contiguous Zone Act which is basically the reflection of what is provided for in the United Nations Convention on the Law of the Sea. Do we carry weapons during our duties? Yes, we do. We have particular rules of engagement which are used in our law enforcement roles which differ from rules of engagement which will be used during military operations. Why do we carry weapons? Because (a) it is part of our character as an Armed Forces and (b) the nature of the work we are doing has mandated the use or at least the threat of the use of these weapons on some occasions. So it is partly based on who we are and it is also partly based on our experiences through the years. As an organisation, we have been doing this for approximately 30 years now—obviously now in a much more formal and organised manner, partly because of the EU accession and the Schengen border code itself. In total, we allocate approximately 350 people to the border control role. These are not dedicated solely to border control; these are dedicated to all our other maritime roles, including search and rescue, fisheries protection, anti-smuggling and anti-contraband operations, but obviously all of them have a role in border control when it comes to blue borders. Regarding the financial allocation which we devote to this task every year, when you exclude personnel costs and also amortised costs of the assets (that is, depreciation) and you also exclude the funding which we have received from Frontex operations which is a particular funding branch, for 2006 we conducted operations to the tune of €1.8 to €1.9 million in border control alone. Again, I repeat, that does not include our personnel costs, because the personnel are not dedicated solely to that task. That does not take into account that appreciation of the assets involved. Those are purely operational costs. Nor does it include Frontex operations which are financed through a particular method which does not fall within our normal financing.
Chairman: Lord Marlesford, would you like to come back on that?

Q372 Lord Marlesford: Yes, indeed. Thank you very much. That is a very helpful introduction indeed. On the funding point, you gave us a clear picture of your marginal extra costs of conducting your own operations. You referred to Frontex being a separate funding operation. Could you give us some indication of the financial provision and source of it for Frontex and, also, presumably you do not get any outside funding towards the €1.8 to €1.9 million for your own domestic operations?

Major Mallia: That is partly correct and partly not. Let me begin with the question of Frontex if I may. Once an operation has been declared a joint operation (that is, is it involves resources of more than one Member State), Frontex will offer to finance the purely operational costs of that operation to the tune of 80%. Obviously that does mean that the particular Member State has to fork out the costs on the front-line but then will receive a refund of those costs. The costs are based on the type of asset you are offering and, until date, are based mostly on receipts and invoices for the various materials and supplies which you would have required to use. There is currently, however, a project ongoing within Frontex, which is called the REM project (the running expenses of means project), which is attempting to establish standard costings for types of assets and types of resources, so that when it comes to refunding the operational costs of those resources it can be done in a much more efficient and quick manner. In regard to external funding for the other tasks, when it comes to recurrent funding, no, we do not receive anything from external services. However, in regard to capital funding, because we are a military organisation we can tap into military financial instruments, such as the US foreign military funding system and funds which we may have allocated in that. We will have patrol boats operating at sea on migrant operations which were funded by the US Government. We have had patrol vessels funded directly by the Italian Government. We are conducting the procurement of our new helicopter also using foreign military sales funding from the US Government. So: operational costs, no; capital costs, yes. Those have totalled about €30 million over the period 2000–07, so they have been a significant factor in allowing us to upgrade our operational means.

Q373 Lord Marlesford: To follow up on that particular aspect, is the setting up of Frontex going to require assets to be available to countries which are going to operate; in other words, not calling on the national force to carry out an operation but to be able to carry out an operation? Will Frontex be financing any such capital assets?

Major Mallia: I am aware that the Frontex regulation does provide for Frontex owning operational equipment. The scope and the nature of that operational equipment are not defined. From a technical point of view, I do not think Frontex as an agency is equipped to be operating aircraft, patrol vessel, helicopters, et cetera. It is quite a complicated task which requires a high level of skill and a high level of infrastructure. As to whether the Commission or the Community as a whole is making funds available for procurement of assets, the answer is yes, and the financial instrument, in particular, is the External Borders Fund, which has only become available in 2007. In 2007, 2008, 2009, if I am correct, there is approximately €140 to €180 million per year. What is interesting about the External Borders Fund is not the total amounts, it is how it is divided. It is divided on the level of risk, which is assessed by Frontex; on the number of illegal entries you may have in proportion to the size of your country; as to the length of the external border which you are policing. As far as Malta is concerned, therefore, it is a slightly more level playing field than other financial instruments because the risk level and the external border which we are policing bring us up in the ranking of the amount of funding allocated to us and that will provide substantial funds up until the period to 2013.

Chairman: I do not want to get too deeply involved in Frontex at this stage because we have a good many more questions to come later on it.

Q374 Lord Marlesford: Are you involved in bilateral co-operation with border guards from other Member States or third countries? If so, how does this work out in practice? Also, I think I am right in saying that Malta is not a member of NATO.

Major Mallia: That is correct.

Q375 Lord Marlesford: Therefore, does it mean that you do not have access to the communications capabilities which NATO would have which might be, in certain circumstances, helpful in a Frontex operation?

Major Mallia: To start from the co-operation side, the people we co-operate with mostly at an operational level are obviously Italy, being our direct neighbours and are being our sole neighbour in terms of geography when it comes to the European Union. Admittedly Greece is a peripheral neighbour, if you would like to put it that way, but the distances between us mean that co-operation in this field is not particularly necessary. We have a very good working relationship with the various Italian agencies involved in this issue, and there are a number—there are at least four major agencies involved at sea. That evidences itself not only in our co-operation day-to-day but the fact that we do have an Italian military mission resident in Malta, so we have representatives with some of those organisations to whom we can talk directly. That would be our major co-operation on a day-to-day basis. There are obviously the joint operations in which we are participating. I am not sure whether that will be the subject of later questions, but that is the other area where we are conducting co-operation with other countries. Regarding the NATO aspect, I think what is most needed from NATO will be more of the information capabilities; that is, having the domain awareness at sea, and a lot of that is available to us already, either from bilateral agreements or from special arrangements which are in place.

Chairman: Lord Dear.

Q376 *Lord Dear:* My Lord Chairman, thank you. Major, thank you very much for coming and the point I am making can probably be dealt with very quickly. I am interested in the rules of engagement for armed operations. It may be, rather than taking time out today, that it would be possible for you to let us have a note of how your rules of engagement operate and send that through to the Secretariat.

Major Mallia: I do not think that should pose any major problems.

Q377 *Lord Dear:* You probably carry the card.

Major Mallia: We carry the white card. It is based on the British Army white card which was issued for Northern Ireland operations. That is where it started from. It is very similar to that in concept. It has obviously been updated over the years because of new legal developments. Sometimes we bring special rules of engagement into force for a particular event, but that is the basics. I should think that I will be able to provide that.

Chairman: Thank you. Lord Mawson.

Q378 *Lord Mawson:* My question is really about the funding mechanisms and how they work in practice. How long is it taking for invoices to clear or is it too early to say?

Major Mallia: I would say that at this time it is too early to say. This is the first year that we have been heavily involved in joint operations. As far as I am aware, the refund for the initial phases of joint operation Nautilus II, which was in June/July, have already been received—at least in part—so there does seem to be a moving process, an ongoing process. We are presently working on requesting the refunding of costs for the operation in Spain, Operation INDALO, in which we were involved for three weeks. It obviously does involve a certain amount of paperwork—these things do. I think the REM project which I mentioned earlier, in which Frontex is trying to quantify standard costs, will simplify this because it will mean that you just have a standard claim form and you have to specify the types of assets you are using and you would not have to provide invoices because it has been established beyond

doubt that those are the operating costs for it. When it comes to the capital instruments, those are a lot more complicated. Those require an application stage, an evaluation stage, a project proposal stage. The ones in which I have been involved tended to take two to two and a half years to bring the equipment to the people, but that is the nature of the game and you have to factor that into your planning process and take it as a fact of life. You really plan that you have a two and a half to three year lead time of those items if you intend to fund them with EU funding.

Chairman: Lady Henig, would you like to come in.

Q379 *Baroness Henig:* Thank you very much indeed. Again, I would like to thank you very much for coming here and giving us your perspective on the event. To what extent does Malta co-operate with international organisations such as, for example, the International Organisation for Migration and the United Nations High Commission for Refugees in? What does this co-operation involve in practice?

Major Mallia: Again, I can only answer this question from our perspective not from the perspective of the police. However, in practice, for the Armed Forces it is a very close co-operation on two levels. The first level is during the period in which we are conducting operations at sea and we have information that a migrant boat may be at sea, may be in distress. Many times the UNHCR representative in Malta is the conduit for receiving that information, either from his counterpart in Italy who has been contacted by third parties or he himself may have been contacted by third parties. Many times he will continue to monitor that case and we will provide this information to him. We will provide him with updates so he has a good feel for what is happening. With the IOM, in the case of the Armed Forces of Malta, much less, because the IOM has a different role in the way it is supposed to address the problem once the persons are in country rather than anything else. I can tell you that the office which is responsible for the liaison with both the IOM and the UNHCR is part of the Ministry of Justice and Home Affairs. It is called the Third Countries Nationals Office and their sole job is to conduct this liaison. Obviously the police can give you a much different perspective on that. Our operational co-operation, our practical co-operation with them is limited to the degree that I have told you.

Q380 *Baroness Henig:* If there was a particular emergency in which there was an operation co-ordinated by Frontex, what would be the relationship then with the UN High Commissioner for Refugees? In other words, what is their relationship with Frontex and with the operations?

Major Mallia: The UNHCR have a permanent representative in Warsaw with Frontex, so they already have a very close liaison with the UNHCR.

Q381 *Baroness Henig:* Is that repeated at your—
Major Mallia: It would not be repeated at the ICC (International Co-ordination Centre) level which is conducting the operation. The reason for that is because the ICC has a more operational character and is supposed to concentrate on the conduct of operations. I have personally never experienced anything similar; however, I would assume that the co-ordination can happen very rapidly then at Frontex head office or headquarters level because Frontex is in constant contact with the ICC and if they receive information which they think is of interest for the UNHCR, they have a UNHCR person with them now. That has definitely improved the liaison. As I have said, my personal opinion would be that the ICC is not the place to conduct this liaison because of the operational nature of what is happening. It is possibly too close to events. It is possibly more appropriate that this is happening at Frontex head office level.

Q382 *Baroness Henig:* The Commission say that between January and August 2006 14,567 irregular migrants landed on Lampedusa and 1,502 irregular migrants landed in Malta. I wonder whether you would be happy to comment on these figures.
Major Mallia: I can comment on the figure for Malta. I am not able to confirm or deny the figure for Italy; I can, however, confirm that the figure for Malta for January to August 2006 is correct. For January to August of this year, to offer some comparison, the number was down slightly to about 1,379; however, that was more a seasonal fluctuation rather than any substantial reduction. This year the figures are less than 100 less than last year in total, and the year has not yet finished and there are still boats out there. Obviously you can see the substantial difference for Lampedusa and Malta. The reasons behind that are numerous. First of all, the types of craft used on the two migrations are different. The craft used on the route passing by Lampedusa will be large fishing boats carrying between 200 and 400 people and therefore a single craft means that you have 200 to 400 people on your doorstep. In our case, they are much smaller craft, carrying between 25 and 35 people. It does not reflect any less work. The number of cases which we are having to handle may be the same: their cases are larger and our cases are smaller. The other point is that Lampedusa is obviously recognised as part of Italy and the migrants know they will be spending very little time on Lampedusa, they will be very quickly transferred to the Italian mainland. Despite it being an even smaller island than Malta, and even more remote in some senses,

politically it is part of the Italian mainland, so reaching Lampedusa means that you have reached Italy. It is a more convenient way of doing it because the distances are shorter. Obviously Malta is less targeted, in the sense that arriving in Malta, because of the Dublin II Convention you are staying in Malta. There is nowhere much else to go. The acceptance rates are reasonably high when it comes to applications for refugee status and for protected status but obviously Lampedusa continues to be more attractive. That probably accounts for the difference in numbers.

Q383 *Chairman:* You confirmed that figure of 1,502 for Malta. I know you cannot be precise and you may think it is an unfair question, but what sort of volume is there that you do not know about?
Major Mallia: That is an extremely difficult question to answer. I can say that we do see a number of other craft passing by who refuse assistance, who refuse to allow us to aid them in any manner, and, basically, just want to be left alone. Our actions in this case would be to remain in their vicinity—and in a number of cases this has proved very fortuitous because they have capsized later on in their voyage—and, as soon as they start approaching Italy, to inform our Italian colleagues. But I would say that this year we have had 1,700 almost entering Malta and at least that much again passing by—at least. But it is extremely difficult to put a handle on it, for a number of reasons. We are not aware of all the craft. We are having multiple reportings of the same craft and it is very hard sometimes to separate these into different craft or collate them into a single craft, so it is difficult to put an exact handle on that, my Lord Chairman.

Q384 *Lord Harrison:* A warm welcome, Major Mallia—especially to someone born in Oxford! UNHCR says that three out of ten of those who landed in Malta in 2006 were recognised as refugees or accorded humanitarian status. How does Malta deal with the other seven out of ten? If this is a problem—and I am sure it is—what help is given by other Member States and what further help might we or others, the Italians, give to assist Malta in dealing with that problem of the seven out of ten?
Major Mallia: Before answering this question, I must point out that this is something which I had to go to my colleagues in the police and literally research in detail with them, because, once the case of an individual has been decided then, again, it becomes a police competency as to what then happens to that person. Basically, after the three out of ten have been accepted, either as refugees or have been accorded humanitarian status, in the case of the seven out of ten they will be subject to repatriation. That is obviously a much more complex situation than one would think because the first thing you have to do is

to establish their identity and their nationality. In some cases, that is reasonably easy. In those countries where we have diplomatic representations in Malta, for instance Egypt, the Egyptian Ambassador has become an expert in this regard and he can immediately tell you from which suburb of Cairo that individual has come because of his accent. It is very easy to establish the fact that they are Egyptians and the Egyptians are very forthcoming in issuing travel documents for those individuals. In the case of other countries, it is much more difficult for a number of reasons. First of all, we do not have the diplomatic representations permanently in Malta, so an ambassador or a member of the Embassy would have to come to Malta from either Tripoli or Rome in most cases. Secondly, especially in Central Africa, you will find ethnic groups distributed over a number of countries, so being able to find that the individual is from a particular ethnic group does not give you the country he is from, it narrows it down to maybe three, so then we have to still work further to identify exactly which country. Once you have got to that stage, the issuing of travel documents can take a substantial period of time and sometimes the travel documents have to be returned and updated for new requirements of, for instance, the EU. They must contain other security features, et cetera, et cetera, or they would be inadequate for that person to travel on. The final problem is then making the travel arrangements for that individual, which in some cases can prove difficult. In all cases, it is extremely expensive. This is one area where we are co-operating within Europe, and that is on joint repatriation flights, so you have an aircraft departing from Germany with, say, ten individuals who are being returned to Nigeria, it will be stopping in Italy for another five or six individuals, landing in Malta for another two individuals and then continuing the flight. That does decrease the costs overall. If we cannot identify where a particular person is from, then, at the end of that day, that person becomes an illegal migrant in Malta, with very few rights to work, et cetera, but no possibility of sending him home. That is the major problem here. It is not the genuine refugees who are causing the problem; it is these persons who have no right to any status but cannot be returned because it is impossible to establish where they are from. There was a project at one point, which was funded, if I am correct, by the Commission, to provide expert interviewers to try to establish where these persons had come from but it fell into the same pitfall as the diplomatic representatives: "Yes, I can tell you he is from Mali, Chad or Niger" but that is not much of a starting point. It has narrowed it down but it has not given us the exact information to allow us to be able to repatriate this person. What more can be done at the European level? On an individual basis, there are a number of countries which are assisting us, in that they are taking genuine refugees and already reducing that part of the burden. The Netherlands have been notable in this regard. The Baltic Republics have taken one or two—as a gesture more than anything else, but a much appreciated gesture, I should note. The US is accepting a substantial number as well under a resettlement programme. The danger of that is obviously that it starts to generate a pull factor. It starts to become a target for why you should try to get to Malta, because all of a sudden the United States is offering so many places to get to the US this year. You have to be very careful with that. On the other hand, there is always the question of Dublin II—which remains a problem because Dublin II for us means that whoever applies for asylum in Malta cannot apply anywhere else within Europe, they cannot move anywhere else within Europe. Relaxation of the Dublin II would be another particular area where at least some relief would be felt. Another proposal which happened recently, although a very specific proposal, regarded those persons rescued outside the Maltese Search and Rescue Region—of which we have had a number of cases. While being brought sometimes to Malta, the Maltese proposal, which was made by our Minister of Justice and Home Affairs, was basically that there should be sharing mechanism for these persons: that, because they are not the direct responsibility of any EU state, there should be a pre-established mechanism by where they are shared, so to speak, across the EU Member States, and, therefore, obviously sharing the burden. That is an ongoing process. I would not be competent to speak at what stage that has arrived. Perhaps the High Commissioner can clarify further on that. It is one of the other ways in which we are seeing that we can reduce the pressure which is directly on them.

Lord Harrison: Thank you for the clarity in your answer.

Q385 Baroness Tonge: Welcome and thank you for coming. In May of this year it was reported that 57 Eritreans were lost from a vessel off the coast of Malta and have not been seen since. Could you explain what steps were taken at that time by the Maltese authorities and could more be done in the future to deal with emergencies like that?

Major Mallia: I am very familiar with this particular case. I was the co-ordinator for this particular case, so I can answer that with some authority, so to speak. First of all, the reporting was extremely poor. "Off the coast of Malta" was initially 200 kilometres from Malta, closer both to Libya and to Lampedusa, so you have to put that into perspective. We initially received the call from a third party, likely a migrant who was already in Malta, who called to say that a friend or relative of his was aboard this boat, and, as usual, provided a satellite telephone number which was on board the boat. All the boats are equipped with a satellite telephone, given to them by the traffickers, which allows them to call for help and to call relatives, and, because it has an embedded GPS, it also provides the navigation details. That is standard procedure. On initially receiving the call, which was about six o'clock in the morning, because the position we were given was still within the Libyan Search and Rescue Region, our first step was to inform the Libyan authorities. At the same time the Italian authorities had also received a second call on the same case and at that time we started exchanging faxes and telephone calls of what we knew and what we were doing at that time. We did not receive a response from the Libyan authorities in this particular case, so, as first Rescue Co-ordination Centre—thus that centre still responsible for the case—we continued to monitor the progress of this boat by regular contacts with these people. At one point, they had stated that they were in a position within the Maltese Search and Rescue Region, their craft was adrift and that they required assistance. We immediately deployed a vessel from Malta and, as we normally do, also an aircraft. The reason we deploy the aircraft is because sometimes the positions are not exact and that gives us a very quick handle on the situation. I think two hours after the initial alert we had an aircraft on scene—which also took those pictures which were then shown in the media. The craft did seem adrift. It did not seem to be making way at that time. It took approximately seven hours for our boat to transit from Malta to the position— which also gives you a feel of how far away it was. Obviously during that time the aircraft was withdrawn for refuelling and sent again to the position. On arriving in the position, it did not find a boat, neither in the position where it had been initially sighted nor within a substantial radius around it. We had also alerted merchant shipping in the area to be alert for this craft but we received no reports from merchant shipping of the sighting of this craft and therefore our vessel which arrived in the area began a search. During this search it found a second craft with 25 people on board which had just capsized. It conducted the rescue of those persons and proceeded directly to Malta because a number of them required medical assistance. The next day we flew a further sortie with an aircraft and also liaised with the Italian Rescue Co-ordination Centre in Rome to fly at least one sortie in the area and ask any other aircraft in the area to keep a sharp look out, and they found nothing. Given that a number of the people on board this craft were wearing life-jackets and there were a number of empty fuel receptacles which could be seen visibly in the photo, it is highly unlikely that a boat like that would sink without leaving at least minimal trace. Some three days later

we noted on a couple of Eritrean websites which are of the Eritrean nationalists that this craft had been reported to have arrived again in Libya. Basically they had lost their way and they had landed again in Libya. Obviously we are not able to confirm the veracity of those reports but that is the only information further that we have on the case. Could we have done more? When we look at our search and rescue plan and the way it is set out, I think we reacted fully in accordance with it. The only unknown was that when we got there we found another craft, so, instead of searching for longer, we had to return to base. But that is the nature of the game and there was very little we could do about that. We did search the area extremely well, both ourselves and the Italians. The only thing we cannot allow for is if a boat is continuing on its course. We can find a drifting object quite easily but a boat being driven in a particular direction, God knows which direction, is very difficult to find because we do not know what the person driving that boat is thinking. We could not really have done much more and I have my doubts whether this craft disappeared so completely as was said by the press.

Q386 *Baroness Tonge:* The obvious question is: Did you have any contact with Libya after that? Do we have any idea whether they did in fact arrive? Does Malta have any formal contact with Libya?
Major Mallia: At the time, contacts were not particularly good. We had made a written request, asking whether they could confirm the report that this boat had arrived—and I cannot confirm but I think the Italians did the same as well. We did not receive a response to that. Currently things are improving. We have already been to Libya on a bilateral visit; we hope to host them in Malta in January; and we are working on drawing up a search and rescue agreement between the two sides. We hope that that will improve the relations in general. The problem is more identifying which is the agency responsible rather than any lack of effort on their part. It is just a complicated system.

Q387 *Chairman:* Lady Tonge, before you go on, I wonder whether I could put another question. I visited earlier this year an extraordinary establishment in Stavanger in Norway. Whilst I was there, a report came in of a boat occupied by potential refugees which was drifting without fuel or food or water 200 miles in the Indian Ocean east of Djibouti. The organisation in Stavanger organised the rescue operation, I think through the Seychelles in the end. Do you use that organisation in Stavanger at all?
Major Mallia: The RCC in Stavanger is one of the RCCs within the global SAR system. They are a particularly co-operative one, it must be said. They

are known for the high level of work they do. However, this necessity of co-ordinating out of area operations is something which we are all faced with. RCC Malta will co-ordinate or at least observe any rescue case in the world which has a Maltese registered ship—and that is 27 million tonnes of shipping. We would regularly be monitoring a search and rescue case off Japan or possibly in the Americas, so it is a general feature of the global SAR system that the geographical location of a SAR case does not necessarily dictate who is looking after it. There is also the principle of first RCC. If you are the first Rescue Co-ordination Centre to be advised, then you hold legal responsibility for that case until the competent centre has taken over. Until they send you a written message confirming that they are assuming responsibility, you are responsible.

Q388 *Lord Mawson:* If they had a satellite phone on this boat, was there communication between the aeroplane and the boat? How do you deal with the question of language and understanding the communication? Is there some facility to help you on that?

Major Mallia: To the first question: no, our current aircraft are not fitted with a satellite telephone—it is something we are trying to remedy at this time—so we did not have direct contact with the craft from the aeroplane. The language issue is a problem sometimes. We are fortunate in that, being such a small island, our citizens tend to have reasonably good language skills, so if it sticks to French, English and Arabic we can generally get along, and that covers most of the nationalities with whom we are dealing, either from Francophone Africa or Anglophone Africa or from Northern Africa, which is generally Arabic and we have at least two or three fluent Arabic speakers on each boat, so that is not really that much of an issue.

Q389 *Baroness Tonge:* What is the policy of Malta towards merchant vessels who attempt to disembark unregistered migrants whom they have rescued at sea?

Major Mallia: The last part is a very important clarification, because when it comes to stowaways who have been picked up in another port there are clear international rules for that. Regarding the disembarkation of persons rescued, we basically act in full accordance with international law as we have ratified it. I am sure you are all aware that we have not ratified the 2004 amendments to the SAR and SOLAS conventions, so we act in a manner as provided by the conventions up until that point. If persons are rescued within our Search and Rescue Region we will do everything we can to make sure they are disembarked to the nearest safe haven. For us, the nearest safe haven is that port where they can

be reasonably easily disembarked—it does not require a helicopter disembarkation or something of the sort—where they are assured of medical treatment and all their basic needs will be seen to, and where, if need be, they can continue their voyage be it a legitimate one—there is obviously that issue. If persons are recognised outside the Maltese Search and Rescue Region then we will generally not accept their disembarkation in Malta. That has been the case in a number of cases which have also received much media attention but, again, the media failed to note the fact that these persons were not rescued within our Search and Rescue Region. Generally, we would not. However, that being said, if there are overriding humanitarian reasons, yes, we would disembark those persons.

Q390 *Baroness Tonge:* Could the owner of the merchant vessel not just say, "We have rescued these people at sea"? How can you prove that they have not? Do you see what I mean?

Major Mallia: I do. You have no ability to say, "I can prove that you rescued these persons in this position and not this position." That is completely true. However, generally the information given to you by a captain we find is genuine information. There are a number of reasons for that. Partly it is because the captain knows that there will be an investigation into the case and the migrants themselves can produce some information, being equipped, as I have told you, with GPS embedded phones. Secondly, in the case of merchant vessels there is an insurance question here. They are going to be compensated by their insurers for their rescue activities, so they have to give to their insurers the exact starting time and the exact ending time and the exact starting time position and any position of those activities, and that information can easily be cross-checked. Generally, I find the merchant captains are an extremely honest bunch of people. That is for a number of reasons but also due to the fact that the type of person selected for that job will generally be quite a focused, honest individual. We are not talking about people who are operating on the fringes of society; we are talking about international citizens, yes, because they come from a complete variety of countries, but there is an underlying thread of honesty in all of them, so we very rarely are deceived about where a rescue has taken place.

Q391 *Lord Dear:* I would like to ask you a question about Frontex operations, which switches the focus from what you have been talking about so far. I do not know whether you have been involved in Frontex operations. If you have, I would be very interested in how the duties were allocated between the Malta authorities and the border guards in other Member States—and probably that is Italy, from what you have said so far. How would you split and allocate those responsibilities?

Major Mallia: Frontex operations in general are managed by an ICC (International Co-ordination Centre). Within this International Co-ordination Centre there will be a Frontex representative and there will be a representative from each of the countries which has assets involved in that Frontex operation, be they human resources, such as interviewers, or be they operational resources, such as vessels, aircraft, et cetera. When a joint operation is prepared, it is prepared by a particular host country. Together with Frontex, this host country will draw up an operational plan which will detail the areas where they intend to conduct operations, the type of activity against which they are conducting these operations, what they are trying to achieve with these operations, et cetera, et cetera. At such time as this operational plan is issued and the various other Member States are asked to pledge assets towards the operation, they will also have the ability, if they see fit, to make minor changes to the operational plan if that is in their particular interest. It is an ongoing process until literally the last day sometimes. Once the operation starts, any actions which are to be undertaken by a particular vessel have to be okayed by the national representative, so if an Italian or a Spanish vessel or a Greek vessel is operating from Malta and the overall co-ordinator of the operation, who will be Maltese, as the host nation, wishes to deploy them in a particular manner, in a particular place, for a particular role, that would have to be okayed by the national representative.

Q392 Lord Dear: Who would be there.

Major Mallia: Who would be there in the ICC. If he is not available physically at that time, he would have to be contacted before the tasking is given. Generally, national representatives have the authority to agree on the spot. In some cases, we have seen them referring it back to national authorities to ask whether this is go or no go, but generally they will be on a level that they can okay it on the spot. When operations are happening at sea, in so far as those operations are surveillance or border control operations, the ICC will continue to manage them in this manner. At the time at which the operations become search and rescue, there is a distress case, operational control moves away from the ICC and goes to the Rescue Co-ordination Centre responsible for the geographical area and all the assets will have to put themselves at the disposal of that Rescue Co-ordination Centre. He may not use them all, he may decide that I require only one vessel and one aircraft but they will have to put themselves at the disposal of the Rescue Co-ordination Centre to allow the conduct of the normal search and rescue operations.

That is basically how command and control is organised.

Q393 Lord Dear: Could it be improved? From your experience are there glaring errors in that? Do you find that you are getting by really by making it work rather than because the system is geared up perfectly or is it alternatively working very well and you see little chance of altering it?

Major Mallia: I would always prefer unity of command to a Chinese parliament, I think that is clear, but that is probably something to do with my military background rather than anything else. However, the type of operations which are happening and the fact that there are so many Member States involved will necessitate that this consultative process will have to happen. I have to admit it has worked remarkably well. As long as the national representatives are given the power to take decisions on the spot, that is the important decision which has to be made. Once they are empowered, then things move extremely smoothly. If—as has happened in rare cases, I admit—they have to call home and say, "Listen, the Maltese would like to put our patrol vessel there doing this, that and the other, is that okay?" then the chain of command starts to become too unwieldy and too long. The time periods involved are just too long.

Q394 Lord Dear: You are looking for as much delegation as possible.

Major Mallia: Yes, although, to be realistic, delegation of national competencies down to ICC level is about as far as we will get—at least in the short to medium term.

Q395 Chairman: When we were in Brussels we met Simon Busuttil, who is, as you perhaps know, a member of the European Parliament, and he told us that some Member States which pledge resources towards Frontex operations do not follow those pledges. In particular, Italy pledged 342 ships to a Frontex operation in July but made none available in the event. Would you comment on this. Do you think that Frontex ought to have power to insist that members make resources available which they have pledged already?

Major Mallia: I think the first stage of this is that there was some misunderstanding between Frontex and the Member States when there was the request for pledges, especially in those Member States which were pledging military assets. A pledge does not mean: "I am giving you this asset and it will be there at a drop of a hat." It is saying, "I am making these resources available. Sometimes I will be able to participate; sometimes I will not." That has been the case, frankly, with Malta as well. We have pledged one of our largest vessels to the so-called "tool box" as it was called at the time. We have deployed it on only one operation in Spain. There were other requests, but at the time we were so involved in national operations that it was beyond our means to deploy this vessel. One has to look at these pledges in a very realistic manner, in the sense that they are what could conceivably be available rather than what is always available at the drop of a hat. I do agree that in honouring these pledges there have been some disappointments and possibly some Member States could/should have done more. However, speaking from our point of view, one does also have to appreciate that Malta is not the only Member State which has an immigration problem. Everyone is under severe pressure. In cases such as Spain they are under pressure from two sides, in two oceans rather than just the one, so I understand that at certain times they have a reluctance to release these resources. The options to improve this picture are to provide more resources to the Member States. The External Borders Fund in fact is giving high priority to those projects which are producing capabilities which can be deployed, so we will get more co-financing for such projects and they will be given higher priority. If I am buying, for instance, as an example, an aircraft which not only is useful for local operations in Malta but it allows me to deploy out of area, to Greece and Spain, that would be given more priority. When one comes to the question of coercion, by Frontex or any other part of the Commission forcing Member States to provide these resources, I honestly could not comment on the legal background to that. I am not sure whether that is legally possible but, to give you an idea of what could be done, one could look at NATO and NATO Standing Forces, the Standing Maritime Groups, for instance, where vessels are pledged in rotation. But, again, there you have a 50-year history, a 60-year history of the Alliance working very closely together, there is where you have unified command now because they are so comfortable working with each other, and the pledges were entered into by individual states with the Alliance, not as a blanket measure: "Everybody has to give you something." I cannot really see any coercion of the Member States to give resources happening in the near or medium term.

Q396 Chairman: Mr Busuttil went on to say: "The Italians in the summer when this happened simply said that they thought that Frontex missions would never be sufficiently effective without the participation of Libya because, as you know, Libya has refused to participate in these missions although it was repeatedly invited to do so." Would you like to comment on that?
Major Mallia: I am aware of the Italian position. It is a position which they have not expressed solely at that time but also at later dates. It does hold some

water to some extent. On the other hand, the other option is to do nothing, and that is not an acceptable option for anyone. There are legal problems involved overall with joint deployments—the obligations into which states are entering, the obligations which states may have towards rescued persons, et cetera, et cetera—and these are an issue at this time. So far they have been handled on a case-by-case basis, so when an operational plan is drawn up for a particular operation there will be a set of procedures for that particular operation and they may be different somewhere else. Something in which I will be engaged tomorrow—because unfortunately I am not returning home, I am heading off to Brussels—is that all the Member States, together with the Commission and Frontex, are working on providing clear legal guidelines. These will be provided to all the Member States, to all the joint operations, and these will allow a much more clear view of what obligations each state will be getting into when they get into joint operations. I think they will serve to allay the concerns of a number of Member States. I must also say that, despite that statement by Italy, Italy has been participating in joint operations. In the second stage of Nautilus they were there in a relatively substantial way. They were operating generally from Lampedusa rather than from Malta—but that was for logistical and technical reasons and we had no problem with that—and, as far as I am aware, they participated with at least three boats, one aircraft and two helicopters in the second phase of Nautilus which was in September/October. A practical change of heart has happened for sure. Whether it is a change of heart at the higher levels I cannot comment, but they were definitely there for phase II of our joint operation.

Q397 Lord Hodgson of Astley Abbottts: I wonder if we can drill down a bit and talk about "pledge" as opposed to "conceivably available". Particularly, you sent this very helpful paper, where, in paragraph 13, you say that some of this "reluctance to provide surface assets is related to the fact that no clear solution exists as to where any rescued persons are to be disembarked". In the context of Frontex operations, what relevant directions or guidelines are given? Are they satisfactory to you? Could you give some specific examples of how this works so that we can feed them back into the question of disembarkation and the lack of assets?
Major Mallia: The question of guidance regarding disembarkation has so far been handled on an *ad hoc* basis. For a particular joint operation the participating countries and the effective countries will sit down in a room, discuss the operational plan, which, among other things, will address this issue of disembarkation, and there will be some practical solution to it which is literally working at the lowest

level. It is not something which is based on a general principle. It was made very clear by all parties involved that it does not reflect a general position, it reflects an *ad hoc* arrangement. This obviously is not satisfactory for many of the Member States; it does not provide the stability which they want. That is why now we are looking at it as a working group and trying to identify the exact legal regime so that we can provide a set of blanket rules. Even that itself is not an easy task: there are different interpretations, there are different levels of ratification of legal instruments, so that does also pose a number of problems. On the other hand, we are making very reasonable progress towards it and I think that is the only solution to this issue, having a set of guidelines which provide stability over time, so that any Member State when assessing whether it wants to or does not want to participate in joint operations has a clear legal framework from the word go. The *ad hoc* arrangements, while they generally work, are not sustainable. We cannot continue to make *ad hoc* arrangements for every operation.

Q398 *Lord Hodgson of Astley Abbotts:* You say you are making progress towards the principles. When is that?
Major Mallia: As far as I am aware, the Commission has to report back to the Council either in January or February of next year. I stand to be corrected, however, on that particular date.

Q399 *Chairman:* We are going to move in a short moment to a number of questions about RABITs, but, just to complete the questioning about Frontex, I wonder if I could ask what you think Frontex could do to give more help in safeguarding its borders.
Major Mallia: As you probably know, there has already been a substantial increase in the budget allocated to Frontex for 2008 and that alone will prove of significant assistance to Malta because it has provided for the joint operation around Malta to be extended for a much longer period than was the case this year. We are hoping to conduct the operation for a constant five, possibly six months compared to a total of two and a half months this year with a break in between. That is the first area where we see Frontex definitely assisting us in safeguarding our borders (that is, joint operations). Frontex also has a useful risk-analysis role. We would like to see that strengthened. As far as I am aware, in the business plan for 2008, in the light of the new funding, risk analysis is one of the areas which is going to be addressed. Knowing the trends and what we are going to be facing over the next couple of years will be very useful to us. There is the question of whether Frontex should be operating its own resources. As we have said before, we feel this is a complicated situation, both for Frontex and for the Member States. If Frontex decides to operate ships and aircraft, they will have to carry someone's registration and someone's flag, so someone will be responsible for them and therefore you cannot remove their national nature. We do not see that, therefore, as a particularly practical solution. Training is also another area where Frontex has already delivered and is continuing to deliver more. We are finding very useful training opportunities with Frontex, a lot of which are offered at no cost to us, which is obviously a major incentive. We have a very limited training budget and it has to cover all our competencies, not just border control, so that is another area where Frontex is developing. The one area where we would like to see Frontex move ahead at greater speed is in its role as the contact point between the European Union and third states. Frontex has been empowered to conduct these negotiations with third states, they bring with them the leverage of the Commission, rather than the leverage of a single state, and in addressing the problems on the Northern African rim, most specifically with Libya, we feel that Frontex can take a much more substantial role and should take a much more substantial role because of their supranational character and because of the fact that they bring with them the weight of the complete union rather than just a single Member State. That is one area where we would really like to see Frontex pushing forward at some speed.
Chairman: Lord Teverson, I think you might have another question to wind up on Frontex and then perhaps you might turn to the questions on RABITs.

Q400 *Lord Teverson:* Indeed. Thank you, my Lord Chairman. What is the experience of Malta in receiving the resources it needs to mount operations through pledges from Frontex? I know we have dealt with this to a degree and you sounded a little bit more satisfied with the way things are going. Forgive me for having left the room briefly but I was trying to postpone my next meeting so that I could hear your full evidence, which I am very keen to do. It is clear that you believe this is a young organisation that is developing—and you have gone through some of the areas that you think it should develop to—but do you believe that, despite those issues, it has added value generally to what you are trying to do so far, given its youth? Particularly, this is coming back this area of the resources it needs to mount operations through pledges.
Major Mallia: When it comes to resources, obviously Frontex has to balance the demands of various Member States. The joint operation which is happening around Malta is not the sole joint operation that is happening at sea. We are well aware that operations are happening around the Canaries; the West Mediterranean; the East Mediterranean,

where we have participated. Last week I was in Lisbon and it was stated very clearly by the Director of Frontex, Ilkka Laitinen, that they are trying to rationalise the number of joint operations which are happening. They are seeing that there are many proposals for joint operations but now they are going to have to accept the fact that the resources will always be limited and that they are going to have to prioritise operations in regard to the limited funding available. They are going to do that by risk analysis. That is one step forward. It is clear to us that we cannot expect to be the sole joint operation, or the most important possibly; however, we feel comfortable that with an assessment done on risk analysis we will be receiving adequate funding. Obviously some operations will lose funding, some will possibly lose funding completely and will not occur, and others will gain funding. The manner in which that funding is given, as I have said, is reasonably simple when you compare it to other EU financial instruments. It is a very simple system of funding: it is directly to the operators rather than going through some chain of administrators and it is reasonably prompt. As far as can be expected when you are talking about the sums involved and the bureaucracy which goes with it, we are happy about the promptness. When it comes to the value added by Frontex, if we were to assume for a moment that Frontex did not exist we would still be conducting operations. That is clear. This is not something which is happening because Frontex is in existence. However, where Frontex has helped, at least in the Maltese experience—and I cannot speak for any other Member State—is that, because of our limited size, because of our limited financial resources, Frontex is doing things for us to which previously we could not have dedicated all the resources we would have liked. An example would be risk assessment. We are a military organisation. We do have an intelligence organisation within the military organisation, but they are not solely involved in migration. We cannot dedicate that amount of resources, both human and financial, and time to assessing that particular problem. Frontex is doing that for us as a third party—as a subcontractor, if you would like to put it that way. If I might turn to joint operations: joint operations happened before Frontex, mostly on a bilateral basis, but happening on a multinational basis did not exist before Frontex. I think Frontex has been the vehicle for that. We have yet to see the real rewards of conducting business in this manner. I cannot tell you now whether we have found joint operations to be a very, very good thing or a very, very bad thing. They have definitely had some positive effect but to give you a real assessment would have to be a couple of years down the road— they are still too new—but they would not have happened without Frontex, I firmly believe. The final

area is that Frontex has got more people talking to each other and, strangely enough, both within Member States and between Member States. To give you the example of Italy, the organisations in Italy did not have particularly good co-operation before Frontex. Their co-operation has improved. I have heard it said by Italians themselves, because they are sitting at the same meetings and having to co-operate. This has happened in Malta: our co-operation with the police has improved because of Frontex, because now we are involved in joint conferences, we are involved in joint projects, we are involved in working groups together. This has improved both inter-force liaison within the Member States and, most definitely, the liaison between the Member States. We are talking on a much more regular basis. Sometimes it is just talking shop, just talking general trends, but sometimes it is talking very, very important issues which normally would not have been handled. As a clearing house, in a way, Frontex is adding value. It now remains to be seen in which direction Frontex decides to go. I personally— and this is something which we have also submitted in our written evidence—do not think Frontex should go down the operational path. Frontex should not be an operational organisation, it should be an organisation which co-ordinates, which brings people together, which looks after relations with third countries. That, I think, is where its strengths should lie.

Q401 *Lord Teverson:* That is very interesting. Thank you very much. Finally, could we turn to "RABITs"—the terrible term for the Rapid Border Intervention Teams. Have Maltese border guards participated in RABIT operations? What is the future for that? Do you see RABITs as a positive, added value? Perhaps I can ask you at the same time the other question which you will have seen which is about the carrying of weapons. In which scenarios would you envisage weapons would be needed to be used in the exercise of border operations? You have said you carry weapons but how they are used or the context is very different between civilian and military. Do you think the safeguards are adequate?
Major Mallia: Let me start by speaking about RABITs in general. Regarding RABIT deployments: as far as I am aware, none have as yet happened—and I received an update on RABITs again last week in Portugal. What has occurred is a test deployment to Portugal of a RABIT team, which, as far as I am aware, was approximately 20 people and was an air borders team. That was just a test exercise, a test deployment. RABITs would probably have their major applications on land and air borders, but I say that because, when you look at the pledges of Member States to RABITs, how many experts they will be giving, you do not see the ships which come

with them. They are not equipped to operate in the maritime environment. Operating on the maritime/land interface, yes—possibly interviewing people who have been brought in, et cetera—but I see their main role on land and air borders. They will be useful as a rapid reaction force in cases of real emergencies. The example which was given at the conference last weekend is an actual example: when you have a sudden influx, for instance, of South American citizens towards Spain, trying to pass through the airports, but that is a very particular scenario and the RABITs are a very particular tool. They can only be deployed for very short periods—28 to 30 days, if I am correct—and, again, they are literally the warm bodies. They are not the equipment, really. They are the people. It cannot be an equipment-intensive task which they are going to do, unless they are operating the equipment of the host nation. It remains to be seen how often Member States will ask for a RABIT deployment—because I am sure you are aware it is something which has to be asked for by a particular Member State. Also, on effectiveness when they deploy: there were a number of minor issues in this test deployment, one of which was associated with weapons—and I will speak about that in the answer to the second part of your question. I do think, however, that they are a useful concept, in that you may need to get a number of experts to a place in a hurry to advise on a particular issue or a particular situation. As an operational force patrolling the borders I see less of a value for it, but it remains to be seen. They are a very, very new institution and I think the proof of the pudding will be in the eating. Regarding weapons: one of the contentious issues in the RABIT regulation was this issue of carrying of weapons in a third country by border guards from another Member State. There were a number of restrictions placed upon this. The first of those was that only if the Member State border guards are carrying weapons should the RABIT team carry weapons and they should be of a similar level as those for the host nation. So it is not to be expected that the host nation will be carrying side arms while RABITs roll up in a tank, obviously. The other issue which, unfortunately, was not so clear in the RABIT regulation, if I am correct, was the issue of what we would term a status of forces agreement. There has to be a very clear legal chain and a clear jurisdiction to which these deployed forces are subject, because, if something happens, as it inevitably one day will, we will have to see the liability of that deployed border guard. Is he liable to the host state? Is he liable in his Member State? He definitely cannot be liable in both. That would lead to a number of problems. There does need to be a certain clarity in the status of the individuals deployed. Weapons do have a role in border control, unfortunately. It is an unfortunate fact but it is a fact. Speaking from personal experience, we regularly conduct rescues of in excess of 100 migrants, by a boat which has a crew of 20 people. So you immediately have a law and order issue: you have 100 people on one side and 20 on the other and you have to keep a very strict control of matters. It is a fact that we have often found these people carry weapons: knives, shanks (a sharp object with a wooden handle) and various other bits and pieces. So far, there have been no firearms, I am glad to say. The weapons have two roles in such a scenario. The first is, literally, the visual impact of the fact that the people are carrying weapons. It immediately acts as a deterrent: if somebody is going to do something silly, he will certainly think about it twice. The second reason we carry weapons—and it comes from our rules of engagement—is for self-protection, protection of third parties (that is, when there is an act happening), or, if it is the last resort, to prevent that act even happening, so as a deterrent. These are issues which are rarely talked about but unfortunately do exist. There is a security threat on board a small boat when you have rescued 100 people. You have to keep the situation well under control. There are enough hazards on board as it is. There are the medical hazards involved in picking up these people, who carry a number of diseases which are no longer present here in Europe—and this has also been another issue which we have had to address. So weapons are unfortunately a necessity when conducting such operations. There is one area where I think this could be improved upon. I am sure you are all aware of the common core curriculum, which is another Frontex project to try to give a basic level of training for border guards. I think it would be very reassuring for all Member States if the common core curriculum contained weapon safety training and rules of engagement, because then I am assured that the RABIT being sent to my country has a basic knowledge of which I know exactly what the points are: I know how he is using his weapon; how he will be handling his weapon; what his safety procedures are. That would be much more reassuring. It is a simple tool of training but it would be a common training for all EU border guards.

Chairman: Are there any other questions.

Baroness Henig: I would just like to say that was excellent clarification of all the issues.

Chairman: Major Mallia, I would like to thank you for what I think has been an outstanding presentation. You have been clear, you have been helpful and you have been most interesting. I would like to say that I think many ministers I have known over many years in this House, at both ends of it, could well have taken advantage of sitting and listening to the way you have answered our questions. I can only think you will not be a Major for much longer and I congratulate you very warmly on the way you have answered our questions. Thank you very much.

WEDNESDAY 5 DECEMBER 2007

Present   Dear, L   Teverson, L
                 Harrison, L   Tonge, B
                 Jopling, L (Chairman)   Young of Norwood Green, L
                 Mawson, L

Memorandum by Immigration Law Practitioners' Association (ILPA)

1. ILPA welcomes this inquiry by the sub-committee into Frontex. ILPA is a professional association with some 1,000 members, who are barristers, solicitors and advocates practising in all aspects of immigration, asylum and nationality law. Academics, non-government organisations and others working in this field are also members. ILPA exists to promote and improve the giving of advice on immigration and asylum, through teaching, provision of resources and information. ILPA has provided written and oral evidence to the Select Committee on the European Union on many occasions. This response focuses on areas where ILPA considers it can be of most assistance to the Committee.

Question: *Whether the institutional and legal framework ensures adequate accountability of Frontex*

2. In ILPA's view the founding instrument of Frontex (Regulation 2007/2004/EC) is deficient in legal terms on two points:

     (i)   the legal obligations governing Frontex are uncertain; and

     (ii)   the territorial remit of Frontex is uncertain.

The legal obligations governing Frontex are uncertain

3. Frontex is a first pillar agency. However, its role in such operational activities as the co-ordination of operations and the exchange of information makes it look much more like a third pillar agency such as EUROPOL or EUROJUST. Changes to the structure of decision-making in Title IV (including in the mandate for the Reform Treaty),[1] may affect the extent of scrutiny of the activities of Frontex. There is reason to suppose that scrutiny will in any event be extremely weak.

4. Regulation 2007/2004/EC sets out that Frontex is a body of the Community and has legal personality.[2] However, it treats Frontex as a management agency and makes scant reference to the legal framework for its work, including on such matters as the applicable law (including human rights law) and the jurisdiction of the European Court of Justice (ECJ) over the work of Frontex. It envisages Frontex setting up "specialised branches in the Member States"[3] but fails to indicate whether or not such branches would have separate legal personalities.

5. Article 10 of Regulation 2007/2004/EC states that the "exercise of executive powers by the Agency's staff and the Member States' experts acting on the territory of another Member State shall be subject to the national law of that Member State". No definition of "executive powers" is provided and there is nothing further to indicate the legal obligations governing Frontex activities. By contrast Article 9 of Regulation 863/2007 on Rapid Border Intervention Teams provides that "while performing the tasks and exercising the powers as referred to in Article 6(1), the members of the teams shall comply with Community law and the national law of the host Member State".

---

[1]   Draft Treaty amending the Treaty on European Union & the Treaty establishing the European Community, 23 July 2007.
[2]   Council Regulation (EC) 2007/2004/ (26.10.2004, OJ L 349/25.11.2004)., Art 15(1).
[3]   Article 16(1). See also Preamble, Recital 13.
[4]   House of Lords EU Select Committee Report, *Illegal Migrants: Proposals for a Common EU Returns Policy*, 32nd Report, Session 2005–06, HL Paper 166 (Q591).

6. This leaves open the question of obligations stemming from public international law. The Director of Frontex, in the context of questions about Frontex' role in returns, told the House of Lords Select Committee that "it is up to Member States" to check compliance with the European Convention on Human Rights'.[5] But who will guard the guardians?

7. See further our answer on how Frontex should develop in the future, below.

Territorial remit of Frontex

8. The territorial scope of Frontex action is unclear. Article 2 of Regulation 2007/2004 defines the tasks of Frontex. The list includes to:

— "coordinate operational co-operation between Member States in the field of management of external borders"; and

— "assist Member States in circumstances requiring increased technical and operational assistance at the external border".

For this purpose, the notion of "external border" is defined by Article 1(4) of the Regulation, as now amended by Regulation 863/2007 on Rapid Border Intervention Teams, as "the land and sea borders of the Member States and their airports and seaports, to which the provisions of Community law on the crossing of external borders by persons apply".

9. Articles 2 and 1(4) together appear to mean that the activities of Frontex are limited to the territories and border of the Member States. That conclusion is not altered by the permission given to Frontex by Article 14 of Regulation 2007/2004 to co-operate with third countries. If this interpretation is correct, Frontex lacks legal authorisation to engage in activities—such as in the context of HERA II and HERA III —which concern activities on the high seas or on the territory (including the territorial sea) of other States.

10. The external sea, land and air borders of the EU are not subject to a coherent or common definition. The most important aspect of variation is the Schengen acquis, which provides for the abolition of intra-Member State border controls among certain Member States. From January 2008 this should include all the pre-2004 Member States, with the exceptions noted below, and the Member States that joined on 1 May 2004. It is not yet clear to us whether this will also include the two Member States that joined the EU on 1 January 2007.[6] The exceptions are Denmark, which continues to apply the common internal border control-free area with the others via the Schengen Implementing Agreement and to apply the other aspects of the Schengen acquis; and Ireland and the UK, which do not participate in measures which are a development of the Schengen acquis except to the extent that agreement has been reached in the Council for their participation.[7] A number of non-EU states participate fully in the Schengen acquis by virtue of agreements with the EU. Iceland and Norway participate fully and Switzerland is in the process of doing so. An agreement reached with Iceland and Norway permits those two countries to vote on measures that constitute the extension of the Schengen acquis. The governance of the external border is thus not exclusively within the hands of the Member States. Non-Member States are involved in Schengen while Ireland and the UK are not, and Denmark participates by way of an international agreement rather than EU law proper. Thus, the EU's external border runs through the internal market but embraces third countries. The control of the internal borders is unclear, with the continuing application of internal controls at only some of them. The controls at external borders are far from uniform, with some, such as those with Iceland and Norway, having no controls, while others are heavily controlled. Other developments such as enlargement change the nature of the external borders. As the internal borders are the subject of considerable fluidity, the definition of the external borders is also less than obvious.

11. The objective of Frontex to coordinate joint operations by Member States at the external sea, land and air borders is thus complicated insofar as the identification of those borders is not self-evident. How are Frontex and others to interpret its mandate?

12. When Frontex was established, its mission of coordination of joint operations by Member States at the external sea, land and air borders was not underpinned by any EU law clarifying how people should cross that border. EU Regulation 562/2006 (the "Borders Code"), where these rules are set out, applied only from 13 October 2006. Thus Frontex was established to carry out a function about which there was little, if any, satisfactory legal clarity. Since the establishment of Frontex, Bulgaria and Romania have become Member States, changing the external border.

---

[5] House of Lords EU Select Committee Report, *Illegal Migrants: Proposals for a Common EU Returns Policy*, 32nd Report, Session 2005–06, HL Paper 166 (Q591).
[6] "Citizens without a Constitution, Borders without a State: EU Free Movement of Persons" in Baldaccini, Guild & Toner *Whose Freedom, Security and Justice?* EU Immigration & Asylum Law & Policy, Hart, Oxford 2007.
[7] See Opinion A-G Trstenjak in C-77-05 *UK v Council*, 10 July 2007, discussed below.

13. The definition of those persons who enjoy a presumption in favour of crossing the external border (and move freely within the internal borders of the Schengen area) is complicated. Article 2(15) of the Borders Code provides for a list of residence permits issued by the Member States that authorise stay or re-entry into the territory. Article 5(1) (b) provides that third country nationals holding a valid residence permit do not require visas to enter the Schengen area. Effectively, where a third country national holds a residence permit issued by a Member State there is a presumption that s/he should be admitted at any external border crossing. The list of residence permits (2006/C 247/01) includes, for example, more than 30 different documents issued by Germany and a similar number issued by France. For Finland, some documents are residence permits for the purposes of the list only if issued before or after specified dates. Each Member State in the Schengen system issues its residence documents in its own language and without translation. Nationals of the Member States have a right, only qualified on grounds of public policy, public security and public health, to cross an external or internal border of the EU's Internal Market, not just the Schengen area. Turkish nationals who qualify as workers and who have accrued rights under the EC Turkey Association Agreement and its subsidiary legislation also enjoy a right to continue to work and to residence and, by extension, to cross the external border to return to the Member State where they work and live.

14. While Frontex is established for the purpose of co-ordination, nonetheless as an EU agency it must comply with EU law. Although it was established before the Borders Code was adopted, following the adoption of the Code it is incumbent on Frontex to ensure that in the context of its co-ordination activities, the Member States that carry the operational responsibilities, faithfully and fully comply with EU law including the Borders Code.[8]

15. While the measures adopted in Title IV EC, including the Borders Code, contain many references to the 1951 UN Convention relating to the Status of Refugees and its 1967 protocol (see for instance article 3(b)), there is no information on how, in co-ordinating external border activities, Frontex is to achieve this. The information available on projects Frontex has co-ordinated (for example HERA I, II and III)[9] gives no adequate account of how the principle of *non-refoulement* has been observed. UNHCR has expressed concern about the respect for refugee protection in Frontex' activities.[10] EU texts refer to Member States' obligations under the Refugee Convention, but in operations the EU institutions and agencies seem leave it to Member States to sort out how to resolve the tensions between international obligations and the EU ones. The result may too often be a responsibility gap—the EU institutions and agencies deny responsibility because they do not have an obvious operational role, the Member States' institutions and agencies deny responsibility because they are bound to carry out faithfully their obligations in EU law.

(Lack of) accountability—the Management Board

16. Because Frontex is an agency there is limited opportunity for scrutiny of its activities and thus limited accountability.[11] Prior to the creation of Frontex, ILPA had voiced similar concerns about the Strategic Committee for Immigration, Frontiers and Asylum (SCIFA), its lack of transparency, and the secrecy about its activities and the lack of democratic control of those activities.[12] The status and work of Frontex, and its activities, must be understood in the context of the Hague Programme[13] which views the establishment of secure borders as necessary not only in the context of preventing illegal immigration to the European Union, but also as part of counter-terrorism activities. The exceptions to normal levels of scrutiny, accountability and constraints, for example on the retention and sharing of information, that are seen in the context of Counter-Terrorism measures, can be expected to be prayed in justification of lack of scrutiny of Frontex.

---

[8] "Danger—borders under construction: assessing the first five years of border policy in an area of freedom, security and justice" in J de Zwaan and F Goudappel, *Freedom, Security and Justice in the European Union: Implementation of the Hague Programme* Asser Press, The Hague, 2006, pp 45–72.

[9] S Carrera *The EU Border Management Strategy: Frontex and the Challenges of Irregular Immigration in the Canary Islands* CEPS, Brussels, March 2007.

[10] "UNHCR and Frontex have begun discussions on cooperation, as foreseen in Regulation 2007/2004/EC and proposed by the Commission in its Communication on Reinforcing Management of the EU's Southern Maritime Borders, COM(2006)733. UNHCR is willing to collaborate with Frontex to ensure that personnel deployed on joint operations are trained in principles of international law and refugee protection. Guidance would appear also to be needed on how respect for international refugee law can be ensured in carrying out border operations. See UNHCR's Recommendations for Portugal's European Union Presidency July–December 2007, 24 July 2007.

[11] See Dehousse, R, "Regulation by networks in the European Community: the Role of European Agencies" (1997) 4 *Journal of European Public Policy* 2, 246–261.

[12] ILPA Evidence to House of Lords Select Committee on the European Union, *Proposals for a European Border Guard*, 29th Report, Session 2002–03, HL Paper 133, reproduced therein.

[13] The Hague Programme: strengthening freedom, security and justice in the European Union, European Council [2005] OJ C53/1, 3 March 2005.

17. As an Agency the work of Frontex is coordinated by a Management Board, made up of representatives of participating Member States and of the Commission[14] consisting of one representative per participating Member State plus two representatives from the Commission[15] and a representation of associated Schengen States. The Management Board approves Frontex's annual work programme and appoint its Executive Director—these require a three quarters majority vote. Decisions, on a case-by-case basis, to allow the UK and Ireland to participate in Frontex activities require an absolute majority vote. A Management Board is a weak method of scrutiny and for accountability at the best of times, but is particularly weak in the context of Frontex. The Annual Report of the Management Board is to be made public.[16] In addition, an annual work programme must be sent to the Council and Commission[17] and an independent external evaluation of the Agency must be commissioned within the first three years of its operation.[18] None of these amount to mechanisms for accountability, and they offer precious little opportunity for scrutiny, in particular for prospective scrutiny of Frontex' work.

(Lack of) accountability—accountability to Member States

18. Individual States have a measure of control over the activities of Frontex. They must consent to joint operations and pilot projects.[19] In addition, Members of the Management Board representing a Member State must vote to approve specific activities to be carried out at the external border of that State.[20] However, this provision is more about protecting State sovereignty than providing scrutiny of Frontex's own activities.[21] The provisions in the Regulation should be read in the light of the agreement reached between Member States reflected in Protocol 21 to the Treaty establishing a Constitution for Europe,[22] which provides that the provisions of the Treaty will be without prejudice to Member States' competencies to conclude agreements with third countries, subject only to those agreements respecting EU law and international agreements. Again, the question is: who guards the guardians? If there were increased safeguards, scrutiny and accountability of Frontex, it is arguable that this would merely increase the likelihood that member States would go it alone, under bilateral or other agreements with third countries.

Extent of Frontex' competencies—operations

19. It is a mark of the weakness of the mechanisms for scrutiny and accountability of Frontex that is has so far proved impossible to determine Frontex' competencies, their extent and legal basis, and the extent to which Frontex will have an operational role.

20. The title of Regulation 2007/2004/EC refers to the "management of operational co-operation". The question of whether Frontex will have a role in operations has been left very unclear,[23] as is demonstrated by the summary of its activities on the EUROPA website:

> "Frontex coordinates operational cooperation between Member States in the field of management of external borders; assists Member States in the training of national border guards, including the establishment of common training standards; carries out risk analyses; follows up the development of research relevant for the control and surveillance of external borders; assists Member States in circumstances requiring increased technical and operational assistance at external borders; and provides Member States with the necessary support in organising joint return operations".[24]

---

[14] Article 21. The UK and Ireland will be invited to attend meetings, see Article 23(4).
[15] Article 21(1).
[16] Article 20(2)(b). To be forwarded by 15 06 of the year following its adoption to European Parliament, Council, Commission, Economic and Social Committee and Court of Auditors.
[17] Article 20(2)(c). This report is to be sent by 30 September each year.
[18] Article 33.
[19] Council Regulation 2007/2004/EC Art 3(1).
[20] Art 20(3).
[21] See also Art 2(2), protecting Member States' entitlement to cooperate other than through Frontex. Without clarity on the competencies of Frontex itself, the sphere of action preserved for Member States and their obligations to report such action to Frontex under Article 2(2) are unclear.
[22] [2004] OJ C 310, 16 December 2004.
[23] The original proposal for such an agency COM (2003) 323 final, calls for the creation of a "much more operational body" but see House of Lords Select Committee on the European Union, *Illegal Migrants: Proposals for a Common EU Returns Policy*, 32nd Report, Session 2005–06, HL Paper 166 (Q581) evidence of Mr Laitinen, Director of Frontex.
[24] http://europa.eu/agencies/community_agencies/Frontex/index_en.htm, accessed 7 September 2007.
[25] *Commission proposal for a Regulation establishing a mechanism for the creation of Rapid Border Intervention Teams and amending the Border Agency Regulation* (COM (2006) 401 final, Brussels, 19 July 2006, Art 12.

21. The view that Frontex and teams operating under it will have a role in operations is reinforced by the proposals to amend Regulation 20007/2004/EC to allow for the creation and deployment of Rapid Border Intervention Teams (known, rather unfortunately, as RABITS).[26] RABITS would be able to carry out surveillance activities at the border.[27] Border guards from other EU Member States, are entrusted with a series of wide-ranging tasks of border checks, but also border surveillance, including prevention (Arts 7 and 8). This proposal will perhaps receive more scrutiny than the regulation establishing Frontex, because the European Parliament will have a role in passing the amending legislation. Operational activities also appear to be envisaged under Art 9 of 2007/2004/EC, which relates to the role of Frontex in return operations.[28]

Data Protection

22. Particular attention should be given to whether the institutional and legal framework ensures accountability of Frontex on matters of data protection. There is no Data Protection framework for Frontex. Article 11 of Regulation 2007/2004/EC is very much an enabling provision and does not spell out constraints. These disappeared during the drafting process—the Commission's original draft limited cooperation with EUROPOL to the sharing of strategic information, not of a personal nature. Articles 13 and 14 provide for co-operation with EUROPOL and other international organisations and merely require that arrangements for this are in accordance with the relevant provisions of the Treaty.[29] This must be considered in the context of proposals to ensure increased "interoperability"between different European Union information systems and databases, such as the Schengen Information System II (SIS II), EURODAC and the Visa Information Service (VIS).[30] This is very much linked with the question of whether Frontex has an operational role. If it is seen merely as coordinating and managing the activities of States, this is likely to reduce the questions asked about its own access to, and use of, an increasingly sophisticated database.

Question: *Does the AG's Opinion in the case challenging the UK's exclusion from Frontex affect the UK's current position?*

23. The UK has challenged the Council's refusal to allow the UK to opt into the Biometric Passports[31] and Frontex[32] regulations. The dispute raises a key interpretative question concerning the Schengen Protocol. The respective mechanisms for opting into measures under Title IV of the EC Treaty, on the one hand, and Schengen measures, on the other, differ. The United Kingdom and Ireland may opt in to measures under Title IV of the EC Treaty as of right. In contrast, their opting in to measures that form part of the Schengen *acquis* must be approved by the Council unanimously, in accordance with Article 4 of the Schengen Protocol.[33] The dispute has immediate wider relevance, for example in relation to the UK's access to immigration aspects of the Schengen Information System and future Visa Information System. The Council and Commission argue that for the UK to access this information, it would have to opt in to the entire body of related Schengen measures.[34]

24. Pursuant to Article 4, the Council in 2000 approved the UK's opt in to various Schengen measures on illegal immigration, policing and criminal law.[35] However, where measures build on the Schengen *acquis*, Article 5 of the Protocol appears at first reading to allow Ireland and the United Kingdom to participate

[26] *Commission proposal for a Regulation establishing a mechanism for the creation of Rapid Border Intervention Teams and amending the Border Agency Regulation* (COM (2006) 401 final, Brussels, 19 July 2006, Art 12.
[27] COM (2006) 401, Arts 7 and 8.
[28] See the Explanatory Memorandum submitted by the Home Office to the House of Lords Select Committee on the European Union for their report *op. cit.*
[29] The first Frontex Annual Report states that so far the Agency prepared a contribution to Europol's first Organised Crime Threat Assessment. *Frontex General Report for the year 2005*, Council document 10438/06, Brussels, 13 June 2006 which describes work with EUROPOL.
[30] See eg the European Council *Declaration on combating terrorism* 25 March 2004 and see the European Commission Communication COM (2006) 402 final, 19 July 2006 on the fight against illegal immigration., which makes extensive reference to Frontex. See also Levi, M and DS Wall, "Technologies, Security and Privacy in the post-9/11 European Information Society" (2004) 31/2 *Journal of Law and Society*, 194.
[31] Council Regulation 2252/2004 of 13 December 2004 on standards for security measures and biometrics in passports and travel documents issued by Member States ((2004) OJ L 385/1).
[32] Council Regulation 2007/2004 of 26 October 2004 establishing a European Agency for the Management of Operational Cooperation at the External Borders of the Member States of the European Union ((2004) OJ L 349/1).
[33] Art 4 of the Protocol Integrating the Schengen *Acquis* into the Framework of the European Union:
  "Ireland and the United Kingdom of Great Britain and Northern Ireland, which are not bound by the Schengen *acquis*, may at any time request to take part in some or all of the provisions of this *acquis*. The Council shall decide on the request with the unanimity of its members referred to in Article 1 and of the representative of the Government of the State concerned".
[34] See S Peers, Statewatch Analysis: EU Reform Treaty Analysis no 4: British and Irish opt outs from EU Justice and Home Affairs (JHA) law, 16 August 2007, p 6.
[35] Council Decision 2000/365/EC 29 May 2000 concerning the request of the United Kingdom of Great Britain and Ireland to take part in some of the provisions of the Schengen *acquis* (OJ 200 L 131, p 43).

without such approval.[36] On the basis of this reading the UK argued that the Schengen Council acted illegally when it refused to allow the UK to participate in the impugned regulations. It advocated a narrow conception of the scope of Article 4, being those measures that are "integral" to Schengen, while Article 5 should be read broadly, encompassing all "Schengen-related" measures.[37]

25. When Advocate General Trstenjak gave his opinion[38] in July, he supported the Council and Commission's interpretation, that Article 5 is subject to Article 4, and so participation in Schengen building measures is only permissible if the United Kingdom (or Ireland) has, pursuant to Article 4 of the Protocol, already sought and obtained the approval of the other member states for participating in those parts of the *acquis* on which the subsequent regulations are based. This interpretation (the "subordination thesis") was also supported by the Commission, on the basis that it was necessary to preserve the integrity of the Schengen *acquis*, and avoid a "patchwork of cooperation and of obligations".[39]

26. The AG noted of the UK's selective participation "Legal writers describe the United Kingdom's position as appearing to involve a total rejection of the free movement of persons without checks at internal borders, accompanied nonetheless by a wish to cooperate in the repressive part of the legal regime governing free movement".[40] He noted that Article 5, in granting a right to participate, would in effect allow the UK or Ireland "to slow down or even completely block the adoption of any Schengen measure".[41] However, it granted a right to participate "narrower than at first sight",[42] allowing the UK (or Ireland) to participate in some Schengen measures which were not subject to a prior authorisation from the Council under Article 4, but only if the measures were capable of being applied "autonomously".[43] He opined that both regulations were not amenable to autonomous application, given the links between external border control, passport control and the abolition of internal borders.[44]

While notionally this reasoning leaves open the space for the independent application of Article 5 should a Schengen building measure be deemed autonomous, he also explicitly referred to the subordination thesis as "correct".[45] That the Advocate General supports the view of the Council and Commission is of no immediate relevance because the European Court of Justice is not bound to follow this opinion.

Question: *How the agency's role should develop in the future*

27. In ILPA's view, Frontex itself should be governed by a clause similar to Article 9 of Regulation 863/2007, providing that while exercising its powers and performing its task, Frontex shall comply with community law and the national law of the host member State.

28. ILPA also favours the amendment of the list of obligations applicable to Frontex and RABITs, to include those which stem from public international law. This category would include both customary principles, and treaty-based obligations for which there is a large consensus among member states. Many public international law principles anyway bind the EC/EU and its institutions.[46] An express provision would avoid any doubt as to the applicability to the EC/EU of international obligations binding upon the Member States.

29. The following principles of public international law in particular ought to bind Frontex. In each case, they are binding on all or most member states, and there has been at least some recognition given to the principles at the EC/ EU level.

---

[36] Article 5 of the Protocol Integrating the Schengen *Acquis* into the Framework of the European Union provides, insofar as relevant, as follows:

> "1. Proposals and initiatives to build upon the Schengen *acquis* shall be subject to the relevant provisions of the Treaties . . . where either Ireland or the United Kingdom or both have not notified the President of the Council in writing within a reasonable period that they wish to take part, the authorisation referred to in Article [11] of the Treaty establishing the European Community or Article [40] of the Treaty on European Union shall be deemed to have been granted to the Members States referred to in Article 1 and to Ireland or the United Kingdom where either of them wishes to take part in the areas of cooperation in question . . ."

[37] Opinion, para 44.
[38] Case C-77/05 *United Kingdom v Council ("Border Agency Regulation")* and Case C-137/05 *United Kingdom v Council ("Passports Regulation")*, Opinion 10 July 2007.
[39] Opinion, para 71.
[40] Opinion, para 94.
[41] Opinion, para 96.
[42] Opinion, para 99.
[43] Opinion, paras 97 and 101.
[44] Opinion, paras 102—105.
[45] Opinion, para 105.
[46] See eg the statements in Case C-286/90 *Poulsen and Diva Navigation* [1992] ECR I-6019, para 9 and Case C-162/96 *Racke* [1998] ECR I-3655, para 45.

30. *Assistance in cases of distress.* It is an established customary law principle that a state must ensure that both its own vessels and those under its flag should give assistance to this SHIPS ?? in distress at sea. The obligation is codified in Article 98 of the UN Convention on the Law of the Sea 1982 (UNCLOS), to which the European Community and all 27 Member States are party and in Regulation 10(a) of Chapter V of the International Convention for the Safety of Life at Sea 1974 (SOLAS), to which all 27 member states are party.

31. *Search and rescue.* The Search and Rescue Convention of 1979 (SAR) requires participating coastal states to maintain search and rescue facilities, engage in search and rescue operations, and co-operate with other states in doing both. SAR has been ratified by 24 EU member states, and the three exceptions (Austria, Czech Republic and Slovakia) are landlocked states. While the EC/ EU is not itself a party to the SAR Convention, the Council of Ministers adopted a recommendation in 1983 calling on all member states to ratify it, including because that would improve safety in the Community's coastal area.[47]

32.   *Freedom of the high seas.* The customary law of the sea recognises the freedom of the high seas for all vessels flying a state flag. This principle is codified in Article 87 of UNCLOS (above). In the immigration context, the Protocol against the Smuggling of Migrants by Land, Sea and Air of 2000 must also be taken into account. This allows for government vessels to intercept other vessels which they have reasonable grounds to suspect are engaged in the smuggling of migrants by sea. It is however a pre-condition to interception that the vessel either has no effective flag, or that the permission of the flag state for interception has been obtained. The Smuggling Protocol has been ratified by 22 member states. (The exceptions are Austria, the Czech Republic, Greece, Ireland and Luxembourg.) It has also been ratified by the EC, on the basis of its competence over external borders.[48]

33. *Non-refoulement*: It is generally agreed that Article 3 of the European Convention on Human Rights prohibits action at sea or in another state's territory which risk the return of an individual to a place where they are at risk of torture or inhuman or degrading treatment. There is also support for the view that, under the Geneva Convention on the Status of Refuges, a state must take responsibility for the asylum application where (i) a vessel of that state has intercepted or rescued an individual who wishes to seek asylum, and (ii) the alternative(s) risk direct or indirect return to the state of alleged persecution.[49] All Member States are bound by Article 3 ECHR and the Geneva Convention. These have also been recognised at the EC/ EU level: the principle in Article 3 ECHR is covered by the general statement in Article 6(2) EU, and is recognised specifically in Article 4 of the Charter of Fundamental Rights, while the Geneva Convention is referred to expressly in Article 63(1) EC, and the right to seek asylum is set out in Article 18 of the Charter of Fundamental Rights.

34. In ILPA's view, it is desirable that these public international law principles be clearly binding on Frontex. If that were done, it would ensure that the principles governed both its own activities and also those of member states when participating in Frontex operations.

35. The mandate of Frontex should be clarified to place the correct application of EU law, in particular the Borders Code, at the heart. Simply ensuring that the issue of appeal forms and information to every person refused admission at the external border as required by the Borders Code would be an excellent addition to the rule of law in the EU to which Frontex should address itself. Co-ordinating the full and effective application of the Member States' obligation of *non-refoulement* in respect of refugees is another task that Frontex ought to undertake as a matter of priority. Member States remain responsible for the correct application of EU and international law in control of the EU's external frontiers. Frontex should have a role in ensuring that Member States correctly carry out those duties and should refer to the Commission any breaches that might found the Commission's commencing enforcement proceedings against the failing Member State. The legitimacy of the EU's external border depends on the proper implementation by the relevant Member States of their international human rights obligations. Frontex, as the EU's Agency responsible for co-ordinating these activities must place these obligations at the heart of its activities.

26 September 2007

---

[47] Council Recommendation of 25 July 1983, [1983] OJ 237/34.
[48] Council Decision 2006/67/EC [2006] OJ L 262/34.
[49] On both the ECHR and the Refugee Convention, see European Commission, Study on the International Law Instruments in relation to Illegal Immigration by Sea, SEC (2007) 691, Annex, section 4.1.2.

Memorandum by Refugee Council and ECRE (European Council on Refugees and Exiles)

1. INTRODUCTION

1.1 The Refugee Council is the largest charity working with asylum seekers and refugees across the UK. We campaign for their rights and help them to rebuild their lives in safety.

1.2 ECRE is a European network of 76 key non-governmental organisations in 31 European countries, working for the protection and integration of refugees, advocating for a humane and generous European asylum policy. Our strength lies in working together at the European and national level as a united, pan-European network. Together with a broad range of stakeholders, including refugees themselves, we seek to improve asylum and refugee rights in Europe.

1.3 The Refugee Council and ECRE welcome this timely inquiry and the opportunity to comment on the European Agency for the Management of Operational Cooperation at the External Borders of the EU Member States, Frontex. We share the view that the Agency's mandated powers are expanding fast and consider that this is happening without due attention to the establishment and/or clarification of the Agency's role and responsibilities in relation to human rights. We are particularly concerned with the right to seek asylum as enshrined in the Universal Declaration of Human Rights and the extent to which this may be violated as a result of Frontex activities.

1.4 Our comments focus primarily on whether the procedures and operations of Frontex are carried out with full respect for international legal, political and moral obligations, with particular reference to individuals in mixed migration flows who may be in need of international protection. We have also addressed a number of the Committee's questions pertaining to accountability, the legal framework for exercise of border guards' powers, the nature of working agreements, risk analyses, monitoring and evaluation, and the participation of the UK.

2. SUMMARY

2.1 Frontex fails to demonstrate adequate consideration of international and European asylum and human rights law including the 1951 Convention relating to the Status of Refugees and European Community (EC law) in respect of access to asylum and the prohibition of *refoulement*.

2.2 There is a worrying lack of clarity regarding Frontex accountability for ensuring compliance with international and EC legal obligations by Member States involved in Frontex coordinated operations. This is compounded by the lack of transparency, and the absence of independent monitoring and democratic accountability of the Agency.

2.3 The relationship between the UK and Frontex requires further clarification, in particular with regard to the applicability of the Schengen Borders Code.

2.4 Frontex involvement in extra-territorial operations raises questions regarding jurisdiction, accountability and responsibility towards asylum seekers.

2.5 All training provided by Frontex should include international human rights and protection principles and obligations.

2.6 Frontex risk analyses and feasibility studies, as the basis for operations and the distribution of resources under the External Borders Fund, must be publicly available.

2.7 Frontex should assist Member States involved in joint operations, to collect data on asylum flows and the impact of Frontex operations on migratory trends.

2.8 Frontex should not advance its involvement in joint return operations until the EU adopts common standards on return.

3. GENERAL COMMENTS

3.1 Frontex must necessarily be viewed in the context of today's increasing and sophisticated barriers to physical access to the EU. Such measures affect all migrants, including amongst them, persons who need protection. With the mandate of *"facilitat[ing] . . . the application of . . . Community measures relating to the management of external borders . . . by ensuring the coordination of Member States' actions in the implementation of those measures"*,[50]Frontex is becoming an increasingly important actor in Member States'

---

[50] Council Regulation (EC) 2007/2004, Article 1.2.

efforts to prevent irregular migration to Europe. The Agency is growing very quickly and has seen its budget increase from €12.4 Mio in 2006 to €35 Mio for 2007.

3.2 Between July and August 2006, Frontex was involved in detecting and diverting over 6000 "*illegal migrants*" from the Canary Islands,[51] which have also seen a 60% drop in arrivals of undocumented migrants by boat in the past year.[52] Any decreases in the number of irregular entries into the EU stemming from the implementation of immigration control measures are presented as a success by the EU and as a factor that contributes to saving human lives.[53] This interpretation fails to acknowledge the consequences of these measures for individuals fleeing persecution.

3.3 Notwithstanding international protection needs, it is unclear whether there are mechanisms in place to deal with the wider humanitarian needs, particularly medical requirements, of persons rescued, intercepted or diverted during Frontex operations. We would like to see a commitment by Frontex to help ensure adequate reception facilities are available to meet the needs of all migrants wherever they are taken. These could be based on the current model in place at a reception centre on the Italian island of Lampedusa, for example.

3.4 We are extremely concerned that the interdiction of all potential irregular entrants from physical access to the EU at its external borders is indiscriminate. In lacking any specific measures to safeguard the rights of people who are potentially in need of protection, this undermines the right of refugees to seek asylum.

3.5 The result of preventing the arrival of refugees in Europe, is that EU Member States fall short of their human rights values and obligations and leave the responsibility to take care of refugees to developing countries which often struggle to do so.

3.6 We urge this inquiry to address the following key questions:

— How does a border guard functioning under Frontex coordination respond when encountering someone who wishes to seek asylum? How is this different when in EU territory, at the external border, in international waters or on third country waters for example?

— How does Frontex ensure that the operations it coordinates do not breach Member States' obligations, for example when diverting boats back to their place of departure?

— How can Frontex ensure that operations carried out beyond EU borders do not lead to systematic violations of international law?

— If violations do occur, who can be held accountable for them and how?

3.7 We are concerned that Frontex border control activities, if not managed properly, could lead to breaches of human rights as serious as *refoulement*. Transparency is called for in Article 28 (2) of Frontex's founding Regulation; lack of public accountability in practice may be giving Member States the opportunity to avoid fundamental human rights obligations.

4. LEGAL FRAMEWORK

4.1 We understand that, just as obligations stemming from international and European refugee and human rights law, as well as European Community law, are incumbent upon the relevant authorities of Member States, compliance is also required by these States when their agents participate in Frontex operations. This obligation extends to any other border control mechanisms, such as the Rapid Border Intervention Teams (RABITs) and the newly agreed Coastal Patrol Network, in which states may participate.

4.2 International human rights law stipulates that there can be no exception to the prohibition on directly or indirectly sending persons to a place where they may face torture, inhuman or degrading treatment or punishment. This is outlined in the UN Convention Against Torture[54] and International Covenant on Civil and Political Rights[55] as well as the European Convention on Human Rights to which Member States are bound. The prohibition on return to persecution for reasons contained in the 1951 Refugee Convention itself is often said to form the "cornerstone" of refugee law.

4.3 However no mention is made in Frontex's founding regulation or operational reports of the prohibition on *refoulement* as contained in all of the above instruments to which Member States have signed up. This is evidently of concern given that Frontex's task is to control international borders. Welcome reference is made

---

[51] Frontex Annual Report 2006, p 13.
[52] EU Observer: EU border agency cuts African migrant numbers.
[53] Presidency Conclusions of 21–22 June 2007, paragraph 18. and Frontex press release *Joint Operation Nautilus 2007—the end of the first phase*" 6 August 2007
http://www.frontex.europa.eu/newsroom/news—releases/art28.html
[54] Article 3.
[55] Article 7.

to Member States' obligations concerning *"international protection,*[56] *in particular as regards non-refoulement"*[57] in the subsequent Council Regulation establishing Rapid Border Intervention Teams (RABITs) although no specific reference is made to the 1951 Refugee Convention.

4.4 Turning to European Community law, the Schengen Borders Code sets out the rules on border control and border surveillance and is applicable wherever these activities take place. The Code states that refugees and people in need of protection represent an exception to the requirements normally demanded of third country nationals crossing external borders and that refusal of entry must be substantiated with reasons and accompanied by a right of appeal.[58] There is no indication as to how this may be put into effect in the context of a Frontex operation.

4.5 The Asylum Procedures Directive[59] applies to applications for asylum made in the territory (including territorial waters) of Member States as well as at the border or in transit zones.[60] The Directive requires states to guarantee access to the asylum procedure and affords asylum seekers the right to remain in the territory, at the border or in a transit zone pending the examination of the claim and the right to an effective remedy, including against a decision of inadmissibility.

4.6 The European Commission's view is that *"asylum must be an important feature of the response, and an effective option for persons requiring international protection. To this end, it is necessary to ensure coherent and effective application of the Member States' protection obligations in the context of measures relating to the interception and rescue at sea of persons who may be in need of international protection, as well as the prompt identification of persons with protection needs at reception sites following disembarkation."*[61] Yet there is no evidence to date indicating that any consideration has been given to this in Frontex joint operations in the Mediterranean. All exercise of border control which fails to take into account that refugees and people in need of international protection represent an exception to the ordinary requirements for admission to EU territory runs counter to international and European refugee and human rights law, as well as EC law.

4.7 As a new EU agency, there is a particularly worrying lack of clarity and transparency concerning the exact scope of Frontex's coordinating role and the way in which its operations are conducted. Ultimately *"responsibility for the control and surveillance of external borders lies with the Member States"*,[62] and most Frontex operations are undertaken following a request from an EU Member State and can only be realised with the involvement of Member States. However Frontex also has the power to *"launch initiatives for joint operations and pilot projects"*[63] and the Agency's staff have some *"executive powers"*.[64] The separation of tasks and the issue of proper accountability therefore lack clarity in theory and in practice.

4.8 *Recommendations*

4.9 As an EU agency acting with and on behalf of Member States, Frontex should explicitly demonstrate on a regular basis, how its activities fully respect Member States' obligations of non-refoulement under international and European refugee and human rights as well as EC law.

4.10 Frontex should seek support from joint "Asylum Expert Teams",[65] which could be deployed at short notice alongside Rapid Border Intervention Teams.

4.11 The legal framework and mechanisms available to hold Frontex accountable for possible breaches of international and European refugee and human rights as well as EC law should be clarified.

4.12 Frontex should be required to demonstrate what mechanisms it has in place to comply with the Schengen Border Code requirement to ensure access to an appeal procedure upon refusal of entry.

---

[56] The EU defines international protection as referring to refugees and those with subsidiary protection status, Council Directive 2004/83/EC of 29 April 2004 on minimum standards for the qualification and status of third country nationals or stateless persons as refugees or as persons who otherwise need international protection and the content of the protection granted, Art. 2(a).

[57] Regulation (EC) No 863/2007, establishing a mechanism for the creation of Rapid Border Intervention Teams and amending Council Regulation (EC) 2007/2004 as regards that mechanism and regulating the tasks and powers of guest officers, Article 2.

[58] Regulation (EC) No 562/2006, Article 13.1, 13.2 and 13.3.

[59] Council Directive 2005/85/EC of 1 December 2005 on minimum standards on procedures in Member States for granting and withdrawing refugee status, Member States bound by it shall have or bring into force domestic legislation necessary to comply with the Directive by 1 December 2007.

[60] Council Directive 2005/85/EC, Article 3.1.

[61] Commission Communication on Reinforcing the Management of the Southern Maritime External Borders of the EU, paragraph 12.

[62] Council Regulation (EC) 2007/2004, Article 1.2.

[63] Council Regulation (EC) 2007/2004, Article 3.1.

[64] Council Regulation (EC) 2007/2004, Article 10.

[65] As proposed by the European Commission Communication on Reinforcing the Management of the European Union's Southern Maritime Borders, COM (2006) 733 final of 30.11.2006.

4.13 Any revision of EU legislative instruments under the development of the Common European Asylum System should incorporate respect for the principle of non-refoulement into the Frontex regulation. Any reviews of Frontex's mandate should be subject to the co-decision procedure (as in the case of the Schengen Borders Code) which would give equal power to the European Parliament and thus increase democratic accountability.

5. Extra-territorial Operations and Working Agreements with Third Countries

5.1 The issue of responsibility and accountability is further complicated when Frontex coordinates operations which take place beyond EU borders. Article 14 of its founding Regulation allows for "*integrated border management*" in the form of operational cooperation with third countries in the framework of working arrangements concluded with the relevant authorities. The 2006 Frontex Annual Report refers to a number of working arrangements that are being negotiated and concluded with international organisations and third countries.[66] These agreements could significantly impact on Frontex operations in the Mediterranean and West African areas with regard to control and surveillance, readmission, or training of border guards. Working arrangements between Frontex and authorities of a third country agreed to date[67] do not appear to provide any solid legal framework for operations beyond the EU borders.

5.2 In addition, there is evidence to suggest that Frontex has already been involved in operations beyond the EU borders, in the territorial waters of Senegal and Mauritania where "*informal contacts*" have been established.[68] It is not clear what legal jurisdiction Frontex is acting under when providing assistance with such operations. Furthermore, unlike Frontex Working Agreements with third countries, Member States' agreements are often not publicly available and therefore beyond scrutiny for compliance with international, European and EC law. While international obligations of EU Member States still apply, we are concerned that extraterritorial activities carried out under the framework of bilateral agreements may prevent the applicability of EC law such as the Schengen Borders Code and the Asylum Procedures Directive.

5.3 *Recommendations*

5.4 The legal framework for Frontex-assisted operations in the territory of non-EU states should be clarified. The framework decision on how Frontex can cooperate with third countries, as referred to in the Frontex Annual Report 2006, should be publicly available.

5.5 All Frontex agreements, whether political or technical, which are liable to have an impact on the physical access to the EU for refugees and people in need of protection, should adequately address the issue of responsibility towards people who wish to seek asylum. This is particularly important in light of plans to intensify operational cooperation with third countries in Africa and Asia. Working agreements must not be concluded with countries that have not signed up to key international instruments that guarantee protection for those seeking asylum. All future working arrangements with third countries must be publicly available and therefore subject to scrutiny for compliance with international and EC law.

6. Independent Monitoring

6.1 At present there is no independent monitoring of the workings of Frontex. Since it is not known whether any of the thousands of individuals that have come into contact with Frontex coordinated border guards wanted or attempted to seek asylum, we cannot be satisfied that adequate safeguards are in place to ensure that access to asylum is guaranteed.

6.2 Urgent formulation of measures is required to ensure independent oversight that guarantees operations under the coordination of Frontex facilitate access to asylum and that the principle of *non-refoulement* is being respected in the context of their duties to implement immigration control. The involvement of NGOs with expertise in refugees, as well as UNHCR, would go some way to safeguarding the right to asylum and enhancing refugee protection in Europe, in view of their existing experience in this area.[69]

---

[66] Permitted under Council Regulation (EC) 2007/2004, Articles 13 and 14.

[67] Working arrangements were concluded with Switzerland, the Russian State Border Guard Service and the Ukraine State Border Guard Service.

[68] Frontex Annual Report 2006, p 13.

[69] Examples include a project co-ordinated by the Hungarian Helsinki Human Rights Committee, the project monitors six major airports: Amsterdam—Schiphol, Budapest—Ferihegy, Madrid—Barajas, Prague—Ruzyne, Vienna -Schwechat International, and Warsaw—Frederic Chopin and ECRE's current AENEAS-funded project 'The protection of refugees, asylum seekers and forced migrants' which includes monitoring and training of Ukrainian border guards.

6.3 *Recommendations*

6.4 Member States and Frontex should allow the independent monitoring of their border operations by relevant NGOs and international organisations, according to a jointly defined framework.

6.5 The European Union should develop or support pilot projects with this aim under the EU External Borders Fund.

6.6 Frontex should establish regular cooperation with international organisations with a mandate in the areas of asylum and/or human rights as allowed by its founding regulation (Art 13).

6.7 Frontex should ensure maximum transparency of its activities and operational rules. This should include the publication of all annual reports by the specialised branches of Frontex.

7. THE UK AND FRONTEX

7.1 The relationship between the UK and Frontex set out in its Regulation and its 2006 report requires further clarification. The current situation appears to be that since Frontex constitutes a development of the provisions of the Schengen *acquis* in which the UK is currently not taking part, the UK is, therefore, not bound by or subject to the Regulation establishing Frontex.[70] However, the UK has been involved in a number of Frontex-assisted operations, including Operation Torino at Heathrow, Operation Poseidon in Greece and Operation HERA I in the Canaries, which all took place in 2006.

7.2 Our main concern is that this creates a possible vacuum of accountability. While the UK clearly remains bound by its international and European obligations, it must be clarified what EC rules the UK is bound by when acting collectively under Frontex auspices. It is also unclear if it will be possible for Frontex to undertake any operations on UK territory in the future and how, given that Member States are subject to the Schengen Borders Code and the UK is not.

7.3 *Recommendation*

7.4 The exact nature of the UK's role in Frontex needs to be clarified, crucially, the accountability of the UK under EC law *vis-à-vis* participation in Frontex.

7.5 Details of the agreement that Frontex has concluded with the UK, setting out the framework for cooperation including its meaning and scope should be made public.[71]

8. TRAINING

8.1 Frontex currently provides extensive training and assists the development of a Common Core Curriculum and the establishment of common training standards. We wish to emphasise the imperative for adequate training of border guards in the identification of asylum and protection needs and in particular amongst vulnerable persons—notably women and children—given the additional hurdles they may face in articulating an asylum claim. There is a high risk of failing to recognise specific forms of persecution or underestimating the particular fears of women and children as well as elderly persons. Furthermore, it is essential that officials are trained in their approach towards trafficked persons, some of whom may also be able to establish a refugee claim.

8.2 *Recommendations*

8.3 Any training provided by Frontex should enable Member States to fulfil their duty under Article 16 (4)[72] of the Schengen Borders Code by offering specific guidance on the legal rules that border guards must comply with when exercising their duties, taking full account of international human rights principles and responsibilities.

8.4 Relevant existing capacity building programmes provide training on international protection principles with an emphasis on the early identification of asylum seekers and persons with special needs.[73] A similar commitment to instruction on safeguards and protection needs should be applied to Frontex training programmes, including in particular, a focus on gender and age-sensitivity.

---

[70] Council Regulation (EC) 2007/2004, Preamble (25).
[71] Frontex Annual Report 2006.
[72] Article 16 (4) states that "*Member States shall provide for training on the rules for border control and on fundamental rights*".
[73] *Ten point plan of action for refugee protection and mixed migration for countries along the eastern and south eastern borders of European union member states*, UNHCR, 29 June 2007 and UNOG press release "*Committee against Torture hears response of Hungary*", 16 November 2006 at
http://www.unog.ch/80256EDD006B9C2E/(httpNewsByYear_en)/18A5E5A949271D3FC1257228005937C7?OpenDocument

8.5 Training on international protection principles and obligations should be extended to all Frontex officials to ensure decisions made at all levels are informed by an adequate knowledge and understanding of the principles of asylum and international protection.

9. RISK ANALYSES AND FEASIBILITY STUDIES

9.1 The 2006 Annual Report states that the Frontex Risk Analysis Network (FRAN) has compiled a risk analysis covering all the external borders which will be used to inform the distribution of resources under the External Borders Fund. It is unclear what precise risks are being identified with regard to a particular region or country.

9.2 Frontex has also been exploring the technical feasibility of establishing surveillance systems covering the southern maritime border of the EU and the Mediterranean Sea, as well as a Mediterranean Coastal Patrols Network involving North African countries.

9.3 We would like to know whether Frontex includes in its risk analyses and feasibility studies, an assessment of the security situation and humanitarian context within migrants' countries of origin and transit. The management of external borders, design of surveillance systems and distribution of funding can only be confidently undertaken with a full understanding of the causes and contexts of migration flows, including forced migration.

9.4 *Recommendations*

9.5 Consideration of the root causes of migration, including forced migration should be built into any future risk analysis programmes.

9.6 Frontex risk analyses provide an assessment of the context, the need and the modus operandi for all Frontex operations and, as such, must be declassified in due course. All feasibility studies undertaken by Frontex (such as BORTEC) should be made public.

10. DEVELOPMENT AND DISSEMINATION OF RESEARCH

10.1 There is currently a significant lack of collection, analysis and exchange of reliable data on migratory and asylum flows within the regions targeted by Frontex. This should improve with the permanent establishment of the European Migration Network (EMN) and implementation of Regulation (EC) No 862/ 2007, which calls on Member States to produce statistics on third country nationals refused entry at the external border, beginning in 2008. However, this does not include statistics on third country nationals intercepted and diverted before they reach an EU border. As such, there will continue to be an unclear picture of migratory trends and patterns, and the consequences of Frontex operations on access to attempts to make claims for asylum in Europe.

10.2 *Recommendations*

10.3 Frontex is well placed to coordinate the collection of data on migrants intercepted or diverted by Member States during Frontex joint operations and we urge the Agency to develop mechanisms to do this.

10.4 In this way, Frontex could usefully support the analysis and dissemination of more reliable data and research related to migration trends, and contribute to Member State compliance with Article 13 (5) of the Schengen Borders Code.[74]

11. RETURN OPERATIONS

11.1 Provisions for joint return operations to be assisted by Frontex are provided for in Article 9 of the Regulation establishing Frontex. We remind the Committee of their previous inquiry into the draft returns Directive[75] at which the Refugee Council raised its concerns with regards to safeguards in return operations, pre-removal detention, judicial remedies, monitoring and return to third countries.[76] The Directive is of direct relevance to the role of Frontex in return as the preamble to the Regulation establishing Frontex stipulates that return assistance is "*subject to the community return policy*".

---

[74] Article 13 (5) places a duty on Member States to "*collect statistics on the number of persons refused entry, the grounds for refusal, the nationality of the persons refused and the type of border (land, air or sea) at which they were refused entry*".

[75] Directive on common standards and procedures in Member States for returning illegally staying third-country nationals, COM(2005) 391 final, 1 September 2005.

[76] See also ECRE Comments Proposal for a Directive of the European Parliament and the Council on common standards and procedures in Member States for returning illegally staying third country nationals (COM(2005) 391 final), CO2/5/2006/ExtPC.

11.2 *Recommendation*

11.3 Until the EU adopts common standards for return, the role of Frontex in joint return operations should not be developed as a priority. A Directive should not only facilitate cooperation on an operational level but also establish safeguards. This would provide a more consistent set of standards framing any Frontex- assisted return operations.

12. We urge the House of Lords to put some of these important concerns to Frontex and the UK Government. We will be pleased to provide any necessary clarification, including oral evidence upon request.

Sarah Cutler
Head of International and UK Policy
Refugee Council

Patricia Coelho
Senior Policy Officer
ECRE

24 September 2007

Examination of Witnesses

Witnesses: Ms HELEN MUGGERIDGE, Refugee Council, Ms PATRICIA COELHO, European Council on Refugees and Exiles and DR BERNARD RYAN, Immigration Law Practitioners' Association and University of Kent, examined.

Q402 Chairman: Good morning, and welcome. As you know, this Sub-Committee of the House of Lords European Committee is conducting an inquiry into Frontex. You have sent us two papers, one a joint one—thank you very much for those. This evidence session is broadcast over the internet. We shall send you a transcript of the evidence in case you feel there are any corrections to be made in the way it has been put together, and if there are any questions that you find it difficult to answer or any answers you would like to supplement, you are most welcome to write to us after this session. I do not think there is any point in asking you to introduce yourselves, that is clear from the papers, so perhaps I can begin and say to you that most of our witnesses so far in this inquiry have given us an overall positive assessment of Frontex's operations, particularly in terms of their deterrent effect on illegal immigration, which obviously concerns us all. The question is how do you assess the work carried out by Frontex so far, and we have read what you put in your two papers so there is no need to repeat all that, but maybe you could summarise it and add anything to it. Who would like to begin?
Dr Ryan: I am happy to start. From ILPA's perspective we are obviously not competent to comment on the policy side or the actual operations of Frontex. Our expertise is in relation to the legal framework within which it is conducting itself. In relation to that, we have some specific concerns about the framework governing Frontex operations within the territory of the European Union—although there clearly is a legal framework governing that—and externally. Clearly, there are provisions set out in the Frontex regulation with respect to the activities of Frontex in so far as they relate to the territory of the

European Union. Our main concerns are with respect to activities that are Frontex co-ordinated but take place outside of the territory. We think there are a number of very important issues that that raises which are not adequately addressed, either in the legal framework or in the broader policy discussion with respect to Frontex.
Ms Coelho: From ECRE's perspective, again, as a network of NGOs we are not privy to all the information that would be necessary to sit here and say whether Frontex is being fully successful in what it is trying to do. Our question is are the positive assessments that have been put forward to you to date taking into account the full picture and the full impact of Frontex's operations. Some of the questions we would therefore expect to be asked in an assessment of Frontex's operations are questions such as if irregular entries to the EU have been reduced, at what price has this been in terms of human costs; how many people have been stopped from coming who had protection concerns and what has happened to them since Frontex has prevented their entry? How many people have simply been forced to undertake more dangerous journeys and, as a result, have lost their lives? Then how many people have tried several times to come in, and this is a factor that may be affecting the picture in terms of how many people have actually been prevented from entering. We know for a fact from our members working on the ground in reception centres on the borders of the EU that people they talk to say they have tried two, three, four, five times and they have sometimes been turned back, some of their colleagues have never made it and some of them have made it. This needs to be considered within any assessment. Also how many people have been given the

opportunity to appeal their refusal of entry, which is something I think we can come back to, been given reasons and felt that that was satisfactory. For us, where we have seen the assessments, they have not taken these issues into account, so our question is if the world's numbers of refugees are rising, but the number of refugees claiming asylum in Europe is going down, what is affecting that and is prevention of entry into the EU a factor in the statistics?

Ms Muggeridge: From the point of view of the British Refugee Council we found it quite hard to obtain public information about Frontex in preparation for this evidence session, and one of the issues we had with assessing the success of Frontex was the lack of information available. Our general impression is that success is hard to quantify and even if the indicator of success is deterrence, which would be about numbers, the full picture from our colleagues and NGOs throughout the EU is that the numbers of arrivals are actually increasing in Greece, and this could be because of Iraqis arriving to Greece. Numbers are not decreasing in Italy and in Malta the Jesuit Refugee Service has confirmed that the number of boats arriving has increased but the number of people arriving has decreased. This may be because the boats are arriving with sole survivors on them or two or three persons arriving on them, which is obviously of great concern to us. The information that we have been able to obtain from colleagues with regard to recognition rates of persons arriving leads us to believe that there are people arriving with protection needs who have founded and genuine refugee claims. For example, in Malta, 48% of the so-called boat people arriving actually receive protection and, in Italy, half of those who arrived by sea asked for protection and 25–30% of those were granted protection which leads us to believe that some people who may be coming into contact with Frontex operations may have protection needs, and this does not seem to be reflected in the Frontex reports that we have seen.

Q403 *Baroness Tonge:* Could I just clarify what actually is the involvement of Frontex with individual people coming over the border.

Ms Muggeridge: From the information we have seen they are national border guards, co-ordinated by Frontex, so people would come into contact with people, either on the high seas or elsewhere.

Baroness Tonge: I just wanted to make it clear; thank you.

Q404 *Lord Harrison:* Could I put the question the other way? That is, in your recent experience has what has happened with the borders been different distinctly as a result of the advent of Frontex? In other words, you may well have concerns of the kind that you would describe in your evidence, but have

those concerns been reinforced or has there been a perceptible change in atmosphere as a result of those who are applying which you think you could attribute to Frontex coming to maturity?

Ms Coelho: There is a similar strand in what you are saying and we are very much aware of the fact that the Member States are the ones working on the front line and, obviously, these border controls were in place beforehand. We may come on to this when we look at the operations of Frontex beyond the EU territory. What Frontex is doing is reinforcing certain practices that perhaps only some EU countries have been at the forefront of, such as the UK, in terms of extraterritorial border controls, and is introducing and trying to develop various types of border controls across Europe and along the EU border that maybe we did not see on such a scale. Seeing Frontex operating in African waters is something that certain individual countries may have been doing, but what I think is the interest of Member States in the use of the Frontex operation is to see this on a much more consistent basis and in a much wider area of territory. Either Spain or Malta have asked for some of the Frontex operations to actually be permanent and not to be missions and, with time, if this were to be the case, we would see a distinct change in the way that border controls are undertaken.

Q405 *Lord Young of Norwood Green:* Given the dangerous nature of those crossings, I did not quite understand where you were coming from on that, as though it was a bad thing for Frontex to try and co-ordinate with third countries to deal with the situation. I mean, what they are trying to do is to regularise it, to have a consistent approach. Surely we should not be in a situation where we are actually encouraging those kinds of crossings; they are innately dangerous, they are not exactly the normal passenger ferry type approach, as we know, so I did not quite understand where you were coming from there. I can understand the concern about how people are treated, but are you seriously complaining about Frontex in respect of those kinds of activities so that there is a consistent approach, an approach that does have accountability. We might argue about the level of accountability and transparency, but they are subject to report.

Dr Ryan: If I approach that as a policy question, I would say it all depends on what happens next. If you say that migrants at sea are going to be returned, diverted, maybe rescued but then sent back to countries which have limited resources, which do not have the same political traditions as in Europe, then there are grounds for concern about what happens next as regards their treatment. In the context we are talking about around the Mediterranean, off the Canary Islands or journeys towards the Canary Islands, there are grounds for concern about Frontex changing the nature of the operations that Member States are engaging in.

Ms Muggeridge: Just to add to that, we acknowledge quite clearly that states do have a right to control their borders. Within that, our main concern is that there is some opportunity left open for refugees and asylum seekers and, at the end of the day, refugees have to use the same routes as everyone else as there is no legal way to travel as an asylum-seeker, so by its very nature it involves some form of irregular travel. One additional point that we wanted to make is that in terms of border control there have been routes that have been diverted because of the activities of Member States, for example in pushing people to embark further and further south, for example in Senegal, and this actually results in a longer route, a more dangerous route and a more expensive route, so actually border control can have the effect that people have to travel for longer distances and take more risks.

Q406 Chairman: With regard to Frontex operations what is your view about the relationship between Frontex and Member States' border guards, and in what way would you like, if any, to change the legal framework which controls that relationship, or are you satisfied to leave it as it is?

Dr Ryan: We had concerns about the initial Frontex regulation, that it did not indicate what the legal regime was to be with respect to officials of other states that were sent to a given state in order to assist. It is fair to say that the RABITs regulation, both in itself and also in its amendments of the original Frontex regulation, has improved things because it does make clear that in any event the law which applies is that of the state that has called for assistance or on whose territory the operations are taking place. We think that that is essentially the right answer. We would still have concerns, however, about Frontex itself. There ought to be greater clarity about Frontex being subject to the obligations of public international law; that is left at the moment as something that is implied but it ought, in our view, to be express—including of course human rights guarantees within that. Again, I would return to the point I made earlier and I suspect we will come to again in more detail, which is that there is almost a complete lack of provision for the legal framework where there are activities organised by Frontex outside of the territory of the European Union.

Q407 Lord Teverson: If I could just explore that argument, which I do not fully understand, normally when there are obligations or an organisation set up—say it was in the UK—you would not write down all the laws and obligations and treaties that that particular organisation had to abide by because that is the law. Why is it quite so important—I am

sympathetic, but is there not a risk if you start listing things that it is the things that are not on the list then that become vulnerable in terms of the context within which you are operating? I take the point that on RABITs you have got those obligations in there, but are those obligations not implied and to list them somehow suggests that the ones that are not listed are not important. Do you see what I am swaying?

Dr Ryan: I do. I would say with respect to Frontex that at least what ought to be done is to make it express that it is subject to the ordinary principles of international law, including international human rights law, without necessarily listing each and every obligation. It might be possible to list some, perhaps the more important ones, let us say as regards non-refoulement or the Law of the Sea, but those would just be examples and there could be other principles unspecified. I think your concern about listing could be addressed in having a more simple formulation, but one which addressed the current lacuna that exists with respect to Frontex.

Q408 Lord Teverson: I can see from almost a public relations point of view or for the management committee, yes, it is in there in the regulation and it is clear, but surely the officials would see those as international obligations anyway, would they not, because you cannot avoid them, or am I wrong?

Dr Ryan: You are almost now asking me how Frontex sees itself or thinks and we do not have the capacity to know that. One would hope so, I suppose is part of the answer, but it would be better in terms of its internal culture if things were express rather than simply left to general principles of community law.

Q409 Baroness Tonge: I am quite confused actually—and maybe it is me—about how you are actually seeing Frontex; could you give us a concrete example and if you think that Frontex, whatever that is, is breaking humanitarian law or not respecting human rights, do you have any examples, can you make it into a concrete thing instead of just saying Frontex?

Dr Ryan: We could talk about Libya, for example, and Frontex is itself directly negotiating with Libya. It also is co-ordinating Member States' operations that probably already and certainly it hopes in the future will involve returns to Libya. Libya is not a party to the Refugee Convention; we just do not have guarantees about what is going to happen if migrants are returned.

Baroness Tonge: That is a good example; thank you.

Q410 Lord Mawson: Following on from that, how do you know what you know about Frontex? Is it simply from reading papers or have you actually ever sat down with Frontex and had these sorts of practical discussions about how it works. How do you know what you know?

Dr Ryan: As I indicated right at the beginning, we do not feel competent to talk about Frontex operations or Frontex thinking, we are looking at the legal framework and what is in the public domain about the operations that Frontex is involved in.

Ms Coelho: We talk regularly to the European Commission, we talk regularly to UNHCR who has a person posted in Frontex. I have also had direct conversations and was invited to meet with an official of Frontex but was not able to, but we have started a dialogue and have access to what is public in terms of papers and information and then I have my colleagues on the ground who can talk generally about border controls, some of which may have been co-ordinated by Frontex and some of which may not have been. I want to emphasise that while we cannot comment on the relationships during the operations between Frontex and Member States we are very clear about what Frontex is doing: it is co-ordinating, it is planning, it is doing risk analysis, it is not implementing the border controls. But we think it is important for some clarification of responsibilities, my sense is that when you talk about Frontex, you say it is implicit—

Q411 *Lord Teverson:* I am asking, not saying.

Ms Coelho: The impression we get is that Frontex says "We do not have these responsibilities, Member States have these responsibilities" and for us Frontex is an EU agency. The question therefore is not if it has responsibility but to what extent it has as a result of its planning and co-ordination role. Surely in the way that it plans an operation it has a responsibility to ensure that Member States can respect their human rights and refugee obligations. They are having an influence on how those border controls are taking place, even if they are not actually undertaking them themselves, that is why we are keen on clarification.

Ms Muggeridge: I think Lord Mawson has actually hit the nail on the head; part of the problem that we have had is engaging with Frontex and finding out information about it, and that is exactly what we would like to do, is have more contact with Frontex and engage so that we can contribute and make a positive contribution to their work.

Lord Harrison: I know you are anxious to move on, My Lord Chairman, but you said something very interesting, Dr Ryan, in response to Lady Tonge's question when you identified Libya as an example of where Frontex has introduced a qualitative difference. I think you actually said that Frontex had, as it were, negotiated with or spoken on behalf of, presumably, countries like Italy and Malta to Libya and the Committee would be very interested to learn that because clearly that would move beyond a co-ordinating role to one where Frontex becomes an

entity in and of itself. Could you just say a little more about that, what your evidence is that they have so acted?

Baroness Tonge: Before you answer can I just add to that because I was going to ask you later on actually about involvement with third countries such as Libya and Morocco and this question has come up now, so maybe we could have that discussion now, My Lord Chairman, as we have got onto this topic.

Q412 *Chairman:* Yes, why not, but would you like to come back to what Lord Harrison was asking?

Dr Ryan: The information that I have in relation to Libya is that Frontex has had a technical mission to Libya with a view to putting in place arrangements for the future. I do not know, the state of play with those negotiations, as that is not information that is clear—at least, not in detail—on the Frontex website. There is a Frontex report that is in circulation—I confess I do not know how it got into the public domain—which contains details about the Libyan mission.

Baroness Tonge: I was going to ask you about arrangements between Frontex and third countries and we would be particularly interested in Morocco, Libya, Egypt and Senegal and whether you saw it as a positive step for Frontex to be negotiating with third countries. You actually implied a few minutes ago that you thought it was not a very positive step because Libya was not signed up to the Convention on Refugees.

Chairman: Lady Tonge, you are moving into a question which you are hoping to ask later on. I am perfectly happy to take it now.

Baroness Tonge: Yes, because we raised it I just thought that we ought to finish this topic now really rather than stop. Are you agreed, Lord Harrison?

Lord Harrison: Indeed.

Chairman: I am perfectly happy to do this; do you want to enlarge on what you have said in view of the fact that you are going to ask a question towards the end.

Q413 *Baroness Tonge:* I have used that question because we are already on that subject and I thought we should ask it now.

Dr Ryan: If I could give a general answer, there would have to be guarantees about the treatment of those returned to any of those states given the lack of resources and also the traditions in those states. As I said, I do not feel that we as an organisation are competent to speak about the specifics of what may or may not be happening there, but the general answer is pretty clear. It is probably best if I bring in my colleagues to speak about some other aspects.

Ms Coelho: I will say something and then I will pass on to my colleague, Helen, who has been speaking to our colleagues on the external border who have lots of contacts and sometimes staff in some of these countries and have given us quite a good picture of the problems. There may be some positives, it could add value to have Frontex Working Arrangements with third countries if the results are that good practices on border controls that are undertaken by European countries are shared with these countries that may not be implementing adequate border procedures and may not have the resources either. However, the way that different people are talking about these Working Arrangements is quite important. We find that they are very much put forward as technical agreements between the different border services but, as my colleague Dr Ryan has said, if there is an agreement on working arrangements between Frontex and Libya while the EU has not been able to formalise and agree on its political relationship with Libya, this cannot be seen as two separate things. A Frontex Working Arrangement with Libya by default is part of a political relationship between the EU and Libya and therefore has important political implications, and we are concerned that these Working Arrangements are put forward as very technical, low-level operational agreements but they do have significant political implications. I should say that they would not necessarily determine that relationship. Countries like France and Italy, for example, have already given equipment for border management to Libya and there are several bilateral types of arrangements in place. An arrangement with Frontex would amount to legitimisation of certain practices by the EU, it could perhaps be seen as the EU agreeing that the way Libya treats people as it does on its borders and within its detention centres is acceptable.

Ms Muggeridge: Just to give some concrete examples of what might be happening in some of these countries, we spoke to a colleague in Morocco and UNHCR is not informed if ships are intercepted or if they are going to receive, possibly, persons with protection needs. UNHCR is not systematically informed and actually to claim asylum one has to go to Rabat, to the UNHCR office, so it would imply that it would be very difficult for people who might need to claim asylum. Even more worryingly, we have heard reports that people are expelled to the border with Algeria, which is 30 to 40 kilometres from a town called Oujda, and whilst there may not be direct refoulement, persons who, for example, cannot be returned to their country of origin or who may not have had a chance to claim asylum could be expelled to this region, and it is very, very dangerous on the frontier where there are a lot of bandits and gangs roaming around and there have been allegations of human rights abuses such as rape occurring on that border. With regards to Egypt, we have heard from our colleague Michael Kagan at the

American University in Cairo that whilst UNHCR has a long-established operation in Cairo and persons who have refugee documents from the UNHCR in Egypt are not usually refouled, the situation is quite different for people who arrive at the border. He described that there are Eritreans crossing from Sudan into Egypt because of the worsening protection situation in Sudan and these people can get arrested at the border and can be taken to a military court where the situation is that things are done behind closed doors. These people may be refugees and that is a concern. He did think that persons who left Egypt illegally, who may be returned back, are subject to prosecution and up to a year's imprisonment in an Egyptian prison where there are poor detention conditions. I should say that the situation in Senegal, where there is a UNHCR presence, is that we have heard slightly more positive reports. I would concur with what my colleagues have said about the situation in Libya.

Q414 *Baroness Tonge:* But those arrangements have been directly negotiated by Frontex.
Ms Coelho: Yes. If I could add one thing, it may be small numbers but there are people originating from Senegal or Morocco—the Western Sahara as some prefer to call it—who are themselves refugees, so some of these border controls may be preventing people from these primarily transit countries from actually leaving their own country, which is clearly against international law.
Chairman: It has been very helpful to have a general session up to this point, but we will now move if we can to more particular points and go through those, but you have given us a good start. Lord Dear.

Q415 *Lord Dear:* Thank you, My Lord Chairman. It is a question really for Dr Ryan: in paragraph 8 of your evidence to us in writing you talked about the territorial scope of Frontex being unclear and I am interested in this. I wondered if you have got any examples that would show us what is or could be happening vis-à-vis Frontex externally. We know what they do on the border and internally, that is clearly understood—at least, we understand what they should be doing—but do you see them performing a role in your view beyond the border, out into facing countries? It is a direct follow-on in a sense from what we have just been discussing.
Dr Ryan: It is clear that Frontex does have a co-ordinating function, both in relation to activity on the high seas and also in territorial waters of other states—we know about Senegal and Mauritania in particular. I should just add a footnote to the previous discussion if I may, which is that my understanding is that Spain negotiated with Senegal and Mauritania but then Frontex does the co-ordinating subsequently, whereas in the case of Libya

it is Frontex doing the negotiating rather than particular states.

Q416 Lord Dear: If I understand your written evidence correctly you think there is a lack of clarity as to what Frontex may or may not do beyond the border, outside the border, and I wondered if you had any examples of that and particularly how you think it should be altered, because clarity is important.

Dr Ryan: The issue is not so much about examples, it is rather the legal position: what is the legal mandate given to Frontex? Reading the regulations that exist, it is very difficult to see that Frontex has, as a matter of European Union law,, a mandate to operate beyond the external borders of the European Union. The Frontex regulation speaks of "integrated management of the external border" and then it talks about surveillance and control. I think you could say that surveillance can take place outside of the territory but it must be somehow linked to attempted entry or anticipated entry to the territory. The reference point is the external borders and I think again we would say that there must be control with respect to those borders and not control taking place somewhere else entirely. I feel that what has happened is that Frontex has stretched its mandate beyond what is set out in the initial regulation and that needs to be addressed. The reason to address it is that if there was a legislative process which looked at the question of whether Frontex should be acting extraterritorially or not, whether the mandate should clearly extend that far, then that would open a space within which the kind of question we are raising would get posed, of what guarantees must then govern Frontex in so doing. It is not that we are saying it should be absolutely ruled out but it must be explicit that there is such a role and then the terms of that role should be defined in the governing instruments as well.

Q417 Lord Dear: I can see the desire for clarity, which I am sure all my colleagues share; I wonder if you would like to give us a view on where you think the law should settle. If you were redrafting or revisiting the law, what would you like to see in order to address this? Quite apart from clarity, which is one point, where would you like to see—using the word very broadly—the boundaries set?

Dr Ryan: I take your point that there is a distinction between clarity and substance, shall we say. On the substance I have indicated previously that our view is that respect for international law principles, including human rights principles, ought to expressly govern what Frontex does in the extra- territorial domain. That would open a policy discussion about the kinds of guarantees that are sought and obtained with respect to what happens next to those who are

either prevented from leaving particular states or are returned to those states.

Q418 Lord Dear: I understand that and I follow the line of reasoning, but to put it in very simple terms do you welcome or not welcome an enhanced or extended role for Frontex beyond the borders. Do you think it is a good thing that Frontex should be up there negotiating with, taking a part in, acting on behalf of or not, or would you prefer to see them simply as it were pinned down on the EU borders and within it?

Dr Ryan: We do not rule out Frontex having such an extraterritorial role, so it is not that we are saying no, that should not happen. Our concern is about the context, the actual context in which Frontex is doing that, which is that it is co-operating in the Mediterranean area with states where there are insufficient guarantees about what happens to those who are returned. So it is not a simple yes or no to extraterritorial action by Frontex, it is a question of looking at the specifics to see whether it is desirable.

Q419 Lord Dear: You would have to identify what it is they are going to do, but the question is a very simple one, if I may say so, and that is that given all the guarantees in place do you see a role for Frontex extraterritorially or not?

Dr Ryan: Given all the guarantees in place, yes—but that may be somewhat difficult to achieve in many cases.

Ms Coelho: Can I just say that in the short term we do not agree with Frontex having an extraterritorial role, but we are not saying we would rule it out, seeing how the agency develops, but we all are very aware that it has been in place for two years, there are lots of issues around its mandate to be clarified and there are a lot of challenges on the EU external border that can be addressed, and it can be very usefully focused on that at this stage. The reason why I say that is because my understanding of some of these activities in third country territory is that the legal basis being put forward is the bilateral agreements that exist between EU states and that third country. I fully agree with my colleague who says there is no legal basis for Frontex to operate beyond where the European Community law applies at this stage, but also these bilateral agreements are not available, we cannot see them, there is no transparency whatsoever, so to be able to know whether those agreements comply with all these guarantees is not possible at this stage and until those kinds of agreements become more fully public I do not think it is possible for us to be in favour of Frontex operating under their mandate in the current situation.

Q420 *Lord Dear:* I did have a second question which can probably be answered quite quickly because it is quite specific and it does indeed go over broadly the same ground, and that is about rescue at sea—you have alluded to it even if you have not addressed that in particular. There is a degree of a lack of clarity in terms there, particularly so far as the question of disembarkation and asylum issues are concerned. I wondered if, just to help us, you wanted to focus specifically upon rescues at sea and the ensuing problems vis-à-vis Frontex.

Ms Coelho: You mean rescue and disembarkation and the responsibility for asylum. There has been some debate within the Committee as to whether Frontex should have specific responsibilities around rescue at sea. Those responsibilities exist and rescue at sea takes place, as far as we understand, during Frontex operations because Member States have the responsibility to do that when that situation arises. So we do not see that as a major issue; rescue at sea clearly has to be part of Frontex operations when it is needed. The issue around disembarkation and who is responsible for asylum applications I think needs to be taken separately. From our analysis it is clear that there may be a gap in the international maritime law in terms of which country must agree for people to be disembarked but there is no such lack of clarity on who is responsible for the asylum applications which are governed by a whole other raft of laws—the Refugee Convention, the European Convention on Human Rights et cetera, and if we look at the case law there it is very clear that if a country during its operation or during its rescue meets the threshold of having jurisdiction over the people that it is controlling, then it has the responsibility to deal with any of the asylum applications that may ensue from that group of people. I feel that it is very important to say that the laws are all in place in terms of who is responsible for the asylum applications and we just need to apply them. There is a problem with the issue of disembarkation and it is clearly preventing countries from undertaking rescue; the EU has a role to play in brokering agreements between EU states in terms of responsibility sharing. There are lots of possibilities there but I think that some of the requests to perhaps share the burden more equally are very valid, and we would go along the lines of reforming the Dublin II Regulation, providing people with more freedom of movement once they have a status and possibly also what has already taken place in some cases from Malta, with some Member States agreeing to receive people who have been recognised as refugees once their applications have been dealt with in order to support each other, so we think these sorts of arrangements need to be explored.

Q421 *Lord Dear:* I understand where you are coming from, I think. You are almost saying, if I understand you correctly, that on this particular issue

Frontex need hardly exist, other than perhaps in a very general sense of co-ordination, but it is down to individual states who first pick up the responsibility and then deal with it in its system.

Ms Coelho: Yes, these responsibilities just need to be integrated in all Frontex operations.

Q422 *Lord Dear:* But Frontex should not be playing a leading role in this, it is up to individual countries.

Ms Coelho: Frontex is not the body that needs to consider asylum applications, Frontex does not have the power to agree whether a person goes on one country's territory or another and Frontex is not going to be providing the conditions and the rights for people who are refugees to then be able to integrate and rebuild their lives. I think it is way beyond the Frontex mandate.

Dr Ryan: Could I add something very briefly on that last question, which is a very important one. We would see a possible role for Frontex as regards planning for rescue situations because clearly it is of absolute importance that no state or no vessel is discouraged from engaging in rescue operations. Rescue, particularly in the central Mediterranean, seems to be not an accident, it is part of that situation—I think that is clear from the evidence you have had from Frontex itself. Given that there is detailed planning for those operations, there is a planning system, it does seem to us that it would be appropriate to also address the question of rescue and disembarkation in that planning phase, with a view to burden-sharing as well, in the spirit of my colleagues' remarks. Within the Frontex mechanisms it ought to be one of the elements that is addressed.

Chairman: Lord Young, would you like to move on?

Q423 *Lord Young of Norwood Green:* I have been looking at the papers and quite a lot of analysis at paragraph 13 in relation to the Schengen Borders Code; do you feel that does apply satisfactorily to the activities of Frontex? I was referring to your document there, Dr Ryan, and I notice in the European Refugee Council's document you say "We are concerned that Frontex border control activities, if not managed properly, could lead to breaches of human rights", somehow implying that the Schengen Borders Code does not apply to the activities of Frontex. I would just like to tease out where you think the problems are in relation to this, bearing in mind that Frontex is essentially a co-ordination role and the Member States have their obligations to honour the Schengen Borders Code.

Dr Ryan: I see this question of the Borders Code as a concrete aspect of the wider question, what is Frontex mandated to do, what is its jurisdiction? The Schengen Borders Code regulates those seeking to enter or possibly refused entry to the Schengen area and Frontex is referred to in the code. In that context it is co-ordinating the activities of Member States' officials and then those officials are governed anyway by the local law of the state in which they are functioning, so in its own terms it makes sense, the Borders Code. However, it does not cover activity outside of the territories, extraterritorial activity. To that extent some of the things that Frontex is involved in are not regulated by the code. If I could give one example, the code gives a right of appeal against a refusal of entry; it is a bit hard to see how that is operating in the territorial waters of Senegal, to the extent that Frontex is co-ordinating refusals of entry to the European Union there. The code is not designed to address extraterritorial activity.

Ms Coelho: I fully agree. We believe the Schengen Borders Code applies to Frontex' co-ordinated activities on national territory and in international waters and it very positively recognises that refugees are the exception to entry rules and provides these possibilities for legal remedies, but we have absolutely no evidence, based on the information that we have access to, that this right is in any way implemented and that there are any provisions within the operations to allow for that to happen. That is our concern.

Q424 Lord Young of Norwood Green: If I could address the point that is being made, it seems to me that your primary concern all the time we return to this question of territorial waters—again, I am a bit puzzled because you have accepted that if Frontex were not there co-ordinating activities there are bilateral agreements going on anyway. So Frontex is still carrying out a co-ordinating role, they cannot just act on their own and there is a real, serious problem in the Mediterranean as you know where human lives are at risk every single day; I do not quite understand, therefore, why you believe that Frontex is the cause of the problems. The problems are there anyway and they are trying to co-ordinate their area which we know to be exceedingly dangerous. They cannot initiate activities without the agreement of Member States so they are reacting to real problems that occur in the Mediterranean area and outside those territorial waters, and they are dealing with a situation which actually exists now, bilateral agreements that currently exist and they are simply acting as co-ordinators. Is that not better than having a load of random situations. You have more chance, I would have thought, of ensuring that the kind of things you seek assurances on, that at least those questions can be put on whether people's rights are being abrogated because of these activities.

Ms Coelho: We do not think Frontex is the cause of the problems and I appreciate some of the points you make in terms of the value of the co-ordination. I think there is a question mark as to what extent Frontex can or cannot initiate activities. If we look at

the Frontex Regulation it does have some power to launch initiatives and has some executive powers, and again this is an area where we would like some clarity; to what extent it has some autonomous powers and to what extent it is completely subject to the will of Member States. Frontex is an EU agency and it is as such that it draws its mandate and its powers to act. If we are now saying that a bilateral agreement between a EU Member State and any third country is an acceptable legal framework for Frontex activities you could argue, could you not, that a bilateral agreement between any country around the world might be an acceptable legal framework for Frontex to intervene and there must be some clear boundaries as to where and under which agreements Frontex can operate. I come back to the point that I made: we do not know what the contents of these agreements are, they are confidential agreements on the whole. Some of our colleagues have access to some of them, but they know that often the versions they can see are not the full versions of the agreements—some of which are kept secret. We do not accept that an EU agency can function on the basis of such agreements and the EU has a responsibility of transparency which needs to be met.

Q425 Chairman: Let me just ask a question to clarify your broader approach. Do you, all three of you, support the policy of Her Majesty's Government in keeping the United Kingdom out of the Schengen area?

Dr Ryan: That is a very large question.

Q426 Chairman: It is yes or no, quite frankly.

Ms Coelho: As ECRE I would say we do not have a position on such an issue, we are a European network and we do not take positions on particular government policies in that way so I defer to my colleague.

Ms Muggeridge: I do not think I would be able to answer that, but I am happy to get back to you there.

Dr Ryan: This puts me in a difficult position because I might have my own personal opinion but that is not necessarily the opinion of the organisation I am here to represent, so I would rather not comment on that.

Chairman: I am just surprised you do not have a corporate view on it, all three of you. Anyhow, if there is anything you would like to send us, by all means do. Lord Young.

Q427 Lord Young of Norwood Green: We have touched on this question, if my memory serves me right, Dr Ryan, what is the added value of the RABITs regulation in relation to Frontex. You gave some faint praise—or it might have been more than faint praise—in relation to the way the rapid action activities actually take place. I wonder if you would like to comment further; whether you see this as broadly positive or not.

Dr Ryan: Obviously we are looking at that essentially from a legal perspective. From a legal perspective the RABITs regulation is a distinct improvement on the Frontex regulation because there is a clear legal framework for operations that take place on the territories of participating states, be it in the form of a RABIT, rapid intervention team, or be it in the form of what are called guest officials. Essentially the same legal framework applies, which is the territorial state's legal framework, and that does seem to us to be broadly the correct answer.

Q428 *Lord Teverson:* In the ILPA evidence which I read with great interest you spent a lot of writing on the area of accountability, and of course this is something we are in the process of here, if you like, and certainly as part of the parlance it is something that we are interested in ourselves. I found your analysis very interesting and we have found many of those issues ourselves in terms of finding out information, but what I would really like to understand from your own point of view is how do we solve this thing of accountability. When we talked to Members of the European Parliament they also had that concern, and of course one of the ways that parliaments do these things is that they try to take control of budgets and say if you do not tell us, we do not pay you, therefore you stop working, which is a blunt instrument of accountability in terms of parliamentary processes. What do you see as the key points that must be brought in to make an organisation like Frontex—which I agree could be used as a sort of shadow organisation for Member States' decisions that they do not really want to come out too publicly perhaps—more accountable?

Dr Ryan: Let me say a couple of brief things and then I will let my colleagues answer as well. Generally more structure to the democratic oversight of Frontex would be one element. You may feel exactly the same. Essentially, the oversight is done by its management board but the management board is very close to Frontex in terms of personnel. Although there are reports, beyond that there are not specific structures in place through which Frontex is accountable to and can take guidance from democratic bodies, and I suppose the European Parliament is the obvious candidate. There is a separate issue about transparency within Frontex and preparing for this session I was having to use the Frontex website more than in the past and it is remarkable that there are documents in the public domain with respect to Frontex that are not accessible on its website. For example, its public bulletin—Helen passed that to me and I had not found it on the website; I went back and looked again and I still could not find it. It is intended to tell the public about what Frontex is doing and yet it is not easily accessible.

Q429 *Lord Young of Norwood Green:* It is possibly down to website management, but I agree that it is a particularly bad website.

Ms Coelho: We discovered the problem; you have to register as a journalist.

Dr Ryan: There is also no register of documents on the website. Those are a couple of things. I would also say that there is some sensitivity with the operations that Frontex is involved in co-ordinating or planning. If that is an impediment, or to the extent that that is an impediment, to matters being put in the public domain, then a structure needs to be put in place for evaluation of those things, both on their own terms, and the legal consequences and the legal regime. So, there can be oversight in that manner, it does not necessarily all have to be in the public domain, so long as the right structure is put in place.

Q430 *Lord Young of Norwood Green:* Can I just ask you, before anybody else answers, is there another EU body, agency or institution that you would see as being the model for how Frontex should be accountable?

Dr Ryan: I do not have a model right away that I can identify.

Ms Muggeridge: Just to come in, I agree with my colleague that Member States and Frontex have an interest in ensuring they respect protection obligations and are seen to respect protection obligations. We have some positive ideas about how accountability could be improved: one is looking at the appointment of perhaps an ombudsman or an independent observer which could be a neutral role and could receive information from all sides with respect to Frontex operations and produce reports in the same way that we have monitors here on the domestic front. The other aspects we would recommend are on the management board, given that the protection agenda seems to have been slightly sidelined so far, would be to possibly have UNHCR as an observer on the management board, or to have somebody with protection expertise on the board in order to input on the protection side of things, to ensure that was covered. We would also like to see Frontex engage with civil society organisations, given UNHCR's perhaps limited capacity, especially to monitor and observe operations that are happening on the ground and we would like to feed in in particular to risk assessments, given that the risk is not only to states but also can be to individuals as well. We would also like to see better quality reporting and statistics to move away from what we have gained, which is anecdotal information really, and the numbers that are cited in some of the Frontex reports seem somewhat general and do not include any reference at all to the numbers of people that have needed protection or asked for protection. Then, as I think we said earlier, we would like to see more transparency on return agreements so that we can gain information about them and possibly input, but we are happy to input and would like to really engage with Frontex.

Ms Coelho: Just to say briefly, we understand that there are intelligence elements that sometimes cannot be shared, but that still allows for the suggestions that have been made to be explored. While it may not seem very easy to develop a relationship perhaps between a border agency and civil society, we have some very good examples and practices emerging on the ground in Hungary, in Slovenia and other countries, in the Netherlands, where members of our network are co-operating very positively with their national border guards and with UNHCR through tripartite agreements and are doing monitoring. I was myself in Budapest last week and heard the Hungarian border guards say how much they had been benefiting from this kind of exchange and dialogue and building of trust and confidence. So I see this as a very good practice and something that can certainly be looked at the European level.

Q431 *Lord Harrison:* Very quickly, that sounds very interesting; is there anything written about that relationship with Hungary and Slovenia?

Ms Coelho: Yes, there is a formal tripartite agreement between the Hungarian Government and UNHCR and the Hungarian Helsinki Committee which I can share with the Committee.

Lord Harrison: We would like to have sight of that.

Chairman: Thank you very much. Lord Mawson, did you want to come in on this or move on?

Q432 *Lord Mawson:* I was really wondering about your comment about the sense that democratic structures are more accountable. They are shifting sands in my experience and a relationship with the management board actually might be a far more accountable structure. Do you have any comments on that?

Dr Ryan: Perhaps the question is what kind of accountability are we looking for? The management board in a sense is the stakeholders. The agency is acting on behalf of Member States and the Commission, so the management board it seems is very closely involved—or at least, it is structured in that way—in Frontex's core tasks. It is a different kind of accountability, which is accountability to the public at large or to the political system at large and that is what is lacking; I do not think the management board is really in a position to do that, or it is not going to be its primary concern. The question is to put in place structures that will ensure that the wider polity is familiar enough with what Frontex does,

and what the Member States do under its aegis, and the consequences thereof, and has the opportunity to have input into Frontex.

Q433 *Lord Mawson:* This is for ECRE and the Refugee Council: in paragraph 3.4 of your joint written evidence you express concern that "the interdiction of all potential irregular entrants from physical access to the EU is indiscriminate". What evidence is there to show that Frontex is involved in such interdiction practices, and maybe you could just give one or two practical examples?

Ms Muggeridge: We were a bit confused by this question initially because we thought that the interdiction of entrants in a way was part of the raison d'etre of Frontex itself. In terms of indiscriminate entry or indiscriminate practices, we note that the evidence that was given by Frontex itself, including its annual report, mainly cites the statistics of thousands of people that it has stopped from coming or turned back, there is no reference really to the differences within that large group, the different needs of people and what kind of ages or gender or whether any of them were vulnerable people, or whether any of them indeed wanted to seek protection or did seek protection. Really from Frontex itself the reporting seems to imply that people are seen as a mass of irregular migrants rather than individual people with individual needs, some of which might be a need for protection.

Ms Coelho: If I could just give an example, the way that Frontex concerns around Iraqis are portrayed is a great concern to us when we know that 90% of Iraqis arriving in Sweden are being recognised as people needing international protection and 74% of Iraqis in Austria are, yet we know that Frontex is planning operations to prevent the entry of Iraqis. We all know that what is happening in Iraq is a stark example of the need for that protection element to come into their planning and their way of thinking.

Ms Muggeridge: Just to add on Iraqis as well, as my colleague said 1500 Iraqis arrive in Sweden every month and that number is increasing. We have not really spoken much about people who arrive by land and air, which is more than the people that arrive by sea and the dangers for individuals—we heard from our colleague George Joseph at Caritas, Sweden that they conducted some 260 interviews of persons who have come, mainly in containers, and these are Iraqis who have spent two or three weeks getting to Sweden, paying £40,000 for a husband and wife to come, maybe in situations where they are sitting in containers with dead bodies in those containers during the journey. So there are some quite real concerns about safety and the conditions and the human cost of persons trying to get to the EU that we feel that Member States and Frontex need to take into account in a risk analysis of the risks to the people who are trying to flee their countries.

Q434 *Lord Harrison:* Did I hear you say that Frontex have, as it were, ordained that Iraqis should be wholly excluded?

Ms Coelho: No, the public bulletin that my colleague referred to talks about some analysis being undertaken about the risk of illegal entries from Iraqis and that that analysis is ongoing and is likely to lead to an operation next year as I understand. So there was some quite extensive concern expressed by Frontex and they were clearly planning to target this particular group, and what I am saying is that in addressing that particular group the fact that so many of those who do arrive are recognised as having protection concerns is not recognised—at least not within the materials that I have seen—in the way that they are undertaking their risk analysis. So they are all viewed as illegal immigrants.

Q435 *Lord Young of Norwood Green:* On that last point, Frontex and the Member States have an obligation to deal with the problem of illegal immigration; are you saying that they should not do that? That is the bit where I cannot quite understand what it is you expect them to do. I agree there is a problem with people who are genuinely seeking asylum, genuine refugees, but that does not take away from the problem. If we do not attempt to deal with illegal immigration more people will die in containers; that seems to me the only conclusion one can draw because that is acceptable. Member States and Frontex working together are trying to deter those kinds of routes of illegal immigration, that is what it is about. How we deal with the other side of that human problem, with the genuine people who are caught up in that, is something that has to be resolved by both the Commission and Member States but surely there should be a common aim in deterring illegal immigration because of the very risks. Because Frontex is carrying out a risk analysis, saying that route there is not the popular route these days, this is another route, that is a legitimate aim and activity of Frontex is it not? You seem to be describing it as though somehow that is a distorted objective of the organisation.

Ms Muggeridge: One of the issues is that we have not seen the risk analysis so we actually do not know what it contains, but as I said earlier we would like to input into that—after all, we are talking about Iraqis and it is specifically aimed at Iraqi nationals and we know that many Iraqis are genuine refugees, in fact the majority of them are, and UNHCR actually recognises Iraqis from central and southern Iraq as prima facie refugees. It is a concern of ours, obviously, that we be able to feed into that, and on your point about border control the anecdotal

evidence that we have is that border control and strengthening border control can actually mean that people are pushed more into taking circuitous or longer or more dangerous routes. We would agree, however, with your point that this issue of mixed flows and somehow allowing refugees to come in definitely needs to be addressed.

Q436 *Lord Young of Norwood Green:* That is the point; Frontex is not the organisation that is going to resolve that problem surely, it is about a common European policy on how we deal with asylum seekers and refugees and it seems to me that asking Frontex to do a risk analysis on the basis that you are saying is not their role. They should be more transparent and maybe more accountable, I do not think we would argue with that, but I just wonder whether you are directing your attentions or expecting something from an organisation that it cannot really provide.

Ms Coelho: I just feel that the separation of responsibilities does not match with reality. If we are dealing with mixed flows and refugees are amongst irregular immigrants then operations that are meant to deter irregular immigration have to address the needs of refugees. To say that Frontex is not the right organisation, Frontex is acting on behalf of Member States as we understand it, Member States have those obligations. We are not saying that Frontex does not have a legitimate role to play and we are not saying that there should not be border controls and we should not be trying to tackle to illegal immigration; we are saying that because of the nature of the way people arrive and the fact that refugees have no legal way in, there has to be recognition that they are there and they are being impacted by the activities of Frontex; therefore Frontex's operations have to be sensitive to their needs and to the obligations of Member States. It is about bringing things together rather than either/or from our perspective.

Dr Ryan: Could I offer a quick comment in response to those questions? Firstly on the relationship between Frontex and the Member States, my assessment would be that Frontex is more than a passive co-ordinator of Member States' activity where it is the kind of thing they would have been doing anyway. Frontex has rather led to a step change in the situation because it is initiating the co-ordination that it engages in. I think it is appropriate to look at Frontex somehow separately from the Member States and perhaps, in many ways, as almost more important than the Member States, certainly in some of the contexts in which it is operating. I do agree with you that this is a difficult situation and often a tragic situation that we are dealing with when you are talking about people crossing the sea in flimsy vessels, and stopping that happening is not absolutely a wrong thing to do; I do not think any of us here is saying that. But because it is difficult it is not enough just to say "Push people back" and then not think about what comes after that. A point I have made a couple of times is that they have pushed them back to particular states that we might otherwise have concerns about as to how people are treated and how especially non-nationals are going to be treated in those states. So pushing back and then washing of hands does not seem to me an appropriate response, but that is not to deny however the difficulty of the situation and so the absence of any simple solution to it.

Q437 *Lord Teverson:* Rather than going around the houses, surely what you are saying—with which I would tend to have some sympathy—is that when someone comes into contact with Frontex it should just be from a legal way the same as if they had arrived at the land border control of an EU Member States. That is what we are saying, is it not? It should not be any different that your first call if you like is Frontex as opposed to a border post on the Moroccan/Spanish land border.
Dr Ryan: I would not actually go that far in all circumstances. Are we talking about the high seas or are we talking about the territorial waters of Member States?

Q438 *Lord Teverson:* You think there is a difference, do you? Clearly there is a difference legally but you are saying there should be a difference in terms of the asylum seeker.
Dr Ryan: I think in terms of the starting point, yes, but the second point I wanted to make is that it all depends on the state that is the interlocutor to which individuals may be returned. What is going to happen to them if they are returned to that state? That is a context specific point, it is not a general one. It is about the particular operations of particular states that are in that situation.

Q439 *Lord Teverson:* I will leave it there.
Ms Coelho: My response to that question would be that anybody subject to a Frontex operation should not have any fewer rights than if they were subject to any border controls undertaken by a Member State. That is my response to that, which is agreeing with what you are saying, that all the responsibilities should clearly flow into and through a Frontex operation as it would through the national authorities. We are not convinced that that is actually in place, that the mechanisms are in place to allow that.

Q440 *Lord Teverson:* I understand that.
Ms Coelho: That is not to say that we think that people have actually received their rights at national borders that are controlled by Member States at the moment.

Q441 *Lord Mawson:* This again is for ECRE and the Refugee Council. What, if any, mechanisms to address humanitarians concerns exist in the framework of Frontex operations and has there been any progress in establishing "joint asylum expert teams" to accompany Frontex operations?
Ms Coelho: As I have already mentioned, Frontex operations allow for rescue at sea to take place when the need arises, so I suppose that is one aspect. Development of working arrangements with the UNHCR and IOM may lead to some mechanisms and relationships that can improve the ability of Frontex to respond to humanitarian needs and to see how people, once they arrive at the place where they are diverted to or taken to, can be dealt with on reception. We think that the presence of a UNHCR position in the Frontex headquarters in Warsaw is a positive step towards making suggestions and providing advice on how some of the humanitarian needs of refugees can be addressed. We are concerned that his position is not a secure position, that it is only funded until June and it is actually funded by UNHCR so we would be interested in how that kind of role can be made more sustainable. In terms of asylum expert teams we have been disappointed actually at the lack of progress on those. I think they were proposed in the summer of 2006 and, once again, in September 2007 we saw that the Justice and Home Affairs Council urged for there to be some development of how these teams can be put into place. We think that they have a lot of potential to actually address some of the concerns we have been raising and to work in complement with the RABITs. We have seen a very fast pace in agreeing and starting to implement RABITs, and we know that this week in Portugal they are having a testing mission and, on the other side, the asylum expert teams have not been progressed, so we feel that that has been a bit unbalanced.

Q442 *Lord Mawson:* If they were progressed how would they work in practice; how would you like them to work?
Ms Coelho: We have not gone into a lot of detail because we were wanting to see what more detailed proposals would come from the European Commission and then we would see how we felt those could be implemented then if we felt those proposals could be improved. We do have some ideas in terms of the sorts of people who need to be involved, and it is clear to us that UNHCR need to have a core role in those asylum expert teams. We are not just talking about some people being trained and then forming asylum expert teams, they are people who have longstanding expertise and mandates from UNHCR and also from NGOs around Europe that should be involved with State authorities; perhaps they are a mechanism where some of the very good practices on

the national level that I mentioned could be replicated, for example, but we have not developed a clear model of exactly how these teams should function and on what criteria should they be deployed et cetera.

Q443 Lord Mawson: Would it not be helpful to your cause if actually you did begin to develop something that was practical, that people could actually begin to look at and engage with?

Ms Coelho: Yes, I take your point. I also would like to say that it has been a long hard struggle for civil society to get some positive reaction to our wishes to be involved in these sorts of issues. Authorities that work at borders do not traditionally co-operate on the ground or have a political dialogue with NGOs necessarily, so I would say we are at the beginning of a new phase with lots of possibilities, and that is perhaps why we are looking at some examples on the ground and we have not as such had the opportunity to envisage that kind of mechanism and all the opportunities it could offer us at this stage.

Q444 Lord Harrison: In that case might not Frontex be a beneficial vehicle, for instance, to transmit the example you gave earlier of which you are going to provide us evidence about the relations set up with Hungary and Slovenia, as it were to expand best practice throughout Frontex's operation.

Ms Coelho: My understanding is that UNHCR through its dialogue and through its position is very much sharing that, they are very much at the centre of brokering these kinds of practices in Central Europe, and I think that conversation and sharing of information is starting. We would be very happy to play a role in increasing that kind of sharing of information and good practice, certainly.

Q445 Lord Teverson: If we can continue on UNHCR, when we were out in Warsaw we very briefly met the representative, he had only just recently arrived and everything was just being set up if I remember. I would be interested to know what role you think the UNHCR representative, particularly moving Warsaw alongside Frontex should have, and more generally. It would be interesting to know if you have any feedback on how you think that relationship is working so far and what it should become. Is it sufficient as a major plank of protecting and getting the interests of refugees and asylum seekers on Frontex's agenda?

Ms Coelho: I do not feel we are in a position to comment on how that post is having an impact or not having an impact and how well that relationship is going, I think it is for UNHCR to say. For us it has certainly been seen as a positive step—we learnt of it in September—and we think that there are lots of possibilities. As I said, the building of relationships

and trust on a very human level is very important and having the presence of somebody physically in the headquarters is a first step towards that. I am not sure it is all that is needed and I think it is very important for the Working Arrangement that is being discussed at the moment between Frontex and UNHCR to be concluded and for there to be some exploration of how other entities or actors or agents could help to implement that relationship and the bringing in of the protection issues. For somebody there to improve information-sharing, to provide advice, to provide training—my understanding is that there would be good possibilities for training on international refugee and human rights law and for it then to be considered how operations can respect it—and help with how people can be better identified during the operations for example. That is how we would see the role of UNHCR being useful to Frontex.

Ms Muggeridge: Just on a practical level to add to that, during conversations with UNHCR they have mentioned that, for example, in Morocco it would be helpful if UNHCR was alerted if, for example, a ship or some people were going to arrive and there may be refugees within that group, both in Morocco and Libya. It would be very useful for them if they were alerted as a matter of course. Also, if humanitarian concerns and obligations could be written into operational plans, not just as an add-on to a mandate or something, but actually written into operational plans and for officers to be given real guidance about what they should do if they encounter somebody who is either vulnerable or in distress or indeed wants to ask for protection. In Morocco UNHCR mentioned that the number of refugees compared to the number of migrants is actually quite small and it would actually be good to have help from organisations, perhaps civil society organisations, to assist with the larger number of irregular immigrants so that people were not all forced into the asylum route as well. With regards to IOM, given that they do not have a protection mandate it is difficult to comment on that; our only comment would be that we understand that IOM is involved in voluntary returns and we would simply say that returns should be truly voluntary and not just an option, for example, to get out of poor detention conditions in certain countries.

Ms Coelho: Can I quickly add to that that while we have a protection mandate as an organisation we are extremely concerned about the suffering and violence that migrants encounter on their journeys and the treatment that they receive on arrival, and so we would be very much in favour of there being a more structured look at what organisations need to be in place, dealing with those humanitarian needs. That may be IOM, that may be more an organisation like the Red Cross who provide a lot of humanitarian support on arrival in some countries, such as in Lampedusa, so we are concerned that the needs of this large group of people need to be better taken into account.

Q446 Chairman: A question for Dr Ryan is to ask what your views are on the Advocate General's opinion which led to exclusion of the UK from Frontex regulations. It would be interesting to hear your view as a lawyer on that, and do you see circumstances in which the UK in the future might be able to opt in to Frontex and other similar arrangements?

Dr Ryan: I have to be a little bit careful since I know that the Court of Justice is going to give judgment soon on this case. What I would say, having looked at the Advocate General's opinion and at the different arguments, there is a superficial attractiveness to the UK's position, that there is a part of the Schengen protocol that permits a unilateral decision by the United Kingdom to participate. Equally, with respect to the Frontex agency, you could say anyway is this not something the UK could participate in, without participating in the rest, so it is not somehow central or integral to the Schengen system. When you look at it in a bit closer detail, and particularly look at all of the Schengen protocol and think about all of the Schengen system, it is not quite as straightforward. On the protocol itself, the other parts of the protocol which require unanimous consent, if they are to have any meaning and they are not just a transitional provision, then it cannot be the case that the UK always has a unilateral right and if the other provisions are still applicable, then there is a difficulty with the UK's somewhat selective reading of the Schengen protocol. As to whether this agency is integral or not, that rather depends on how the agency is understood. If the agency is understood as being about the management of the external borders because there is a border-free zone behind the common external border, then it is hard to justify the UK being able to participate unilaterally because the UK is not in that zone and does not have the same stake in the outcome as regards the agency as the states that are in the Schengen zone would have. Of course, if the agency is understood in a somewhat broader sense as just being about the good management of borders, one might take a different view. There is certainly a case on the UK side, but there is equally a good case on the other, and I do not think that the Court of Justice could be criticised if it turns out that it follows the Advocate General and says that the UK does not have a unilateral right in this matter.

Chairman: Thank you very much. I wonder if I could end with a question of which you have not had notice. We have listened to your very understandable concerns about the rights and opportunities for refugees and so on and we understand all that, but if the rules were changed and circumstances were changed whereby the people you are concerned about had a much easier run—you have talked about dangerous journeys, you have talked about all sorts of legal and physical man-traps which make it difficult for the people you are concerned about— would it be fair to accept that if there were changes in that direction it would inevitably bring with it an increase in illegals, in undesirables who might have terrorist intentions and the flow of those sorts of people whom we call overall "illegals" might increase to a flood. Would that be a situation that could arise if you were able, by waving a magic wand, to make life a great deal easier for potential refugees?

Q447 Lord Mawson: Could I add to that? What are the implications of that for inner cities, particularly some of our most vulnerable areas?

Ms Coelho: I will try to address those questions and then defer to my colleague. In terms of if the rules were changed, the rules are there.

Q448 Chairman: And the opportunities were changed.

Ms Coelho: Yes, so what you are talking about if I am right is more the practical implementation of those rules and how they are adapted to that. I do not accept that premise; if you bring in good mechanisms, if your asylum systems are good quality and you are able to screen as you put it people who would not fall into the category of people in need of international protection and that might have other intentions for coming here, I think all the rules and laws are in place to be able to identify those people— the Refugee Convention has very clear exclusion rules. Also, there are some interesting ways in which entry for the people we are concerned about can be explored; one of them actually put in place by some countries is what is called "protected entry procedures" where people can go to embassies or consulates, for example, in third countries and say that they would like to claim asylum, and there is a pre-screening that takes place on that territory, and if they are seen as people who would be admissible for such a claim then their entry is facilitated into the EU. That would be one way of people being able to bypass these kinds of journeys, with the checks that need to be in place as to whether these are people with the right intentions, and those checks can be applied right at the very beginning. From our perspective— and I am not saying that is the only solution but I think it is one mechanism that could be explored—if there are mechanisms to avoid people taking these kinds of dangerous journeys, with the right balances and checks, good quality asylum systems that are able to identify people who are clearly not in any way in need of asylum, then the problems you raise are dealt with. I understand that this is a challenge but the development of a common asylum system at the

European level is supposed to be something which helps EU Member States to be able to do this better in the future. Your question about inner cities is a very broad question about integration and how people who come and are recognised as refugees can be helped to integrate into our societies and make a contribution without placing a burden on societies may be struggling. That is a huge area which my organisation is very active on in terms of looking at how people can be helped to acquire language skills, to re-qualify, to get jobs, be able to contribute to society and how society can see the benefits that come from people arriving and can build up trust and confidence. I would be happy to share any materials you would be interested in on those issues after this session.

Dr Ryan: I do not think we have been arguing for open borders or anything of that nature, we are really focused on Frontex-originating activities or even just Member State activity which exposes people to risks of ill treatment and trying to prevent that from occurring. I would emphasise on that that of course the primary concern is with those who are at risk of ill treatment or have perhaps fled from ill treatment in their countries of origin, and that is a refugee scenario. But there is also another dimension which is people who, if returned, are at risk of ill treatment in the countries of transit. I think both groups are

deserving of attention in the design of the system and in its application. So I do not think we are talking about open borders or under-estimating the challenges which irregular migration presents, it is more of a specific set of concerns that we are bringing forward.

Ms Muggeridge: I would concur with my colleagues; we are definitely not saying that everyone is a refugee or everyone should be a refugee, but unfortunately there are still instances in the world where people will need to flee. All we are saying is that there should be some opportunity for these people to be set apart and given protection. Unfortunately, given that there is no way for an asylum seeker to travel legally as an asylum seeker to reach somewhere, refugees will have to use the same sorts of routes. I would just like to mention Article 31 of the 1951 Convention which allows for refugees not to be penalised for travelling illegally, so what we are asking for really is that attention be paid to safeguard the rights of that group of people, whether that is a large group or a small group.

Chairman: Thank you very much for coming, you have been most interesting and, unlike a lot of witnesses who give evidence before Select Committees in this building, you have been admirably concise, for which we are particularly grateful. We have learned an awful lot and you have given us a lot to think about; thank you.

WEDNESDAY 12 DECEMBER 2007

Present   Dear, L.   Mawson, L.
           Harrison, L.   Teverson, L.
           Hodgson of Astley Abbotts, L.   Tonge, B.
           Jopling, L. (Chairman)   Young, L.
           Marlesford, L.

Examination of Witnesses

Witnesses: MR LIAM BYRNE MP, Minister of State, Home Office (Minister for Immigration), MR BRODIE CLARK, Strategic Director, Border Control, MR TOM DOWDALL, Border Control Director of European Operations, and MR TOM DODD, Policy for Border Control, Border and Immigration Agency, examined.

Q449 Chairman: Minister, welcome. We are at the final evidence session which we are holding with regard to our inquiry into Frontex. You have no doubt been briefed about the way the Committee has been carrying out this inquiry. We did visit Warsaw and we did visit the Ukraine/Polish border, and we have been to Heathrow to look at things going on there. We have had various witnesses as well. Would you like to invite your colleagues to introduce themselves for the record?

Mr Byrne: My Lord Chairman, on my right is Brodie Clark, who is the Strategic Director for Border Control for the Border and Immigration Agency. On his right is Tom Dowdall, who runs our European operations at the Border and Immigration Agency, and on my left is Tom Dodd, who has oversight of our policy for border control in the agency as well. I thought I would bring everybody along this morning so that we could have as informed a discussion as possible.

Q450 Chairman: That is fine. We have met the two outside gentlemen before in this inquiry. This evidence session is broadcast over the internet. We will send you a transcript of the evidence in case there are any corrections or alterations which you would like to make and if there are questions you cannot answer or would like to think about we would be delighted if you would like to write to us afterwards, but fairly quickly please. This Committee is not enamoured with the speed with which the Home Office deals with some of our problems and because we are starting to draft our report very soon I hope you will not delay in sending us additional evidence. You will know that the Court of Justice will very shortly be pronouncing about the legalities of the UK's relationship with Frontex and I wonder if you would like to comment on that and talk about the position of the UK, which is, of course, not a Schengen state, and our aspirations to participate fully in Frontex. It would be helpful if you would talk about the current dispute and the relationship you see between Frontex and the UK.

Mr Byrne: I should start by welcoming your appointment to the chairmanship of the Committee because I do not think we have had the chance to meet in this context before. I should say too that I think this is very auspicious timing because obviously the European Commission is looking in some depth at this question of Frontex next year and so we are very much looking forward to the Committee's considered views and advice on this question to very much help us shape our own perspective on whatever recommendations the European Commission brings forward next year. We are genuinely very grateful for the work you are doing. There are just three things that I would say about the legal position. As the Committee knows, our position is that we think we have the right to participate in Frontex because we think we have a treaty right to do so. Secondly, the test that the Advocate General set out we thought was the right test. We very much welcome the fact that the Advocate General said that we do have the right to participate in Schengen building measures where we are able to participate in those measures autonomously, as it were. What we were then disappointed about was that the Advocate General went on to say that participation in Frontex was not an autonomous measure, so we liked what the Advocate General said about the test but we did not like the way that the Advocate General said the test would be applied. Whatever conclusion the court comes to we think both outcomes are pretty manageable for the UK. Obviously, we would like to be a full member because we think that we have got a great deal to give to strengthening Europe's external border. We think that our border security systems are amongst the best in Europe and we think that we have got the right kind of views about how Frontex should develop over the years to come and we think that those views are shared by a lot of the north European nations. If the European Court says that we cannot participate as a full member then we will obviously continue to seek to involve ourselves in operations on a case-by-case basis, as the Frontex board is allowed to permit us to do, and we will continue to exercise influence in whatever way we can. We have an excellent working relationship with the leadership of Frontex. We think our views are well respected and I think we do have this coalition of interest, in particular with north European states, so, come what may, we are reasonably confident about the future. We think Frontex is important and we would like to commit to it.

Q451 Chairman: Perhaps you would like to expand a little further. What is the downside of our exclusion from full participation? How does it manifest itself? It does seem to us rather curious that we could host Torino and Agelaus, given that the UK is not at the EU external border, which is strictly speaking the remit of Frontex activities. It seems rather curious that we are not in but we can participate.
Mr Byrne: I will ask Brodie Clark in a second to comment on the two operations because he oversees them. What is the downside? I think we can divide this into two. There is the operational and there is the strategic. On the operational side we obviously think that we have a great deal to give. We think that our staff are first-class and we think that in pure operational terms Frontex operations would be stronger for the participation of Border and Immigration Agency staff, so although we can continue to participate as approved on a case-by-case by the management board, there is not the full contribution that can be provided by the UK in the same way as if we were full members, but we think that is pretty manageable. On the strategic side we have obviously got views about the way that Frontex should develop and it would be easier to help influence the development of Frontex along those lines if we were a full member. If we are not a full member I do not think that is a lost cause. I still think that we will be able to influence Frontex quite seriously by sheer force of argument, so, as I say, because we have worked very closely with Member States on a day-to-day level, for example, I work very closely with my opposite number in France, Brice Hortefeux, we have a very close, shared interest in many of the operational priorities that Frontex has because, with the advent of juxtaposed controls in northern France, that does put pressure on the Pas de Calais. Over the next ten or 15 years that particular part of France is seeking to go through some pretty major regeneration and we have a shared interest in helping that part of France prosper and that means that the more we are able to work together with the French government upstream, if you like, the easier that job becomes both in terms of managing the pressure on the Pas de Calais but also in terms of Kent, so I just cite that by way of example to underline this point that we do have a coalition of interest and that is why I think we will continue to be able to exercise a degree of influence over the way that

Frontex develops. I sometimes detect a slightly different agenda between north Europe and south Europe. I think some of the southern European states have perhaps some different ideas about the way that Frontex should develop but, as I say, through the partners we have, particularly in northern Europe and through our own experience, we will be able to exercise quite a degree of influence over the future of Frontex by sheer force of argument and coalition of interest. That might be something the Committee themselves have found.
Mr Clark: If I may add to that, we from the operational side of the Border and Immigration Agency are very keen to retain that position in terms of operational co-operation and collaboration, so in that sense we provide staff on occasion for operations, we provide equipment for operations, we provide expertise and we think in many areas we provide best practice in terms of the operations. You mentioned two particular operations and that really is predicated on the understanding that the border itself is not just the primary arrivals control at the airport or the arrivals area from shipping or from Eurostar. The border increasingly is being extended right back into the hinterlands of countries and much of what we have been achieving in terms of exporting the border is about information and data that we have been able to share and exchange in order to secure the border itself. These two operations, one in respect of the 2006 Winter Olympics and one in respect of unaccompanied children, represent areas where we think there are huge win-wins in terms of our collaboration within Frontex and we continue to look for opportunities so that we can develop those and work positively with Frontex to take those forward.

Q452 Lord Harrison: Good morning, Minister. It is rare for a minister to drop two hints in the first answer to any question but I will follow up what you said about your implied anxieties that the southern states might have a different view of the way forward in the future for Frontex and ask you what you mean on that and to elaborate. I wonder if I could therefore bring forward a question I had in mind to ask later anyway, which might exemplify your anxieties. When we visited the Ukraine/Poland border recently we learned that, of course, the Poles were doing a very good job in learning from and strengthening Frontex, but their objectives, for instance, in terms of unemployment in Poland as a result, interestingly, of the exit of Poles to this country and therefore a requirement to bring some Ukraines into Poland to supply those jobs, might illustrate an example of where the Poles might view Frontex differently because they have a more Polish view of a neighbouring country than they do of the European Union as a whole which might be expressed by us and other countries within the

European Union. What is the nature of your anxiety about the southern states and does that illustrate the possible problem you are alluding to?

Mr Byrne: The thought that I had in mind was slightly different from that one although that is a very interesting perspective. My concern with Frontex is that it tries to run before it can walk, so I am less interested in Frontex leaping ahead and assembling some kind of great bureaucracy at its headquarters where we try and move faster towards any sense of a European border guard that is somehow co-ordinated out of Frontex headquarters. I just think that is a step that is too far. I would much rather see Frontex beginning to strengthen its practical ability to conduct operations which add value to the border security operations of Member States. If you were asking what I would like Frontex to evolve into, I would set three benchmarks before we go too much further. I would like to see much more effective planning of operations. I would like to see much more effective evaluation of operations because, as I think you are about to come onto a bit later in your questions, one of the great difficulties with immigration control is that once you stop one route you begin displacing traffic to other routes and that means that you have to have effective evaluation of your operation so that you understand what the displacement effects are and you can move assets much more dynamically as a result, and we do just need to see that co-ordination of assets and operations conducted in a more effective way. This is a very British perspective but we are very interested in just getting the basics and the practicalities right before we start leaping ahead into bureaucratic headquarters and anything more grandiose. Let us just get the basic operational stuff right, and that has implications, does it not, for the way Frontex evolves and the priorities that it is given over the next three to five years? Those are, if you like, my interests in what Frontex does over the next three to five years.

Q453 *Lord Harrison:* I am very grateful for that. In fact, I think the Minister has answered one of my later questions, but perhaps on the Polish/Ukraine one, which is slightly separate, you might like to give that some thought.

Mr Byrne: Yes, absolutely.

Q454 *Lord Marlesford:* Minister, this very interesting document, *Security in the Global Hub*, I wonder if you like to talk a little bit about it. There are various points that arise. First of all, I do not know if there is a hard copy available. All we were able to get was a photocopy. I found it odd that there is not a date on the front; there is only a tiny date at the back. It seems a rather amateur production. I do not know if you would like to comment on that.

Mr Dodd: It was produced by the Cabinet Office, not by the Home Office.

Q455 *Lord Marlesford:* What I would like to ask is, is it a statement of government policy? I see in the introduction, by the Prime Minister, obviously, that it has 14 recommendations, some of which require legislation, according to the document itself, or is it a Green Paper, a White Paper? What is it and what are you going to do with it?

Mr Byrne: It is a statement of government policy so I suppose it is more akin to a management report about what managerial arrangements will be made with regard to our arrangements at the border and what the consequences are and the lines of direction of further policy development. Just to set it in context, this is part of a sort of multi-part border security architecture which we have evolved over the last 14 months, and that border security architecture starts with much tighter arrangements abroad, what we would call our offshore border. That encompasses biometric visas, which will complete their global rollout in the new year. It includes the visa waiver test which we are now running on every country around the world to check where we need to introduce new visa regimes. The third part of the system is the introduction of passenger screening systems so that in time all passenger manifests will be screened against our no-fly lists and our intercept lists. The fourth part of that architecture is then much tougher organisational arrangements with policing at our ports and airports, and that is where a unified border force comes in, and the fifth part of the architecture is ID cards for foreign nationals here at home so we can acquire much greater purchase over illegal working which we know is the root cause of much illegal immigration. This is part of what has been about a 14-month programme of reform. It is a vital part of it, and I know many members of the Committee have called for these arrangements for some time. The next step will be for me to produce an action plan for the Chancellor, whom I met last week to discuss this, and the Home Secretary, and we will begin making the organisational changes in the new year but we will have a number of follow-up reports which we will need to publish about how the recommendations will be implemented.

Q456 *Lord Marlesford:* Have you any idea of the dates for the publication of the follow-up reports?

Mr Byrne: They will begin in the new year because that is when we start the process of integration. We will start the process of integration by folding in UK Visas to the Border and Immigration Agency and thereby introduce much tighter arrangements between what is effectively Britain's offshore border control and the Border and Immigration Agency. The next key milestone is for Customs operations at the border to be integrated into the Border and Immigration Agency. We have earmarked April/May time for that work, but I suspect there will be five or six reports that we have to publish, including reflections on legislation over the 12 months beginning in January.

Mr Clark: From where we currently are there are huge opportunities around in terms of this report and in terms of the restructuring that has been proposed, and I think the benefits around a much more rational set of processes at the border between the various agencies and the Government make an awful lot of sense, issues around efficiency that can be gained by looking at one workforce rather than a number of workforces make a lot of sense, issues around one face of the Government at the border into the country make a lot of sense, and I think operationally, again, people within the Border and Immigration Agency are very enthusiastic about this, as are many of our colleagues across in the detection part of HMRC.

Q457 *Lord Marlesford:* This leads very well into my next question. Mr Clark referred to huge opportunities. I would like to refer to huge gaps, and in particular the gap when you have given somebody temporary permission to come into the UK and you have no way of knowing whether or not they have departed. I know that in terms of the e-borders system you have just let a big contract, we know about that, and we know that they are going to start doing e-border scrutiny pretty soon and they are doing it quite a lot in coming in, but the information we have been given is that by December 2009 60% of passenger movements will be monitored. That is in two years' time and if about 100% of passenger movements coming in are monitored that leaves a pretty small percentage for the going out, and even by December 2010 when you say it will be 95% of passenger movements, as we know that a lot of the people coming in are going to be done it still leaves a gap going out. How did it come about that you have this enormous gap after 10 years of responsibility for the system?

Mr Byrne: I think the relevant policy dates back even beyond ten years because it was in 1994 that the Government, then under a different party, began dismantling exit controls. It was obviously this administration that finished the job, and I think, frankly, it was a mistake to do so. I think that one of the most basic requirements of a border control is the capability to count people in and count people out of the country, and I think a lot of the debate that we have seen in the media over the last three or four months about numbers, whether the population is growing too quickly or too slowly, has been well informed; much of the debate has been ill informed, but the debate would have been much easier if we had been

able to present to the public a much clearer picture about the number of people that were coming and going. That is why, when John Reid asked me to take this job 14 or 15 months ago, one of the first things that we concluded was that we needed to introduce systems for counting people in and out of the country very quickly. We were also ambitious though to make a second set of changes at the same time. If you are trying to count people in and out of the country effectively, you had better make sure that the person you are counting in is the same person as you are counting out. That is why we do think that the biometric security arrangements are so important because we want to be able to block individuals down to a single identity. We have now rolled out biometric visas in about 110 countries. We are at the point now, I think, of just having issued our millionth biometric visa and some of the results are pretty interesting. We are finding about a 1% hit rate where people are giving us fingerprints which we are able to match against fingerprints we already hold. There are quite a lot of people who are not being straight with us about the identity they possess. We think the arrangements for biometric identification need dovetailing with the arrangements for counting people in and out of the country. It has taken us the best part of the last year to go through the procurement exercise for this new system for counting people in and out and it has taken us the best part of the last year and a half to introduce biometric visas as well. Part of the reason though that it is going to take a bit of time to roll these systems out is that the system depends on the electronic transfer of passenger manifests between carrier systems and the government. There are obviously some carriers, if you take the ferry operators or the Eurostar operators, which are not running passenger booking systems which record the names of passengers. If you take a group of my constituents getting on a coach going to Calais for the day, the ferry operators may not have their names. Part of the requirement of introducing the system is going to be some cost for carriers in building these systems that record people's names and so on. It is an ambitious exercise and obviously the passenger growth in and out of Britain is enormous. We think that by 2015–16 passenger movements in and out of Britain will have almost doubled what they were in 2000, so it is a big exercise and that is why the old paper-based systems were not really going to cut the mustard. I agree with your basic analysis that it is a basic requirement of border control that you count people in and out of the country. I would share your frustration too that it is going to take a bit of time to get the full systems in place and that is why we will probably prioritise which routes these systems will apply to. Candidly, we will look at which routes we are most worried about and we will put the passenger screening systems on those routes first. The point at which we hit 100% high risk groups will be substantially in advance of 2010. We will also be counting in and out the lion's share of foreign nationals much quicker because, according to our analysis, most are moving on planes as opposed to by sea or by rail.

Q458 *Lord Marlesford:* I am very glad to hear that. Your approach is very encouraging. In the meanwhile, with this three year potential gap still, are there any other ways in which you can ensure that you know whether or not people who have been given a temporary permission to come have left other than by counting them out?
Mr Byrne: There are, yes, because we have a pilot system called Semaphore which is already up and running that is slightly ahead of schedule. It is screening about 30 million passenger movements at the moment. What we are now doing as part of the reorganisation of the Border and Immigration Agency is bringing together what was called the Managed Migration Directorate, migration control, that bit of the business that is responsible for extending people's permission to stay in the UK and UK visas so that there is an enforcement resource of their own and an integrated connection with border control. In effect, what the individuals responsible for issuing visas will now be able to do is watch whether people are indeed leaving the country when they are supposed to be leaving the country and begin commissioning enforcement activity if they are not. We are at the early stages of putting together this model. I am sure we will not get it right overnight but to my commitment is that, as we start counting people in and out of the country, we will also be commissioning enforcement activity for those people who are breaking the rules.

Q459 *Lord Marlesford:* Could you at least use for example a driving licence system so that if somebody is stopped for speeding who should have left there is a flag that can be sent to the Immigration Department?
Mr Byrne: Yes, absolutely. There is a strategy that we published in March 2007 called "Enforcing the Rules", which we published just before our strategy for securing the border. We said in that document that we would be exploring with a number of government agencies how we can, in the language we used at the time, shut down the privileges of Britain if you are here illegally. That means looking at how we share data with DVLA, with local authorities, with the National Health Service and the Security and Industry Authority for example. Some of the controversy that we have seen over SIA in the last month or two I am afraid we set out to create. Where the Border and Immigration Agency has data about those people who are here illegally, we should be sharing it. Government

is a big business but it should also work together cohesively where it can. That is hopelessly ambitious I know. It might be helpful for Brodie Clark to comment on the successes which the Semaphore system is already generating because there have been something like 1,400 arrests already as a result of this piece of work.
Mr Clark: It is worth saying that Semaphore and e-borders when fully up and running will be checking people in and out so that covers your point about people leaving the country. It will not just be counting; it will be checking against a number of watch lists which will allow us to identify whether follow-up action or intervention is required. We are at 30 million at the moment and we have quite deliberately within that 30 million sought to—

Q460 *Lord Marlesford:* 30 million what?
Mr Clark: 30 million annualised movements into and out of the UK which then go through this data collection and analysis process of Semaphore which will be part of the full e-borders programme. We have reached 30 million and we have targets over the next two or three years as you have identified. It is a multi-agency operation so we have immigration staff sitting with Customs staff, sitting with Special Branch and UK Visas. It really is a joint agency piece of work which we are all very interested in. The key beneficiaries to date, I would suggest, have been the police. They have followed up over the 18 months of operation of Semaphore with 1,400 arrests, some ranging from quite serious offenders and they have been seeking to lower offenders. These in some degree have been people wanting to leave the country who have been picked up through the data around Semaphore. As the Minister said earlier, part of the issue is around data and how we analyse and act on it. Part is also around identity and making sure we have the right people. Over the past 12 months we have also been doing work on physical embarkation controls in one or two selected sites in line with risk and threat, so in line with the kind of nature of the routes that we are considering. At the moment, about 15% of people leaving Heathrow will go through a physical embarkation control which will not just manage the data but will do the physical check against the document and check for forgeries at that point. Similarly we have some work going at Gatwick on embarkation controls and we will do everything we can in the years ahead to develop and improve the targeting of that and the amount of that which takes place.

Q461 *Baroness Tonge:* Can I just clarify something? We are hoping and attempting to count people in and out of our country. Are those people who go out then going back to their country of origin or may they go into another European country? The second part of my question is: how do European countries with the Schengen agreement in place count people in and out? Presumably, they cannot count people in and out of individual countries; it is just in and out of Europe. Because we are so different from the rest of Europe, how can we ever hope to be recognised as a proper player in the Frontex system and a proper part of it?

Mr Byrne: That is a good question. I think that European border security is catching up. If you look at many of the ambitions of Member States to introduce for example biometric visas, Europe is maybe two years behind where we are but they are definitely heading in that direction. A number of Member States are exploring how to procure and put in place passenger screening systems. I think the French are amongst those Member States, again two or three years behind where the UK is. One of the questions that the European Commission is looking at in its review of Frontex is whether Customs operations should fall within the ambit of Frontex. Again, that is something that we are already addressing with this report which I have in hard copy. Although Britain may be leading the pack in some of the arrangements that we are making, there is a convergence in what is understood to be good practice and maybe in years to come you will see a greater similarity in border control systems. If you look at what is going on in Australia and America, you can see parallels to that integrated border security architecture which I sketched out. It is obviously different. Australia is different to America. America is very airline focused and it is very east coast focused as well. The land borders in the US are much more open. We have had to think much more systematically about air, land and sea. We have perhaps had to move faster in creating a much more holistic architecture for our border security. The truth is that most western states are heading towards the same kind of model.

Q462 *Baroness Tonge:* Where do the people who go out of Britain go to? Do they go back to their country of origin? Do we know where they go or do we just dump them on Europe?

Mr Byrne: No. I would not say we dump them on Europe. People are free to move wherever they choose to after they leave the UK. As the Immigration Minister, I see my day job as being concerned with people leaving the country when they have no right to be here so I am more relaxed about where they are going in some ways as long as they are obeying the rules Parliament is putting through. As long as they are operating according to the rules of Parliament, that is my job done.

Q463 *Baroness Tonge:* What about humanitarian considerations?

Mr Byrne: Obviously, where we have humanitarian considerations, we have the law and I think the law is well administered by the immigration appeals tribunal system. I think they do an extraordinary job and I know that under Igor Judge there are plans for further reform. It is often an extremely difficult and demanding job which I think our penal system does enormously well.

Q464 *Lord Hodgson of Astley Abbotts:* Perhaps I may underline the importance of Lord Marlesford's comments about the gap. My home is in the rural west Midlands on the Herefordshire/Shropshire border and the temporary immigration for fruit picking—raspberries, strawberries, soft fruits—means that mini-towns are established. It is not for me to tell you about political matters but in the saloon bar of the Dog and Duck staying on and not going back to where you came from is a big issue in that part of the world. I think closing the gap that Lord Marlesford referred to is very important. I just give that as an anecdotal, local bit of evidence. I would like to ask you something about the rather narrow issue of rescue at sea because that leads on to disembarkation and the whole issue as far as that is concerned. We have been told that there is a working party looking at EU guidelines on rescue at sea and we are part of that. I wonder if you could tell us where we are on that, of the progress there has been and the likely timetable to be followed and indeed whether or not this should be done at an EU level or at a Frontex level. We have also heard from the Immigration Law Practitioners' Association that it is not clear whether international rescue obligations apply to Frontex or only to countries, whether or not that should be so extended or whether it should remain at a national level, or indeed whether your view is that it is in any case.

Mr Byrne: I share your view about what is going on in the west Midlands. I recently had a meeting with the National Farmers' Union just outside Hereford and they are demanding more migrants from east Europe. It is a difficult balance to strike sometimes.

Q465 *Lord Hodgson of Astley Abbotts:* It is whether they go at the end.

Mr Byrne: We do think it would be helpful to clarify the rules. On the point about Frontex though, we are not sure that there are necessarily changes to the regulations for Frontex which are needed. It goes back to my point about planning that I made earlier on. We do think that Frontex as part of its operational planning needs to be pretty sharp about precisely what legal basis and what laws are going to be used and what obligation is incumbent on who that is going to be germane before they start the operation. We think that the obligation should remain very much with Member States but when we are going into operational planning which Member States and which obligations need to be thought through at the outset, not *ex post facto*. There are two working groups that have been set up. The first one is to discuss the commissioned study into international law as it relates to illegal migration by sea. That discussion has led to a group being set up to discuss the draft guidelines that would apply to Frontex operations. We support it. It has met three times. The guidelines have not been agreed yet but we hope to see the guidelines in the new year. Separately, the meeting that Mr Faull talked about which met in June 2007 agreed that there should be a working group established to develop non-binding guidelines about the law of the sea as it relates to EU States and illegal migrants more generally, but as yet no working group has been set up on that. There is one group which is up and running, which has met three times, looking at the regulations with regard to Frontex operations. There is then a decision to establish a group looking at this question more widely. That has not yet been set up. Do we have a timetable for when that group is going to be set up?

Mr Dodd: We do not have one at the moment. We do believe there is a lack of clarity in the law of the sea and we are quite keen to work with other Member States to clarify that law as soon as we can.[3]

Q466 *Lord Teverson:* One of the areas we have been particularly looking at is around the coordination of the work of the Border and Immigration Agency with the other agencies which you will be well aware of: SOCA, Her Majesty's Revenue and Customs and the security and intelligence services. We would like to understand more about the coordination and how those activities, information and intelligence are shared with Frontex. As we have a passport union and travel freely over the Republic of Ireland as well, let alone the Crown dependencies and I think also Gibraltar, we have a gaping hole in terms of a particular UK e-borders process. I would like to understand also particularly the Republic of Ireland aspect of this coordination and how that is also controlled and how it works.

Mr Byrne: I will ask Tom to talk a little bit about the common travel area in a moment because I know it is an issue that has come up in the House of Lords once or twice now. I think Lord Trimble has raised it once or twice with Lord West. It was an issue that we flagged for review in the document published in March but I will ask Tom to explain a bit about where that has gone. Basically, the coordination of our operations operates at three levels, at the political, at the strategic and the tactical. At the political level, the committee that I worked to is called the DAM, the Domestic Affairs Committee on Migration and that provides government with overall political and

strategic direction on border control and immigration policy. That has met about three times already this last session. At the strategic level, the UK Border Agency will obviously now fold together UK Visas, the work of Customs and the work of BIA. That will create a dual reporting line for me. I will report both to the Home Secretary and to the Chancellor on that. The board that is set out in the document that we talked about a moment ago will have both a Customs Commissioner and a senior police officer to provide that strategic coordination. At the tactical level, there is then a number of different ways in which police, Customs and immigration staff work together. The Joint Border Operating Centre that Brodie talked about a second ago is very important. I do not know if the Committee has had a chance to go to the JBOC at Heathrow. It is well worth a visit because there you can see Customs, Special Branch, immigration officers and police working very closely together in an enormously effective way. A second example would be the Joint Passenger Analysis Unit that is established at Heathrow where again that allows BIA officials and HMRC officials to analyse intelligence and jointly target individuals. There is a similar operation in Kent that brings together Kent Police and others. There are a number of tactical relationships. When we look at SOCA, there is a joint programme of work that is agreed between BIA and SOCA. The Committee probably knows this. There are about 19 different programmes of work that SOCA are running. BIA is represented in about six of them. This is a changing picture because of the advent of the UK Border Agency but in summary that is how it works at the political, strategic and tactical level. Did you have a question about sharing with Frontex?

Q467 *Lord Teverson:* Yes. It is how that coordination relates to Frontex.

Mr Dodd: On the CTA, at the moment we are reviewing the CTA. It is perhaps worth recalling why Ireland and the UK are outside Schengen. It is because we are both islands and we have the benefit of a maritime border. 21 miles of sea is the most effective border control you can have. Successive governments have decided that they want to retain that as our border with contact to Europe. In terms of the CTA, we are very keen to retain the CTA and the benefits of the CTA for CTA nationals. We already have very close operational co-operation with our Irish counterparts. We run joint operations eight days a month at various CTA ports with them and we detect a lot of immigration crime that way which works very well. In terms of the review, we are looking at ways in which we can strengthen the CTA, both externally and round the CTA but also internally at the border between Ireland and the UK. E-borders will apply in due course to sea and air routes between Ireland and

---

[3] (See further supplementary evidence, page 152)

the UK so that will be one way in which we will strengthen our control and analysis of passengers using those routes.

Mr Byrne: On Frontex, effectively there are two ways in which we share intelligence with Frontex. The first is a two monthly strategic intelligence sharing report. There is then a quarterly meeting which brings together the intelligence and risk analysis network, FRAN, which is set up to try and discuss what is emerging from that intelligence.

Mr Dowdall: Those are the main channels of exchange and there are areas we know where there is room for improvement with Frontex. That is very much linked to the build-up of their risk analysis unit and improvement in their analytical capability. In addition to that, there is also the tactical exchange where we are involved in operations such as those mentioned earlier on. There is also a direct feed from a UK central point of contact with Frontex.

Q468 *Lord Dear:* In my previous life, I worked very closely with all of those agencies, SOCA, the security services and so on. I know the problems of all those agencies. They collect data and they guard it very closely. Knowledge is important; knowledge is status; knowledge is power. They never really want to share very much, no matter how much they say they are doing that. I wonder whether you could address that particular issue, as to whether you are satisfied that there is a machinery for data sharing and using it.

Mr Byrne: I will give you a political answer and then I will ask Brodie to give an operational answer. My own sense is that there are tactical initiatives like the Joint Border Operation Centre which have really taken us on quite a long way. When I first visited the Joint Border Operation Centre at Heathrow, I think it was during the World Cup. What the team there were able to show me is how football hooligans that were on travel ban orders were being picked up on passenger manifests. Special Branch was then able to pick up that information and to ask people to intercept those individuals at the border and stop them leaving the country in order to go and potentially cause trouble at the World Cup. There are eight examples like that where information sharing is very good. The work that we are doing with SOCA is in its early stages and that is important because, as you know, what we are trying to do to combat illegal immigration is move further and further upstream, particularly into those transit hubs where SOCA will have assets that nobody else does. There are then particular points of vulnerability on the border where there are extra tactical arrangements that are needed. In preparation for Member States coming into the Schengen zone, I have asked that our activity in the Pas de Calais and in Kent is stepped up. I am especially interested in how our work with Kent Police can be upgraded and how

we can extend into for example the management of covert human intelligence sources because, when I visited Calais—I have been to Calais a few times now—what they will often say is that nobody gets on a truck to Britain without the say-so of either the Afghan gang or the Iranian gang and we have lots of anecdotal experience of would-be illegal migrants being quite badly hurt by those elements of organised crime where they have not paid their dues. The estimates have been given that something like three quarters of illegal immigration into Britain is in the hands of organised crime. I do not know whether that is true or not. You would probably know better than me. There are a number of areas like that where I suspect that the tactical development of joint operation needs to be stronger. That is why I am a passionate advocate of the UK Border Agency because I just think the more we can bring those relationships tighter together the better. I characterise it as operating at three levels. Obviously there is the border experience, the bit that faces out to the public. There is the bit at the top. There is the combined organisation, but there is all the stuff in the middle, that work of intelligence sharing and so on. I do not have the evidence to prove it but in my heart I feel that it is there.

Mr Clark: Firstly, each of the agencies you were referring to have their own intelligence and tasking arrangements in play. Increasingly, we are doing the mix and match so SOCA are part of the BIA tasking and intelligence process and increasingly that swap over is proving very beneficial, not only in understanding what is going on and the priorities of other agencies but also in working with those other agencies. As a consequence of that, particularly with SOCA, we have done some very important work with one particular country. Secondly, the JBOC has been mentioned already. Thirdly, the border management programme which was the precursor to the unified border force document took us a long way down the process of sharing processes and information between the key agencies at the border. Indeed, one of the work streams in the border management programme was about risk assessment and an intelligence-based model for carrying risk assessment out between the agencies, so one shared system to operate at the front line. The other thing that is happening is that agencies are recognising the benefits of sharing as well as wanting historically to protect information. I think some of the work that has come out of our JBOC and the arrests the police have had from that is a real recognition that we cannot do this on our own. No one agency can succeed in this but if we do pull together and begin to trust each other an awful lot more then we will get significant gains. I think there is a climate of that around now. It has been helped by some of the IT developments because that is the point at which often agencies required to make choices about whether to plug in or stay removed. The arguments and the reasoning very clearly for a plug-in because of the benefits you get from it. There is a kind of catalyst around with some of the IT developments that different agencies have taken forward.

Mr Byrne: Another example of that is, when we roll out the full e-border system, the way the roll-out programme will be prioritised will obviously be heavily influenced not just by our own needs but also police and counter terrorism needs as well. Those agencies are at the table. One of the announcements that the Prime Minister made in his security statement a bit earlier on was for example about the inclusion of OPI data in the data that we collect. That is particularly important for the security services rather than for our own needs but it is an example of people beginning to understand the benefits of some of that data sharing.

Q469 *Lord Dear:* You have arrived at the point I wanted to hear about which is data sharing. I guess from what you said that you are going to have some sort of data sharing IT system, not one that will allow you to go into all the back rooms of these organisations but at least to get a flag which will show that there is an interest.

Mr Byrne: Exactly. We will lay regulations in the new year, which will need to be debated in both Houses, which will equip us with the authority to undertake that data sharing. In the current climate it will not be controversy free but it is really important.

Q470 *Lord Dear:* At least you go back into the data.
Mr Byrne: Absolutely.

Q471 *Lord Mawson:* This work is all very new to me because I am quite new to this Committee but the world of inner cities and agencies working together is not new to me at all. One has listened in the inner cities to lots of talk about joined up thinking and joined up action and yet, when you go and look at the devil in the detail, you see the human relationships between the health service, local authorities and other key agencies are not happening in some of the poorest estates in Britain. I know how difficult this stuff is. When you dig further you find that not enough effort has been put into building the human relationships between the various bodies. My experience is that structures are one thing; people are another. Just to push you a bit further, I wonder what is being done. If one does not build the human relationships and learn how to do these complex partnerships—and there is quite a skill to this—at a rhetorical level things may be said to be done and names may change on doors but in reality certain things are not happening. I particularly pick up the concern on recently hearing that some of the

key services in Europe and NATO are not communicating very well. I think, my goodness, if a member of the public knew that, they would be very concerned. How do we ensure that these basic human relationships are happening because all else follows it seems to me? What are we doing about that?

Mr Byrne: Absolutely right. These are human systems and their delicate ecology is like any other human system. Maybe Brodie can add something about the way in which parts of our businesses like intelligence and risk assessment come together. I will say two things. I think we have had to work quite hard in the last 12 months to make sure there are not requirements that are imposed at the top that point people in different directions. The thing that ACPO, people like Ken Jones and Graham Maxwell, who is the immigration leader for ACPO, have been saying to me for some time is that the immigration service's, in their eyes exclusive, focus on failed asylum seekers is not conducive to much more effective joint working at the front line. When we published the enforcement strategy in March 2007 for the Border and Immigration Agency, we changed the framework. We said that we were going to prioritise tackling harm to Britain. All of a sudden, that opens the possibility for a different kind of relationship and often priorities which are stitched together locally. If you take the Met for example, the problem of crime caused by illegal immigrants in Marylebone would be quite different to what it looks like in Waltham Forest. We need to give people the freedom, if you like, to begin assembling what makes most sense locally. We need to provide a framework but if we are providing a framework that allows people to work in common that is quite important progress. When we come to the development of the UK Border Agency, this is another example of how we have to get the human side of the business right. We are very fortunate in that the attitudes and aspirations of staff working at the border, whether they are in Special Branch or Customs or the Immigration Agency, are pretty similar. They are passionate about keeping Britain safe and they are very like minded. That is an enormous advantage. What I have asked for though, as we go into this merger, is we need to think about what is going on port by port. That is what is important to me. It is how these new arrangements are going to be put in place locally. I do not want any enormous, new, bureaucratic frameworks that talk about how I am going to talk to Jane Kennedy and how we are going to report to the Chancellor and the Home Secretary. That is important in terms of our accountability to Parliament but it is the port by port stuff that I am interested in because that is the front line. That is the bit of the system that really has to work if we are to fulfil our obligations to keep the country safe.

Mr Clark: It is people change but it is cultural change. For us, part of the huge learning around this is looking at what other countries have done and what they have not done. We have been over to the US. We have had close discussions with the Canadians. They have made that kind of merge themselves with Customs and immigration together into one. We have seen what they are like three years down the road. We have seen how people are doing a different job but the cultural bloodstream is still as it was in many respects. I think we do well to learn a lot from the lessons of others. That is very important to us as we move into this. The other important thing in terms of this big change is that we are not approaching this in any way like it is the Border and Immigration Agency which is adding something into it. Rather, we are talking about a new agency, a new organisation with a new way of working and a new workforce to deliver that. It is not a sense of unequal partners in this; it is a new development, a new shape and a new organisation. For us, the other important thing is that there is a real belief through the respective businesses that the change we are going into is right. It makes huge sense so we are not having to pull people against the current. We are taking people in a direction that they firmly believe is the right way to go and will make a significant difference to the business at the border. I think that works to our advantage but we must not abuse it of course.

Q472 *Lord Marlesford:* You are talking about learning from other countries. May I suggest you look at Hong Kong because their system, before the British left in 1997, was terrific. I go there quite often and I think it is a very good system. They had full e-border control in 1997 and I do suggest you talk to the person who had been in charge up until then and go and see them again.

Mr Dowdall: I will just try to describe the reality of what happens in an area of strategic importance such as Kent where we have our juxtaposed controls on the other side of the Channel and the importance of the relationships between Customs and the police and the Border and Immigration Agency. I have had to forge strong, personal relationships with my counterparts in the police and Customs. It is important to share the agendas because, particularly for the police, they have a real interest in immigration related issues. It affects their resources and coming to deal with lorry drops or any crime related matters within the Kent area. Therefore, we have our officers who are based in a joint freight intelligence office. We make joint selections of high risk lorries and consignments. We also are involved in jointly searching and also share our relative tasking. We have operations coming up in the next couple of weeks that involve a number of agencies, not only the Border Agency but also VOSA and one or two others. It really has to be based upon

the development of those personal relationships and the development of trust, not only personal trust but also trust that the organisations will do something on behalf of another.

Mr Byrne: The creation of that shared advantage is the key to it. When you talk to front-line border security staff at Dulles Airport for example, they will say that even five years on they feel still very committed to the business that they came from. Two things have been key to front-line motivation going into the changes. One has been that people see that they can do their job better by working with others. The second thing though that was quite interesting was that people also see a whole host of different career paths and specialisms opening up in front of them, so they can see personal advantages and a more interesting career and different opportunities to serve opening up. If you go and talk to our staff in Coquelles where we have been doing some experiments on how we bring Customs and immigration staff together and you talked to quite young immigration officers who are now working together with Customs on some of the deep search capabilities that Customs have, they are really interested in acquiring and the opportunity to acquire different kinds of specialisms. The richness of their career has just multiplied. That is what the Americans found and that is one of the things that we want to be able to bring to the UK.

Q473 *Lord Mawson:* These things do not happen by magic. I just wonder what investment is being made in those processes. Do we know?

Mr Byrne: We have not finalised that yet. I am trying to finalise that for the Chancellor and the Home Secretary over the next month or so.

Q474 *Lord Teverson:* I have one factual question on the common travel area. It is whether the Republic of Ireland is or is going to be doing exit monitoring itself.

Mr Dodd: They are developing the e-border system which they will have in place a few years after us so they will then have an exit system themselves.

Q475 *Lord Teverson:* The next question the Minister has answered to a degree in that you were quite fulsome in your praise for the way that the rest of Europe was catching up. Given that convergence, should that not mean that we should take the full benefit of our European Union subscription and membership and become full members of Schengen altogether, given your excellent prognosis for the future?

Mr Byrne: Possibly but not yet. Speaking candidly, until we have greater confidence than we have today in the strength of the external border, I do not think that would be something that I could recommend yet. The World Bank in *Global Economic Prospects*, which was published last year, forecast that something like a billion people will join the labour market in the developing world between now and 2025. The International Labour Organisation estimates that there is a five fold difference in household income between low income and high income countries. My warning is that over the next 20 years the pressure on Europe's borders will not diminish. It will grow and it will grow sharply. We are already seeing that pressure across the Mediterranean. There is a new risk which Europe is running at the moment with the admission of east European states into the Schengen area. A lot of money is being spent on managing that risk but it is a risk nonetheless. I think it is realistically going to be three to five years before we are really able to take stock of how secure Europe's external frontiers are. The changes in the world and in global migration are that complicated at the moment that that is a realistic time frame for being able to come up with a realistic assessment. That is my own personal view.

Q476 *Lord Dear:* I was interested particularly in looking at the formation of the new agency that we have all talked about and how that will fit into Frontex. Presumably it will not be easy; there will have to be adjustments both ways and I wondered if you could talk a little bit about that nip and tuck, so to speak, and in particular on the question of whether we do arm our own border guards or not and, if not, why not?

Mr Byrne: We do not arm border guards and we are not planning to do so. Border guards, as you know, are equipped with retractable batons and handcuffs at the moment. The report published by Sir Gus O'Donnell tried to draw a separation between protective security functions and border security functions at our ports. We obviously embed a lot of police officers within the Border and Immigration Agency already and we benefit enormously from the capability that police officers bring us but our sense is that at ports and airports today, because there is an armed police presence largely deployed on protective security arrangements, the capability that is needed for armed response is already there. We are satisfied with those arrangements. In terms of the evolution of the UK Border Agency and its relationship with the police, this is obviously a difficult question as you know. I think there was a sense that there needed to be more consensus than there was to date about how police forces themselves coordinated their work at the border. There were obviously in the Met and in Kent questions about abstraction of forces which was going to impact on the flexibility and deployment of resources in those forces, so there were a number of questions there but that is why "Securing the Global Hub" was so explicit about the need for the Home Secretary to take forward those discussions. When it

comes to Frontex, I think we will have to see what the ECJ rules and we expect that on 18 December. Again, I come back to the point I made at the beginning about our ambition to see Frontex evolve in a very pragmatic way. There have been a number of operations, one in particular which was quite effective in reducing the number of illegal migrants routing up through the Canaries. It showed that Frontex is capable of displacing activity. We want to see more of that kind of operation evaluated effectively so that we can understand the displacement effects. That is where we want to participate with Frontex over the next three to five years. We really do want to see Frontex walk before it can run but that is partly why we are going to be quite interested in your report on where you think Frontex should be going, because obviously we will need to put your report alongside what the European Commission says.

Q477 *Lord Dear:* It would help us to know what you think might be the difficult points, the obstacles, in advance. Have you a list of things you have to address?

Mr Byrne: My perspective is that we need to see more effective planning arrangements and more effective evaluation requests. If you take for example the fact that the budget for Frontex is going to double by about 35 million euros, that is a big increase in an organisation's resources in any one year and it is good that the European Parliament has asked for a pretty detailed business plan before it signs that money off. We really need to understand how practically Frontex is going to make a difference because, as you know, tackling illegal migration is not just about those front of field operations that Frontex is able to get involved in. It is also about Member States' effective policing of their borders. It is about a more concerted attack on organised, illegal immigration crime where agencies like Europol are going to be important. There is the work of codevelopment in countries as well as our combined work to shut down the pull factors for illegal immigration in country too, which the French presidency I hope will pick up. I just want to see the specifics around the practical operations first.

Mr Clark: For me, there are issues around the relevance of the operations. They have to be relevant to us, or else there is no point, is there? They have to be effective and they have to deliver something. That is very important to us and there has to be a sustainability about the collaboration in itself. It has to feel solid and as though it is going to endure to a degree. The other thing of interest—maybe concern—is the ambitions of Frontex itself and the way that it manages those ambitions so that it is not trying to do everything all the time. It is the Minister's point about walking before running. The ambition may be very high to do lots of other things and I think for us there is a very big note of caution around that.

12 December 2007   Mr Liam Byrne MP, Mr Brodie Clark, Mr Tom Dowdall
and Mr Tom Dodd

Mr Dowdall: I have a couple of points. One is the evaluation of Frontex by the Commission, which will consider whether it needs to expand its remit in any way. It already focuses on immigration matters. It has also focused on things such as car crime for example. There have been a number of operations over the last year which we have been involved in and we would expect an increase in operations next year. We would certainly urge that there is a focus on the quality of those operations rather than just simply undertaking double or treble operations.

Q478 Chairman: You talked about the budget increase. Can I take it from your answer that the government is content with the very large increase in Frontex's budget?
Mr Byrne: We are content but we will be looking hard at what it is going to be spent on.

Q479 Lord Young of Norwood Green: What do you see as the added value of the Rapid Border Intervention Teams Regulation? What provisions have been made or are intended to be made to allow UK immigration officers to participate in these operations and pilot projects and in what capacity?
Mr Byrne: The added value of RABITs is obviously that they give Frontex that added flexibility to respond to urgent or emergency situations. That is particularly a concern for the southern EU states. I have had a number of discussions with the politicians in Malta for example and they really feel that urgency perhaps more sharply than any of us. The second point is that we will have to wait to see what the ECJ comes back with before we can really think through how we can play. Even if that ECJ judgment is negative, we would like to continue playing a role in an observation and advisory capacity just because we think we are pretty good at this stuff.

Q480 Lord Dear: You mentioned Malta. We took evidence, as you may know, from a Maltese officer earlier on. I wondered how all of that, on which I think we are pretty clear, moves on to where we are not clear and that is the Royal Navy, our own Navy, operating across most of the waters that we are interested in, as you have already signalled, around the Canaries or Malta. If our own ship came across a boat load of what were clearly illegal immigrants, is there some operational procedure for that?
Mr Byrne: There is. The starting point though is to say that obviously there is not a very big Royal Navy presence in the Mediterranean, although exercises will be conducted, that is true. There are two answers to this. The first is that the Royal Navy will typically track rather than intercept boats and therefore observe and alert the relevant Member State authorities but if there was a scenario where a rescue was required the way that we would interpret the law of the sea would be to discharge the individuals who were rescued at the nearest port. That would typically be a port in the Mediterranean.

Q481 Lord Dear: That would be for a rescue. Simply coming across it, they would track but not intercept?
Mr Byrne: They would track and alert, yes.

Q482 Lord Dear: But not interpose?
Mr Byrne: No. It would be about tracking and alerting. Again, we would see the primary obligation as being incumbent on the Member State and therefore the Member State's border security arrangements.

Q483 Lord Dear: We were clear about rescues; it was whether they interposed or not.
Mr Byrne: The philosophy will be track and alert.

Q484 Lord Dear: Could I follow up the evidence we heard from Malta? I am sure others would have said the same thing about the disproportionate burden that falls on places like Malta. I am not sure that they said it to us but clearly there was a desire to share that burden because they have a disproportionate burden in Malta, as an example. Do you have any ideas about how Frontex might ease that pattern away from those who are taking the lion's share of the burden?
Mr Byrne: I am not sure that it is necessarily a Frontex issue. The way that we interpret burden sharing is that we do not think we should be moving people around. We think that would create an enormous pull factor that would compound the problem rather than solve it. We think that financial burden sharing is important. Where there is possibly an area for Frontex is if theoretically Frontex evolved its role and got more involved in returns. That could well be a role that Frontex played. I remain a bit of a sceptic about Frontex getting involved in joint returns and arrangements because I know how difficult organising joint returns arrangements is but there is an EU returns fund of about 35 or 40 million euros which Malta is able to draw from. Logistically, once you get into the business of trying to organise joint charter flights that are stopping at various different points across Europe, it becomes enormously complicated, as you know because you have to coordinate all the detention arrangements and make sure that there are no barriers to removal in any one country. The complexity of trying to organise these things is very difficult. We are committed to trying to organise joint returns flights with the French to Pakistan and potentially to Iraq. We have quite a strong track record at organising return charters to those countries but in practical terms—we have been trying to do it for

about nine or 10 months now—the will is there but it is quite difficult to line up people in any detention estate.

Q485 *Lord Dear:* The will is there. Finding the formula is almost impossible.

Mr Byrne: It is very difficult, yes, and of course we all have different rules as regards detention as well. The French have more limited powers of detention around illegal immigration than we do. The Immigration Act is quite strong. The French often find it difficult keeping people in detention for longer than seven days. We need to continue to try but in practice my experience has been that it is quite difficult.

Q486 *Lord Dear:* To take the hypothetical example of Malta, these are my figures to prove the point, but of those who Malta might stop they are going to six different countries. Therefore, it is fair for Malta to get something as a contribution from those six *pro rata*. It would not be easy to manage. It would probably be impossible.

Mr Byrne: No, but that is an argument for wider cooperation on the financial support that is provided to Malta. Where Frontex probably can add value to a country like Malta, which is obviously a small country and may not have the world's biggest immigration system, for example, we often talk to the French about our experience in enforced returns. Brice Hortefeux has been given very ambitious targets by President Sarkozy for the number of deportations this year. All we are sharing with the French a lot of our expertise in enforced returns. That is exactly the kind of capability and expertise which we can provide to countries like Malta on a bilateral basis but potentially in the future through an organisation like Frontex. It is that capability sharing backed by EU-wide funding that will make the biggest difference and the fastest difference. That is what Malta needs, not bureaucracy.

Q487 *Lord Young of Norwood Green:* If we want to ensure that there is coordinated activity, what equipment has the UK made available to the Central Register of Technical Equipment, with the unfortunate acronym CRATE? What does it plan to make available in 2008?

Mr Byrne: 12 CO_2 detectors, three heart beat detectors, six basic forgery detection kits, six UV lights, 12 magnifying glasses, one document investigation device and a digital camera.

Q488 *Lord Young of Norwood Green:* I am fascinated by the magnifying glasses.

Mr Byrne: They have special lights in them.

Q489 *Lord Young of Norwood Green:* Have you met a proportionate share of demand? Do we feel that we are meeting our obligations in these circumstances?

Mr Byrne: I think so.

Mr Dowdall: Yes. How it has worked to date is that where there have been operations we have been approached and asked to contribute. In the main, our interest particularly on the land borders and also on the southern Spanish border has been the provision of heart beat detectors and CO_2 detectors. Our expertise is very much in the vehicle screening and searching. We can provide that kind of assistance. I met the executive director in Warsaw recently and we discussed the kinds of requests that they would be coming to us with next year so rather than coming to us on an operation by operation basis we have a plan for 2008 which we are considering at the moment. Included within that are the resources and also the requests for equipment. In terms of equipment, they are again interested in us contributing to their land borders freight searching work and I can see that we will be responding positively to those requests.

Q490 *Lord Teverson:* One of the frustrations we came across in a couple of the interviews we have done has been around equipment being available or being declared as part of the CRATE but not being available at the time. Obviously, it is being used elsewhere, but I am interested from the UK's point of view. Have you had to refuse requests ever or have we been able to fulfil all requests that have come in?

Mr Dowdall: We have been able to fulfil all those requests. Some frustration has been expressed particularly by some of the southern states in terms of the provision of maritime equipment. That kind of hardware has been the area that has been of concern.

Q491 *Lord Teverson:* Given that that is a frustration and there is some gap between expectation and delivery maybe, is there a better way that that could be done somehow in terms of the forward planning that you were talking about?

Mr Dowdall: That is the whole issue. In six weeks it is difficult enough to get people assembled. To get the shipping assembled in that time is very challenging. The improvement this year is the fact that all the Member States are having bilateral conversations with Frontex and setting out at this point and now what the requirement is the next year. In terms of the maritime operations, rather than having single exercises, the proposal is to have operations of much longer duration. That allows different countries to contribute at different times.

Mr Byrne: I do not know if the Committee has it but it might be helpful if we provide you with a quick breakdown of the operations that Frontex conducted jointly in 2007 because it underlines the point that most of them have been quite small-scale and often of limited duration. If Frontex is to step up a bit, there is a strong argument for a resource pool that is flexible to which Member States are contributing and from which Frontex can draw down as and when it is needed.

Chairman: I think you are aware of two questions we wanted to ask, one about Frontex training and the other about the lessons learned from Frontex operations. Would you kindly let us have written answers to those two questions?

Q492 *Lord Harrison:* I wondered if you wanted to say anything further about the displacement problem. I think your response was flexibility and resources.

Mr Byrne: I will write on both of those questions but on the displacement there are four principal routes into the UK coming from different directions. That is why understanding displacement effects and how you can flexibly redeploy assets is terrifically important, but so is that sense of realism that just front of house operations are not going to be enough. You do need to engage in development and co-development as well to diminish the push factors in the first place.

Q493 *Chairman:* Explain to us what the government would like to see with regard to the way that Frontex might develop over the next few years to try and take it step by step, including in that what if any assets you think should be possessed by Frontex.

Mr Byrne: Europe collectively needs to think about the work that we need to do on development in Africa and elsewhere, as we set out in the Global Approach to Migration, in a way that helps to diminish migration and illegal migration pressures. Second, there is no substitute for effective Member State border security operations. That is why we do not agree with the argument about a European border guard. We think Member States should be leading that. There is then a question about what happens between the host countries and Europe. Frontex I think has quite an important role to play in coordinating EU activity in

stopping traffic across those routes and that is where the principal focus of expansion should be. My one hesitation where I am not sure in my own mind of the answer is what the future of Frontex is in relation to organised illegal immigration crime. We obviously have European agencies around like Europol which are effective in this arena but one of the questions that I will be seeking advice on from the European Commission's review—and indeed I would be enormously interested in the Committee's view—is on whether there is more that Frontex should be doing to help dismantle the forces of organised crime and therefore diminish the pressure of illegal immigration on Europe's wider borders. I have not answered that question in my own mind.

Q494 *Lord Marlesford:* My concern would be—and I do not know, Minister, whether you would share it—that particularly with some of the new entrants into Europe there would be a real danger of penetration of Frontex by organised crime. I think the vetting of people in Frontex should be done independently by some European organisation.

Mr Byrne: That is a very valid point.

Q495 *Lord Young of Norwood Green:* I wanted to comment a while back but I resisted. We had a recent visit to Heathrow and I wanted to compliment you on what we saw there in terms of a good esprit de corps amongst the UK border guards with smart, new uniforms. I would not say the pay rate of immigration control officers is necessarily the most attractive in the world and I did ask what made them stay. One of the things they pointed out to me was the increased career development activity, as you said, with a wider range of opportunities. I thought you might be interested to hear that.

Mr Byrne: Whenever I get down in the mouth, I try and spend about a day a week of my time on the road visiting with front-line staff. Frankly, there is no greater inspiration than talking to front-line staff in the Border and Immigration Agency. They do an enormously difficult job and they do it with a great deal of passion, pride and professionalism.

Chairman: Minister, thank you very much and thank you to your colleagues for coming. You have been very clear and helpful and we appreciate it very much.

Supplementary written evidence by the Home Office, Liam Byrne MP, Minister of State

I am writing regarding the additional evidence I said I would provide at the oral evidence session before your committee on Wednesday 12 December. I have attached a breakdown of the Frontex operations the UK has taken part in 2007 and have set out below responses to two points which we did not have time to address on 12 December.

Regarding training, the UK makes a significant contribution to production and delivery of Frontex, offering expertise in document forgery detection and use of detection technology. UK Training experts have contributed to developing both the Common Core Curriculum for EU border guards and common standards on forgery detection and use of detection technology, in addition to delivering courses and developing an international CD Rom on forgery detection training.

The UK also lends training and language expertise to ensure that all Member States benefit from our learning and development experiences and practices. We therefore contribute significantly to the enhanced professionalism of all EU Border Guards, whilst at the same time helping to secure the UK border by strengthening the competencies of those guards who operate on transit routes and at the external Schengen borders.

56 days were spent providing UK input to Frontex training in 2007; 21 days for delivery of the mid-level officers' course; and 35 days spent on project development. The cost in staff time has been estimated at £6,517 and 100% of the costs were reimbursable by Frontex.

Regarding lessons learned, Frontex operations have shown that it is possible to coordinate Member States border control efforts into effective common action despite national differences. Participation in Frontex operations has provided the UK with insight into the border management process of others, particularly of maritime borders where we have limited experience. It has provided valuable intelligence and operational information.

We have learnt that the cooperation and, where possible, involvement of third countries of transit/embarkation has proved to be crucial to the success of maritime and land border operations. Frontex is not able to be totally effective on its own. For example, Operation Hera, a maritime operation off the Canaries in 2006–07, was only successful due to the participation not only of several EU Member States, including the UK, but also Mauritania and Senegal. In participation with these third countries, the operation included joint patrolling by air and sea of West Africa, turning back un-seaworthy vessels, debriefing of irregular migrants who survived the journey, and returning those found to be economic migrants. The result was a 50% cut in illegal migration into the Canaries in 2007 compared to 2006.

You will also be aware that we have now received the full judgment of the ECJ on our case challenging exclusion from the Frontex (and Passports) Regulations. The ECJ has found against us in both cases. We are disappointed by the judgment of the Court and are considering its implications.

This judgment does not prevent us from continuing to participate in Frontex measures on a case by case basis with agreement from the management board and we will continue to maintain high levels of passport security in line with the measures introduced by our European partners.

21 December 2007

Supplementary written evidence from the Home Office

UK PARTICIPATION IN FRONTEX JOINT OPERATIONS 2006

Operation	Description	No. of Officers	Duration of Operation
Torino 2006	Air operation to counter illegal migration under the premise of attending the Winter Olympics in Turin.	Italian liaison officer based at Heathrow. UK officers attended planning and evaluation meetings	3–26 February
FIFA 2006	Information collated to assess border risks associated with the World Cup	Information exchange only	9 June–9 July
Agelaus	Focus on minors smuggled or trafficked to the EU by air. Develop procedures for the identification, reception, shelter and protection of the victims.	Information exchange and attendance at planning meeting.	1–28 February
Amazon I	To assess and counter the perceived threat posed by South American nationals to EU airports.	Officer to Frontex HQ and attendance at planning and evaluation meetings.	1–16 November
Poseidon 2006	Land and Sea Op targeting illegal migration from Albania, FYROM and Turkey.	Four officers participating in operation, plus attendance at planning and evaluation meetings.	25 June–5 July
Zeus	Sea Op targeting irregular migrants posing as seamen	Attendance at planning meeting. (Op was delayed until 2007).	27 June
Hera I	Sea Op targeting illegal migration from West Africa to the Canary Islands	Two officers sent to Fuerteventura, plus attendance at planning meeting.	August–September

NB:
Gate of Africa—UK provided two document experts between 17 July and 3 September (funded by ARGO not Frontex)
Support to Malta—UK provided a Chief Immigration officer for one month in September 2006. (Initially a bilateral but Frontex later agreed to provide funding—not classed as a Frontex operation)

UK Participation in Frontex Joint Operations and Pilot Projects 2007

Operation	Description	No. of Officers	Duration	Dates
Amazon II	Air Op targeting South American Nationals.	1 x IO	18 days	19 February–9 March 2007
Amazon III	Follow up of Amazon II.	1 x IO	21 days	7–28 November 2007
Herakles I	Land Op on Hungary/Serbian border	1 x HMI 1 x IO	5 days 5 days	8–17 August 2007
Herakles II	As above	3 x IO's	25 days total	10–19 October 2007
Hydra	Air Op targeting Chinese nationals	3 x IO's	64 days total	11 April–11 May 2007
Gordius	Land Op targeting illegal migration from Moldova	2 x AIO's	24 days total	16–29 April 2007
Poseidon Stage II	Land and Sea Op targeting illegal migration from Albania, FYROM and Turkey.	6 x IO's 1 x CIO	60 days 10 days	26 June–15 July 2007
Poseidon Stage III	As above.	7 x IO's 1 x CIO	70 days 10 days	18 September–7 October 2007
Hera 2007 Stage II	Sea Op targeting illegal migration from West Africa to the Canary Islands	4 x IO's 1 x CIO	45 days 10 days	22 July–30 November 2007
Minerva	Sea Op targeting illegal migration through the western med to Southern Spain	4 x IO's 1 x CIO (co-ordinator)	21 days 33 days	15 August–14 September 2007
Kras	Land Op targeting illegal migration from Croatia	2 x IO's	15 days total	12–22 September 2007
Nautilus II Stage II	Sea Op targeting illegal migration through the central med to Malta and Lampedusa	1 x DC	21 days	10–28 September 2007
Ursus IV	Pilot project aimed at enhancing operational cooperation on border management between EU and Ukraine	2 x IO's	14 days total	26 November–2 December 2007
Zeus	Sea Op targeting irregular migrants posing as seamen	1 x SGT 1 x IO	7 days 18 days	15–30 October 2007
Hermes	Sea Op targeting illegal migration through the central med to Sardinia and the Balearics	1 x IO 1 x HMI	12 days 8 days	18 September–9 October 2007
Extended Family	Air Op targeting Nigerian nationals	2 x IO's Stats also compiled from Heathrow and Gatwick	28 days total	7–20 October and 3–16 November 2007

Pilot Project	Description	Duration	UK participation	Dates
Agelaus	Air Op targeting minors	28 days	Stats compiled from Heathrow, Gatwick and Manchester	1–28 February 2007

Other activities	Description	Duration	UK participation	Dates
Long Stop I	Air Op targeting Bangladeshis, Pakistanis and Sri Lankans	4 days	Workshop to draft a handbook (Not actual operation)	5–8 November 2007

Further supplementary written evidence by the Home Office

Following the Ministerial oral evidence session regarding the House of Lords Inquiry into Frontex on 12 December 2007, you requested further information concerning Liam Byrne's reference to the groups that had been set up to address the issues surrounding the international law of the sea.

I can confirm that there are{two ad hoc groups, one being a subset of the other. The first is the Expert Meeting on the Study of International Law Instruments in Relation to Illegal Immigration by Sea; this group met on 8 June 2007 where it was agreed that a sub-group should be created. That sub-group is the Law of the Sea/ Frontex Guidelines: Drafting Group. This sub-group met three times in 2007: on 19 July, 24 September, and 29 November. It is proposed that a further meeting will take place on 7 February 2008.

31 January 2008

Written Evidence

Letter from the Government of Gibraltar, Office of the Chief Secretary, Gibraltar

We understand that the Committee has expressed a wish to receive evidence relating to Gibraltar in the context of Frontex.

Much to Gibraltar's extreme disappointment Gibraltar has been excluded from the ambit of Frontex.

Article 12(3) of the European Borders Agency Regulation (EU Regulations) provides as follows:

> "The application of this Regulation to the borders of Gibraltar shall be suspended until the date on which an agreement is reached on the scope of the measures concerning the crossing by persons of the external borders of the Member States".

Accordingly we are excluded even from the UK's limited current participation under Article 12 (operational co-operation).

We have expressed to the UK our severe concern that if the UK applies to participate more fully in Frontex, then Spain will demand our exclusion as a condition of agreeing to the UK's wider participation. Gibraltar's exclusion is Spain's publicly stated objective. The Government of Gibraltar has been advised that such exclusion would be (and our current exclusion from Article 12(3) is) unlawful. Litigation by Gibraltar is envisaged.

The European Borders Agency Regulation is a fundamental measure identifying the physical extent of the Union, and it is politically and legally unacceptable for that to exclude Gibraltar once the UK participates more fully in it.

We enclose herewith, for the Committee's information: copies of the following:
[*letters: not printed here*]; press release: dated 30 July 2004.

(1) GOG to FCO, dated 22 December 2003
(2) FCO to GOG, dated 6 February 2004
(3) GOG to FCO, dated 1 April 2004
(4) FCO to GOG, dated 16 April 2004
(5) GOG to FCO, dated 28 April 2004
(6) FCO to GOG, dated 17 May 2004
(7) GOG to FCO, dated 23 July 2004
(8) Press Release by GOG dated 30 July 2004
(9) FCO to GOG, dated 3 September 2004
(10) GOG to FCO, dated 18 May 2005
(11) GOG to FCO, dated 31 May 2005
(12) FCO to GOG, dated 24 August 2005
(13) GOG to FCO, dated 6 February 2007
(14) FCO to GOG, dated 24 May 2007
(15) GOG to FCO, dated 17 July 2007

Accordingly, Frontex does not operate in, or with relation to Gibraltar, either at a practical nor at any other level. It is not therefore possible for Gibraltar to comment on the decision making structure of Frontex, and its lines of accountability or whether Frontex has had an impact in reducing irregular migration.

Gibraltar would wish to be within Frontex, and be concerned by and participate in the Regulation, to the same extent as the UK, and believes that its Treaty right to do so has been violated.

R J M Garcia
Chief Secretary

17 September 2007

Press Release: Government of Gibraltar, Office the Chief Minister

EUROPEAN BORDERS AGENCY

On Tuesday evening the Foreign Office has informed the Gibraltar Government that the UK has agreed to a limited participation in the European Borders Agency, on an operational co-operation basis, but without Gibraltar whose exclusion from the Regulation has been demanded by Spain. This marks a complete departure from the position firmly adopted by successive UK Governments, including the current UK Government, that as a matter of fundamental principle, the UK would not accept any suspension or exclusion of Gibraltar from EU external borders measures, including this one.

As explained by the Gibraltar Government in the House of Assembly at the last question time, the British Government applied for the UK itself to participate in the European Borders Agency Regulation in full and as of right. This was rejected by the EU on the grounds that the Agency was a Schengen external borders measure and the UK had opted out of Schengen external borders measures. The UK rejects that decision, in respect both of itself and Gibraltar, and has informed the Gibraltar Government that it will challenge that decision in the ECJ. The UK claims that as it is not a participant in the decision to set up the Agency it cannot decide how it applies, including Gibraltar's exclusion. The UK has no vote or veto on the matter.

Notwithstanding all of this, the Gibraltar Government's position has been that, even if the UK participated only as an external co-operator, and not fully as of right, it should ensure that Gibraltar could participate with the UK to the same extent as the UK did. All this was explained in the House of Assembly as well.

The Gibraltar Government is disgusted at the UK Government's apparent intention to participate in the Agency, on an operational co-operation basis, but accepting that this does not apply to Gibraltar.

HMG continues to assert that it is Gibraltar's right to participate with UK, if and when the UK's own right to participate as of right and as a full member is established.

The Gibraltar Government takes a very serious view of this unacceptable development in an area which relates to the crucially important issue of external frontiers. This is how our systematic exclusion from aviation measures began. The Gibraltar Government is not willing to sit idly by and see the history of our exclusion from EU aviation measures repeat itself in the area of external frontiers.

The UK is not expecting to conclude these unacceptable arrangements until September. If they materialise as above, the Gibraltar Government will mount such immediate legal challenge in the UK Courts as it may be advised it can.

Commenting on this development Chief Minister Peter Caruana said:

> "The British Government has ridden rough shod over all our arguments and pleas not to participate without us. It is disingenuous for HMG to pretend that its participation, albeit not as a full member, in a measure that contains language excluding Gibraltar, is not severely prejudicial to us now and in the future in relation to other external frontiers measures. The external borders regime will ultimately express the physical, geographic definition of the EU. This early, first precedent for our exclusion from an external frontiers measure will be hugely damaging to the UK's ability to secure our inclusion in this and future external frontiers measures. This is precisely what happened in respect of the Airport and EU aviation measures".

No.163/2004

30 July 2004

Written evidence by Border Control Heathrow/Airline Liaison Officer's Network, Home Office

COMMITTEE VISIT TO HEATHROW & ALON—4 DECEMBER 2007

The committee posed a number of questions before the Heathrow visit and also asked supplementary questions during the visit. We have sought to answer these queries below.

1. *How does the frontier control actually operate? What is the exact step- by-step process that takes place? (Passenger arrives, hands in passport, passport is scanned, etc.)*

The committee observed the end to end Border Control process which included on entry checks at the primary arrivals control including the use of IRIS. They were provided with an overview of the immigration officer's role on the primary arrivals control and a forgery presentation. The Committee were also advised of pre-entry checks by Airline Liaison Officers (ALO's).

2. *What is the difference in the scanning procedures for the EU entry line and the other entry line?*

There is no difference as 100% of passports are checked regardless of the document held.

3. *Are passports of diplomats accredited to UK scanned? Do we distinguish, or in any way treat differently, diplomatic passports (which some countries, but not the UK, issue) held by persons not accredited to the UK?*

All passports are scanned including diplomatic passports, this includes diplomats accredited to the UK

4. *Does the scanning process provide a permanent record of entry? If so how and by whom can this record be accessed?*

Records of the inputs are kept for 12 months. However, these can be accessed by Government agencies only where such access is consistent with UK law, including the Data Protection Act 1998, the Human Rights Act 1998 and any relevant obligations the UK has under international law. For example, Government agencies may be given access to the records where necessary for the purposes of national security and prevention and detection of serious crime.

In all cases, access is via an audited trail which includes a statement of reasons for the request, which is then assessed against the purposes for which the information is sought. Information recorded includes name, nationality and date of birth.

5. *Are all passports now able to be scanned electronically? If not how are those that are not readable electronically dealt with? Which countries do not have electronic passports? Do some offer more or less information than others?*

Not all passports can be electronically scanned. In such cases the name of the holder will be inputted manually. Passport standards vary greatly across the world. Countries abroad are at various stages of upgrading their travel documents. A full current international status list is not available.

6. *How many different kinds of entry visas to the UK are there for non-EU passport holders to the UK? (Permanent, student, work, etc.)*

The categories are as follows: settlement, employment (both work permit and non-work permit categories), students, retired persons of independent means; visits (for stays of up to 6 months); EEA Family Permits; investors; persons intending to establish a business; writers, artists.

7. *What visas need to be obtained ahead of time and which visas can be obtained at the border? (which countries have which visa agreements?)*

A person subject to immigration control may need a visa (entry clearance) to come to the UK. There are two categories, visa nationals and non-visa nationals. There is a list of visa nationals in Appendix A.

A visa national needs entry clearance (a visa) to come to the UK. A non-visa national does not need an entry clearance to come to the UK for less than six months, but does need an entry clearance to come to the UK for more than six months or for a category in the immigration rules which require him to have entry clearance.

Some visa nationals may transit the UK without a visa; however there are circumstances where visa nationals traveling to the UK for the purpose of transiting on to another country require a Direct Airside or Visitor in Transit Visa. Appendix B refers.

It is a requirement under the immigration rules that the person applying for entry clearance must be outside the UK at the time of application.

8. *Will the scan at once reveal anyone who is on the "watch list"?*

The scan will immediately reveal anyone on the watch list. Even where the details of the passenger do not match exactly the watch list will show close matches.

9. *What are the "red flags" that are taken into consideration when reviewing a passport?*

An Immigration Officer will consider a number of issues when interviewing a passenger including the document itself, passengers conduct as well as any previous refusals of entry.

10. *What proportion of individuals are taken aside for additional questioning?*

Only a small percentage of passengers are required to submit to further examination.

For example in October 2007 only 0.08% of passengers arriving at Heathrow were referred for secondary examination.

11. *What kind of "intelligence" is (a) revealed, and (b) recorded, by the swiping of a passport? (name, birth, country of residency, travel patterns, etc?)*

The watch list is based on biographical data and generates an alert for the officer to advise that information is held on the passenger.

12. *Does profiling have any place in entry checks? If not, why not? Are records made of individuals from a certain part of the world/certain religion/certain travel patterns? Does the UK use a similar system to the Passenger Name Record (PNR) system used by USA?*

The routine assessment by an Immigration Officer is a form of risk assessment. The Race Relations (Amended) Act allow Ministers to authorise officials to treat nationalities differently from others.

The UK is developing a full e-borders system which will involve capturing passenger data including PNR. Some PNR data is already captured as part of the e-borders pilot Project Semaphore.

13. *Is there a limit to the number of student visas/tourist visas/work permits etc. that an individual may hold?*

There is no limit and an applicant may hold more than one valid entry clearance, eg a regular traveler already holding a two or five year multiple visit visa can be issued with an entry clearance for a short term work permit. Each application is treated individually.

14. *What, if any, checks are in place at the border to see if someone has previously (a) been refused entry (b) overstayed a temporary entry permit?*

Watch list checks and the signaling of passports will provide the officer with relevant information.

15. *What are the terms and conditions of a temporary resident permit? Terms and conditions of a student visa? Terms and conditions of a work permit, etc?*

There is no set formula and the conditions vary dependant on visa.

16. *If someone tries to enter the UK on an expired temporary residence permit, what happens? Are they turned away? Given a few days to collect their belongings and leave?*

Each application is considered on it merits. There is discretion to grant a short period of temporary admission.

17. *What happens if someone claiming to have a temporary residence permit in a LOST passport tries to enter? Are details of the "lost" permit available on-line at the border?*

Immigration Officers are able to check databases for details of in-country applications and visa applications.

18. *We are aware that at the moment passports are not routinely scanned on departure from Heathrow. When will this change? If passports are occasionally checked upon exit, what "intelligence" is revealed? How is it possible to establish whether a person who has been given temporary permission to enter the UK has departed if there are no routine exit checks?*

E Borders will provide the capability to count and reconcile records of all those arriving in and departing from the UK. We expect to be able to count 95% of passengers entering and leaving by the end of 2010. In the meantime we will continue to mount targeted embarkation controls on an intelligence led basis or at times of emergency. At Heathrow there has been a 100% increase in embarkation checks at Heathrow since July 2007.

SUPPLEMENTARY QUESTIONS POSED DURING VISIT

How many ALO's are there worldwide?

UK ALOs are based overseas at source and transit locations which have been identified as significant points of embarkation for inadequately documented arrivals (IDAs) in the UK. Their role is to offer advice, training and expertise to airlines with a view to preventing or disrupting the carriage of IDAs.

The ALO Network has been significantly expanded since 2005 to 34 ALOs in 31 locations overseas with increased regional coverage. In 10 locations ALOs are now assisted by Deputy ALOs (DALOs). Five ALO floaters provide an additional, flexible resource and the Network is further supported by a response team based in the UK.

The activity of ALOs has played a significant part in reducing IDAs. Over the last five years the ALO Network has assisted in preventing nearly 180,000 IDAs from boarding aircraft.

In the international fora, how do we share best practice?

Border Control engages with partner services through a broad range of international fora and bilateral partnerships.

Examples include:

— Four Countries' Conference: High level engagement with USA, Canada, and Australia on border and immigration issues
— Frontex: a range of meetings from the Management Board through expanding networks on eg risk assessment to working level meetings on the planning and evaluation of joint operations
— International Border Police Conference. An annual meeting supported by working group activity throughout the year focusing on common issues/interests. More than 50 countries are 20 national and international organisations represented
— A broad range of international air transport organisations including International Civil Aviation Organisation, International Air Transport Organisation, European Civil Aviation Council
— A wide range of bilateral contacts which exist between individual UK ports and the control authorities at destination ports and airports.
— Regular meetings between managers in Border Control European Operations and their counterparts in the French, Dutch and Belgian equivalent services.
— Border control is able to promote capacity building and the sharing of best practice through:
— Participation in Frontex operations and the loan of equipment made available through the Frontex Central Register of Available Technical Equipment (CRATE).
— The involvement of BIA Learning and Development staff in Frontex training activities and in preparation of the common core curriculum for border guard training. UK involvement is regarded as being particularly useful because English is accepted as the common language of European Border guards.
— A rolling programme of training activity carried out by the BIA National Document Fraud Unit either by hosting or delivering training overseas.
— Bilateral work with non-EU states who are interested in learning from UK experience and use of technology eg in 2007 Border Control both hosted and returned a visit from the State Border Service of Azerbaijan who were particularly interested in the concept of juxtaposed controls and in the development of detection technology for use in freight searches.

What is the basic pay for an Immigration Officer?

The starting salary for an Immigration Officer working in the London area inc. Gatwick receive £20,864 per annum. Starting salary for Immigration Officers based elsewhere is £20,445 per annum. Immigration officers regardless of location receive an additional 16.5% of their wage as a shift disturbance allowance.

Appendix A: Visa requirements for the United Kingdom

1. Subject to paragraph 2 below the following persons need a visa for the United Kingdom:

   (a) Nationals or citizens of the following countries or territorial entities:

Afghanistan	Ethiopia	Niger
Albania	Fiji	Nigeria
Algeria	Gabon	Oman
Angola	Gambia	Pakistan
Armenia	Georgia	Peru
Azerbaijan	Ghana	Philippines
Bahrain	Guinea	Qatar
Bangladesh	Guinea Bissau	Russia
Belarus	Guyana	Rwanda
Benin	Haiti	Sao Tome e Principe
Bhutan	India	Saudi Arabia
Bosnia Herzegovina	Indonesia	Senegal
Burkina Faso	Iran	Sierra Leone
Burma	Iraq	Somalia
Burundi	Ivory Coast	Sri Lanka
Cambodia	Jamaica	Sudan
Cameroon	Jordan	Surinam
Cape Verde	Kazakhstan	Syria
Central African Republic	Kenya	Taiwan
Chad	Korea (North)	Tajikistan
People's Republic of China	Kuwait	Tanzania
(except those referred to in sub-	Kyrgyzstan	Thailand
paragraphs 2(d) and (e) of this	Laos	Togo
Appendix)	Lebanon	Tunisia
Colombia	Liberia	Turkey
Comoros	Libya	Turkmenistan
Congo	Macedonia	Uganda
Cuba	Madagascar	Ukraine
Democratic Republic of the	Malawi	United Arab Emirates
Congo	Mali	Uzbekistan
Djibouti	Mauritania	Vietnam
Dominican Republic	Moldova	Yemen
Ecuador	Mongolia	Zambia
Egypt	Morocco	Zimbabwe
Equatorial Guinea	Mozambique	
Eritrea	Nepal	

The territories formerly comprising the socialist Federal Republic of Yugoslavia

   (b) Persons who hold passports or travel documents issued by the former Soviet Union or by the former Socialist Federal Republic of Yugoslavia.

   (c) Stateless persons.

   (d) Persons who hold non-national documents.

2. The following persons do not need a visa for the United Kingdom:

   (a) those who qualify for admission to the United Kingdom as returning residents in accordance with paragraph 18;

(b) those who seek leave to enter the United Kingdom within the period of their earlier leave and for the same purpose as that for which that leave was granted, unless it

    (i) was for a period of six months or less; or

    (ii) was extended by statutory instrument or by section 3C of the Immigration Act 1971 (inserted by section 3 of the Immigration and Asylum Act 1999);

(c) *Deleted*

(d) those nationals or citizens of the People's Republic of China holding passports issued by Hong Kong Special Administrative Region; or

(e) those nationals or citizens of the People's Republic of China holding passports issued by Macao Special Administrative Region.

(f) those who arrive in the United Kingdom with leave to enter which is in force but which was given before arrival so long as those in question arrive within the period of their earlier leave and for the same purpose as that for which leave was granted, unless that leave—

    (i) was for a period of six months or less, or

    (ii) was extended by statutory instrument or by section 3C of the Immigration Act 1971 (inserted by section 3 of the Immigration and Asylum Act 1999).

Appendix B The UK's DATV Regime

1. Appendix 1 of the Immigration Rules lists the countries or territories whose nationals require a visa for the United Kingdom.

There are exceptions to the United Kingdom's visa requirement. In some circumstances passengers who are visa nationals may travel to the United Kingdom without visas under the *Transit without Visa* concession.

A visa national who is traveling to the UK simply to travel on to another country may enter without a visa (at the discretion of the immigration officer), provided that they meet all the following requirements:

— They arrive in the UK and depart by air,

— The intended onward flight has been confirmed and departs within 24 hours of arrival,

— The individual is properly documented for their destination and has obtained the appropriate visa if required.

2. The *Transit without Visa* concession does not apply to the nationals or citizens of the following countries or territories. Unless they qualify for exemption—see Note 3) below—they must obtain a *Direct Airside Transit Visa (DATV)* if they wish travel to the UK in order to transit airside—or a Visitor in Transit Visa if they need to pass through UK immigration control see Note 5) below:

Afghanistan	Ghana	Palestinian Authorities
Albania	Guinea	Rwanda
Algeria	Guinea-Bissau	Senegal
Angola	India	Serbia and Montenegro
Bangladesh	Iran	Sierra Leone
Belarus	Iraq	Somalia
Burma	Ivory Coast	Sri Lanka
Burundi	Kenya	Sudan
Cameroon	Lebanon	Tanzania
China, People's Republic of	Liberia	Turkey
Colombia	Macedonia (FYR of)	"Turkish Republic of Northern
Congo-Brazzaville	Malawi	Cyprus"[2]
Congo, Dem Rep of[1]	Moldova	Uganda
Ecuador	Mongolia	Vietnam
Eritrea	Nepal	Yugoslavia[3]
Ethiopia	Nigeria	Zimbabwe
Gambia	Pakistan	

[1] Including travel documents issued by the former Zaire

[2] The "Turkish Republic of Northern Cyprus" is not recognised by HM Government. Visas are issued on an EU uniform format "Form for Affixing the Visa"

[3] Documents issued by the former Socialist Federal Republic of Yugoslavia, the former Federal Republic of Yugoslavia, by present Yugoslavia authorities or by the UN mission in Kosovo.

3. Passengers Exempt from the DATV Requirement

Holders of certain documents are, regardless of nationality, exempt from the requirement to hold a Direct Airside Transit Visa when transiting the UK.

A transit passenger is not required to hold a transit visa if he holds or a person with whom he arrives in the United Kingdom holds on his behalf:

(a) a valid visa for entry to Australia, Canada, New Zealand or the United States of America and a valid airline ticket for travel via the United Kingdom as part of a journey from another country or territory to the country in respect of which the visa is held;

(ab) a valid visa for entry to Australia, Canada, New Zealand or the United States of America and a valid airline ticket for travel via the United Kingdom as part of a journey from the country in respect of which the visa is held to another country or territory;

(b) a valid airline ticket for travel via the United Kingdom as part of a journey from Australia, Canada, New Zealand or the United States of America to another country or territory, provided that the transit passenger does not seek to transit the United Kingdom on a date more than six months from the date on which he last entered Australia, Canada, New Zealand or the United States of America with a valid visa for entry to that country;

(c) a valid USA I-551 Permanent Resident Card issued on or after 21 April 1998;

(d) a valid Canadian Permanent Resident Card issued on or after 28 June 2002;

(e) a valid common format Category D visa for entry to an EEA State;

(f) a valid common format residence permit issued by an EEA State pursuant to Council Regulation (EC) No. 1030/2002;

(g) a diplomatic or service passport issued by the People's Republic of China; or

(h) a diplomatic or official passport issued by India; or,

(i) a diplomatic or official passport issued by Vietnam.

Notes:

(1) a valid U.S. immigrant visa packet (form 155A/155B) is a "valid visa" for DATV exemption purposes.

(2) an expired I-551 Permanent Resident Card issued on or after 21 April 1998 when accompanied by an I-797 letter issued by the Bureau of Citizenship authorising its extension, exempts the holder from the DATV requirement.

(3) holding either an I-512 Parole letter or an I-797C (Notice of Action) instead of a valid U.S. visa; or a Transportation Letter instead of a valid U.S. Permanent Residence Card issued on or after 21 April 1998 does *NOT* qualify for exemption from the DAT visa requirement.

(4) holding a valid travel document with a U.S. ADIT stamp worded—"Processed for I-551. *TEMPORARY EVIDENCE OF LAWFUL ADMISSION FOR PERMANENT RESIDENCE VALID UNTIL. . . .. EMPLOYMENT AUTHORIZED*" does NOT qualify for exemption from the DAT visa requirement.

(5) whether holders of *non-national (including refugee) travel documents* require a DATV depends on their nationality and whether they qualify for one of the exemptions listed above. So, for instance, the holder of a non-national travel document (eg a refugee travel document) who is a national or a citizen of one of the countries listed on the DATV list (eg Afghanistan) will require a direct airside transit visa if they are travelling to the UK to transit on to a third country. Persons recognized as stateless under the 1954 UN Convention Relating to the Status of Stateless Persons are not required to hold a DATV and may TWOV.

4) *Transiting to the Republic of Ireland*

Passengers must pass through immigration control in order to take a flight to Ireland. *Visa nationals (and passengers qualifying for DATV exemption above)* may Transit without Visa providing they fulfil the TWOV conditions and are properly documented for entry into Ireland.

DATV nationals transiting to Ireland must obtain *a visit visa*—not a Visitor in Transit visa which is only for transit to a destination outside the Common Travel Area (Rules HC395 paragraph 47 refers).

5)   All Visa nationals wishing to transit the UK but spend longer doing so than the 24 hours permitted under the TWOV concession must obtain *a visitor in transit visa for stays up to 48 hours* or *a visit visa*.

11 December 2007

Written evidence by the Home Office Border Controls at Calais and Coquelles

COMMITTEE VISIT TO COQUELLES AND CALAIS, 8 JANUARY 2008

1. *What is the basis in domestic law for juxtaposed controls in France and other countries?*

For all Tunnel-related matters the basis is the Channel Tunnel Act 1987 and various statutory instruments which fall out of this, primarily the Channel Tunnel (International Arrangements) Order 1 and the Channel Tunnel (Miscellaneous Provisions) Order 1994.

For sea-related matters, the basis is the Nationality, Immigration and Asylum Act 2002 and the Nationality, Immigration and asylum Act 2002 (Juxtaposed Controls) Order 2003.

2. *Are UK immigration officers in Calais exercising the same powers as those guarding borders at Heathrow airport?*

Yes and also searching vehicles but under the same Immigration Act 1971.

3. *Are French immigration officers exercising equivalent powers on UK soil?*

Yes.

4. *With what other countries does the UK currently have juxtaposed control arrangements?*

The UK has a juxtaposed arrangement with Belgium. Border and Immigration Agency (BIA) staff are stationed at Brussels, Gare du Midi.

5. *Do the respective duties and responsibilities flow from specific bilateral agreements between the countries concerned with responsibility for asylum applications, care duties for minors etc?*

The Sangatte Protocol (Eurotunnel Ops).

Additional Protocol to the Sangatte Protocol (Eurostar ops).

The Treaty of Le Touquet (ferry operations).

6. *How many people have been refused entry to the UK by immigration officers stationed in Calais since the juxtaposed control arrangements have been in place? What happens to people refused entry—are they handed over to the French authorities?*

The French authorities are obliged to take back all persons refused entry to the United Kingdom at the juxtaposed controls.

There have been 10,766 refused leave to enter the United Kingdom by Immigration Officers in Calais.

7. *Who is in charge when people are held in Calais following a refusal of entry by the UK border authorities? Does HM Inspector of Prisons have any statutory powers to inspect{holding centres in connection with juxtaposed controls?*

All persons detained are in the care of Border & Immigration Agency with the responsibility contracted out to G4S. Our holding facilities are subject to inspection by HMIP and have been so inspected.

8. *How do the French immigration authorities check that those to whom they have given temporary consent to enter France have left?*

They do not. The only check is when someone is detained and discovered to be unlawfully there.

9. *For what sorts of periods do the French immigration authorities allow people to enter? Do they alert the British authorities to names of over-stayers?*

Persons admitted to France for a limited period are allowed to stay for 90 days. To stay longer they have to apply to their local prefecture for a residence permit. Such permits tend to be renewable annually.

No. Firstly, the law relating to data protection in France is very strict and the possibility for the exchange of data very limited. Secondly, it is only recently that the French interior ministry has sought to establish a database of those who are known to be liable to removal. This database, called ELOI, was in its initial form ruled to be unconstitutional by the courts in 2007. A revised set of data, smaller than the first version, has now been adopted. The database remains a sensitive issue and any suggestion that its contents could be shared with the British authorities would be controversial. Public debate on ELOI was re-ignited in the last week in an article in *Nouvel Observateur.*

16 January 2008

Memorandum by Immigration Advisory Service

INTRODUCTION

The Immigration Advisory Service (IAS) is the UK's largest charity providing representation and advice in immigration and asylum law. We are independent from the Government. Our asylum and immigration advice is provided confidentially.

The IAS' main role is that of providing community legal advice and representation to immigrants and asylum seekers. Many of the clients we represent have had to pass through borders in very difficult circumstances, and our legal staff hear the detailed accounts of these clients. While there is an understandable concern about the numbers involved in what is termed illegal or irregular migration, we would wish to emphasise the importance of looking after the interests and safety of the migrants involved with due understanding to the serious problems many of them face. These concerns should not be overlooked by focusing on enforcing a strict regime of immigration controls and restrictions (in some instances arguably effectively criminalising the seeking of refuge by rigorous entry and application procedures). Adequate resources and access to proper advice and representation (independent from government) are a vital part of safeguarding the rights of vulnerable migrants, many of whom are refugees.

The IAS is a member of the European Council on Refugees and Exiles (ECRE) and fully supports their position in collaboration with the Refugee Council.

The Sub-Committee F (Home Affairs) of the House of Lords Select Committee on the European Union inquiry into Frontex, the European Agency for the Management of Operational Cooperation at the External Borders of the EU Member States, is welcomed by the IAS; and it is hoped that our comments are duly considered.

The Sub-Committee has invited comments on a variety of aspects of Frontex, but IAS would particularly like to comment on the following issues:

— whether the institutional and legal framework ensures adequate accountability of Frontex activities;
— the legal framework for border guards' exercise of control and surveillance powers in the course of Frontex operations;
— whether and how international obligations with regard to search and rescue at sea affect the Agency;
— whether it is practical to retain a distinction at operational level between preventing irregular immigration and preventing crime;
— the number and nature of working agreements Frontex has in place with Member States, third countries, EU agencies and international bodies; and
— how the Agency's role should develop in the future.

Whether the institutional and legal framework ensures adequate accountability of Frontex activities

While it is advancing in the preparation of a legal framework to establish a Common European Asylum System within its Member States,[1] the European Union (EU) is making it increasingly difficult for refugees and people in need of protection against human rights abuses to access their basic human right to claim asylum,[2] particularly through the use of agencies such as Frontex.

---

[1] Commission of the European Communities, Green Paper on the future Common European Asylum System, COM(2007) 301 final, 6.6.2007.
   The Hague Programme Action Plan foresees the adoption of the proposal for the Common European Asylum System (CEAS) by 2010.
[2] Universal Declaration of Human Rights, Article 14 (1).

There is uncertainty as regards the legal framework and mechanisms for holding Frontex accountable—politically and legally—for breaches of International, European, and Human Rights law that might occur during the operations that it coordinates.

The fundamental principle of non-refoulement,[3] obliges Member States to grant individuals seeking international protection access to the territory and to a fair and efficient asylum procedure. Compliance with this principle would be difficult in the course of current Frontex operations, given that targets are set around the number of people kept out of Europe's borders, and insufficient opportunity is given to migrants to have their protection issues addressed.

The Schengen Borders Code[4] states that refugees are exempt from the usual border control requirements, and must be served with a decision if they are still refused entry, against which there is a right of appeal. It is also stated that human dignity should be respected at all times. The asylum procedure directive[5] obliges Member States to guarantee access to the asylum procedure for those who arrive at the borders of its territories. Frontex operations span beyond these borders, but as an agency of the Member States, the jurisdiction of these States should still be respected.

There is also no doubt that the obligations stemming from the European Convention on Human Rights (ECHR) and the jurisdiction of the European Court of Human Rights (ECtHR) cover areas where, outside its territory, a State party exercises jurisdiction.[6]

The legal framework for border guards' exercise of control and surveillance powers in the course of Frontex operations

There is evidently concern about the legal framework that holds Frontex accountable for its actions. On the ground (or in the sea) these actions relate to the border guards' exercise of control and the surveillance powers used in the course of Frontex operations.

Frontex surveillance operations can take place in various territories:

— in the territory of an African country;

— in the territorial waters of an African country;

— in international waters; and

— in the territorial waters of a Member State.

HERA II was a joint sea surveillance operation, including vessels and aircraft, aimed at enhancing the control of the area between the West African coast and the Canary Islands. For the first time an operation was carried out in the territorial waters of Senegal and Mauritania, in close cooperation with their authorities. The 2006 Frontex Annual report does not provide any further details as to the legal basis for conducting an operation in third countries' territorial waters nor the exact role played by their authorities.

> "During the operational phase of HERA II, 3887 illegal immigrants on 57 cayucos (small fishing boats) were intercepted close to the African coast and diverted. During HERA I and II operations, close to 5,000 illegal immigrants could be stopped from setting off for a dangerous journey that might have cost their lives".[7]

Although required by International, European and Human Rights law to address the issue of differing migrant flows, including refugees and people fleeing human rights abuses as well as economic migrants, there seems to be a blatant disregard for the former in this reporting.

Further incidents of heavy handed border control recorded mainly in the media include the following:

— In July 2006, three people were shot and killed in Melilla as they attempted to cross the fences into Europe. The details of the deaths on the border between Spain and Morocco have yet to be cleared up.

---

[3] Article 33(1) of the 1951 Geneva Convention relating to the Status of Refugees.
[4] Regulation (EC) No 562/2006 establishes a Community Code on the rules governing the movement of persons across borders (Schengen Borders Code), 15 March 2006.
[5] Council Directive 2005/85/EC of 1 December 2005 on minimum standards on procedures in Member States for granting and withdrawing refugee status.
[6] ECtHR judgment in *Bankovic*, 12 December 2001.
[7] Frontex Annual Report 2006, page 12.

— Greece remains under suspicion of having thrown refugees into the sea in September 2006. At least six people died, according to statements by survivors, because officials of the Greek coastguard pushed around 40 people they picked up near the island of Chios back into the sea.

— At the EU's external eastern borders, virtually unnoticed by the public, Chechen refugees have been sent from Slovakia via Ukrainian internment camps back into the Russian Federation, the very state persecuting them.

— In March 2006, UNHCR reported serial deportations. Chechens seeking protection who had managed to reach EU territory in Slovakia were refused access to asylum procedures—contrary to the law. Instead, they were sent back to Ukraine and deported from there to the Russian Federation.[8]

It is concluded that interception operations like HERA II, which are conducted in the territorial waters of third country with a poor human rights record, risks exposing refugees and migrants equally to a risk of human rights violations. Similarly, such operations should not be performed where the third country does not have an asylum procedure in place of a standard equivalent to the procedures applied in Member States.

Whether and how international obligations with regard to search and rescue at sea affect the Agency

Under general international law, States have an obligation to render assistance to persons and ships in distress at sea wherever they encounter them in the course of navigation.[9] There also exists a SAR Convention[10] which obliges some Member States to coordinate search and rescue operations (including transport to a safe place[11]) of vessels in distress within a determined area along their coasts (the so-called SAR region).[12] However, the Frontex director Ilkka Laitinen has stressed that Frontex' role was to protect borders rather than to conduct search-and-rescue missions.

Earlier this month, 27 shipwrecked Africans said they had spent three days clinging to the tuna nets of a vessel in the Mediterranean while Malta and Libya argued over who should rescue them. The case prompted sharp criticism from Franco Frattini, the EU commissioner in charge of migration issues, who accused the tiny island nation of putting bureaucracy ahead of human life.[13]

Whether it is practical to retain a distinction at operational level between preventing irregular immigration and preventing crime

IAS believes that the issues of managing migration and fighting crime should be considered separately.

IAS' concern is that most refugees are forced to commit a crime by attempting to enter a safe country illegally in order to seek asylum there. The criminality of such acts also has negative impacts on their asylum claims where credibility is (in almost all claims considered) damaged as a result. The agencies of the European Union in relation to its border controls, of which Frontex is a main player, are forcing migrants and potential asylum seekers to enter Europe illegally and take greater risks in doing so.

We are also concerned that anti-smuggling and anti-trafficking instruments are applied by Frontex without taking account of the protection needs of migrants themselves. UN Protocols exist for both smuggling and trafficking[14] but they do not provide any guidance for dealing with refugees who are smuggled or victims of trafficking when they are intercepted before reaching a safe country. Nor do they provide for screening measures to determine if such persons may need international protection. IAS views human trafficking in terms of human rights violations as opposed to an immigration control issue,[15] and may well have valid asylum claim.

---

[8] http://www.proasyl.de/en/bleiberechtsb-laendererlasse/index.html
[9] This obligation is also codified in the Montego Bay Convention, the International Convention for the Safety of Life at Sea and the Search and Rescue Convention.
[10] International Convention on Maritime Search and Rescue, 1979
[11] It should be noted that "as a safe place" for these purposes is not necessarily meant dry-land (it could be a ship).
[12] For clarity, the SAR region does not necessarily coincide with the territorial sea or the contiguous zone.
[13] http://www.iht.com/articles/2007/06/12/news/migrate.php
[14] The Protocol against the Smuggling of Migrants by Land, Air and Sea, supplementing the UN Convention against Transnational Organized Crime; and the UN Protocol to Prevent, Suppress and Punish Trafficking in Persons, Especially Women and Children, Supplementing the United Nations Convention against Transnational Organized Crime calls on Party States.
[15] IAS Anti-Trafficking Toolkit by the Research and Information Unit and Tribunal Unit, Immigration Advisory Service.

The number and nature of working agreements Frontex has in place with Member States, third countries, EU agencies and international bodies

IAS is concerned as to the number and nature of working agreement Frontex has in place, particularly those agreements with countries that do not subscribe to the ECHR or the Geneva Convention as they lack transparency and it is not clear whether or not they are even lawful.

In such cases, where the actual interception is carried out by African authorities (who are well paid for this "service" by Spain and the European Union), Frontex argues that the guarantees of internationally recognised border codes don't apply. It is submitted that these border controls are in conflict with the fundamental right that everyone shall be free to leave any country, including his own, as guaranteed by, among others, Article 12 of the International Covenant on Civil and Political Rights and Article 13 of the Universal Declaration of Human Rights.

In a cynical division of labour, non-EU countries like Libya, Morocco, Mauretania, Ukraine, Turkey, etc, are given the job of "bouncer" at the doors to "Fortress Europe". Morocco, for example: more than 400 sub-Saharan refugees and migrants were arrested between Christmas 2006 and the New Year and released on the Algerian border. There were cases of severe ill-treatment by Algerian and Moroccan security forces. Several women were raped during the police operation. A pregnant woman lost her baby. These violations of human rights form part of a chain of violence against people seeking protection in Morocco—whilst Europe remains silent and looks away.[16]

For example, the EU has intensified cooperation with Libya in recent months and is taking forward measures to reinforce Libya's border controls and to send Immigration Officers from EU member states to Libya to intercept irregular migrants and prevent them moving on to the EU. This cooperation is progressing despite the fact that Libya is not a signatory to the 1951 Convention, does not have an asylum law, and routinely violates and disregards its obligations towards refugees and asylum seekers, including by being responsible for refoulement.[17]

IAS believes that there is a pressing need for EU action to support third countries to meet their obligations towards refugees and asylum seekers, particularly where the EU and its Member States are supporting those countries to strengthen their borders and prevent onward movements to the EU.

The lack of transparency around Frontex' agreements, which are labelled as working arrangements or technical agreements, as well as the lack of democratic scrutiny of them, are not acceptable: all agreements, whether political or technical, which are liable to have an impact on the physical access to the EU for refugees and people in need of protection should be subjected to democratic oversight.

Whether there is, or should be, any involvement of, or assistance from, the military in Frontex operations

IAS strongly believes that there should be a reduced involvement of the military in Frontex operations as there already appears to be a degree of it in the spirit and management of the agency.

Frontex has received some highly controversial suggestions from a maritime squadron commander: Major Cauchi Inglott has written a paper suggesting radical measures for tackling the issue, such as confiscating fuel and turning boats back to Libya, which could be against international law.[18]

According to one media source there comes news, or rather accusation; *that illegal immigrants have been put on board a Greek coastguard boat and thrown overboard in Turkish waters. Six—out of the 39—reportedly drowned in the incident. A private television station, NTV reports that the Turkish Foreign Ministry has expressed concern over the allegations, and the UNHCR representative in Ankara is said to be investigating.*[19]

How the Agency's role should develop in the future

One gets the impression that the aim of the Common European Asylum Policy and in particular Frontex' operations, is not to protect refugees, but to protect Europe from refugees. The comments of Frontex Director Colonel Ilkka Laitinen "They aren't refugees, they're illegal migrants"[20] seems to epitomise the attitude of the current Frontex approach, and this attitude needs to be seriously addressed.

[16] http://www.proasyl.de/en/bleiberechtsb-laendererlasse/index.html
[17] http://www.refugeecouncil.org.uk/NR/rdonlyres/83E745F4-DD29-46A7-A541-81BEC1AD2AF7/0/EUasylumlegislation_Sep06.pdf
[18] http://www.icar.org.uk/?lid = 7423
[19] www.ntvmsnbc.com/news/386257.asp
[20] www.goethe.de/ges/pok/prj/mig/mgr/en2081562.htm

The EU has established the Frontex agency and implemented a plethora of border management measures. Such measures have not, however, been matched by efforts to identify and respond to the needs and entitlements of the proportion of irregular migrants who are refugees. Blunt instrument that do not distinguish between those fleeing persecution and irregular migrants seeking to enter a country for other purposes.

Of particular concern is the need to build within Accession States the capacity of NGOs (either existing or new) involved in providing legal advice and assistance and practical welfare help to asylum seekers and refugees. This is important not only so as to ensure that asylum seekers know their rights and are treated fairly by agencies such as Frontex but also are able to monitor whether such agencies are acting in conformity with human rights and other instruments. IAS is well positioned with its expertise to assist in this capacity building given appropriate funding and we hope that the Committee will advocate the strengthening of NGOs as we suggest.

CONCLUSIONS

— a more human rights based approach where refugees can be identified properly and given the opportunity to have their claims considered;

— a legal migration system into Europe to meet labour shortages and to take some of the pressure off EU borders; and

— NGO's strengthened and facilitated to operate in regions where EU funds may not reach.

There is much evidence that significant improvements are still required in relation to national asylum procedure, but in relation to this inquiry, of more pressing concern is the access to the EU for those in need of protection.

Miss Kathryn Warner
European Liaison Officer

6 September 2007

Memorandum by the Standing Committee of experts on internation immigration, refugees and criminal law (the Meijers Committee)

In response to your call for evidence on the functioning of Frontex, the Standing Committee of experts on international immigration, refugees and criminal law ("the Standing Committee") would like to draw your attention to a number of concerns regarding operations of sea border controls coordinated by Frontex in the recent past which the Standing Committee put forward earlier to the European Parliament and Dutch Parliament. This is a synopsis of letters sent to these Parliaments. You find attached the letter and memorandum sent to the European Parliament in October 2006. (Annex 1 and 2) The Standing Committee is worried in particular about measures of pre-border control coordinated by Frontex which have the potential to jeopardize access to protection of those who according to international law are entitled to protection. The Standing Committee observes that the current institutional and legal embedding of Frontex does not properly address the issue of mixed flows of migrants, practices of pre-border controls and operational cooperation with third countries.

FRONTEX ACTIVITIES: REFUGEE CONCERNS

Under the header of operations Hera-II and Hera-III, started in May 2006, Frontex coordinated operations of sea border control carried out by several Member States in sea areas surrounding the Canary Islands. Part of these operations took place in the territorial waters of third countries and in close collaboration with third countries (Senegal and Mauritania) and were targeted at the prevention of departure of migrants towards the Canary Islands and at intercepting and sending back migrants before they left the territorial waters of the African States. According to statistics released by Frontex, in the period August–December 2006, 3.887 immigrants were intercepted and denied further passage towards the Canary Islands. In the course of the recent operation Nautilus coordinated by Frontex in the Central Mediterranean (June–July 2007), search and rescue missions also extended to Libyan territorial waters. According to several accounts, migrants intercepted in Libyan waters have been sent back to Libya without a prior screening procedure or determination of the identity of migrants.[21]

---

[21] See eg *Migration News Sheet*, Migration Policy Group, Brussels, July 2007, pp. 11–13.

The Standing Committee would like to point out that it cannot be ruled out beforehand that refugees who are entitled to protection according to international and community law are also subject to these intercepting measures. It is not guaranteed that refugees or other persons entitled to protection returned to African ports receive appropriate protection in the third countries with which EU Member States, coordinated by Frontex, cooperate.[22] The Standing Committee is worried, in particular, that an increase of operations of pre-border control—in intensity and/or geographical proliferation—could sincerely jeopardize access to international protection for refugees and would deprive the right to asylum as provided for in EC asylum legislation of its practical meaning, since a situation is created whereby all migrants, including refugees, are effectively denied access to the territory of the European Union.

Member States taking part in pre-border control operations apparently operate under the premise that migrants still within the territorial waters of third countries fall under the exclusive responsibility of third countries. This is also the premise underlying the (partly public accessible) Operations Plan Hera III, drawn up by Frontex, according to which the following actions should be taken to fulfill the operation objectives [paragraph 19.1]:

> "— Carry out an optimal maritime and aerial surveillance of the waters close to Mauritania and Senegal, with the authorization of the Mauritanian and Senegalese authorities, carrying onboard the E.U. vessels personnel from these countries that are the responsible of the operations and are the people that must send back the immigrants to the national authorities in the coast.
>
> — Avoid the departure of the illegal immigrants towards the Canary Islands and in the case of the departure, intercept the small boats and return the immigrants to the national authorities."

The Standing Committee would like to point out that EU Member States participating in such operations may be equally accountable under international law for possible human rights violations ensuing from these operations. It can be inferred from the international legal regime on State responsibility for acts taken in conjunction with other States and doctrine on the extra-territorial assertion of jurisdiction that States may remain responsible for human rights violations which are the result of acts taking place extra-territorially and/or of concerted actions with other States.[23] In the attached document, a legal analysis is presented of applicable Community legislation regarding refusal of entry at the EU's external borders (especially Article 13 Schengen Borders Code) and relevant international instruments (the prohibition of refoulement as enshrined in Article 33(1) Refugee Convention and Article 3 ECHR); which raise serious concerns about the legality of the modus operandi of the operations described above. In sum, the Standing Committee is of the opinion that the physical transfer of border controls towards the high seas or territorial waters of third countries may not be used as a means to circumvent international obligations or norms laid down in Community law regarding border controls and asylum applications lodged at the border or within the territories of EU Member States. The Standing Committee regrets that the strategy of pre-border controls is increasingly used without an accompanying legal and operational framework which pays due account to international and community law on asylum. This accompanying framework should in particular address the issue of effective monitoring mechanisms regarding compliance of third States with international human rights and refugee law; specific consideration for persons in need of international protection at the operational level of border management; and an explicit guarantee that all border controls[24], ensure access to the asylum procedure for those who apply for asylum, in accordance with the Dublin regulation (Article 3(1)) and the procedures directive 2005/85/EC, irrespective of whether the border controls are employed unilaterally, under the coordination of Frontex, or in conjunction with third states; and irrespective of where they are carried out.

FRONTEX ACTIVITIES: ACCOUNTABILITY CONCERNS

Search and rescue missions and operations of pre-border control go beyond traditional concepts of border management and should only be applied within an appropriate institutional framework ensuring accountability and democratic control. According to the regulation establishing Frontex (Reg. 2007/2004), an annual activity report has to be made public and a work programme for the coming year has to be forwarded to the European Parliament, the Council and the Commission, which has to be adopted according to the annual Community budgetary procedure. Regular supervising over Frontex activities takes places within the Management Board of Frontex, in which each participating Member State appoints a representative on the

---

22 This is especially so for Libya, but it is notable that neither Frontex, nor the European Commission or Member States taking part in these border controls have made an assessment of the refugee protection regime in other African States cooperating with the EU in taking in intercepted migrants.

23 See in particular Articles 8 ("conduct directed or controlled by a State") and Article 16 ("Aid or assistance in the commission of an internationally wrongful act") of the Articles on State Responsibility; on extra-territorial responsibility for intercepting measures taken at sea, see in particular ECtHR 11 January 2001, *Xhavara a.o. v Italy and Albania*, Appl. 39473/98.

24 Functionally defined in the Schengen Borders Code as activities carried out in response to an intention to cross or the act of crossing that border for the purpose of preventing unauthorised entry; see Article 2(9) Reg. 562/2006.

basis of their degree of high level relevant experience and expertise in the field of operational cooperation on border management. As of December 2006, a vast majority of members of the Board are high ranking officials from national border guards and the aliens police, without necessarily having a legal or asylum expertise.[25] The Standing Committee observes that although the European Parliament may invite the Executive Director of the Agency to report on the carrying out of his/her tasks (Article 25(2) Regulation 2007/2004), an institutionalised mechanism of prompt democratic oversight over operational activities of Frontex is non-existent and the one-sided composition of the Management Board may turn out not to be instrumental for the set up of protection-sensitive border management strategies or for ensuring appropriate scrutiny of the legality of proposed or ongoing operations, for example regarding the drafting of operational plans or the conclusion of working agreements with third countries.

In sum, the Standing Committee signals the following deficiencies with regard to current Frontex activities:

— There is currently no adequate legal, nor operational framework at Community level for conducting border policies targeted at mixed migratory flows of illegal migrants and asylum seekers which guarantees access to international protection for those entitled to protection (paragraph 3, Annex VI Schengen Borders Code remains silent on the matter).

— There is currently no adequate legal, nor operational framework at Community level laying down under which conditions (taking account of human rights obligations) cooperation with third countries regarding border controls may take place.

— There is currently no adequate mechanism of democratic accountability on Community level which ensures a pro-active scrutiny and/or a prompt reactive scrutiny of individual operations coordinated by Frontex.

The Standing Committee takes great interest in the House of Lords inquiry into Frontex and is prepared to provide the House with further information on this subject.

Prof. dr. C.A. Groenendijk
Chairman

5 September 2007

Annex 1

Letter to the European Parliament

PROPOSAL FOR A REGULATION ESTABLISHING A MECHANISM FOR THE CREATION OF RAPID BORDER INTERVENTION TEAMS AND AMENDING COUNCIL REGULATION (EC) NO 2007/2004 AS REGARDS THAT MECHANISM (COM (2006) 401 FINAL)

The Standing Committee of experts on international immigration, refugees and criminal law ("the Standing Committee") has a number of concerns regarding the proposal for a regulation establishing Rapid Border Intervention Teams. While the Standing Committee agrees with the Commission that guarding the EU's external borders is a common responsibility for the EU Member States, the Committee is worried about current practices employed by a number of Member States regarding pre-border checks and the processing of illegal immigrants intercepted at sea. These practices include the categorical refusal of entry into EU territory of third country nationals, without granting access to a determination procedure or the possibility to lodge an appeal against the refusal of entry. As outlined in attached Comment, such practices run counter to international law and principles of Community law. The Standing Committee is worried that the adoption of the proposed regulation will result in EU mandated teams of border guards being engaged in these practices. Therefore, amendment of the proposal is necessary, as will be explained hereunder.

PRE-BORDER CONTROL AND SURVEILLANCE

The Standing Committee is of the opinion that access to durable solutions for asylum seekers is a fundamental principle of International Human Rights Law, Refugee Law and Community Law and that this principle should be adhered to in legislation relating to external border controls of the EU. The present proposal provides for an extremely speedy decision-making procedure with regard to the deployment of Rapid Border

---

[25] Frontex Annual Report 2006, pp. 25–26.

Intervention Teams, without prior approval for individual operations by either the European Parliament or Member States who make border guards available to the teams. While the management of external borders has been proclaimed a common Union activity as a principal means to prevent illegal immigration and human trafficking, which should, according to the Council, include the "stepping up of pre-border checks and joint processing of illegal immigrants intercepted at sea", at present there is no Community framework laying down individual rights of migrants subject to these policies, since the instrument of pre-border controls falls outside the scope of the Schengen border code (EC Regulation 562/2006) which entered into force on 13 October 2006.

The risk of EU mandated teams of border guards being engaged in practices of pre-border controls which run counter to international and Community law is not mere academic, as evidenced by the current border guard operation coordinated by the EU external border guard agency Frontex under the header of operation Hera-II. In this operation, in accordance with agreements concluded between Spain and Mauritania, Senegal and the Cape Verde, border guards from various Member States patrol the territorial waters of these West-African countries in order to intercept illegal migrants and send them back to shore without any form of screening procedure. Only if the vessels are intercepted outside the 24-miles zone, are the migrants being escorted to the Canary Islands and allowed to lodge a claim for asylum. Currently, talks are under way between the European Commission, Italy and Libya, in order to set up a similar operation off the coast of Libya.

AMENDMENT OF PROPOSAL

The Standing Committee is deeply concerned about the proliferation of practices of pre-border controls and the supporting role played by the EU in this regard without the existence of a set of Community rules applicable to these controls. The Standing Committee considers amendment of the current proposal necessary, in order to explicitly guarantee that teams of EU border guards will not participate in border policies employed by individual Member States which amount to categorically refusing entry to third country nationals without allowing them to lodge a claim for asylum or an appeal against the refusal of entry.

This amendment should preferably take the form of insertion of an additional subsection in Article 6 of the proposal:

Article 6:

5. When the tasks referred to in Articles 7 and 8 are carried out in operations of pre-border control and surveillance, guest officers and members of the teams shall comply with provisions applicable to regular external border controls, in particular special provisions on refusal of entry and the right of asylum. Guest officers and members of the teams shall under all circumstances guarantee international protection in accordance with the European Convention for the Protection of Human Rights and Fundamental Freedoms and the Geneva Convention relating to the Status of Refugees.

Additionally, the European Parliament could consider inserting a provision explicitly requiring prior approval for an individual operation agreed upon by Frontex and the host Member State by the European Parliament and/or the home Member State of guest officers.

COMMUNITY FRAMEWORK REGARDING PRE-BORDER CONTROLS

Moreover, the Standing Committee would highly recommend the drafting of new EC legislation, and/or amendment of the Schengen border code in order to lay down the conditions under which the instrument of pre-border controls may be used by Member States. These conditions should prevent Member States from using the instrument of pre-border controls to circumvent obligations applicable to regular border controls and include the guaranteeing of access to a determination procedure in accordance with provisions as laid down in the Common European Asylum System and legal safeguards as already applicable to persons who are refused entry at the EU's external borders (see especially Article 13 Schengen border code).

The Standing Committee is prepared to provide you with further information on this subject.

24 October 2006

Annex 2

COMMENT ON PROPOSAL FOR A REGULATION ESTABLISHING A MECHANISM FOR THE CREATION OF RAPID BORDER INTERVENTION TEAMS AND AMENDING COUNCIL REGULATION (EC) NO 2007/2004 AS REGARDS THAT MECHANISM (COM (2006) 401 FINAL)

1. INTRODUCTION

Although worded in terms of general applicability, the proposal for a regulation establishing Rapid Border Intervention Teams has clearly been prompted by the humanitarian crisis which is currently going on along the West African migration route. From January–September 2006 approximately 23.000 Africans have reached the Spanish Canary Islands with an estimated number of 3.000 who have died during the journey. Back in 2003, the Civipol research institute concluded that the West African migration route became increasingly popular due to the increased deterrent effect of improved surveillance mechanisms of the Spanish authorities in the Strait of Gibraltar.[26] The passage from Mauritania, the Cape Verde and Senegal towards the Canary Islands is significantly longer and riskier. It can be added here that a similar shift in migration routes has taken place with regard to illegal migration from Libya towards Italy. Increased surveillance of the Sicilian Channel has diverted illegal migrants to the considerable longer passage through the Gulf of Sirte.

The Standing Committee believes that guarding the EU's external borders, as well as providing durable solutions to asylum seekers, should be a common responsibility for the EU Member States. At present, Mediterranean Member States (most notably Italy, Spain, Malta, Greece and Cyprus) suffer a disproportionate burden in taking in asylum seekers. Practices in these countries show that individual Member States are insufficiently capable of dealing with sudden influxes of large numbers of illegal migrants, potentially leading to overcrowded reception facilities, rushed determination procedures, collective expulsions and a lack of judicial guarantees offered to asylum seekers.[27] The Standing Committee therefore welcomes developments amounting to a common approach, as long as they are undertaken within the appropriate refugee protection and human rights framework.

The creation of Rapid Border Intervention teams must be seen as supplemental to the creation, in 2004, of the European Agency for the Management of Operational Cooperation at the External Borders of the Member States of the European Union (Frontex), by EC regulation 2007/2004. Frontex' main tasks exist of coordinating Member State cooperation in the sphere of external border controls and the supply of expertise and technical equipment to individual Member States. The proposed regulation adds another task to the Frontex mandate: the deployment of "Rapid Border Intervention Teams to Member States requesting assistance when faced with situations of particular pressure, especially the arrivals at points of the external borders of large numbers of third country nationals trying to enter illegally into the European Union."[28]

In summary, the rapid intervention teams consist of a list of officers of national border guards whom Member States put at the disposal of Frontex. They will be offered training by Frontex and can be deployed "in circumstances requiring increased technical and operational assistance at its external borders" in the territory of a Member State at a temporary basis. The tasks of the Rapid Border Intervention Teams consist of both surveillance of external borders and the participation in border checks. Art. 7 of the proposal lists the competences relating to border checks, art. 8 lists the competences relating to surveillance. Included in these competences are: (1) the check of travel documents of persons crossing the border; (2) checking that a person is not the object of alert for refusal of entry in the Schengen Information System (SIS); (3) searching means of transport and possessions of persons crossing the border and; (4) preventing persons from illegally crossing external borders. Art. 7 (3) stipulates that decisions to refuse entry shall be taken by members of the teams only after consultation with, and subject to the agreement of, a commanding officer of the border guard of the host Member State. It is up to each Member State to decide whether it wants to make officers available to the intervention teams and, furthermore, the teams can only be employed in a Member State at the latter's request.

---

[26] "Feasibility study on the control of the European Union's maritime borders" by Civipol Conseil to the European Commision, Doc. 11490/1/03, Rev. 1, FRONT 102, COMIX 458, 19 September 2003, at p. 15.

[27] See eg Human Rights Watch report "Stemming the Flow: Abuses Against Migrants, Asylum Seekers and Refugees", vol. 18, no. 5(E), September 2006; Commissioner for Human Rights of the Council of Europe, Country Report Italy, CommDH(2005)9, pp. 37–44.

[28] Art. 12 (1) draft proposal.

The joint execution of external border controls and the proliferation of EU activities in this field raises—at least—two legal issues to which the Standing Committee would like to draw attention. The first one is the question of State responsibility for possible human rights violations emanating from actions undertaken by members of multinational intervention teams; the second one is the issue of pre-border checks and the joint processing of illegal immigrants intercepted at sea.

2. LIABILITY FOR CONDUCT OF RAPID BORDER INTERVENTION TEAMS

According to the proposal, members of the Rapid Border Intervention teams remain officers of the national border guards of their Member States. They are allowed to wear their own uniform and will be continued to be paid by their own State, but must also wear a blue armband with the insignia of the European Union. They shall perform activities as laid down in the operational plan concluded between Frontex and the host Member State and fall under the direct command of officers of the national border guard of the host Member State. The members of the teams are bound to comply with Community law and the national law of the host Member State. Article 10 of the proposal holds that home Member States are liable for any damages caused by their officers (*civil liability*), although the host Member State shall compensate this damage to the victims on behalf of the home Member State. Art. 11 confers the *criminal liability* with respect to offences committed against or by guest officers to the host Member State. With regard to *administrative liability*, the proposal envisages that appeals against decisions to refuse entry shall be addressed to the authorities of the host Member State.

This approach serves the principle of effective judicial protection and is in conformity with both the case law of the European Court of Human Rights[29] and the Articles on State Responsibility adopted by the *International Law Commission*. Article 6 hereof holds that: "The conduct of an organ placed at the disposal of a State by another State shall be considered an act of the former State under international law if the organ is acting in the exercise of elements of the governmental authority of the State at whose disposal it is placed". Since the proposed regulation envisages that guest officers will operate under the direct command of the host Member State and shall only take instructions from the host Member State, it is appropriate to confer responsibility for actions of these guest officers to the host Member State.

This does mean however, that, while wearing the uniform of their own Member State and being continued to be paid by the home Member State, the home Member State effectively loses control over conduct undertaken by its border guards operating abroad. Since the regulation stipulates that guest officers need to comply with Community Law and the national law of the host State, they are—*a contrario*—not bound to comply with the national laws of their home State. Art. 4 (1) of the proposal stipulates that members of the teams shall *only* take instructions from the host Member State. This can result in border guards practicing competences which they do not have when active in their own State. This is potentially problematic, especially when the host country conducts border policies which run counter to principles adhered to in the home Member State. In this regard, one cannot overlook current practices of pre-border checks and the processing of illegal immigrants intercepted at sea.

3. PRE-BORDER CHECKS AND THE (JOINT) PROCESSING OF ILLEGAL IMMIGRANTS INTERCEPTED AT SEA

At present, off the shores of Mauritania, Senegal and the Cape Verde, Frontex is already coordinating a joint external border operation under the header of operation Hera II—started in May 2006. This operation takes the form of pre-border surveillance and interception. In accordance with agreements made between Spain and Mauritania, Senegal and the Cape Verde, patrol boats and planes from Spain, Italy, Portugal and Finland patrol the contiguous zones of these West African countries (24 nautical miles) and assist the local coast guard in intercepting illegal migrants and sending them back to shore. Only if the vessels are intercepted outside the 24-miles zone, are the boats being escorted to the Canary Islands. Although the United Nations Convention on the Law of the Sea normally does not authorize inspections outside ones own territorial waters by a State other than the flag State, the Convention makes an exception when the vessel has no nationality or its nationality is in doubt, or when the flag State has consented to the inspection (Article 110). The Hera II headquarters in Tenerife has reported that the joint operation inside the contiguous zones of Mauritania, Senegal and the Cape Verde has resulted in approximately 1.250 people being returned to African shores in the period May-September 2006. Currently, talks are under way between the European Commission, Italy and Libya, in order to set up a similar operation off the coast of Libya. Already in July 2003, the Italian Ministry of Interior issued a decree that enabled the Italian navy to intercept ships carrying asylum seekers and migrants and, if possible, to force the vessels back to the

---

[29] Eg ECtHR 26 June 1992, *Drozd and Janousek v. France and Spain* (Appl. 12747/87), ECtHR 14 July 1977, *X and Y v. Switzerland* (joined appl. 7289/75 and 7349/76), DR 9, p. 57.

territorial waters of the countries from which they came without consideration for identifying asylum seekers.

The Programme of measures to combat illegal immigration across the maritime borders of the European Union adopted by the JHA Council in 2003 expressly calls for "International cooperation between Member States, as well as between them and non-member countries, which will in particular have to involve stepping up 'pre-border' checks and joint processing of illegal immigrants intercepted at sea."[30] Extraterritorial border enforcement activities of the EU and its Member States raises refugee protection as well as broader human rights concerns. The Standing Committee is particularly worried about the practice of pre-border checks resulting in migrants immediately send back to a third country without some form of individual assessment, nor any possibility of access to a determination procedure. Such a practice is, as will be underlined below, in conflict with both international law and standards developed in Community law.

Although the extra-territorial application of the Refugee Convention is much disputed (eg US Supreme Court in Sale, *Acting Comr, Immigration and Naturalisation Service v Haitian Centers Council Inc 509 US 155 (1993)*; Inter-American Commission on Human Rights, Merits Report No 51/96, Case 10.675, *Haitian Boat People (United States of America)*, 13 March 1997; House of Lords, *R. v. Immigration Officer at Prague Airport*, [2004] UKHL 55, 9 December 2004) and the Refugee Convention at any rate seems to exclude persons from protection who are still inside their country of origin, both the European Convention on Human Rights and the International Covenant on Civil and Political Rights do have extra-territorial effect. The ECtHR held in Loizidou that " . . . the responsibility of Contracting Parties can be involved because of acts of their authorities, whether performed within or outside national boundaries, which produce effects outside their own territory."[31] In Issa, the ECtHR elaborated the reasoning behind the extra-territorial application of the ECHR: "Accountability in such situations stems from the fact that Article 1 of the Convention cannot be interpreted so as to allow a State party to perpetrate violations of the Convention on the territory of another State, which it could not perpetrate on its own territory."[32]

In *Xhavara and others v. Italy and Albania* (No 39473/98), the ECtHR considered a case of Albanian citizens who were trying to enter Italy illegally when their boat sank following a collision with an Italian warship whose crew was attempting to board and search the vessel. The Italian operation took place as a consequence of the wave of Albanian citizens immigrating illegally into Italy, after which Italy decided to set up a naval blockade and signed an agreement with Albania authorising the Italian navy to board and search Albanian boats. Although the ECtHR held that Italy did not act contrary to the right of a person to leave one's country (art. 2(2) prot. 4), the ECtHR did rule that the interception activities which extended to international waters and to the territorial waters of Albania fell under Italian jurisdiction and that Italy therefore, had to take "all the necessary measures to avoid, in particular, drowning."

The extra-territorial application of the ECHR and the ICCPR implies that, when dealing with illegal immigrants at high seas, States must also comply with the principle of non-refoulement as embedded in articles 2 and 3 of the ECHR and may not send back immigrants without allowing those who make a credible showing of political refugee status from access to a determination procedure. In this respect, the current practice in West-African waters seems to comply with international law: persons intercepted at the high seas or in Spanish territorial waters are escorted to the territory of Spain and allowed to make a claim for asylum.

With regard to the practice of intercepting illegal migrants in the territorial waters of African countries without allowing further passage towards the Canary Islands, the following remarks can be made. The Refugee Convention seems to exclude persons who are still inside their country of origin—albeit in the territorial waters—from protection, since, according to Article 1, a person can only fall under the refugee definition when he is "outside the country of his nationality". The UNHCR has interpreted this clause as "a general requirement for refugee status that an applicant who has a nationality be outside the country of his nationality. There are no exceptions to this rule. International protection cannot come into play as long as a person is within the territorial jurisdiction of his home country."[33] On these grounds, the House of Lords in a case concerning the conduct of British immigration Officers operating at the airport of Prague, whose main tasks consisted of not allowing Chech Roma asylum seekers from boarding plains heading for the UK, ruled that these asylum seekers could not invoke the Refugee Convention.

---

[30] Doc. 13791/03, FRONT 146, COMIX 631, 21.10.2003), para. 26.
[31] ECtHR 23 March 1995, Case 15318/89 (*Loizidou v. Turkey*), par. 62.
[32] ECtHR 16 November 2004, Case 31821/96 (*Issa and Others v. Turkey*), par. 71. See with regard to the extra-territorial application of the ICCPR eg HRC 29 July 1981, Case CCPR/C/13/D/52/1979 (*Lopez Burgos v. Urugay*), par. 12.3. and HRC 29 July 1981, Case CCPR/C/13/D/56/1979, (*Celiberti de Casariego v. Uruguay*), par. 10.3.
[33] UNHCR *Handbook on Procedures and Criteria for Determining Refugee Status* (1992).

This reasoning, however, does not automatically apply to the principle of non-refoulement as enshrined in the ECHR and the ICCPR. Although this principle is commonly understood as referring to the return, expulsion or extradition of persons to a country where they face a real risk of suffering serious harm, neither the ECHR nor the ICCPR explicitly makes a territorial reservation analogous to the Refugee Convention. In fact, the word "return" (or "refouler") is absent in the relevant provisions in both the ICCPR and the ECHR. The ECtHR has repeatedly stated that the absolute prohibition of torture or inhuman or degrading treatment—which includes the prohibition of refoulement—is an obligation which State parties have to adhere to with regard to anyone who falls under their jurisdiction, regardless of where this jurisdiction is asserted.[34] This implies that the principle of non-exposure to prohibited treatment is applicable to the handover of illegal migrants from the jurisdiction of one State to the other, even if the handover concerns an immigrant which has physically never left his country of origin but who only temporarily has been brought under the jurisdiction of a foreign State acting within his country of origin. In these cases, the transferring State may not proceed with the transfer without appropriate enquiry into the risk and seriousness of the harm the claimant fears.[35]

In this regard, it must moreover be mentioned that, contrary to the *R. v. Immigration Officer at Prague Airport* case, not all immigrants intercepted within the continguous zones of Mauritania, Senegal and the Cape Verde, hold the nationality of these countries. The West African migration route is used by persons coming from across the African continent and even beyond. Late September it was reported that a ship of Asian asylum seekers, mostly Pakistani, had managed to reach the Canary Islands. It falls beyond dispute that these persons can invoke the Refugee Convention and that, when asserting jurisdiction over these persons, European countries are bound to adhere to the principle of non-refoulement.

Furthermore, the Standing Committee would like to draw attention to Recommendations 1645 (2004) and 1737 (2006) of the Parliamentary Assemblee of the Council of Europe, in which the Committee of Ministers of the Council of Europe were invited to call upon member states to:

(Recommendation 1645 (2004) Access to assistance and protection for asylum-seekers at European seaports and coastal areas)

a. ensure that those who wish to apply for asylum at seaports and coastal areas are granted unimpeded access to the asylum procedure, including through interpretation in their language or, if this is not possible, in a language they understand, and to free and independent legal advice;

b. ensure that every person seeking entry at seaports or coastal areas be given the possibility of explaining in full the reasons why he or she is trying to do so, in an individual interview with the relevant authorities;

[. . .]

i. accept responsibility for processing asylum applications of clandestine passengers when the first port of call on the planned route of the ship is on their national territory;

j. in the context of their responsibilities for immigration control, conduct sea patrolling operations in such a way as to fully comply with the 1951 Geneva Convention on the Status of Refugees and the 1950 European Convention on Human Rights, by avoiding sending people back to countries where they would be at risk of persecution or human rights violations;

(Recommendation 1737 (2006) (New trends and challenges for Euro-Mediterranean migration policies)

8.3 comply to the letter with international human rights protection conventions in all operations to prevent or deal with illegal migration and, in particular:

8.3.1 guarantee the right to leave one's country;

8.3.2 guarantee unimpeded access to asylum procedures for people in need of international protection;

8.3.3 ensure that return measures are applied in keeping with human rights standards and with due regard for safety and dignity;

8.3.4 avoid returning irregular migrants to countries where they would be at risk of persecution or human rights violations;

8.3.5 avoid secondary migration movements by sending back migrants to non-European countries, whose nationality they do not have and by which they have merely transited;

8.3.6 examine and take account in all cases of the root causes of these migration movements.

---

[34] Eg ECtHR 7 July 1989, case 14038/88 (*Soering v. United Kingdom*), par. 88.
[35] See also E Lauterpacht and D Betlehem, "The scope and content of the principle of non-refoulement", in: Feller, Türk and Nicholson (eds.), *Refugee Protection in International Law*, Cambridge, 2003, at. para 67.

The Standing Committee would like to recall that access to the asylum procedure is one of the cornerstones of the Common European Asylum System as shaped by the asylum regulations and directives adopted under title IV of the EC Treaty. Article 3 (1) of EC Regulation 343/2003 holds that "Member States shall examine the application of any third country national who applies at the border or in their territory to any one of them for asylum". The Procedures Directive (2005/85/EC) obliges Member States, with as controversial exception the "European safe third countries concept", to allow for an individual examination of asylum cases when employing either the safe country of origin or the safe third country concept. These provisions must be seen in the light of Article 18 of the Charter of Fundamental Rights of the European Union which holds that Member States are to "guarantee the right to asylum". Although this provision cannot be read as obliging Member States to grant asylum themselves, Member States must guarantee that durable solutions are available.[36]

The practice of refusing access without an individual screening procedure or the possibility of a legal remedy against such refusal also runs counter to the approach taken in the recently revised Schengen border code (regulation EC No 562/2006), which, with regard to the "Control of external borders and refusal of entry" holds that:

> "Persons refused entry shall have the right to appeal. Appeals shall be conducted in accordance with national law. A written indication of contact points able to provide information on representatives competent to act on behalf of the third-country national in accordance with national law shall also be given to the third-country national (Article 13 (3))."

The Schengen border code furthermore stipulates that all decisions of refusal of entry must be substantiated and in written form (Article 13 (2)).

The Standing Committee is of the opinion that the physical transfer of border controls towards the high seas or the territories of third States may not be used as a means to circumvent international obligations or norms laid down in Community law with regard to border controls and asylum applications lodged at the border or within EU Member States. The Standing Committee regards the practice of pre-border checks and surveillance, if amounting to categorically excluding groups of persons from access to EU territory without an individual examination of asylum claims or the possibility to lodge an appeal, as running counter to (1) (the spirit of) the Refugee Convention (2) the ICCPR and ECHR and (3) principles of Community law.

4. CONCLUSION AND RECOMMENDATIONS

Although the Standing Committee welcomes increased Member State cooperation in the sphere of external border controls, the Committee notes that, at present, a clear Community framework with regard to the practice of pre-border controls and surveillance is non-existent. The Schengen border code narrowly defines the EU's external borders as "the Member States' land borders, including river and lake borders, sea borders and their airports, river ports, sea ports and lake ports, provided that they are not internal borders" (Article 2 (2)). The absence of explicit provisions relating to the use of the instrument of pre-border checks could lead to EU agencies and individual Member States making use of this legal vacuum in Community law by engaging in activities which run counter to International human rights law. As a minimum, international human rights law applicable to the instrument of pre-border controls should be defined in a Community framework whenever the EU participates or condones Member State participation in these controls.

The Standing Committee is worried that the setup of Rapid Border Intervention Teams will lead to the participation of border guards from across Europe in practices of pre-border checks and surveillance, including the practice of sending back potential refugees without a screening procedure. Therefore, either (1) the proposed regulation should be amended or (2) new legislation on EU level should be drafted which fully guarantees that in pre-border situations potential refugees will never be denied access to a determination procedure.

The draft proposal on Rapid Border Intervention Teams does not contain a provision on express agreement granted by the home Member State for the participation of its border guards in an individual operation. The proposal provides an extremely speedy decision-making procedure on the deployment of Rapid Border Intervention Teams. Frontex has to decide on a request for deployment by a Member State within five working days (Article 12 amending Regulation 2007/2004 Article 8 f (2)). If Frontex decides to authorize deployment, it has to draw up an operational plan together with the requesting State immediately (amended Article 8 f (3)). The Rapid Border Intervention team shall then be deployed no later than five working days after the date of agreement of the operational plan (amended Article 8 f (5)). The role of Member States whose border guards are deployed in this decision-making procedure is reduced to a minimum.

---

[36] see also H. Battjes, *European Asylum Law and International Law*, Leiden: Brill Publishers, 2006 at p. 114.

Amended article 8 f (4) merely holds that "As soon as the operational plan has been agreed, the Executive Director [of Frontex] shall inform the Member States whose border guard officers are to be deployed." With regard to the composition of the teams, Frontex will take into account both the relevant professional experience of the officers (in particular the knowledge of languages) together with the circumstances the requesting Member State is facing (amended Article 8 b), without any provision referring to consultation or preferences of home Member States. This means that, after the provision of a list of available officers for joint operations to Frontex, participating member States effectively lose control over the actual deployment of their officers and the conditions under which they will operate.

The Standing Committee therefore recommends:

1. The drafting of EU legislation concerning the use of the instrument of pre-border controls which guarantees that the use of that instrument should not circumvent existing obligations emanating from human rights treaties and Community law. Access to durable solutions for asylum seekers must under all circumstances be guaranteed. This legislation can also take the form of amendment of regulation 562/2006 (Schengen Borders Code) by inserting a chapter on "pre-border controls and surveillance".

2. As long as legislation mentioned under (1) does not exist, the current proposal on the establishment of Rapid Border Intervention Teams should be amended by way of insertion of a provision ensuring that access to durable solutions for asylum seekers is under all circumstances guaranteed and that activities engaged in by Rapid Border Intervention Teams shall never preclude access to a determination procedure.

3. Additionally, the insertion of a provision in the current proposal requiring explicit approval prior to the deployment of Rapid Border Intervention Teams in a Member State by the European Parliament and/or the home Member State whose officers will be deployed in another Member State.

As a final note, the Standing Committee would like to underline that although border patrols in itself can be useful instruments in the fight against illegal migration, they do not take away root causes for illegal migration and—as long as these root causes exist—can realistically not be expected to prevent the ongoing influx of illegal migrants into the EU. Answers must be found in an integral approach, encompassing issues of prevention, conditions for granting asylum, effective return policies and the fight against human trafficking. In this regard, not only further harmonization and coordination of policies in the area of Justice and Home Affairs, but also an intensification of cooperation with third countries is desirable; within the human rights framework as provided by *inter alia* the European Convention on Human Rights and the 1951 Refugee Convention.

24 October 2006

Memorandum by Spanish Embassy

I. INTRODUCTION

Migrations are a complex social phenomenon due to their causes and consequences, their origins and destinations, and the challenges that they pose both to the societies where immigrants come from and the societies where they settle. Yet, with varying degrees of intensity depending on the point in history, all societies have experienced both incoming and outgoing migratory movements. It is the sedimentation of successive migratory currents in a given area that makes all contemporary societies mixed and plural. Migration therefore contributes to moulding the host societies while leaving a deep mark on the societies of origin.

Until recent years, Spain and other southern European countries have been areas of emigration. And the emigrants who left Spain and other European countries moved to the Americas, to Northern Africa and to other European countries over different times in modern history, making a positive contribution to both the development of the host countries and the welfare of the overall population in their countries of origin.

For the last two decades, Spain has become a country of immigration. This has been the case since the mid eighties in terms of annual flows, and since the beginning of the nineteen nineties in terms of the number of immigrants residing in Spain compared to the number of Spaniards residing abroad. Moreover, with the acceleration of migratory flows registered over the last five years, the proportion of foreigners residing in Spain has reached the high range among European Union countries.

The opportunities and challenges posed by immigration are very similar to those faced by our surrounding countries whose experience in receiving immigration is longer standing. Spain has the advantage of being able to learn from their experiences, from what they did well and from their mistakes when integrating immigrant population. However, aside from the brisk pace of this phenomenon in Spain, our immigration also has specific traits that should be taken into account.

As regards the fight against illegal immigration, the Government is making a great security, diplomatic and political effort, not only on a bilateral basis but also on a regional and international level, in order to stop the arrival of illegal immigrants, fight agains the mafias involved in this activity and to increase the surveillance and control on borders and airports.

In this sense, we have increased:

— the means of control and surveillance on the borders;

— the number of patrolling units on the coast of origin of this kind of immigration;

— the rescue effort of people who risk their lives in their journeys;

— humanitarian and health services; and

— care and repatriation of these people to their countries of origin.

II. Measures Adopted Within this Framework

A. *Operational Measures*

— Significative increase in the National Security Forces (FCSE). For instance, there has been a near-50% increase in the National Police Corps (CNP) and border posts and a 65% increase in the foreign departments.

— The Commissariat-General for Aliens and Documentation of the CNP has design a Plan to combat Illegal Immigration, creating the Illegal Immigration Squad (BRIC) and reinforcing the Central Unit of Immigration Smuggling and Fraudulent Documentation (UCRIF) and the Central Unit of Expulsion and Repatriation (UCER).

— At the "Guardia Civil", important reinforcement of 285 members of personnel in the Territorial Fiscal Patrol (PAFITEs) in 2006 on the Ceuta and Melilla land borders, raising of the fences and building of a tridimensional wire structure.

— Extension of the Integrated External Surveillance System (SIVE). It's been finished in Lanzarote and Fuerteventura and between Cádiz and Almería. It's being continued in the rest of the Canary Islands and it will be installed in Huelva at the end of 2007. **Planning and development continues in Murcia, Alicante and Valencia.**

— National and European border control forces have been established: Seahorse (2006–08), Seahorse network (2007–09), "Paso del Estrecho" (Strait of Gibraltar Crossing), Operations HERA.

— **Spain has sent and is sending help to other State Members that are also affected by illegal immigration in joint operations: Nautilus (Malta-Sicily) and Hermes (Sardinia-Balearics).**

— The permanent deployment Spain has in Western Africa not only is going to continue but it is going to be increased sending planes and ocean-going vessels to Mauritania, Senegal and Cape Verde.

— **In September the "Guardia Civil" was given the "Río Miño" ocean-going vessel, a more efficient tool to fight against illegal immigration both on international waters and anywhere in Africa.**

— *Proceedings regarding the control of common borders:* Together with the cooperation with Morocco, cooperation and training actions regarding border control are being developed in Mauritania, Senegal, Cape Verde **and Gambia**: joint patrols, cooperation in training, liaison officers and joint investigation of mafias. So far all of this has resulted in the special repatriation of third country nationals and the building of a refuge in Mauritania.

— The "Guardia Civil" has worked on a Five-year Plan ("Plan Atlántida") for the reinforcement of staff and equipment to purchase ocean-going vessels, surveillance planes, and unmanned planes and satellite surveillance.

— The Council of Ministers approved a Contingency Fund on 7 December 2006 to the value of €31,075,349.81 to finance various expenses such as improvement works for the CIEs, equipment and travel expenses of the National Security Forces officers both in and outside Spain.

B. *Structural Measures*

— The Ministry of Interior has created the Directorate-General for International and Foreign Relations (Royal Decree 991/2006 8 September).

— Interior attachés have been deployed to contribute to the fight against illegal immigration in Mauritania, Senegal, Cape Verde, Guinea-Bissau, Mali and Guinea Conakry.

— The Regional Coordination Centre in the Canary Islands has been created. Its Director has become the Coordinating Authority.

— A National Coordination Protocol is under consideration. This would affect all ministries that are involved in case there is a possible crisis when making a decision regarding immigrant boats. **With the experience of the Regional Coordination Centre in the Canary Islands, the Centre of Sea Borders Surveillance will be created. The Ministerial Order draft is being studied by the different Ministries.**

A general Royal Decree which will regulate the help and subsidies that are given in the field of international police cooperation is being elaborated. The purchase of equipment to reinforce border control and the help to these countries will be directed faster and more efficiently. Thus, once the decision for special help is taken, it will not be necessary to publish a Royal Decree for each case.

— *Agreements regarding immigration:*

— Bilateral Readmission Agreement in force: Algeria, Bulgaria, Cape Verde, Slovakia, Estonia, France, Gambia, Guinea Conakry, Guinea Bissau, Italy, Latvia, Morocco, Mauritania, Nigeria, Poland, Portugal, Romania, Switzerland, Ghana and with the Former Yugoslav Republic of Macedonia.

— Agreements in hand with Cameroon, Ghana, Mali, Niger, Sierra Leone, and Senegal.

C. *Economic and International Measures*

— Approval of the Integral Security Plan of the Canary Islands 2006-2008. It is coordinated by the vice-presidency and eight ministries are involved. Five of the eight goals it contains are related to immigration. It has meant an increase in the officers of the National Security Forces.

— Efforts are being made to negociate with the countries of origin or transit to achieve greater efficiency and speed in the immigrant identification and repatriation processes.

— Spain has signed MOUs with Senegal, Mauritania and Cape Verde so that they accept the deployment of Spanish or European forces on their territorial waters.

— These countries have been offered operative cooperation and technical assistance, and equipment too.

— Spain has been able to make immigration a world priority for the European Union at the moment.

— Spain, together with France and Morocco and the cooperation of the European Commission organised the Rabat Euroafrican Conference on Migration and Development. Its Action Plan has already been started.

— Spain has contributed decisively to the promotion of four new EU funds regarding Borders, Asylum, Return and Integration (more than €4,000 million for 2007–13). Spain is particularly contributing to the European Border Fund with €1,800 million. **During 2007 and 2008 Spain has been the first recipient in the border fund, and it is waiting for a 60 million allocation. Spain is also the first recipient in all four funds, where it is expected to receive 87 million euros in funds. The Ministry of Interior is developing a specific structure to manage border and return funds.**

— Spain has been one of the countries that have strongly led the support and promotion to start the Agency for the management of the Operative Coordination of Member States External Borders (FRONTEX). The Deputy Director of the Agency is Spanish.

— **Spain has promoted the development of Article 7 of the Regulation of FRONTEX, which sets out an inventory of equipment for the control and surveillance of external borders that each Member State provides the Agency with. This inventory already exists. Spain has contributed with two helicopters (one from the Police, another one from the "Guardia Civil"), eight ships (five coasting vessels—17 metres, three seagoing vessels—30 metres) and some equipment (six thermal cameras, one of them being a mobile camera, one CO_2 mobile detector, one mobile radar). Spain is one of the countries at the top of the list of contributors.**

III. STRATEGIC PLAN FOR CITIZENSHIP AND INTEGRATION (not printed here)

19 October 2007

Printed in the United Kingdom by The Stationery Office Limited
3/2008   383572   19585

ISBN 978-0-10-401232-1